Syrian Gulag

Syrian Gulag

Inside Assad's Prison System

Jaber Baker
and
Uğur Ümit Üngör

I.B. TAURIS
LONDON • NEW YORK • OXFORD • NEW DELHI • SYDNEY

I.B. TAURIS

Bloomsbury Publishing Plc

50 Bedford Square, London, WC1B 3DP, UK

1385 Broadway, New York, NY 10018, USA

29 Earlsfort Terrace, Dublin 2, Ireland

BLOOMSBURY, I.B. TAURIS and the I.B. Tauris logo are trademarks of Bloomsbury Publishing Plc

First published in 2022 in Dutch as *De Syrische goelag: De gevangenissen van Assad, 1970-2020*, by Boom Uitgevers Amsterdam

First published in Great Britain 2023

Cover design by Mijke Wondergem
Cover image: The Empty Chair, 2014 by Fadia Afashe

A catalogue record for this book is available from the British Library.

A catalog record for this book is available from the Library of Congress.

ISBN: HB: 978-0-7556-5020-0
       ePDF: 978-0-7556-5021-7
       eBook: 978-0-7556-5022-4

Typeset by RefineCatch Limited, Bungay, Suffolk
Printed and bound in Great Britain

To find out more about our authors and books visit www.bloomsbury.com and sign up for our newsletters.

Contents

Illustrations

Figures

Plates

Preface

This book is an attempt to understand the world of the Syrian prison. It examines the history, functioning, impacts, perpetrators, and victims of the veritable Gulag that the Assad regime has set up since it seized power in Syria in 1970. The book is based on a wide range of sources, including archival documentation, oral histories, novels, memoirs, newspaper clippings, government files, leaked materials, social media content, human rights reports and most importantly, interviews with former prisoners, and defected regime agents. And yet it is still only the tip of the iceberg: the world of the Syrian prison remains elusive, at times unfathomable and impenetrable.

This book has been long in the making. In 2017, we met in Amsterdam at the presentation of Jaber's book on Hospital 601, the brutal detention site in Damascus that was featured in the infamous Caesar photos. That day, we asked ourselves a simple but essential question: Why is there still no overview book of the Syrian prisons after half a century of Assad rule? This discussion evolved over time, we pondered how we can even probe deeper into the nature of these prisons, and we arrived at the idea of building a map of all Syrian prisons. Thanks to the indispensable input of many friends, in particular Annsar Shahhoud, we decided to work on such a book and set the periodization between 1970 and 2020. Our cooperation went exceptionally smooth, and we worked hand in glove. Uğur's familiarity with theories and the broader context of mass violence in the Middle East and Syria complemented nicely Jaber's profound expertise and personal experience in the Assad regime. The first core draft of the manuscript was completed by Jaber in Arabic, then translated capably and patiently by Mrs. Lara Al-Malakeh into English, and finally complemented, edited, and finished by Uğur.

This book leans heavily on archival materials and oral history interviews. Both of us conducted interviews with former detainees. Jaber wrote a questionnaire for use in interviewing survivors, which exceeded 130 questions, including details of their lives before, during, and after detention. We interviewed over a hundred individuals, most of which conducted by Jaber in Arabic over a period of four years, and almost all of them recorded in audio or video. Then Uğur came across the archive of a Dutch asylum lawyer, Mr. Pieter Bogaers, whose career spanned four decades and whose archive included a rich depository of details of over 1000 asylum cases, including dozens of Syrians. The Bogaers archive provided us with a unique set of life stories of Syrian refugees, most of whom were former detainees, who fled to the Netherlands. This archive gave us a broader picture of the impact of imprisonment on Syrian society. We quote from this archive anonymously to protect the privacy of the individuals involved.

All in all, we hope the reader will gain a better understanding of the impact of the Syrian Gulag, and a vivid picture of its brutality. We also hope this book does justice to the memory of the victims and human dignity of the survivors. Any and all mistakes belong solely to us.

Jaber Baker and Uğur Ümit Üngör

1 May 2023

Introduction

'Behind the Sun'

In Damascus stands a grim building in a grim compound. Mezze military airport is tucked in between the working-class neighborhoods of Moadhamiyya and Darayya on its south, and the upscale Mezze area to its north. The air base is Syria's most important strategic installation and plays a crucial role in the regime's military activities. Historically, it was used by Syria's air force, but also its elite troops: the Defence Companies, the Republican Guards, the Special Forces and it serves as a private airport for the Assad family. On the north side of the air base, right on the highway, sits the compound of the Air Force Intelligence. It consists of several buildings, some administrative, some recreational, but most crucially, an underground world full of terror: its prison.

In the summer of 2011, a young Syrian man we will call 'Akram' was enjoying his summer break. He hailed from a middle-class Damascene family from Midaan. He was in his last year of university, dressed well, had a girlfriend, was into rock music and basketball, and spoke fluent English. In any other country he could have had a fairly normal, almost boring bourgeois life: graduate from university, get married, buy an apartment, have children, go on occasional holidays to Lebanon or Turkey, and live happily ever after. But on one fateful day, which he remembers like nothing else, Akram was arrested on the streets of Damascus, shoved into a car, blindfolded, and beaten all the way to the compound. Before he realized what was happening, he found himself in a torture dungeon, hanging from the ceiling by his wrists. As a computer geek who had never even been spanked by his parents or been in a fist fight, Akram was known as a gentle boy who was 'homely' (*baytuti*). The only reason he had been arrested was because he had liked a social media post criticizing the Assad regime. The power cable swooshed through the air, thick with cigarette smoke and the smell of sweat, and landed on his skin like a hornet bite. It took his breath away, at first shocked him into an involuntary, bestial scream, followed by the excruciating pain a second later. 'You want freedom, right?!' yelled the torturer sardonically, as he whipped him again, using his full force, 'here's your freedom!' Blood flowed down Akram's tender back and legs and dripped on the dirty cement floor. He remained at the Air Force Intelligence branch at Mezze military airport for three months, a stay which changed his life forever.

The man who was torturing him, for our purposes 'Amjad', was originally from a poor village near the coastal town of Jableh. When he was an infant, Amjad's parents had moved to Damascus, where his father served in the Syrian army and achieved the rank of captain. Amjad was roughly the same age as his victim, whom he did not known personally, but tortured enthusiastically anyway. He tortured him on behalf of the Air Force Intelligence; a sinister, brutal organization run by the implacable hardliner Jamil al-Hassan. Amjad had joined the organization in the early 2000s, having failed to become a pilot. From the outbreak of the 2011 Syrian uprising on, he worked overtime to 'process' the large numbers of detainees who passed through Mezze military airport. Whenever he was not in sessions when he hanged, whipped, beat, burnt, electrocuted, and strangled countless victims like Akram, he passed his long days and often long night shifts by smoking cigarettes and drinking *maté* or whisky with his colleagues at the branch, which was like a second home to him. His comrades and his bosses were his social network, his wife and child increasingly a sideshow. Nobody knew exactly how many people he had tortured and killed; perhaps somewhere in the archives of the Air Force Intelligence it was registered. He never thought about it, with a few rare exceptions: once he tortured an old classmate. Him he remembered. The calluses on his knuckles and on the palms of his hands were a silent witness to his many years of violent routines. For the rest, as far as he was concerned, everyone passing through his underground torture chamber deserved the treatment meted out to them. That included Akram, whom he tortured and forgot about.

Akram's predicament is known in Syria as being 'behind the sun' (ورا الشمس). His story is a microcosm of the catastrophe that has befallen Syria since 1970 in general, and since 2011 in particular. Akram and Amjad are two Syrians whose fates met in the torture room. Akram had expressed support for the popular protests against the regime, whereas Amjad had pledged to his superiors to repress that uprising. Their story is not unique: there are hundreds of thousands of Akrams, and possibly many hundreds of Amjads out there. The process of mass imprisonment and torture that the Assad regime has unleashed on Syrian society, has made a profound, irreversible, and indelible impact on millions of Syrians. The prison network has become an intrinsic part of mainstream Syrian identity, much like the struggle against the sea is an aspect of Dutch national identity, or beef is a core element of Argentinian identity. The Gulag is omnipresent inside Syria and its relevance reaches beyond simply the prisoners and the guards. In the torture chamber, many topics come together: postcolonial state power, authoritarianism, sectarianism, sexism, revolution, resistance, and violence. Its relevance even reaches beyond the country itself, since the Syrian occupation of Lebanon, the imprisonment of non-Syrians, and the presence of countless survivors and even some perpetrators outside of Syria has made it pertinent as a global political, moral, societal, and legal problem.

To provide a sense of perspective on the Syrian Gulag, it is useful to sketch a broad overview of imprisonment worldwide. At the time of writing (2023), approximately 11 million people are imprisoned across the world. The highest absolute numbers are in the United States (2.1 million), China (1.7 million excluding a million Uyghurs in camps), Brazil (750,000), and Russia (700,000). The countries with the highest prison population rate (the number of prisoners per 100,000 of the population) are the United States (629), Rwanda (580), El Salvador (564), Turkmenistan (576), Cuba (510), Russia (445), and the global average is 144 per 100,000.[1] Two cases that are often mentioned when Syria is discussed are Israel, which keeps approximately 4,500 Palestinians in its prisons, and the American base prison of Guantanamo, where a total of 775 prisoners were kept. We lack precise numbers, but if there were clear statistics, Syria would doubtlessly figure at the top of this chart. Even if we use the conservative estimate of 300,000 Syrians having been in prison at some point since 2011 (including those who died in prison), it amounts to about 1,200 prisoners per 100,000 of the population.[2] This catastrophe is of an unprecedented scale in Syrian history: never before have so many people been arrested, imprisoned, tortured and killed in prison as in the past half century in general, and the past decade in particular.[3] The violence is of such a degree and nature as to pose a threat to the viability and stability of Syrian society. It generates pervasive fear, collective trauma, economic stagnation, sectarian polarization, stifling of talent, persistent injustice, and prevention of alternative futures for the country.

A recent paper by the International Center for Transitional Justice mentions the detained and disappeared in one breath:

> In most cases, to be imprisoned in Syria is to disappear. Whether detained by the regime or abducted by one of the many armed groups involved in the Syrian conflict, in many cases the result is the same. A person is suddenly taken from their home or place of business in secret or seized at a checkpoint, usually by one of Syria's security agencies or sometimes by an armed group of unknown affiliation. Occasionally, families can locate the place where they are being held and visit once or twice. Sometimes, a release is possible, perhaps after a payment or a prisoner swap. More often, the person is never heard from or seen again.[4]

Indeed, one interpretation of the Syrian Gulag argues that the detainees are to be considered disappeared and not imprisoned, since in many cases the regime has arrested them but denies officially that it has them. This has brought the centrally important discourse of forced disappearances into the fray, with a well-organized advocacy group of family members, and the International Commission on Missing Persons (ICMP) getting involved. However, we chose not to use the term 'disappeared' for the detainees in the prisons, because even though most detainees are held incommunicado, within the prison system they are known to exist. Detainees have to be distinguished from the victims that the regime took, executed, and buried somewhere in a deliberate attempt to cover up the murder.

Aims of the book

This book aims to provide an overview of the Syrian Gulag, the vast and complex system of arrest, imprisonment, and torture that the Assad regime uses to maintain its grip on Syrian society. It aims to explain why the Assad regime set up and developed its prison industry, how it used the Gulag to construct its power, why it tortures people, and what impact this has on Syrian society. This system was not built in a day but rests on a history that can be divided into four distinct periods. First, the Ottoman Empire ruled Syria for four centuries (until 1918) and established a number of prisons in which judicial and political prisoners were incarcerated. Some of these fell into disrepair or were discontinued, others were adopted by consecutive Syrian governments, such as the Citadel Prison. Under the French Mandate (1923–1946), political dissidents, activists and militants were imprisoned in some of the inherited prisons, but the French also built and developed their own prisons, such as the military prison in Palmyra. The democratic period (1946–1963) then saw an acceleration of political imprisonment, as each coup d'état saw the successful plotters throw their opponents in prison; Mezze prison was developed in this period. But the final coup d'état of the Baath Party (1963) and the internal coup by Hafez al-Assad (1970) was a rapid transition that saw two trends: the gradual expansion of and increased relevance of the prison system as a tool of governance, and the development of a four-dimensional Gulag: intelligence prisons, military prisons, civil prisons, and secret prisons.

The Assad regime perfected the art of arrest, detention, and incarceration, and one can argue that imprisonment *defines* the regime. Therefore, we aim to contribute to a better understanding of the Assad regime, especially the key debate on how its practices of violence have impacted Syrian society. Research on the regime was traditionally constrained by strict limitations on sources and access and, therefore, historically we knew very little about the workings of the various intelligence agencies. Since the story of the Syrian Gulag is the story of the Syrian intelligence agencies, referred to in the Syrian vernacular as *Mukhabarat*, writing this book would not have been possible a decade ago. An encyclopedia on Middle Eastern intelligence, published right before the Arab Spring, admits about Syria that 'it is impossible to precisely analyze the exact structure of the country's intelligence apparatus'.[5] Indeed, the Mukhabarat does not provide information, it gathers information, to the extent that a most common Syrian maxim is 'the walls have ears' (الحيطان لها أذان). Traditionally, there was a 'conspiracy of silence', as many victims refuse to tell their stories, whereas the perpetrators are bound by secrecy. Therefore, very little information reached the outside world about the prison system.[6] However, since 2011, the conflict has inadvertently made possible unprecedented levels of access and insight into the regime's inner workings. Survivors have fled abroad and spoken up about their experiences, defectors have exposed their former bosses, and a wealth of digital information has leaked and is now available. Never before has it been possible to take such a good look at the Assad regime, including through the prism of the prisons.[7] Perhaps for that reason, or because the Syrian prisons are black boxes, anybody who has been imprisoned naturally feels the need to describe their story.

This book is a first, but certainly not definitive, overview of the Syrian Gulag. As a book for a general audience, it is primarily descriptive, synoptic, and introductory. None of these chapters purport to constitute the final word on any prison. For example, Saydnaya prison has received a good amount of interest from both Syrian and international media and researchers. Writing its history could easily fill a library of its own, and we hope that these chapters lay a foundation of future, more elaborate studies on each and every prison. We earnestly acknowledge the excellent work conducted by a number of individuals and organizations, such as the Association of Detainees and Missing in Sednaya Prison. We also benefited from critical media covering, such as the captivating Syria TV series 'Oh Freedom' (يا حرية), in which each episode focuses on an individual survivor and her/his testimony and paints a complex picture of the prison experience.[8] In a similar vein, the podcast 'Branch 251' has covered the trial of two Syrian intelligence officers in the German city of Koblenz. It has fleshed out, in great detail, how the two men operated Political Security Branch 251 in Damascus and how the survivors pursued justice in Europe.[9] Individual writers, of whom there are too many to name, we owe a specific debt of gratitude – see the bibliographic appendix for a comprehensive but not exhaustive list. If this book manages to provide an overview of the Syrian Gulag to laypersons, while also offering new insights to experts, it means it has succeeded.

Sources

This book rests on a broad source base, in particular five types of sources. First and foremost, it relies heavily on oral histories of survivors and eyewitnesses. Without their courage, openness, and trust, this book could not and would not have been written. For this book, we conducted over 100 interviews with former detainees about their experiences in prison, as well as eyewitnesses and family members of detainees, and even a few perpetrators.[10] In order to gather as many different vantage points on the prisons as possible, we contacted Syrians from different backgrounds, classes, neighbourhoods, and political persuasions in various countries and had several long interview sessions with them. These semi-structured, in-depth interviews were mostly videotaped and audiotaped but, in some cases, notes were taken upon the request of the interviewee. We asked for informed consent and respected the interviewees' wishes for anonymity: some wanted to remain fully anonymous, others sufficed with initials, while others insisted on being mentioned using both their name and surname. In our selection of interviewees, we attempted to avoid the well-trodden paths of former detainees who had already received lots of media attention. Rather than revisiting the fairly well-known stories of these (often middle-class, English-speaking) survivors, we devoted attention to others, including some who have spoken for the first time about their experiences for this book. In 2021, these interviews were archived at the NIOD Institute in Amsterdam.[11] These interviews render a complex, rich, and colourful picture of the prison phenomenon and beyond. Beyond these interviews, we relied on a number of other interviews published online, either in the Syrian, regional or international media.

Second, we have used a number of reports by international and non-governmental organizations, such as Human Rights Watch, Amnesty International, the Syrian Network for Human Rights, the Association of Detainees and Missing in Sednaya Prison, EuroMed Rights, the International Center for Transitional Justice, the Office of the United Nations High Commissioner for Human Rights, Physicians for Human Rights, Pax for Peace, the Syria Justice and Accountability Center, the International Commission on Missing Persons, Families for Freedom, the European Center for Constitutional and Human Rights, and others. Their work in general, including reports, policy briefs, social media posts, and other publications were very helpful in offering a deeper understanding of the dynamics of the prison system in Syria. Many of these reports focus on the survivors' experiences only during their imprisonment, but this book looks at their biographies in a broader sense. It also looks at the perpetrators, the relations between the four distinct prison systems, and the impact on Syrian society more broadly.

A third body of knowledge that has proven very useful are leaks. Due to the secrecy of the Assad regime and its strict censorship on the prison system, leaks are an important source to rely on. These videos, documents, and files that were either stolen from or (even deliberately) leaked by the regime have a different provenance, as they offer an unredacted perspective on the realities of regime violence. The Syrian Justice and Accountability Center (SJAC) and the Commission for International Justice and Accountability (CIJA) have in their possession sizeable archives of the Syrian intelligence agencies. These archival collections were smuggled out of Syria after the regime lost territories to the rebels and contain unique materials that the two organizations aim to utilize in prosecuting Assad's crimes. Once they become accessible to research, they will resolve many unknowns regarding the Syrian Gulag. In August 2013, a photographer for the Syrian military police, code-named 'Caesar', defected, and smuggled 53,275 photographs out of Syria. The photos show at least 6,786 detainees who died while imprisoned by the intelligence branches.[12] Caesar's job was to document the dead, including anyone who died in a traffic accident or military attack. The photos are horrific: they are close-up shots of dead victims who bear marks of torture on their bodies. The emaciated bodies are black and blue, there are marks of whipping, beating, and strangulation, and some of them have their eyes gouged out. These men (and a few women) had not only been tortured; they had been executed through torture. The Caesar photos demonstrated, for the first time, the undeniable fact of the brutality of the Syrian Gulag and confirmed what survivors and eyewitnesses had been saying all along.[13]

A fourth repository of primary materials emanated from an unexpected source. From 1975 to 2015, the Dutch immigration lawyer Pieter Bogaers practiced law and took up the cases of almost 800 refugees who fled to the Netherlands in that period. Among these refugees were about 40 Syrians of all walks of life: Communists, Islamists, liberals, Kurds, and regime insiders – all of whom sought asylum in the Netherlands. Many of the Syrians in these files are former detainees, and their reasons for fleeing Syria were often the threat of prison, torture, or worse. Bogaers' method was to hold long interviews with his clients upon first contact, often right after their arrival in the Netherlands. These interviews were meant to give him a better biographical sketch of the person sitting across him, so he could build his cases effectively. These biographical interviews are exceptionally rich in detail, cover a broad range of topics, and are therefore a unique source for modern Syrian history. The dossiers also contain other sensitive information, such as medical files, personal letters, photos, and even official documents taken from Assad regime functionaries (most likely through bribes). In 2015, Bogaers donated his archive to the International Institute of Social History in Amsterdam and we are grateful that he granted us permission to conduct research in the files. His archive has proven a vital source of survivor narratives for the period before the Syrian uprising. Since many of these former detainees are still alive, we used only their initials.[14]

Our fifth source type is also sensitive: published and unpublished memoirs. Many survivors of the Syrian Gulag have written memoirs, notes, novels, fictionalized accounts, reflections, articles, observations, and autobiographies. Indeed, the infamous Arabic genre of 'prison literature' (*adab al-sijoon*) is particularly well stocked for the Syrian Arab Republic.[15] Some of these authors have become known for their brutally honest, beautifully written memoirs that would not be out of place with the great memoirists of other prisons and camps, such as Primo Levi, Olga Lengyel, Imre Kertesz, Margarete Buber-Neumann, Alexander Solzhenitsyn, or Yevgenia Ginzburg. Many of these memoirists have become voices for the disenfranchised, the forcibly disappeared, those who succumbed or were killed before they could put pen to paper, and those who did not have the eloquence to articulate their pain.[16] Former detainee Mansour Omari formulated this well:

> It took me years to finish writing my memoir, and I believe it had a devastating toll on my life. However, I am satisfied that I documented my memory before years go by, and I forget more and more of its details ... After all these years, my trauma has got worse, not better. With the years passing by, this toll on me started to deepen and to be permanent. Gradually, I felt that I could not go on anymore. I began to avoid everyone and do traumatising work or interviews as little as I can. But I can't stop. I made a promise to those left behind. Many detainees and their families would not want me to give up hope that there will be justice one day. Syrian detainees are tortured and killed every single day, and I will keep speaking up for them even if the world ignores all our pleas to save the rest. I dedicate my life to this work.[17]

This means we also have to think of the flip side of the story, which is the photo negative of the history of the Syrian Gulag: we have to picture the countless victims who died horrific deaths, or were too traumatized to express themselves properly. We have to imagine the depth of stories untold, repressed, and unremembered. Over the years, we have met dozens of survivors of the prison system who we wanted to interview, or who we felt should tell their stories, but who were too destabilized mentally and disappeared into the mist of time. For this reason, it has been difficult deciding between writing the book in present tense or in past tense. Not only are most prisons mentioned in this book still operative and the events described in this book very much ongoing. But for the survivors and their families none of this is over, and they continue to suffer. As William Faulkner said: 'The past is never dead. In fact, it's not even past.'

The Syrian Gulag in context

The Soviet term 'Gulag', short for *Glavnoe Upravlenie Lagerei* ('Chief Administration of Camps'), refers to a vast canvas of camps, prisons, transit centres, secret police, informers, spies, interrogators, torturers, and executioners. It is therefore entirely appropriate to use for the Syrian prison system.[18] That system, too, was set up to eliminate the regime's perceived political enemies; it. too, forms an archipelago across a country with a wide carceral geography; it, too, has an inordinate impact on the society on which it operated; and it has similar levels of mortality. Furthermore, Solzhenitsyn's concession that he did not have access to any documents and therefore built his work on his own and other prisoners' memories counts for us too.[19] Long-time Soviet Gulag prisoner Anatoly Marchenko opened his memoirs with a passage that might symbolize one of the most important parallels between the two prison systems. Marchenko writes that every time he felt seized by despair, hunger, illness, and helplessness, 'one thing alone gave me the strength to live through that nightmare: the hope that I would eventually come out and tell the whole world what I had seen and experienced'.[20] Every single Syrian ex-detainee we have spoken to, expressed this exact same deep desire.

But the parallels run much deeper. After spending three separate periods of imprisonment in the Soviet Gulag, in 1961 Varlam Shalamov wrote a list of everything that he had learned in prison.[21] Three of his observations are highly relevant for the Syrian Gulag. His first major lesson was: 'The extraordinary fragility of human nature, of civilization. A human being would turn into a beast after three weeks of hard work, cold, starvation and beatings.' This transition from peaceful, civil life to the dark, brutal universe of the prison is the major transformative experience of all Syrian prisoners. Nothing resembles life in prison, and no rules from outside apply on the inside. Another one of Shalamov's points was: 'I learned the difference between prison, which strengthens character, and work camps, which corrupt the human soul.' This distinction between camps and prisons applies to the Syrian Gulag as well, which consists of four separate but interconnected systems: the intelligence branches, the military prisons, the civil prisons, and the secret prisons. The former two cannot be considered prisons in the mainstream understanding of prisons, but must be seen as camps – mostly for concentration, sometimes for extermination. Finally, Shalamov noticed: 'The lust for power, for unpunished murder is great – from big shots down to regular police operatives with rifles.' Syrian detainees, too, saw the perpetrators in their worst moments, and therefore fulfill a dual function: they testify to their own experiences of what it means to be in prison, but they also bear witness to the perpetrators and their personalities, acts, and ideas.

Prisons and camps have been the focus of much thought and theory, especially after Nazism and Stalinism. Hannah Arendt famously argued that as part of a totalitarian system of government, the Nazi and Soviet camp systems were experiments in 'total domination'.[22] Michel Foucault, who spent much of his intellectual energy in understanding the prison as a phenomenon, was categorically critical of imprisonment: 'Prison is the only place where power is manifested in its naked state, in its most excessive form, and where it is justified as moral force.'[23] But Foucault neither distinguished nor theorized the relationship between prisons and camps, and even in his work on biopolitics, did not write much about the Nazi and Soviet camps as mass imprisonment. The Syrian Gulag straddles the grey zone between concentration camps and prisons: its scale, levels of violence, and impact on society transcends a regular penal system and approaches that of a concentration camp industry. It is a massive phenomenon, an enormous institution that touched the lives of a tremendous portion of the Syrian population. Salwa Ismail rightly uses the hybrid term 'prison camp' to depict the dual reality of the Syrian prison industry.[24] Former detainee and writer Yassin al-Haj Saleh notes that we cannot speak of prisons in the Syrian case but must rather contextualize it within the Nazi and Stalinist universe of camps, further arguing that besides the actual prisons, 'Syria at large was a giant prison'.[25] Even those 'who made it out', were never really out.

In a riveting analysis of the concentration camp phenomenon, Wolfgang Sofsky wrote that the camp was 'a specific form of society' where 'absolute power . . . liberates violence from all inhibitions and restraints'.[26] For him, at the centre of the camp stood 'arbitrary terror and routine violence', which 'destroyed personal identity and social solidarity, disrupted the very ideas of time and space, perverted human work into torture, and unleashed innumerable atrocities'. These cogent descriptions fit the military prisons in Syria well. There too, the guards 'did what they were permitted to – and they were permitted to do everything'. They acted on 'implied orders' which ambiguously outlined what must be done but did not specify how the order should be carried out, allowing for personal initiative in which camp personnel anticipated what their superiors meant.[27] So, too, the spy bosses, wardens, and torturers in Syria might never have received a direct order from Bashar al-Assad to torture detainees to death, but they did so nonetheless. The Syrian Gulag is a prime example of totalitarian prison and camp systems, and its impact is going to be long-lasting and irreversible.

Structure of the book

This book consists of two parts of five chapters each that can be read separately, but only collectively constitute the Syrian Gulag: the intelligence apparatus, and the prison complex.

Part I provides a comprehensive overview of the detention system within the main Syrian intelligence services: Military Intelligence, Air Force Intelligence, General Intelligence, and the Political Security Directorate. This order closely follows the order of power held by the various services: the Military Intelligence undisputed at the top, followed shortly by the Air Force Intelligence and, at noticeable distance thereafter the two civilian intelligence services, the General and Political. Together this ominous quartet makes up what is commonly known in Syria as the secretive, omnipresent Mukhabarat, whose tentacles are tightly wrapped around Syrian society. The ramifications of the intelligence prison system are so numerous and complex that no thorough overview of its workings exists to date. Even people who work in the system as officers, prison guards, or torturers often do not have a clear overview of their own place in the entire apparatus or of the precise tasks of the other intelligence agencies. This book on prisons begins with the intelligence services for this very reason, because they represent a number of central issues: methods of arrest, torture, structure of the various departments, forms of cooperation and competition among the agencies, and impact on society. The Syrian intelligence services are the backbone of the Assad regime, and therefore of this book. The final chapter in this part includes a description of the Military Police, which is responsible for surveillance of the prison system independently of the four services.

Part II outlines the landscape of the prisons whose mere mention struck terror into the hearts of generations of Syrians: the military prisons of Mezze, Tadmor (Palmyra) and Saydnaya. In addition, the volume deals with the civilian prisons and secret prisons. These prisons profoundly influenced political and cultural life in Syria; a very large group of detainees traversed them and wrote about them. Even the prisons that were later closed, Mezze and Palmyra, continue to reverberate in the individual and collective traumas that haunt survivors. Hence, these chapters warrant a longer look at these three prisons. The next two chapters complete the tour d'horizon of the Syrian Gulag. The fourth chapter of Part II paints a picture of the civilian prisons, which fall under the Ministry of Interior and the civilian judiciary. The living conditions and level of violence in these prisons were certainly not pleasant. However, they never reached the level of inhumane treatment that dominated the Mukhabarat prisons or the military prisons, as evidenced by the testimonies of former detainees who went through both. Finally, the last chapter in this volume explores the hidden world of the secret prisons, dark places of lawlessness and unlimited violence that were transformed into makeshift prisons, especially after the uprising broke out in 2011. The three prisons examined in this chapter offer a glimpse of the impunity enjoyed by various agencies (outside the Mukhabarat and the military) to set up their own prisons.

Finally, the appendices aim to provide context to a number of relevant themes: methods and means of torture, diseases and medicines, prison jargon, food in prison, and a biographical listing of main perpetrators. The four intermezzos should be seen as vignettes; short impressionistic scenes that, in a nutshell, paint a telling picture of a particular moment within the Syrian Gulag.

The Guilty Dream

Abu Hassan Sawalha was arrested for having seen a dream. The accused arrived at Tadmor, Palmyra's desert prison, awaiting trial in the early 1980s. When it was his turn to meet the representatives of the Second Military Field Court, an argument erupted between him and the judge, Major General Suleiman al-Khatib. The latter asked him, 'So you saw in a dream the Prophet Mohammed, who said to you, 'Be patient ... By God, salvation is near.' Then you spread the story among the people of the village, that the Prophet said to you, 'Wait only until three. For the fall of this regime.''

Blindfolded, Abu Hassan replied, 'Sir, the last sentence, I did not see that in the dream, nor did I tell it to people, nor was it part of a dream. This sentence was added by the informant who told you this, and the interrogator insisted by force, pressure and torture, on adding it to my exact statement.' Al-Khatib interrupted him: 'Shut up, you're a dog. Our informant never lies, and our interrogators do not fabricate your confessions, nor do they have any interest in adding to them. You said "wait until three", and this is what the Prophet said in a dream. You said, "The whole village is a witness", and you know that the Prophet told you to "wait until three" for the fall of the system.'

After the controversy and Abu Hassan's attempts to dismiss the accusation, his tongue overpowered him, and he sharply objected to the judge's accusations: 'Sir, am I the one who had the dream, or you?' Al-Khatib exploded with anger: 'By God, I will educate you, and I will teach you a lesson if you ever dream dreams that harm the security of the state.' Abu Hassan felt so helpless and frustrated that he cried out desperately and pleadingly, 'But this is unfair. By God, this sentence was not part of my dream, and I did not receive it in my dream.' To this Major General Suleiman Al-Khatib calmly replied: 'Don't worry, son. Here we have never wronged anyone.'

Abu Hassan was sentenced to 15 years in prison with hard labour and was deprived of all civil and military rights.

Part One

The Intelligence Agencies

Introduction

The concept of a Syrian nation state was developed during the French mandate (1920–1946). In the same period, the Syrian army was formed from the *Armée du Levant*, a nascent Syrian army recruited predominantly from sectarian minorities. During the Mandate period, French military power always loomed large, but civil authority also retained a modicum of liberal governance in Syria, as it exercised its colonial administrative functions through its commercial and financial influences. Civil authority was confined to the rich and middle classes in Syria. When the French left Syria, the separation between the Syrian army and the central authority continued.[1]

The army emerged on the political scene with the coup d'état of 1949 led by General Husni al-Zaim. Civilian forces maintained a clear presence in state institutions and considerable space was granted for freedom of speech and the formation of parties and associations. The consecutive military coups in the following years did not weaken civilian life in Syria until the union with Egypt in 1958.

The attempted United Arab Republic was the decisive blow to the remnants of Syrian democracy. The Syrian side implemented the demands of former Egyptian President Jamal Abdel Nasser: parties were disbanded and the newspapers closed. Syrian public and political life was completely neutralized in the interest of the unity between the two countries. Syrian security forces grew exponentially and the name of military officer Abdulhamid al-Sarraj began to be heard. The *Second Department* (*al-shuba al-thaniya*), the main intelligence agency, was turned into a torture and detention centre for political opponents. This phase brought military forces to the forefront of Syrian politics and society, as the militarized government invaded public life in both the economic and social spheres. The central government in Cairo also nationalized Syrian industrial enterprises and companies. The middle class and the national bourgeoisie were sidelined in favour of socialism and the welfare state system.

The coup d'état that led to the break-up with Egypt in 1961 was led by Damascene military officer Abdulkarim al-Nahlawi, and his coup ringleaders tried to bring civil forces back to life. However, the Baath party coup of 8 March 1963 took place shortly afterwards, and with this coup, Syria began to be ruled by a military junta and entered a state of emergency that lasted *de jure* until 2011 but *de facto* continues until today.

Figure 0.1 Abdul Hamid al-Sarraj, from a private collection.

The Baath Party and its security culture

The Baath Party, represented by its military committee, relied on intelligence as a tool to strengthen its rule and establish its popular base. In 1967, the head of the newly established National Security Service, Abdulkarim al-Jundi, expanded the repressive state apparatus considerably. Torture stories that had never been heard before in Syria began to spread and strike terror in the hearts of ordinary Syrians.

The Baath Party realized that controlling the entire state was best done through controlling the army and security services. It became mandatory that personnel in the military, the Ministry of Interior and the police must become members of the Party.

Figure 0.2 Abdul Karim al-Jundi, from a private collection.

The Party's National Security Office became a major institution under which other military and civil security institutions operated. The Baath regime issued several authoritarian security arrangements. It took the Decision to establish the State Security Court based on Legislative Decree No 47 of 1968. It founded the Department of State Security based on Legislative Decree No 14 of 1969. The legislation establishing these departments remained in the dark and was never promulgated. These semi-public transformations were accompanied by a series of administrative, military and security measures that helped impose a disproportionate Alawite control over the army. An elite strike force was formed to protect the Party's military wing. The members of this force were elected from among those considered the most loyal and was led by Military Committee member Mohammed Omran. These troops were later known as the Defence Companies (*saraya al-difa'a*), led by Hafez al-Assad's brother Rifaat al-Assad, following the removal of Omran from power.[2] At the request of the then Air Force

Figure 0.3 Mohammed Omran, from a private collection.

Commander Hafez al-Assad, the Air Force Intelligence was established under the command of military officer Mohammed al-Khouli.

These massive security transformations were accompanied by economic changes, led by Assistant Secretary-General of the Baath Party, Salah Jadid, in 1964. He re-nationalized the country's economy, which hoped to return to liberalism after breaking up the unity with Egypt. Jadid attempted to develop a welfare state with all its economic and social consequences. The major Syrian cities ruralized, as mass migration from the countryside to the cities caused bloated central cities and abandoned villages and small towns. State institutions were inflated to accommodate the growing number of government employees, which later became known as 'masked unemployment'.

Figure 0.4 Rifat al-Assad, from a pro-regime social media site.

By the late 1960s, the Baath was well settled in power. Its institutions pursued the implementation of monolithic politics, that is, painting everyone in one color: Baathist. During this period, the Party witnessed shifts and conflicts among its rival wings. One of these conflicts brought Hafez al-Assad to power, when Assad carried out a coup d'état against his comrades in November 1970. Assad tightened the security's iron fist on public life in Syria – politically, economically, culturally and even religiously. He turned the security forces into a powerful arm of domination that infiltrated the state and society.[3] Eventually, under Assad, four intelligence agencies would grow into all-powerful security bodies: the General Intelligence Service or State Security, the Air Force Intelligence, the Military Intelligence, and Political Security.

On 12 November 1970, Hafez al-Assad had his former comrades Salah Jadid, Prime Minister Youssef Zuayyin and Head of State Dr Noureddin al-Atassi arrested and sent, along with their supporters, to Mezze military prison. Assad then tried them in staged treason trials between January and August of 1971, putting the founder of Baath Party and 100 of his most faithful followers, most in absentia, on trial. The main charge was conspiring to overthrow the Syrian government with financial and military assistance from Iraq. Michel Aflaq, former President Amin al-Hafiz and three others were sentenced to death, while 99 others received varying terms of imprisonment.[4]

The changes within the Party were reflected within the army and the security establishment. In a real purge, Assad arrested all officers loyal to Salah Jadid along with

Figure 0.5 Mohammed al-Khouli, from a private collection.

officers assumed to side with his oppositional factions within the Party. He used this opportunity to carry out a clean-up operation of the army and the security establishment. His own loyal comrades took over these institutions and positions within a matter of days. Colonel Mohammed al-Khouli officially became commander of the Air Force Intelligence. Major General Hikmet al-Shihabi became head of Military Intelligence. Brigadier Ali Dabbagh was handed the General Intelligence Service and Hafez al-Assad himself became the 'General Commander of the Army and Armed Forces'.

Hafez al-Assad's movements were an unprecedented unilateral turn in the political history of Syria. This unilateralism was reinforced by his 1973 war against Israel, aimed at restoring the Golan Heights. Assad's propaganda apparatus presented this war as a victory, but the Golan Heights remained under Israeli control. Over time, Assad's personality cult established him as the hero of 'Correction and Liberation' (*al-tasheeh*

Figure 0.6 Hafez Al-Assad flanked by Prime Minister Mahmoud Al-Ayoubi (r), and Mufti of the Republic Ahmed Kaftaro (l). From a private collection.

wa al-tahreer), 'correcting the Party's path' and the grand 'Liberation War of October'. This period witnessed some protests, particularly in 1973, which later became known as the 'constitutional protests', because they addressed the infractions Assad committed against the Syrian constitution.

Assad's dictatorship did not leave Syrian society unaffected. There was widespread political protest as Assad was slowly becoming involved in the Lebanese Civil War which escalated in 1976. To stifle dissent, the Syrian security services launched a massive campaign to 'cleanse' Syrian society of opponents to Assad. The regime began framing any form of dissent and opposition as hostile, labelling the opposition as the Muslim Brotherhood or parties cooperating with it.

Assad based his harsh moves against the full spectrum of civil society on the infamous artillery school incident of 1979, when Islamists stormed the artillery school in Aleppo and massacred mostly Alawite cadets. The security services arrested anyone believed or accused to be a member of the Muslim Brotherhood. Thousands were killed, detained, or went missing because of this massive military and security campaign including religious army officers, all left-wing opponents, as well as members of various trade unions. The bloody climax of the offensive was a chilling massacre on the morning of Sunday 28 February 1982, in which a massive infantry and artillery operation laid waste to the town of Hama in central Syria. No one knows the exact number of the victims of this massacre. However, the Syrian Commission for Human Rights estimated that about 40,000 people were killed.[5]

Figure 0.7 Atassi Assad Jadeed 1968, from a private collection.

The consolidation of a security mentality in Syria

The memory of the military coups that followed independence, the subsequent unity with Egypt, the ascent to power of the Baath Party and its internal struggle for the presidential chair, the bloody conflict between the Islamists and the Baathists during the mid-1960s and the ultimate battle in the early 1980s, and the severe economic transformation that has befallen Syrian society. All these elements provided Assad with a solid basis from which to enforce security control over the Syrians. Political forces were eradicated and opposing military powers were either locked up or laying in graves. From this perspective, as a security mastermind, Assad started by promoting the concept of *al-sutra*, which became a metaphor for wanting to stay out of trouble, or just 'getting by'. The concept came to symbolize the notion of 'positive neutrality', which the security services used to describe citizens in their security reports, usually submitted on request. In these reports, positive neutrality meant 'a citizen who does not get involved in politics, someone who just wants to make a living, even if a bare minimum, someone with no negative feelings towards authority, not even by means of a joke, someone who believes in the desire of the authorities to improve conditions and raise the standard of living'.[6]

The so-called 'security report' (*taqrir*) became the regime's most prominent form of intelligence intervention in the daily lives of the Syrian people. These studies or reports showcased the philosophy of Syrian intelligence: establishing a set of rules, norms and standards and rendering civil society inactive and fully dependent on the security apparatus, creating a mindset that drives society to devise the limits of what is permissible and what is forbidden.

All security departments functionally fall under the Office of National Security. However administratively, they fall under either the Ministry of Defence or the Ministry of Interior, or they form a separate department, such as with the General Intelligence. Despite their different functional and administrative affiliations, they all adopt an intrinsic duality to recruit operatives and officers: they are inherently loyal to the regime but advance their own particular interests.[7] This duality was the real guarantor to allow those departments to remain as the main actor in all domestic interactions; and the strongest support base of the regime. The most important features of this dual philosophy were absolute power and tying the movement of Syrian society to the security services. The consequences of this duality were that it gave the security services full independence and expanded their powers to cover every aspect of life. Granting security officials full power over all corners of the state allowed them to pursue their own interests. This allowed the heads and senior staff of these departments to accumulate unprecedented power and wealth. This wealth could and would subsequently be used against them in the form of corruption charges when there was a need to remove them from their posts. In other words: Assad created the moral hazard of extreme empowerment of his cadre, and then used its consequences to compromise those same men. These powers were accompanied by competition for loyalty to the regime and hostility between the departments. Hafez al-Assad maintained that hostility to tighten his control over security. He linked good performance to the criteria of loyalty and absolute obedience to his person.[8]

When Bashar al-Assad came to power in 2000, he worked on growing the conflict and competition over the areas of security influence and control. For example, control over border access points became divided: Iraq's access points belonged to the General Intelligence department, but Jordan's were under the Air Force Intelligence, whereas the crossings with Lebanon were controlled by Military Security, and Political Security oversaw access points with Turkey. The structural competition and loyalty to the regime were accompanied by a layered security fear, best exemplified by the 'Intelligence Report'. The phenomenon of the Intelligence Report perpetuated a state of terror among both civilians and security personnel alike. Everybody feared everybody. Anyone could be denounced in an intelligence report at any time.

This compound security administration magnified the size and role of intelligence services. Huge security structures mushroomed in the capital, Damascus, and in the major cities. Immense concrete buildings emerged that cordoned off entire streets and neighbourhoods with cinderblock walls and checkpoints. The administrative flooding of Syrian cities by the security services led to a state of despondency and terror and established the complete shutdown of the political scene, debates, and practice.[9]

Order, security, and society

The Assad regime has maintained its security mentality since 1970. It has not sought to establish either a security college or academy that can produce qualified officers to fill leadership positions in the military and civil security services. As confirmed by security studies research and field interviews we have conducted, every security commander in Syria has been assigned from the military. They control the levers of the military and civil security services via delegation mechanisms. All personnel working in these services are subject to the military system, its code of conduct, penalties, etc. This strict military mentality ensured these departments remained loyal and cohesive during their encounters with Syrian society.

The bureaucracy of these departments formed a powerful shield protecting them from collapse. The most obvious example is the Idlib Intelligence branches, who sustained their functions and remained intact throughout the Syrian civil war, although the entire province has been ruled by Syrian armed opposition for many years. The function of these branches is to follow up on cases of dissidents and people from Idlib wanted by the central security services. Those branches maintained their functional and administrative system, publishing circulars, naming the head of the branch, or periodically adjusting the salaries that get paid

The four security departments are involved in everything, from freelance licenses and kiosk permits to municipalities to the appointment of ministers and candidates for the Parliament. They are busy fighting opposition political parties or acts classified as hostile. This systematic overlap enshrines the concept of a security state and fortifies strict security management. However, these security forces also have their boundaries known to all: the Presidential Palace, the Republican Guard, and the Fourth Division.[10] These three power centres in Syria are autonomous and enforce their own jurisdiction, thereby dividing the security sector into two levels:

- *Control tools*: Air Force Intelligence and Military Intelligence departments are the tools of the military and the armed forces. The General Intelligence is a joint control tool of the National Security Bureau and the ruling Baath Party, while Political Security is the control tool of the Ministry of Interior.
- *Paramilitary networks*: The Republican Guard, the Fourth Division, and the Tiger Forces. These are tasked with engineering the security process and setting its relationships and governing rules, as well as ensuring the security of the regime and carrying on processes and operations within society should any threatening indicators emerge. Their main function is establishing and enhancing the stability of the ruling regime.[11]

This vast security complex required a massive number of personnel. At the beginning of the Syrian Revolution in 2011, there were about 65,000 full-time employees and several hundred thousand part-time employees in the various Syrian security services. This amounts to one intelligence operative for every 257 Syrian citizens. As 59.5 per cent of Syrians are over the age of 15, the ratio then becomes one in every 153 Syrian citizens – one of the highest percentages in the world.[12]

The deeply enshrined security arrangements require several legal and constitutional supporting pillars devised perfectly by the Assad regime. The General Commander of the Army and the Armed Forces is, at the same time, the State Secretary of the ruling Baath Arab Socialist Party. He appoints the director of the National Security Bureau –

the highest security authority in the country – and appoints the heads of the security services. He also appoints the Prime Minister and the president of the Supreme Court. Hierarchically, as head of the Party, he is head of the civil and military security forces, which in turn controls the National Security Bureau. He is the Supreme Commander of the Army, which in turn runs the Air & Military Intelligence, while its affiliated officers head the rest of the civil security departments. Looking at the biographies of most of these officials, their strong military affiliation is evident. All this executive authority means that the Syrian President is nearly omnipotent in overseeing the security sector.

Continuity

Changing the heads of the security services does not change their functional role or mechanisms, which are based on a small army of operatives and non-commissioned officers who form the real engine of those services. Sergeant-Majors, Sergeants, and Corporals occupy active administrative posts within this security system. They manage correspondence, investigation or interrogation offices, studies, research, tracking, patrols, and detention centres.

The effective military model through which Syrian security services operate, guarantees the continuity of their functions, regardless of the change in their leadership. For example, recent changes have only affected the security forces in terms of personnel, not in terms of strategic policies or levels of violence. The head of the National Security Bureau, Ali Mamlouk, became the Vice President for Security Affairs. He was replaced as a Director of the National Security Bureau by Major General Mohamed Deeb Zeitoun, while the General Intelligence Service was headed by Major General Hussam Luqa. Replacing Luqa as Director of the Political Security department, Major General Nasser al-Ali was appointed. The head of the Air Force Intelligence, Major-General Jamil al-Hassan, was released into retirement and was succeeded by Major General Ghassan Jawdat Ismail. These appointments included the placement of Major General Nasir Deeb as Head of the Criminal Security Department, succeeding Major General Safwan Issa. The names might have changed, but the realities of surveillance, control, and repression have not. The intelligence services continue to rule Syria with unchecked and unchallenged power.

1

The Military Intelligence

Introduction

The Syrian army is comprised of intelligence arms as well as military divisions of an intelligence nature. This situation arose within the Syrian military following the arrival of the Baath party into power in 1963. On that day, the Baath Military Commission established a special military force, later known as the Defence Brigades. The current Fourth Division, special forces, was established from the remnants of the Defence Brigades, which were dissolved following the disagreement between Hafez al-Assad and his brother Rifaat, who was subsequently expelled permanently from the country and for decades lived a life of luxury in Paris. In addition to the Fourth Division, the Republican Guard received special attention from Hafez al-Assad. The Guard is formed from a clear Alawite majority and its main task is to protect Damascus and the Presidential Palace.

Besides these teams that are a mix of military and intelligence, the army has its own exclusive intelligence service, Military Intelligence, which is more distinct in terms of its history, scope, and massive deployment. Military Intelligence is the security and intelligence division under the Syrian military establishment. Its role emerged as the army infiltrated public life, starting with the 1949 coup, and continued during the union between Syria and Egypt. The authority of the Division expanded vastly with the Baath's assumption of power. Its role increased in power and visibility on Syria's domestic political scene. The Air Force and Air Defence also have their own Air Intelligence department, established by Mohammed al-Khouli.

According to Figure 1, the army can be considered a purely Baathist force. The Supreme Commander of the Army and the Armed Forces is at the same time the State Secretary of the ruling Baath Arab Socialist Party as well as the President – currently, Bashar al-Assad. Reporting to him in the pyramid is the Minister of Defence, who serves as a member of the Party's Central Committee, the highest authority in the Party. Then come the commanders of the army corps, where every commander is also a Party Branch Secretary because each corps is considered a branch of the Party. The military divisions are considered Party divisions and consist of three Party divisions representing the brigades and military departments within the division. Party presence within the army continues into the military brigades, which represent a Party section that adopts a weekly Party meeting system, similar to Party branches and divisions.

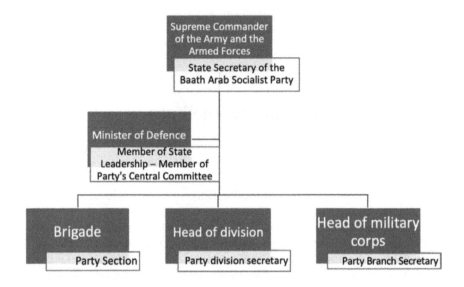

They submit periodic reports to Party leadership within the army. What is true of the army applies to its security institutions as well.

The Military Intelligence

The roots of the immense Military Intelligence apparatus of the current Syrian government go back to the 'Second Office' of the French Mandate's Syrian army (*le deuxième bureau*). It was transformed into the Military Intelligence division after decolonization and became known among the Syrians as 'Military Security' (*al-amn al-askari*). Like other security services, this division was taken over by the Baathists in 1963. When Hafez al-Assad turned against his party comrades and took power in 1970, the division was headed by his close friend, Mohammed Ali Zaza. Succeeding him in heading the division in early April 1971 was Hikmet al-Shihabi, who had obtained his Soviet intelligence certificate from the KGB in 1970. Shihabi remained Division Head until 1974. He was succeeded by Ali Douba, one of the most prominent and notorious commanders in the history of Syrian Military Intelligence. He remained the head of the division from 1974 until 2000, where he was forced to retire in preparation for the arrival of Bashar al-Assad in power. His successor as Division Head was his deputy, Hassan Khalil, whose term ended in 2005 and who was succeeded by his deputy, Assef Shawkat, the husband of Hafez Al-Assad's daughter Bushra, who remained head of division until 2009. The Military Intelligence Service was then led by Abdul-Fattah Qudsiyeh (until 2012), Rafiq Shehadeh (until 2015), Mohammed Muhalla (until 2019), and Kifah Mulhem (July 2019 to date).

The Military Intelligence Division reports to the Ministry of Defence administratively and financially, but the Minister of Defence does not have any authority over it. The

Figure 1.1 Assef Shawkat, from a private collection.

division intervenes in the appointment of the Minister of Defence, his deputies, Chiefs of Staff, and movements of all officers and operatives in the army. The head of the division is appointed by a direct decision of the President. The division was established to take charge of the security of military sectors, the borders, operatives, and officers, as well as military buildings. Over time, the division started interfering in the public life of Syrians much more broadly. Its role was increased during the first battles of Assad against his opponents in the mid-1970s, specifically as armed confrontations with the Muslim Brotherhood escalated in the early 1980s. The division led a massive campaign to regain control of Syrian society. It threw thousands of opponents in its detention centres, first in the cellars of its branches, and later into political prisons such as Mezze and Tadmor, and then Saydnaya. In earlier times, it had used the prisons of the Citadel of Damascus and Karakon al-Sheikh Hassan.

The division comprises several central branches, located in Damascus. Some do not have prisons, such as the Information Branch, which specializes in gathering and evaluating information. It contains many different sections, including one on religions and political parties. It also monitors the activity of local and global printed

Figure 1.2 Rafiq Shahadeh, from a pro-regime social media site.

and audio-visual media, including the internet. It deals with these directly or indirectly, based on whatever aspect is considered important to the work of the Military Intelligence.

Other branches that do not have any known prisons are:

- Branch 211: in charge of monitoring the military's radio signals for security and encryption, in addition to technical surveys.
- Branch 225 (also known as the 'Computer Branch'): responsible for monitoring all the military's telecommunications lines.
- Branch 294: responsible for monitoring movements of the army and armed forces, excluding the air force and air defence, which have their own intelligence agency. It holds files on the military camps and corpses, their state, combat readiness, and the extent of their loyalties. Security officers of military corpses are more associated to this branch than to their own lines of command. It is alleged that any movement of troops must be carried out with the approval of, and in coordination with this branch. It supervises the Military Police Service and its units attached to the military corpses. It is suspected that there is a detention centre in the Patrol Branch 216, which executes all commands, central or subsidiary, related to the implementation of the field security functions.

As for branches that have known prisons, or that oversee detention centres, the most infamous are:

- Branch 235: known as the Palestine Branch;
- Branch 248: known as the Military Investigation Branch;
- Branch 293.
- Branch 215: known as the Raid and Incursion Force. This branch has approximately 4,000 operatives trained in all special forces' tasks such as kidnapping, assassination, and arresting the most wanted, hard to incarcerate, individuals.

All these branches are based in Damascus, but there is a Military Intelligence branch in every province of Syria: Homs Military Branch 261, Hamah Branch 219, Idlib Branch 271, Deir ez-Zor Branch 243, Hasakeh Branch 222, Aleppo Branch 290, Palmyra/

Figure 1.3 Kifah Mulhem, from a pro-regime social media site.

Figure 1.4 Map of Military Intelligence Damascus, Google Maps.

Tadmor Branch 221, Deraa Branch 245. These provincial branches contain all the previously mentioned divisions, but in a smaller format, as well as their own detention centres. One special branch is the Front Intelligence Branch, 220, also called Sa'sa' Branch, which specializes in the intelligence affairs of the occupied Golan Heights, the forces at the front and also monitors the International Emergency Forces operating there.

Since the mid-1970s, Military Intelligence became active in Syria as a major arrest and detention apparatus. The reason it emerged lies in the varying weights of the intelligence services on the Syrian domestic scene, which follow a very complex equation. In the 1970s, the biggest player in the world of intelligence was the Air Force Intelligence. Its main aim was the removal of the Baathist leaders who Hafez al-Assad turned against in the autumn of 1970, by detaining them in al-Mezzeh prison. At the beginning of the 1980s, Military Intelligence began operating with assertiveness and had *carte blanche* to commit violence. Military Intelligence became the primary department among the Syrian spectrum of intelligence agencies, and some big names emerged, such as Mazhar Faris, Kamal Yusuf, Hisham Ikhtiar in Damascus, and Ghazi Kanaan in Homs. This major shift was accompanied by Ali Douba's arrival to the leadership of the Division in 1974. We will see what a pivotal role these men had in arresting, detaining, and torturing tens of thousands of Syrians.

The role of Military Intelligence grew to the point where, in 1987, Hafez al-Assad, directed all intelligence divisions to abide by the decisions of Military Intelligence. After this, it became the strongest and most aggressive of all security departments and had the highest level of control over the country's files.[1] In order to build a complete picture of this security apparatus, and to understand the methodology of its work in its detention centres, we have examined and documented testimonies from forty former Military Intelligence detainees. We have analyzed dozens of legal reports as well as testimonies published in articles or literary journals. We have reviewed the (auto)biographies of the senior officers and conducted interviews with people who knew and were close to them. We have also discussed the major shifts in this apparatus with a number of deserters and dissidents of the intelligence services and security researchers.

The wide reach, profound power, and deep personal and societal impact of the Military Security is demonstrated well in the life story of M.A.K., a man from Aleppo, born in 1958 and detained from August 1979 to March 1980 on suspicion of Muslim Brotherhood activity. At the Military Security branch in Aleppo, he was hung from the ceiling in a car tyre and beaten for over four hours. The interrogator asked him: 'Who is your God?' When he responded 'Allah', they lunged at him with sticks and power cables yelling that his God is Hafez al-Assad. He described the guards as 'illiterates, who only carried out orders, as devils, who continuously pushed, kicked, and punched him. They tried to insult me verbally and swear at my religion and my mother. Through practicing my belief and prayer I tried to stand my ground.' MAK suffered from a lifetime of amnesia as a result of being tortured, even after he fled to Europe. Former detainees such as him suffer from a certain speechlessness, as the violence they suffered was literally unspeakable and they remain at a loss for words. From personal letters between M.A.K. and his son, we know that the Syrian intelligence agencies arrested at least three of his family members in Syria and tortured them, while asking about M.A.K.'s fate. They also told those family members that if M.A.K. returned to Syria voluntarily, all of them would be released. Consequently, the pressure on M.A.K., who by now was in the Netherlands, was immense. For the rest of his life, he suffered from sleeplessness, irritability, and pain in his back, hands, and ankles. When it rains, the pain in his bones reminds him of prison, decades after his imprisonment.[2]

Branch 261: Homs

The oldest arrest documented by Military Intelligence was one of the followers of Marwan Hadid, the most prominent Islamist figure of the time. Hadid himself was arrested at his home in the Adawi district of Damascus on 30 June 1975. A number of his followers, including Abu Ibrahim,[3] were arrested on Friday 15 August 1975 by the Military Intelligence branch in Homs and transferred to the Military Investigation Branch in Damascus, eventually ending up in Mezzeh military prison.

This incident highlights the power of the Homs Military Intelligence Branch led by Ghazi Kanaan. The Branch arrested Abu Ibrahim and interrogated him, taking on the role of the 'Quartet Committee' and the Central Investigation branch in Damascus. The Quartet was then based in the Mezzeh military prison, and was responsible for the investigations in the case of Hadid and his followers. In our interview with him, Abu Ibrahim said: 'I ran away from home in fear of being arrested. The Badia guards caught me around Tadmor. I was transferred through the Badia Military Intelligence branch to the Homs Military Intelligence branch. Ghazi Kanaan interviewed for me seven days before he transferred me to Damascus.[4]

The first attempts to extract detailed confessions from Abu Ibrahim were violent. At the time of his arrival at the branch, a number of operatives immediately started beating him with their hands and feet. He was held in solitary confinement for the duration of his stay at the Homs branch. The torture lasted about 12 hours on the first day. Six operatives took turns in his torture using 'bamboo and wooden sticks. Back then the quad cable was not yet in use'. The quad cable shows up as a torture device in the early 1980s.

Ghazi Kanaan performed 'the good cop' act with Abu Ibrahim. He acted as the protector. When the operatives took Abu Ibrahim to meet Kanaan, he immediately started berating his men for torturing the prisoner. Abu Ibrahim was able to see Kanaan, as back then blindfolding prisoners had not yet implemented as a mandatory procedure. Abu Ibrahim was almost carried into Kanaan's office –he was not able to walk because of the torture he had suffered. Kanaan served him a meal and tried to extract information in a nice way.

He conversed with the then 18-year-old Abu Ibrahim but got nothing.

That's when he summered two operatives and asked them to bring the 'telephone' – an old manually operated telephone device – which was the instrument of electric torture at the time. The electric current is generated by the dynamo of the phone and its power is connected to the speed of spinning. I refused to confess, so he became more ferocious, yet without getting angry or nervous. He put the electricity in my ear and on my pinky fingers. The scars from those stainless-steel clamps are still visible on my hands to this day. Then they stripped me down, put electricity on my private parts, and I passed out. They beat me unconscious and repeated the procedure. I woke up the next day naked in the cell, after they opened the door and splashed me with cold water.

Abu Ibrahim was tortured again with electricity; again he passed out. He was transferred to Homs Military Hospital Al-Wa'er and stayed there for four days with his hands and feet tied to the bed. He was then transferred to the Military Investigation Branch 248, which was led by Mazhar Faris. He stayed in the Military Investigation for four days without being asked a question. He was then transferred to the Mezzeh military prison. Abu Ibrahim stated: 'The official investigation was led by a high-level security committee comprising Major General Naji Jamil, the Head of the National Security Office, the Head of the General Intelligence Service, Adnan Dabbagh, the Chief of Military Intelligence, Ali Douba, and the heads of the other security departments. The direct interrogator was Captain Hisham Jamil, the brother of Major General Naji Jamil, along with First Lieutenant Hamid Esber.'

The interrogation of the commission did not differ much from that of the head of the Military Intelligence branch in Homs. The same violent methods of electricity, bamboo sticks and cold water continued for three days. Abu Ibrahim was placed in the cell adjacent to that of Hadid's. Apart from taking him to Homs Military Hospital and transferring Hadid to the Military Hospital 601, Abu Ibrahim does not recall any health support during his arrest and investigation period. He was not asked if he had any illnesses, nor was he checked by a doctor in the branch or in prison.

The food in the Mezzeh military prison during his investigation was the same as the military's, the food allocated to the Syrian army. It comprised of 'Halawah and olives or hard-boiled eggs or thick yogurt with a loaf of *sammoun* bread for breakfast. Cooked bulgur or rice with vegetable gravy with bread for lunch. For dinner, boiled potatoes or boiled eggs with lentil soup and bread.' However, food and drink were used as tools of pressure and torture during the interrogation. The interrogator allowed them or prevented them from eating and drinking, depending on the pressure he wanted to exert on the detainees.[5] The malnutrition and torture suffered by the group's leader, Marwan Hadid, was extreme. He was transferred to Hospital 601, but his body was in a such a deplorable state, as a result of torture and starvation. that he died at the military hospital in June 1976 at the age of 42.[6]

On 25 October 1980, the Homs Military branch, led by Ghazi Kanaan, arrested a group of high-school students on charges of affiliation with the Muslim Brotherhood. Among them was Mohammed Nader Diab, who was 16-years-old at the time. After his interrogation, he was transferred to the Baloni[7] military prison in Homs. He was then transferred to Tadmor military prison directly. This process was repeated with other detainees in Aleppo. In Hama, the detainees were grouped at the 49th Brigade and then transferred to Tadmor. 'Before the Hama massacre, the intelligence services' branches were authorized to send anyone to Tadmor prison as they please . . . After the massacre, Hafez al-Assad withdrew this authorization, keeping it in the hands of the central branches of the capital.'[8] During the same period, i.e., before February 1982, the Military Intelligence branch in Tartous arrested a group of students, but transferred them to Military Investigation Branch 248 in Damascus; from there they were transferred to Tadmor.

The Military Intelligence branch of Homs arrested Mohammed Nader Diab along with fifteen students from Abdul Hamid Al-Zahrawi high school. They were arrested by a patrol led by the head of the Raid Department of the branch, Captain Mohammed al-Sha'ar. The 'reception' at the branch at the end of 1980 was no different from that at the end of 1975: The operatives immediately started striking, this time with cables. They interrogated them immediately, asking questions about their visits to mosques and their attendance at roundtable religious discussion circles. The interrogation was over in an hour. The next day, they were made to seal their written statements with their fingerprints, without knowing what they contained, as they were blindfolded.[9] The practice and policy of blindfolding had been introduced in the middle of 1976.[10]

The Military Intelligence branch in Homs is located near the train station, between the City Customs and the headquarters of the Iraqi Petroleum Company, which was building Iraq's oil pipeline. There are no dormitories in Homs prison, only individual cells. Using the toilet is permitted only twice a day. The food provided is sandwiches purchased using the detainees' own money. Until 1980, there was a nurse in the branch who functioned as a medical officer to heal the wounds resulting from torture, however many detainees did not survive.[11]

The lucky interview

Diab said in our interview: 'Three days after we were transferred to the Baloni prison, they moved us back to the branch. Patrol operatives told us that the 'master' (*moallem*), meaning the head of the branch, Ghazi Kanaan, will meet us in preparation for our release. Kanaan saw some of us, while others, me included, waited in vain. They sent us back to Balouni. The next day, the Fighting Vanguard group carried out a military operation against the regime. The Homs branch released those interviewed by its head Kanaan. The rest, me included, were transferred on Thursday, 30 October 1980 to Tadmor prison in the desert.

Branch 271: Idlib

Treatment and torture methods are similar in the various Military Intelligence branches in the provinces. A former prisoner told the story of his detention in the Military Intelligence branch in Idlib in 1980:

My hands were pulled behind my back and tied with a strong rope. I was blindfolded and taken to an underground chamber. The methods of torture began mutilating my body. Whipping with cables and electrocution. I was put on the 'Magic Carpet' (*bisaat al-rih*) and the confessional chair (the German chair). They used to wet my body with water and put an electrical wire on parts of my body. On my fingers and toes. It's like I'm in a parallel life filled with nightmares. My screaming was shaking the walls of the room. Charges I'd never heard of before were thrown at me, which I denied. The torment grows and then the question is asked again. Every re-interrogation means an hour and a half to two hours of torture. After which they would take me back to the 80 x 180 cell. Its floor is covered with a blanket filthy with urine and excrement residues. The cell's previous resident was not allowed out to the toilet, so he had to relieve himself in the cell. I spent three months in a Military Intelligence cell in Idlib, during which I was exhausted from the severity of the torture.[12]

Branch 219: Hama

Anyone who knows anything about Syria's contemporary history understands the importance of the security grip in Hama. The city revolted against Baath rule in 1964, and its population played a prominent role in protests against the authoritarian constitution in 1973. In 1976, this escalated into armed conflict and ended up in the unprecedented massacre of February 1982. The security grip, however, did not end with the massacre. Arrests increased and became even more vicious.

A university student, Baraa al-Sarraj, was arrested at the gates of his college. On 5 March 1984, Military Intelligence transported him to the district branch in its old headquarters in the Adawi District of Damascus. He stayed there a few hours and was transferred to the Military Intelligence branch in Hama. In an unpublished memoir which Sarraj shared with us, he paints a particularly evocative image of his ordeal:

> The car entered the building of the Military Investigation branch of Hama, led by Colonel Yahya Zidane ... So many steps down to a cellar ... I heard the noise of food distribution, and threats from time to time, until a warden led me to cell number three and locked the door ... I couldn't even see my hand ... I was exhausted ... the cell was 2 metres long by less than a metre wide and had a vent on the ceiling that allows no more than a fist to pass. The ceiling is lower than 180 cm, my height ... A stinky toilet by the door. A stench of mold and moisture ... It wasn't too long before the door was opened again and I am led by a warden, blindfolded, through a metal door. My feet hit a frame. I entered a lit room. I heard the music of the evening news on T V. I knew it was 8:30 pm. The interrogation room smelled of cigarettes and orange peels; I had chills of fear that I will never forget ... I heard the voices of more than three people.[13]

And so, the journey of al-Sarraj's torment began; it was not dissimilar to those in all the other branches. The violence continued during the interrogation in the branch. The Military Intelligence prison in Hama maintained its brutal reputation until the beginning of the twenty-first century. On Sunday July 23, 2000, Iraqi-British athlete Hilal Abdul-Razzaq Ali was taken to the branch regarding his residence papers in Syria.

> I went with the operatives to the Military Intelligence Centre in Hama, headed by Brigadier Ahmad Hallum. A three-storey building with a big gate, no other buildings neighbour it on the way to Damascus.[14] Brigadier Mohammed al-Sha'ar met him without asking him any questions. I went down to the branch jail, where I was received by a horrid warden named Imran. His voice was so rough. He yelled at me for intimidation: 'Asshole ... Stand straight, boy!' He dragged me to solitary cell number four and locked the door behind me. I turned around to see a tight, filthy cell. It had a stinky toilet ... I woke up the next morning on mixed voices of beatings, insults, groaning and cries for help. I learned that it was the first shift of savage torture that detainees were subjected to within the branch. The wardens used to come early in the morning. They opened the cell doors violently and took their victims out, with their hands cuffed and eyes blindfolded. They steered them like sheep. I used to look at them and tremble in terror. Shortly afterwards, the cable whipping begins on their backs and all parts of their bodies, indiscriminatingly ... The torture started every day at 8:00 am and stopped at 2:00 pm. It started again at 8:00 pm until 11:00 pm. Although I have not been tortured, the cries and groans of the detainees whipped my soul. The cables make a terrifying whistling sound before they land on the backs of the prisoners as they groan in pain. I kept myself together but faced an extreme panic episode when a female prisoner in her solitary cell had a nervous breakdown. She was screaming hysterically before they took her to the hospital.[15]

A torturer speaks: Branch 211

MT, from the eastern town of Muhassan, worked for Military Security, Department 211 in Qaboun. In 1991, he defected to Switzerland and was elaborately interrogated by the Swiss authorities. These are excerpts from his testimony.

'They kept passing on reports about me to the leadership that I did not let them torture me so brutally. I was then questioned daily, they wanted to know why I did not brutalize the prisoners. I was insulted and sometimes beaten during the interrogations, and psychological pressure was also put on me. There were many people tortured in front of me, 90% of these people were innocent. That put a lot of pressure on me, I am a human being and I had to witness the torture.'

Q120: Were you ever present during an interrogation session when a detainee was being electro-tortured?

A: During the torture, yes.

Q121: Was this an integral part of your job that you had to be there?

A: Yes, I supervised the forces carrying it out.

Q122: How many volts and how many amperes can a human body endure?

A: That was simply by means of a device. The detainee is connected to a cable at the genitals and receives an electric shock.

Q123: How strong is this shock?

A: Undefined. Depending on the person. 40, 50 or 60 volts, you can die from it.

Q126: How many electric shocks could be given per interrogation session?

A: Depending. One person will testify to everything before being hooked up to the device. The other dies and says nothing at all.

Q129: How does a human body react when it is connected to such a device by means of a cable?

A: Some bodies react by twitching, the others faint, the third keep their eyes open and bite their teeth, but they faint at the same time. These will die.[16]

Branch 227: 'District Branch'

One of the most infamous Military Intelligence branches in all of Syria, the District Branch, is in charge of Damascus province and its countryside. Its old headquarters was in the Adawi district, close to Abbasiyeen Square in the centre of the capital. From the beginning of the 1970s until the end of 1984, it was headed by Major Nizar al-Helou. After the escape from the branch of members of the Islamic Vanguard,

Figure 1.5 Map of Branch Location in City 227, Google Maps.

al-Helou was sacked and his deputy, Hisham Ikhtiyar, became head of the branch. At the end of 1984, the branch's headquarters were moved closer to the Military Investigation branch in a large security cluster comprising dozens of military buildings and security branches.

The late poet and political prisoner Adnan Misbah Al-Miqdad (1959–2019) said:

A Military Intelligence patrol raided my neighborhood near Damascus, at about 3 in the morning on 16 October 1980. They broke into the house in a brutal way. They knocked on the doors with rifle butts. I tried to escape through the roof of the house, but found dozens of guns pointed at my house from neighbors' rooftops ... I gave in. Ten operatives invaded our house. They lined my mother and siblings to the wall. They thoroughly searched the house looking for the Secretary-General of the Communist Party's Political Bureau, Riad al-Turk. They thought he was hiding in my house. I learned the identity of patrol later at the branch. They didn't say why I was arrested, but I knew what it was about. I arrived at the branch in its old headquarters in Adawi district. I spent there 15 days which were more hell than my 15 years of imprisonment. I was admitted to the prison registrar. They took my personal data and everything I had in my pockets. I was immediately taken to the cellar where the detention centre was. We did not have the luxury of a medical examination, nor were we asked about our health condition.[17]

Al-Miqdad was not subjected to severe physical torture during the interrogation. He was new to the Party. However, the torture of his superior, journalist Ridha Haddad, remained engraved in his head. Haddad refused to say his real name. They brutally tortured him. He didn't give them any information, so their brutality increased. The torture led to his hospitalization where he stayed for several days. Al-Miqdad remembered: 'Watching the torture of your comrades and colleagues is a thousand times more difficult than being tortured yourself.'[18]

Mock Execution

We were called upon by numbers as usual. We were crammed in a small lounge. They told us shortly afterwards that they were going to transfer us to Tadmor prison to carry out execution sentences against us. We were glad to hear about the execution. We believed that death was going to be a relief from our prison. We learned each other's identities by peeking from under the blindfolds. As we climbed the stairs towards the car, intelligence operatives started beating us. We started racing up the stairs and were certain we were going to our execution in Tadmor. We're trying to decipher the route and directions. Knowing the streets of Damascus, we knew they were not going to take us to Tadmor. We recognized the city noises near al-Hamidiyah old market downtown. The destination was Karakon al-Sheikh Hassan. When we arrived, they lifted our blindfolds and removed the handcuffs. I was finally able to see the world and light after 15 days of darkness. I fell unconscious from the majestic light. A warden hit me with his foot to wake me up.[19]

Branch 227: the old headquarters

The former Jordanian detainee, Suleiman Abu al-Khair, writes in his memoir:

> They violently led us into an underground corridor. I counted over 20 steps of stairs. I descended, blindfolded, barely able to make my way. A small passage overlooked a room to hand personal belongings. To its immediate left, stood a room for judicial prisoners (non-political ones). The corridor overlooks another room called the 'Salon'. To its right is a toilet. On the other side is the 'Buffet', as they call it. It's a room where they prepare our dirty food. They stopped us in this narrow corridor for a while, then led us into the personal belongings room. The branch officially 'received' us from the patrol that brought us in. The handcuffs and blindfolds were removed. The admission cards were written, then we were ordered to take our clothes off for inspection. They took us to the Salon. Its far end and right side were lined with the black doors of solitary cells. We were told to take our places laying on mattresses; I have never seen, nor will I ever see, anything dirtier. I lay among the heaps of human bodies stacked motionless, like mummified corpses.[20]

Detainees in the branch are not allowed to remove the blindfolds or the handcuffs. They are assigned numbers instead of their names. Abu al-Khair's was 11. They were denied long periods of sleep. 'There was a warden who would curse us even during his sleep. When he wakes up, if he doesn't find someone to hit, he hits the wall. He was a horror for everyone. Once, while I was asleep my blindfold was tilted out of place. The guard started hitting me with a quad cable so hard that he almost broke my leg.' The guards systemically blocked any communication between the detainees. They punished whoever broke the rules.[21]

Abu Al-Khair reported: 'Once I fell into a coma, from which I only woke to the voice of the doctor. I was drenched with water; something I was already used to. The doctor ran full checks. He confirmed I was in a good shape, and I could stand on my own two feet, but I didn't get up on my feet. I didn't let them know I was awake. So the doctor yelled: 'Put him back on the wheel, apparently he's an actor, but we will not fall for his games!'[22] In addition to the wheel as a torture device, electricity was used with a dynamo, quite similar to that used by the Military Intelligence branch in Homs with Abu Ibrahim in 1975.

The great escape

The most prominent event that occurred in the new HQ of the District branch was the escape of members from the Fighting Vanguard in 1983. In 1986, the following people arrived at Dormitory 15 in Tadmor prison: Mohammed Nihad Boshi, Mohammed Fahad Na'al, Mahmoud al-Jassim and Mohammed Ghazal from Aleppo, accompanied by Abu Hammoud Zalkhi and Abdullah Bakrjan from Jisr Al-Shughour. Mahmoud Ashour remembered:[23] 'I was close to Mohammed Nihad al-Bushi.' He entered Syria from Turkey with members of the Vanguard, who were lured by an agent of the regime. They were arrested immediately and transferred to the District Branch in its new headquarters in Damascus. In total, 55 young men were arrested along with their Commander Adnan Akleh. Ashour tells the story as related to him by al-Boushi, who was later executed in Tadmor:

> We were placed in two dormitories in the branch, each with 22 young men. Adnan Akleh and the spokesman of the Vanguard were placed in solitary cells. Once as they took us to the bathrooms outside the room, we found small pieces of an iron saw. We collected them and decided to use them to escape the branch. We studied the place carefully and discovered that the net in the ceiling leads to a second roof. Between the two roofs and along the diameter there were windows from which we could escape. We started sawing the net. Everyone in the dormitory, 22 detainees, escaped through the net we cut, and we passed through the window between the two roofs. We attacked the guards securing the perimeter of the branch and we took their weapons. We divided ourselves into two groups. The first one got into a military ZiL jeep and drove away. The second swirled between the streets and allies accompanied by a Damascene young man. Eight made their way to the Jordanian border and crossed it. Security was on maximum alert and immediately launched search operations which resulted in capturing the remaining 14. They were all executed in Tadmor prison.

Divisie 227: het nieuwe hoofdkwartier

The new building became the official headquarters of the District Branch by the end of 1984, with Hisham Ikhtiyar at its head. In addition to the dormitories and cells, the new headquarters had an area which detainees called 'the net' (*al-shabak*). The former

Palestinian detainee, Haitham Shamlouni describes it as 'a space used as a dormitory in mid-1985. It's about 20 x 8 metres with a sky roof. It was supposedly designed as a 'breathing' space for prisoners, but it was covered with a metal mesh with only the sky above it.'

The prisoners' food at the new headquarters was different. The daily allowance for detainees was similar to those for Syrian army soldiers.

> We were eight young men, the night we were arrested. They brought us a *sammoun* loaf of bread, an egg and about ten olives for breakfast. They told us the amount was low because we hadn't entered the prison records yet. Lunch was red broth with little portions of potatoes, cauliflower, or eggplant with rice or bulgur. On national holidays, they brought chicken which we used to call 'handicapped', as it had no thighs. More often than not, they told us that the food had ran out and we had nothing left to eat.[24]

The administration of the branch's prison at its new headquarters resorted to the same old mechanism of keeping the detainees handcuffed and blindfolded. This time they were tying us in pairs. This prevented Shamlouni from defecating for the duration of his stay in the branch – 23 days. 'Going out to the toilets was a trip of torture. The warden whipped us all the time. Added to that, you're tied from the hand to another human being while in the toilet. How can you do anything but pee? I became severely constipated. The first time I was able to defecate was in the Military Investigation Branch the day we were transferred there.'[25]

Shamloni was tortured in various forms during interrogation sessions. He said:

> We were arrested following the disagreement between President Hafez al-Assad and the commander of the Palestine Liberation Organization, Yasser Arafat. The lack of clarity of the reason for the arrest did not prevent torture. Torture sessions were very harsh. They just wanted to hit us; the detective didn't want any information. They used whips and the German Chair on me. I was put in the Chair three times. I survived the German Chair which caused paralysis to an engineer detained with us. In one of the torture sessions, the nerve of my right thumb was damaged. The cable strikes caused the flesh and skin to be ripped from my hands and feet. Three nails fell off after being inflamed as a result of receiving the beating. Continuous starvation due to lack, or theft of the allocations added to the agony of the torture.[26]

A new system

By the end of 1987, the food system and treatment of the warden in the branch changed. Former Lebanese detainee, Ali Abu al-Dihn said:

> I was transferred from al-Suwayda Branch to the District Branch. There they took my personal belongings and took pictures of me with a number. They admitted me to cell no 6: 2 metres x 1.5 metres x 3 metres. I stayed there for four-and-a-half

months. They took me to the toilet twice a day. If I asked to go more, they allowed it. The food was good. Breakfast was an egg or yogurt with olives and a loaf of Arabic bread. Dinner was soup and potatoes. Lunch was bulgur with hummus or rice and some gravy. Tea was good. On the third day of my arrival of the branch, a doctor visited, asked me if I was sick and examined me to make sure.

A further change in prison life occurred in the District Branch in the beginning of the 1990s. Prisoners were dressed in uniforms. Former detainee Pierre Adam Yohanna says:

I was transferred from the Syrian Intelligence headquarters in Lebanon – in Anjar – to the District Branch in Damascus. I gave them my belongings and the wardens searched me. They made us shower. We received a military uniform as they took our clothes. This uniform became our official attire in the branch. It was washed once a week during the scheduled hot shower. They took the dirty ones and handed us clean, sterilized ones. The District branch was quite clean. Cleaner than any other branch I've been transferred to. The blankets and uniforms were washed well. They were boiled in water with chemicals to sterilize them.

The District branch maintained the system of replacing the name with the number of the cell in which the prisoner is held. Yohanna says: 'I was placed in cell number 42, and from that day on, my name became the cell number. No one from the warden called me by my name.'[27]

Branch 248: Military Investigation Branch

Branch 248 is the main investigative body of the Military Intelligence service. Mustafa al-Shughri was held there and said: 'In 1981, I was transferred from the Military Intelligence branch of Tartous to the Military Investigation Branch. The branch, led by Kamal Yusef, was one of the most violent branches of Military Intelligence. I stayed there for about five months. A detainee or two died every three days as a result of the ferocity of torture during the interrogation.'

There are conflicting views on the severity of the torture among leftist and the Islamist detainees. The leftists believe that the situation in the branch became easier with Kamal Yusuf, contrary to Islamists' views of that period.

A few days we spent in this abyss – in reference to the solitary cells – after which we were transferred to dormitory no.11 overlooking the interrogation offices and torture yards. We got to learn what really happens in the branch cellars. You would only sleep to the sounds of torture, and you would only wake up to that. Throughout the day all you hear is the sounds of torture and the cracks of whips on the bare backs... We once saw how they took turns beating a man who kept standing and made no sound; we counted 800 cracks. Then we heard a loud bang; we looked and he was lying on the floor. That was the sound of his head as it hit the ground. He fell a martyr and went to a better place.[28]

Al-Shaghri received special treatment in this branch because one of the wardens knew his family and helped him to become a labourer inside the prison. Al-Shaghri recounted:

> The branch prison is very big. It is divided into large groups of cell clusters and a big number of dormitories. Those were infested with diseases, like scabies and lice. Prisoners in solitary confinements were taken out to the toilet once or twice a day. The intervals lasted no more than 15 seconds. There are no bathrooms and no hygiene. The detainee could spend months without a shower. Breathing breaks happened only once every two months. To get to the breathing square we had to cross many passages, the last of which was a long corridor that led to stairs then to the square. I didn't see any doctors at the branch throughout my detention. But sometimes they'd give us drugs for scabies, benzoate. They did not use starvation, in the literal sense, as a tool of torture. Most of the detainees became frail due to their deteriorating psychological state from hearing the sound of torture around the clock.

As the Military Investigation branch is considered a central one to which all military intelligence branches from the provinces and the capital transferred their detainees, its prison cells were congested throughout the year. Testimonies claim the prison is shaped as the letter L and, of course, like the other branches, it is located in the cellar of the building. The management of the branch made barely any effort to combat scabies. The health officer distributed some benzyl benzoate medicine to those infected. However, the al-Azbakiyah bombings in Damascus on 29 November 1981, transformed the branch into a station for receiving and transferring. Every day it received dozens of detainees from provincial branches, while dozens of others were transferred out to Tadmor prison twice a day, in the morning and in the evening. Al-Shagri and his comrades were transferred to Tadmor during this campaign.

Dormitory no. 6

10 metres after the management room, you see a cluster of dormitories located on both sides of the corridor. Their doors are perfectly aligned opposite one another. Among these dorms was dormitory no. 6 ... It was overly crowded. Stepping in there for the first time felt like stepping into a public bath, or a field hospital filled with injured survivors from a war still raging. They were over 150. Piles of people, pale as death. Almost none of them was without a deformity from severe torture.[29]

With these difficult conditions, prisoners needed some form of management. Detainees divided themselves into food groups. Mealtime was the second most important event in the branch after torture. Each group was headed by a food supervisor, who acted like a lord. He reported administratively to the head of the dormitory, who acted as the link between the prisoners and the wardens. However, prison hardships do not end with torture, food, or illness. The daily details enshrine the prison state into the life of the prisoner. Abu al-Khair writes:

> Just as crowded with prisoners, the place was packed with strange types of rats. When I first saw them, I thought they were a type of rabbit species due to their big size. They were awful. I mastered capturing them … The dormitory had two ventilation outlets, in and out. These cylinders were hanging from the ceiling. We hung our clothes on them to dry after washing. This centrifuge system gave this group of people the only hope of life. If it stops working, we are annihilated. It's operated by electricity, so if the power goes out, the lack of oxygen throws us into a state of extreme fatigue that almost takes our lives away. In these cylinders and between them, the rats lived.

The role of the Military Investigation has its own role in arrest and interrogation. Former detainee, Mohammed Issam al-Dimashqi, says: 'I was arrested by the Military Investigation Division patrol from my work in Damascus. The moment I arrived they started interrogating me. It was bad and physically and psychologically exhausting. During the torture, they used the wheel, the German chair, suspension by the hands (*shabah*), as well as threat of using electricity and of rape.'[30]

Branch 235: Palestine Branch

The start of the 1980s saw the rise and expansion of the central branches of Military Intelligence, such as Military Investigation, District Branch 227, and Palestine Branch

Figure 1.6 New Map of Palestine Branch, Google Maps.

235. Branch 235 grew to a point where it became more like an independent intelligence service. The branch's offices held most of the sensitive files regarding Syria, both internally and externally. The office of 'Commando Control', is responsible for following up on Palestinians and their organization within Syria. Its first office is responsible for espionage and intelligence affairs, while other offices have different competencies. The Branch functions have expanded to include chasing, infiltrating, directing, and controlling Islamist movements. These tasks are carried out by the branch's 'counter-terrorism' department. The violence, the ferocity of torture and keeping detainees in their cells for years without any legal representation, established, for the Palestine branch, an especially dreadful reputation in the collective memory of the Syrians.

Poet and former political prisoner Faraj Bayrakdar talked extensively about his detention in the Palestine branch:

> I was blindfolded. A man came, they called the Doctor. . . He examined me and told someone: 'Boss, most likely he has a fracture in his right foot, and possibly a broken rib. He must be transferred to Harasta Military hospital.' The beating during the interrogation was sometimes targeted, mostly random, and other times vindictive with ideological, sectarian, or regionalist motives . . . Some of the torture tools were the wheel, suspension by the hands (*shabah*), hanging upside-down on a ladder, the German chair, electrocution on sensitive areas of the body, splitting the legs violently which led repeatedly to dislocating the pubic symphysis.

During the first 11 months of his arrest, Bayrakdar was subjected to almost daily torture, except for when he was taken to the hospital. The torture stopped when he passed out.

The Department of Investigation was the highest level in the Palestine branch. Interrogation and torture sessions were attended by senior officers. Bayrakdar says:

> Sometimes I sensed, while blindfolded and hearing voices, that there are about ten interrogators. And sometimes I could assess they were no more than three. Towards the end of torture sessions they would remove the blindfolds, and I could see there were only two . . . Interrogators were of different ranks . . . Among them were the then Chief of Military Intelligence, Major General Ali Douba, and the Head of the Palestine branch, Brigadier Mazhar Faris.

A medical presence during torture was customary in the branch during that period. Former detainee Lena Wafai says: 'They brought the doctor during the interrogation. They threatened to do a gynecological check to see if I had intercourse with my husband the night before when I wasn't home.' Wafai was arrested as a hostage in place of her husband. Despite his arrest three weeks after hers, she remained in the Palestine branch prison under the pretext of 'sympathy and complicity'. She spent three years of her life there. The regime's practice of violence does not differentiate between male or female, but the physical differences may play a role in the types of torture used. Wafai continues: 'They took me straight from the branch door into torture. They dressed me in pants and put me in the Wheel. The session lasted about five hours, during which they used the wheel and electrocution. The only question was: 'Where is Adnan?' My husband. The next day, the head of the Parties Office, Abdul Mohsen Hilal – who was from a Sunni background – tried to stir the interrogation into a personal context. He played the bad cop and gave the good cop role to another officer called Ismet Hilal – who was from an Alawite background. The former accused Wafai of breaking the customs by marrying an Alawite, while the latter praised her freedom of choice and progressiveness. They both agreed to release her if she promised to hand over her husband. Wafai refused. After 12 days in the interrogation room on the first floor, Wafai was taken down to cell no. 9 in the basement. They summoned her a few days later in a strange festive manner. Wafai says:

I heard them scream: 'Bring the 9th cell inmate!'. They entered the cell with all their rage and extreme enthusiasm. They dragged me into a room with many agents and officers. I walked in, and my husband was in the middle of the room on his knees. I didn't know how to act. I didn't know if they knew then his real identity. The officer's words pulled me out of my dismay: 'Here's Adnan, we brought him to you.' I crouched down to him and I held him. He whispered in my ear not to be afraid and that they would scare no one. They beat him on the eye so I burst into their faces, so they beat me back into the cell.

Adnan was subjected to severe torture, during which interrogators insisted on keeping the door of Wafai's cell open at all times so that she would hear her husband's torment. They took her out again to see him as he was very frail from the torture.[31]

Wafai was not the only woman taken hostage in exchange for a husband or a father. The general doctrine of Syrian intelligence during that period allowed for the taking of hostages. Wafai says:

The head of the Palestine branch at the time, Mazhar Faris, arrested us. With his departure and the arrival of Mustafa al-Tajer to head the branch in 1990, the latter immediately got rid of us. We were transferred to the Military Investigation branch, which automatically transferred us to the women's prison in Douma. The prison refused to take us in because of space constraints. They sent us back to the Investigation branch. We met its head, Kamal Yousef. We were all crying and totally devastated. He heard our stories as hostages. He re-interrogated us and within two months we were released. We were 12 women; they started to release us in batches.

Three months after Wafai was arrested, Bassam Yousef entered the Palestine branch coming from the Latakia, following his arrest by the Military Intelligence branch there. He stayed in interrogation rooms for five days until they closed his file. He was then taken to dormitory 2, overlooking the interrogation rooms, through a window at the top of its inner wall. Yousef says: 'On that day there were 54 people in the dormitory. The dormitory is four metres by four. In its corner was the toilet and the sink. On top of the bathroom there was a shed where some detainees slept.'

Political detainees reported significant differences in levels of interrogation between provincial and central branches, such as the Palestine branch. The officers of the main branches have considerable experience in political parties and movements. The tasks of the branches are limited to the arresting wanted persons and transferring them to Damascus. This central investigation mechanism increased the number of detainees in the Palestine branch prison. The large numbers of detainees, coupled with a minimum level of medical care caused the spread of disease. Yousef says:

> The doctor would come to the dorm door and ask if anybody was sick. We would keep quiet in fear of the wardens and their warnings. But this silence does not prevent the spread of scabies which was widespread. Some people got tuberculosis. There were inflamed and rotting wounds, as well as injuries caused by torture by the German chair like temporary paralysis or fractures. Despite all this, we remained silent when the health officer passed by.

The tiniest political infraction could get someone to be imprisoned and tortured. On the night of 5–6 October 1992, Kurdish activists in a number of Syrian cities distributed banners and flyers critical of the Assad regime. O.D., a Kurdish man, was arrested that night in Aleppo by Military Intelligence, who caught him fly posting. Pistols drawn and pushed into his back, he was whisked away to the branch in the Suryaan neighbourhood of Aleppo. There, when the standard treatment of *dulab* and *falaqa* did not extract any information, the torturers began pulling his front teeth with pliers, which ripped off a part of his jawbone and caused heavy bleeding. After five days of torture, the Military Police in Aleppo transferred him to Palestine Branch 235 in Damascus, where he was beaten with a cable and subjected to malnourishment. After two years, he was released, but his problems were far from over: his political party monitored him as they thought he had been recruited by the intelligence services, and the intelligence services monitored him as they suspected he was still politically active. The physical and psychological trauma, being ostracized from society, and the lack of a 'certificate of conduct' issued by the Mukhabarat led him to joblessness, marginalization, and ultimately, flight. In August 1996, he fled – of all places – to Sarajevo.[32]

Sexual torture

Inserting solid tools into the anus. Touching women's genitals. Complete stripping during inspection, interrogation, or torture. Tying the penis to prevent a detainee from peeing. These were methods of torture observed in the Palestine branch. The former Lebanese detainee Ali Abu al-Dihn says:

> I was transferred from the District branch to the Palestine branch in May 1987. A few days later, an officer named Muneer al-Abras called for me. A new torture session started as was customary in the District branch. I didn't respond to their interrogation. They sent me back to the cell, keeping my hands cuffed to the back, except during mealtimes. That remained my situation for two weeks. I was called for interrogation again. The officer ordered me to sign confessions he had written down, but I refused. He sent me back to the cell, handcuffed, but this time with my penis tied to prevent me from urinating. I put my feet up to counter the urge to pee.

I stayed like this for hours. I started banging on the door and screaming. I couldn't talk, I just screamed in pain. As soon as the warden came, I asked to see the detective. I stood in front of him screaming that everything he wrote in the investigation was true. That I did meet Sharon, Begin, and other Israeli leaders during the invasion of Beirut. The warden took me to the toilet. The moment he cut the string off, urine exploded out. He took me back to the detective's room. I put my fingerprint, acknowledging whatever he wanted immediately. After that I was never asked to interrogation again.[33]

A prison diary

Abu al-Dihn stayed in cell no 9, which three months later became Wafai's cell. Abu al-Dihn talks about his cell:

The urination time was limited to two minutes in a toilet across from the cell, so I had to use a special bottle to urinate in the cell. I used an empty box of Halawah (sweets) for drinking water and food when it arrived ... The cell was filthy and stunk bad, so I used to put my head on the floor to breathe clean air coming from under the door which was hanging about 18 centimetres above the ground. The call to the toilet was as follows: 'Six, seven, eight and nine.' Those were the cell numbers. 'Open the door!' That meant getting ready and preparing yourself to go out to the toilet. Once you go in the toilet, the countdown starts, so sometimes we replaced peeing with washing hands and face.[34]

Wafai and Abu al-Dihn shared the same specifics of the cell, which was no more than 190 cm long, 90 cm wide and about two metres high. However, Wafai reports differences in treatment as women seem to have received a different, less physically violent, treatment to men. Women were beaten based on the specific orders of a detective or prison chief.

What about the dorms? Qusay Nazim al-Jundi says: 'I was transferred to the Palestine branch from the Military Intelligence branch in Tartous. I stayed in Palestine branch for more than three years. After two days in the interrogation rooms, I was placed in dormitory 8 on the left side of the prison's main corridor. It accommodated about 45 people.' Al-Jundi worked with a number of detainees to organize life in the dormitory. They formed food groups and organized bathing sessions. They coordinated daily details to help relieve prison stress. However, the overall situation was difficult, and they decided to carry out the 1989 strike, two years after al-Jundi's arrest. The demands of the strike were specific: 'A newspaper, breathing breaks, pens, copy books, organizing visits and transfer to a place above the ground.' The strike included refraining from food and water.

Al-Jundi says:

They were trying to force us to eat, but we insisted. The strike lasted four days after which two strikers were taken to Military Hospital 601. There, they received harsh treatments. Doctors and nurses treated them similar to how the wardens did. They gave them medicine, but they scolded them for what they did. We remained on strike, so we were moved to the ground floor. They started bringing us *Tishreen* newspaper. We were placed in dormitory 10, which is a big one with a view over the breathing space. There were some Palestinian detainees in it.

Following this breakthrough in treatment received by al-Jundi and his colleagues in the dormitory, they founded a magazine called 'The Beginning' (*al-Bidaya*). It was written on the packets of cigarettes. Detainees were also offered the opportunity to access an impromptu mini-market to buy necessities with their own money. During his detention, which lasted about four years, Al-Jundi received a visit approximately once every two months; however there were no legal visits in the branch. The visits took place across the metal Net, not in a private room.

The custom of holding detainees for many years in the cells of the Palestine Branch continued even when the head of the branch was changed. In 1990, Mustafa al-Tajer succeeded Mazhar Faris. He released Wafai and other women, but kept al-Jundi and his companions for an extra year. During his administration, he received Pierre Adam Yohanna, detained by the First Bureau and transferred from the District Branch in early 1993. Yohanna remained in solitary cell no 19 for about 11 months without any interrogation, until officer Muneer al-Abras called for him. Yohanna says: 'Al-Abras met me, after which I was left in the solitary cell until the day that they moved me to Saydnaya prison on 25 May 1996.'

Kurdish prisoners: between Qamishli and Damascus

The long-term impact of Assad's penal system is best demonstrated by family histories, as one can see the damage it caused across generations. The 'S' Family from Qamishli is a Kurdish extended family, part of which had been expelled from the Turkish Republic after Kemal Atatürk crushed the Sheikh Said rebellion of 1925. As they settled down in Qamishli, the family continued to till the land as peasants and opened a furniture workshop. On 5 October 1962, the Syrian government implemented Legislative Decree No 93 to conduct a random census in Hasaka province, stripping some 120,000 Syrian Kurds (20% of the Syrian Kurdish population) of their Syrian citizenship and dividing them into either 'foreigners' (*ajanib*) or 'unrecorded' (*maktumeen*). The 'S' Family were also affected by this 'Arab Belt' (*al-hizam al-arabi*) policy, a clear attempt at demographic Arabization of the Jazeera region. As known sympathizers of the KDP in Iraqi Kurdistan, Father was arrested in 1961, and again in 1973. In total, he was imprisoned for over a year, during which time he was tortured frequently. Throughout the 1980s, his eight children would also suffer from the Arab-nationalist policy of the Baathist state.

His son RS was arrested for organizing Kurdish folkloric and musical events, and his unrecorded son AS was arrested for being involved in the KDP-S. In April, September, and December 1981 he was called in by the National Union of Syrian Students. Due to his refusal to act as informant for the intelligence agencies, he was expelled from Damascus University in June 1982 and banned from studying. He was only able to register in September 1985 after paying bribes totalling 40,000 Syrian Lira. After returning to live in Qamishli, Military Security visited him frequently to 'have a cup of coffee'. Returning to Damascus to live in the Ruknaddin neighbourhood, he participated in a demonstration on Newroz 1986 for Kurdish cultural rights. The demonstration was violently dispersed by the Mukhabarat and Republican Guard, and one young man was killed. When his body was sent to Qamishli to be buried, the funeral procession turned into a demonstration, and a faction led personally by Mohammed Mansoura arrested at least 60 Kurds.

His own arrest was around 23:00, when Military Security agents banged the door of the family house, cuffed him, and dragged him out by the hair into a white Peugeot 504. Upon arrival at the department, he was placed in a basement room, and a man in civilian clothing asked him some questions about members of Kurdish political parties. He was tortured by four men in the *dulaab* but, before he lost consciousness, he heard one of the men say: 'Don't kill him, we also want to bring him to Damascus'. The next day he woke up in a cold cell. Two men put him, blindfolded, into a car that drove about eight hours to a different prison. His blindfold was removed in a hall containing other prisoners. In a separate room, two men told him they wanted to interrogate him without torturing him and asked him who he knew in the Communist Labour Party. When he professed his ignorance, he was beaten down and tortured for over an hour in a dirty room where he saw bloodstains, chains, and whips everywhere. First, he was beaten in the car tyre (*dulab*), then stretched on the German chair.

He was released after 38 days with the admonishment that he should pass on information about political activities in Qamishli to the Military Security branch. He was driven to a quiet street in central Damascus and thrown out of the car. In excruciating pain, he stumbled to the roadside and tried to flag down a taxi to go home, but none of them would stop. When he arrived home a Kurdish doctor and friend of the family treated him for his swollen feet. Traumatized, depressed, and plagued by back and stomach pain, it took him over a year to get back to Damascus. He befriended a man from the Communist Labour Party, and on 21 August 1989, he was arrested by Military Security. He was again tortured with the routine methods (*dulab, falaqa*), but this time he was also subjected to cold water, and electrocution on his fingers, penis, toes, and ear lobes. He was freed on 28 August 1989, but was unable to walk as his feet had been smashed. He went into hiding, as the Mukhabarat arrested, questioned, and released his wife and his elderly father, beating and whipping them until they had bruises all over. As a result of the torture, his wife suffered internal bleeding and lost a pregnancy. Fearing that the next arrest might be fatal, he fled across the Turkish-Syrian border to Diyarbakır, from where he travelled to Istanbul, and onward to Europe. He never had a 'normal' life, nor did his wife and two children.[35]

He was not the only Kurd who was tossed back and forth between Damascus and Qamishli in this period. SA, came from a family that traditionally supported the Kurdistan Democratic Party-Syria. His father had already been arrested in the 1970s by the Political Security Directorate and tortured for two months. SA himself studied Economics at Damascus University for two years and successfully applied for a scholarship to study in the Soviet Union. In September 1982 he moved to Kiev and switched from his Economics degree to a specialization in pediatrics at the Faculty of Medicine of Lomonosov University. He graduated in 1989. During his stay in the Soviet Union (and later Ukraine), he participated in meetings that promoted Kurdish rights among the Russian-speaking public. His problems began when he returned to Syria in April 1994, where he was arrested and transferred to Military Security acused of draft-dodging. During the first three days, his interrogators were mostly interested in his activities in the Soviet Union and subjected him to a barrage of questions and beatings. As part of the standard procedure, he was subjected to *falaqa* in the *dulab*, insulted, and humiliated. On 1 June 1994 he was transferred to Military Intelligence in Qamishli, where he was tortured for another two days. On 1August 1994 he was released, with the express condition that he would come into the branch weekly and report any suspicious information. Suffering from depression he fled to Turkey, and from there moved to Europe.[36]

The period 2000-2010

At the end of the 1990s and the beginning of the 2000s, just before Hafez al-Assad's death, informal propaganda swept Syria promising a relaxation of internal security. Assad Jr., posed as the reforming heir who would revamp the Syrian state and its institutions.

Around that period, the security services witnessed some minor changes in their function because of the evolution of their role and relationship with society. The arrest and interrogation of people on various charges continued, while new political and religious groups emerged on the domestic scene. The country witnessed notable events such as Damascus Spring, the proliferation of cultural and political forums and birth of cross-border Islamic Jihadist groups, particularly following the invasion of Iraq. That stage called for a special security mentality, one that transformed personal relationships into organizational forms in a state that was no longer distinguishable from the Assad family.

The 'Diniyeh Call' was an example of this new security mentality. A former detainee, Ramadan Hamad stated:

> 29 February 2000 was a regular school day. I entered the school building to find intelligence operatives there. I wasn't given a chance to ask about anything. I was handcuffed in front of my students and put in a car that transferred me to the Military Intelligence branch in Aleppo, which was led by Brigadier Hassan Khalouf. I stayed in the building's corridor with others arrested with me for a few hours, after which we were brought to the head of the branch. He presented me with a number of pictures and started asking me about the people in them. Among the photos was one for Dr. Firas al-Absi. He was then a medical student in Aleppo and his family lived in Saudi Arabia. I knew him through friends in the neighborhood. Al-Absi had a jihadi mindset. I explained this information to the officer in detail, yet he placed me in jail.

Twenty people were arrested people, five of whom were teachers. What they had in common was political and religious discussion sessions, during which they discussed general issues from Islamic parties and their experiences to extremist Islamic organizations and their actions and behaviour. These meetings were never of an organized or missionary nature, so those teachers did not anticipate that their fate was linked to the arrest of an Aleppan called Obeid al-Sharif Darwish. Darwish was captured on the border trying to illegally escape Lebanon to go to Syria; his brother had been involved in the al-Diniyeh events.

Darwish was transferred to the Palestine branch which requested him from the Aleppo branch to investigate the case. Arrests started on relatives from the same family. One of the detainees met with teachers periodically and engaged with them in discussions, after which they were all arrested. Hamad said:

> The investigations attempted to link us to the jihadists in al-Diniyeh as some were said to be from Aleppo. Establishing a connection between us and them was required, even if by force … Once, during the interrogations, I heard Brigadier Hassan Khalouf on a phone call saying: 'I secured the two swords on my shoulder', in a reference to the upgrading to the rank of Major General (based on the insignia of the rank), and this is what happened later.

The irony in this case is that Military Intelligence only used minimum torture with Hamad and his companion. Hamad said: 'I was never tortured inside the branch. All questions were based on the knowledge of the other members of the group arrested. They didn't search my house, but any name mentioned was immediately arrested … They were looking for ten organized people in Aleppo, they arrested twenty and we were transferred to Palestine branch in the beginning of March 2000.'

They were put into cells as soon as they arrived: 20 cells for 20 detainees. They were not called for interrogation for two weeks. The Palestine investigations were no different from Aleppo's. The target remained to link the group to jihadist individuals. Hamad said: 'The interrogation was more intellectual than it was torture, with discussions in books and Islamic groups.' Hamad and his companions were presented to the then head of the Palestine branch, Mustafa al-Tajer. Al-Tajer spoke to them about Islam, Qaddafi, and various topics. Seventy days later, the branch released half of the group. The rest were transferred to the Military Investigation branch. Their photos were taken and days later they were transferred to Saydnaya military prison to wait for the Military Field Court.

The fact that Hamad and his comrades were not tortured in the Aleppo and Palestine branches does not negate the tradition of violence in Military Intelligence. In Spring 2002, the Palestine branch saw dozens of cases of torture, during which methods such as the wheel, suspension by the hands, and whipping while standing were used, not to mention punching, slapping and kicking.[37]

Abu Iyad[38] said:

> I was arrested at the Naseeb crossing on the Syrian-Jordanian border on 21 May 2005. The following day I was transferred to Palestine branch. I stayed there for three months until I was transferred again to Saydnaya military prison. The first days of the Palestine branch were not without beating, but three days later, the situation changed completely, as the interrogation began, and with it the torture. They used the wheel, they would leave you standing barefoot for long inside the torture chamber, blindfolded, anticipating punches or kicks at any moment. This lasted from early morning until late night, with the presence and participation of Mohammed, the health officer in the branch. Hearing the sounds of detainees being beaten throughout my detention brought me a great deal of suffering.

Sexual torture was also used during the interrogation. Abu Eyad remembered that 'the torturer targeted private parts during the beating. The director of the Terrorism Bureau, Brigadier George Diab, threatened to arrest my family, meaning the women. These torture and threats didn't aim to extract information, the goal was insult and humiliation. The penalty was for having a different opinion'.

The Palestine branch became very overcrowded. Abu Eyad again:

I was admitted to the fourth dormitory without any medical examination or questions. We were over 70 in the dormitory which was no bigger than 4x4 metres including a toilet in one of the corners. The arrest of the members of what became known as the Islamist group Jund al-Sham added to the crowd. Skin diseases like scabies and lice spread, especially with the use of old, dirty dormitory blankets. These diseases did not receive any attention or health care. The nurse used to come, ask for a patient, hand him an aspirin and leave without any examination. Disease was coupled with malnutrition.

Palestine Branch: a new location

By the end of 2007, the Palestine Branch moved to a much larger building. Its new prison consisted of dozens of solitary cells as well as dormitories, all of which were monitored by cameras. Ibrahim al-Olabi said:

Political Security arrested me on 21 August 2008 for browsing Muslim Brotherhood websites. The investigation was closed and I was transferred to Damascus central prison. Palestine Branch took me from the civilian prison. The first thing you face in the Palestine branch is humiliating strip searches and routine 'security movements'.[39] And then an 'intern' interrogator enjoys slapping, punching and kicking you. He only tortures you to get your civil brief. He documents the details of your life from your day of birth, asking the names of all your first- and second-degree relatives.[40]

The food and hygiene in the new branch prison did not change. Al-Olabi said: 'The food was very bad. Raw lentil soup that is inedible. Potatoes were the only thing we could eat. Bulgur and rice were off and smelled terrible. Chicken was served once a week on Tuesdays. One's share was no more than a few grams.' Despite the new building, the prison remained catastrophic. Al-Olabi says:

I was admitted in dormitory 12. Across from us was the women's dormitory, no 13. Numbers of detainees in the room ranged from 22 to 30, but the problem with this dormitory was that the lighting was very weak, and sleeping was only possible on your side. In addition to tight space, the dorm was wet and very dirty. Cockroaches crawled over those sleeping near the toilet. In addition to cockroaches, body lice spread widely, causing scabies. I remained allergic even long after leaving prison.

Paracetamol for all

During the two and a half months of my detention at the Palestine Branch, four deaths occurred due to medical negligence. Prisoners would knock on the door asking for the doctor to come, but by the time he shows up, with intentional delay, the ailing prisoner dies. After this incident, the prison chief asked the deceased's dormitory colleagues about the details of the incident. They told him he suffered headache and asked for painkillers, but the nurse didn't give him any and his condition suddenly worsened and he died an hour later. The nurse knocked on the dorms the next day and gave us all Cetamol pills for headaches.

Al-Olabi spoke about diseases in the prison: 'In addition to scabies, there were detainees with tuberculosis. They were isolated in solitary cells. I met one of them, Amer Aad al-Sati, before he died in Saydnaya prison. This Lebanese detainee contracted tuberculosis in the Palestine branch. His poor health did not spare him from being constantly handcuffed to the back and sleeping directly on the floor without any blankets that can fend away the cold.'

Transferring detainees of Islamist ideological backgrounds, like Ibrahim al-Olabi, from the custody of civil intelligence departments to Military Intelligence ones was repeated in the fall of 2010. Former detainee Mahmoud Hilal was transferred from General Intelligence custody to the Military Intelligence. He was imprisoned in the Palestine Branch until May 2011, two months after the start of the Syrian uprising. Hilal believes that at that time the branch was under international control. The situation was so relaxed that the detainees could talk to the wardens and request the purchase of items. However, visits were still prohibited.

Abu Khaled did not experience this relaxed approach towards Islamists.[41] He was arrested by the District Branch twice, in 2008 and 2010. Both times he was transferred to the Palestine Branch. Abu Khaled recounted:

During those arrests, I did not undergo any medical examination and was not asked if I had any health problems. During the second arrest, in the last month of 2010, a man died in cell no 4 opposite my cell. He banged on his cell door for a doctor because he was peeing blood. The wardens came and started beating him hard then returned him to the cell. They opened the cell door shortly afterwards to find him dead ... Access to a doctor, an impossible dream for us, came with the beginning of the Arab Spring, and a doctor came and asked about our health. We started feeling like things were changing ... However, as the Syrian Revolution broke out, conditions inside the prison gradually became catastrophic. Wardens intentionally gave us bad, old food. Most detainees, me included, suffered gastrointestinal diseases.

Cell 33

Mahmoud Hilal narrated: 'The day we arrived at the Palestine Branch, they treated us well. They put me in solitary cell no 33, and that number became my name. The dimensions of the solitary cell were 2.5 metres long and 2 metres wide. The wall with the door is completely made of metal. They took me out of the cell to the toilet twice a day, at 6:00 and at 18:00. I stayed in this cell for about two months after the first day of interrogation. On 26 November 2010, I woke up from a dream I don't remember. I started banging the door of the cell hard. The wardens came and dragged me to an area I later learned was a blind spot, uncovered by the cameras. I was hit until my head was cut. They then gave me a drug claiming it was a painkiller. From that moment on, everything became completely different. I started hearing voices talking to me and I couldn't tell where they came from. The voices spoke in a clear Alawite accent. I got into discussions with a nail on the ceiling, thinking it was talking to me. The voice asked me what I wanted, and I answered: 'Salt'. All of this was an internal dialogue – it promised me a good amount of salt. It told me it was going to put it in a specific place in the bathroom, and that's what happened. The incident was repeated several times with regards to food. I lost sleep. I started writing poetry. I wrote a poem of 50 verses on the wall using the tin wrapper of a yogurt box as a pen. I drew the world map with country borders, except for African countries. I think I was possessed. After a while, and without prior warning, I fell asleep and slept for a long period of time. I woke up normal again. Two days later, a warden called Ramadan threatened me with torture, because I was talking to my brother who was in cell no 28 in Urdu. Strangely, Ramadan's voice is the voice I kept hearing during the time I was 'possessed'.'[42]

After this experience in cell 33, Hilal was reunited with his comrades of the same cell in dorm 14. They were moved into several dormitories, the last of which was no 8. They were treated very well compared to the recent prisoners of the 2011 uprising, who started pouring into the branch. Hilal and his group were transferred to the Patrol Branch in mid-April 2011 and were released the following month, two months into the start of the Syrian uprising.

After 2011

March 2011 was an unusual month in Syrian history. Some Syrian youth took to the streets calling for freedom in an old *souq* in central Damascus; they were arrested by the General Intelligence, particularly Branch 251. As the demonstrations spread from Deraa in the south of the country across the country into various Syrian governorates, the Syrian security departments intervened. Assad's vast intelligence apparatus, especially Military Intelligence, was not only involved in arrests and repression operations, but also took the lead in rounding up, torturing, and executing countless Syrians throughout the decade of conflict.

This arrest campaign caused catastrophic congestion in the prison system. For example, Human Rights Watch examined hundreds of arrests in Military Intelligence branches in 2012 and concluded: 'To manage the thousands of people detained in the context of anti-government demonstrations, the authorities also established numerous temporary unofficial holding centres in places such as stadiums, military bases, schools, and hospitals where the authorities rounded up and held people during massive detention campaigns before transporting them to branches of the intelligence agencies.'[43] The congestion caused severe food shortages, immense suffering, and an expansive denial of necessary medical assistance.

The illusion of death

Former detainee in Palestine Branch, Ma'an Mousselli said: 'After my arrest on 14 June 2012 from the centre of Damascus, I was transferred to a giant branch along with my car and all the equipment therein. After the humiliating inspection in complete nudity and safety movements, I was placed in dorm 16. We had a child in the dormitory, held hostage in place of his cousin, no more than 14 years old. They took him once to the interrogation and he came back after a long time, silent and stunned. He lay next to me and started crying hysterically. This repeated the next day, so I asked him why he was crying. He told me they were taking him in a small passenger car to an open place outside the branch. They lift the blindfold off his eyes and played the scene of his slaughter by passing the knife back across his neck in a serious and strict manner, as if it were entirely true. After this play, they brought him back to the branch. To this day, I don't know what else I should have done for him other than crying with him. I was not in a better shape. The ten days of my interrogation were not without humiliation. They'd blindfold me and put me in the middle of the room completely naked. They took turns hitting me from side to side and from hand to hand until I hit the wall . . . Then they would laugh hysterically.'

Mousselli lost over 15 kilograms in his 16 days of detention in the Palestine branch. He recalled that 'the food was very bad and scarce. A quarter of a loaf of bread with a few olives for breakfast. At lunch, a badly cooked bulgur and a broth that I didn't eat because they peed in it'. The prison became more crowded with the arrival of new detainees transferred from the Idlib and Deraa branches.

The Palestine Branch reinforced its brutal reputation during the Syrian uprising. Ayada al-Haj Yusuf said:

I was arrested by the Military Security branch of Hama on 27 January 2016. I was moved for health reasons to the Criminal Security Branch – following pressure from senior officers in my family. Then I was transferred from Criminal Security to Adra prison in Damascus. Then Jaish al-Islam[44] included my name in the lists for prisoner exchange with the regime in September 2016. Security discovered my relationship with the rebels and my disagreement with my pro-regime family. I was transferred on the alleged day of my release to the Palestine Branch. They told me that it was just for a small question. I stayed at the branch for two weeks. After the inspection, I was placed in a large room with over 40 women with their young children. The first torture session lasted more than three hours. It was just hitting by the hands. It wasn't severe torture. The following day I was suspended by the hands. They tied me next to another detainee, after stripping me from my clothes, keeping my underwear. The prisoner next to me begged them to take me down and beat him in my place. So they started beating me with the green plastic water hose. Less than 15 minutes later, I lost consciousness. They woke me up with water and then suspended me by the feet.[45]

Al-Haj Yusuf was transferred to solitary confinement after her torture session. She said:

The next day they took me to the same interrogation office – on a floor above the ground. A person who said he was an officer from South Damascus lifted my blindfold. I don't know why he introduced himself as such?! He tied my hands and feet to the bed and sexually assaulted me. He reeked of alcohol. He was calling himself the filthiest of names every time as he started his assault. He did it three times that day. After that, my daily routine became going from solitary cell to torture, and from there to the officer who assaulted me. I would wake up unconscious in my cell, with cigarette burns on my body ... on my heels, thighs, and genitals, as well as sharp cuts in my private parts. I stayed like this for almost 12 days. They didn't ask me anything. I was then transferred to Military Investigation Branch, then to the military prosecutor's office and then to the street.[46]

Torture was better than staying in solitary confinement

At the beginning of October 2012, a Military Intelligence checkpoint near the Syrian-Jordanian border stopped Ali/Ola Hamidi.[47] He was transferred to a nearby military barracks for several days, then to a solitary cell at the Military Intelligence branch in Deraa where he was tortured with water pipes, cables and even an electric stick. His health deteriorated considerably. Ali/ Ola recalled: 'As a result of my poor health, they got rid of me by transferring me to the Palestine branch. They first put me in room 12 with more than 113 detainees. Scabies were all over the place. I banged on the door, three days later, asking for the interrogator. When he came in, I revealed to him that I had the identity of a man, but I was in fact a girl named Ola. The interrogator went crazy. He started beating and torturing me. He sent a patrol out to my old place of work and they found my real ID. After this I was placed in a solitary cell, where I stayed for three months. The beating never stopped for one day. They used all available torture on me. The interrogator left me hanging by the hands for six days. Torture was better than staying in solitary confinement. I got into a weird psychotic episode. I started banging on the door and begging the interrogator to take me to a dormitory. On that evening I was placed in the women's room. I walked in after three months without a shower. My wounds were inflamed and festering, and I was a mess. I stayed put in this dormitory for a whole year without movement, not even an interrogation. I came across so many stories ... Violence, torture, fear, injustice and rape.'

Back to the District Branch

Sohaib Jaamour was arrested by Military Intelligence for the second time in the summer of 2011. Jaamour says:

My second arrest experience began on Saturday 25 June 2011. I was arrested by a mobile checkpoint of the Military Intelligence as I was on my way to Damascus. I was transferred to the Military Intelligence detachment in Al-Qutaifeh district of rural Damascus. I was brought in handcuffed and blindfolded. The head of the patrol told them I tried to escape so they immediately started hitting me. Operatives from the detachment interrogated me about my connection to the revolutionary movement in Jayroud. I refused to confess so they tortured me in my cell. Hours later, I was transferred to the District Branch 227.

Jaamour was placed in cell 12 after the customary nude inspection procedures and 'security movements'. The warden took him the next day for biometrics: a picture and fingerprints. He was returned to the cell and the daily routine: out to the toilet twice a day, awaiting mealtime and the wait as he listened to the sounds of torture in the Net area close to his cell. Jaamour says:

Three days later, they took me to the interrogation. One of the interrogators led me, with my hands cuffed to the back and my eyes blindfolded. He took off the blindfold at the Net to see the detainees tortured. The interrogator was accompanied by an assistant who mispronounced almost every letter of Arabic, and who said: 'Look, this is how an interrogation works, so make your choice... Confession or. . . .' The scene was horrifying inside the Net, approximately 5 metres wide and 12 metres long with a metal mesh ceiling opened to the sky. This space was packed with detainees and interrogators at the same time. Some detainees were being tortured in the wheel while others were lying on the floor getting beaten on the feet (*falaqa*). After few minutes before this scene, he took me to the third room, near what is known as 'the basement'. They started the interrogation, and before even asking a question he hit me with a stick wrapped in rubber and then ordered me to sit. This session was to write the civil brief.

A uniform

The District Branch maintained its custom of wearing a uniform. A week after Jaamour arrived at the Branch, he was given the blue military service suit. Jaamour said: 'They gave me that suit and took all my clothes, even my underwear and put them in a bag with my name and no 213 and kept it in deposit with them.' The earliest recorded account of the use of uniform in this branch goes back to the 1990s; however, in the summer of 2012, the custom began to disappear. Abu Abdurrahman[48] was arrested in August 2012 and reported: 'The moment we arrived at the District Branch we were greeted with such cruelty and violence that I passed out. As a result, I was carried with my brother to bathroom-like rooms, where they stripped us naked and 'bathed' us with high pressure water. I was with my brother and many other detainees in this space. It was a quick shower after which we wore only briefs. We remained in our underwear throughout the period of our detention in this branch. We were placed in a solitary cell, 2 metres long, and less than a metre wide with five other people. Some days nine of us were crammed in that solitary cell.'

After Jaamour was given his uniform, he was moved to solitary cell no 6, which was isolated from the rest. After interrogation sessions that proved useless to them, he was severely punished and prevented from going to the toilet. He peed in his cell, which incurred the wrath and punishment of the wardens. Jaamour narrated:

After 14 days of punishment in that solitary confinement, I was called to interrogation again. After which, and with no apparent clear reason, I was moved to solitary no 3. On that day, branch patrols arrested a large group from the rural areas of Damascus, so the branch became overcrowded. I knew from the new arrivals that it was Sunday 10 July 2011. The prison administration began cramming 7 to 8 detainees in one solitary cell. They kept some detainees in prison corridors because of the scarcity of places. Three young men were brought into my solitary cell. The only way we could sleep was either squatting or by taking turns.

The congestion in the branch in the summer of 2011 was addressed by transforming the Net area from a torture and interrogation space into a large dormitory. A rights report talks about the prison of the District Branch: 'An underground facility that contains solitary cells and a large room of about 100 square metres, which housed nearly 400 people.'[49] Kheder Ramadan, who was arrested in June 2012, says: 'As soon as we entered the branch, they exchanged our clothes with blue suits. Before that they shaved our heads and beards and bathed us. We were the only ones who received this treatment during that period. We were then placed in the Net area which contained around 600 detainees. There was a toilet without a door, so urinating and defecating became difficult, if not impossible.'

Due to the congestion, Ramadan was moved to a second place of detention called 'the basement' (*al-sirdab*):

At times they would stop the ventilation system for an hour or two as a punishment. Then the situation became catastrophic and caused the death of some detainees. After that you would hear the guards calling: 'Stand up and face the wall', which means they were going in to take the dead who suffocated out. Every day they brought out dead bodies from solitary cells and the dormitories. Afterwards the situation became even more gruesome, reaching intended murder under torture due to suspension by the hands, the German chair, or electricity.

Overcrowding, violence and the scarcity of air and food resulted in a psychological state known as 'switching off', where the detainee enters a state of an almost complete absence of the mind. It starts with a visible lack of focus in the detainee's eyes, his facial features then change, he falls in a state of delirium. Mutayyam al-Taweel was arrested in August 2012 for commenting against Bashar al-Assad's regime at his workplace. When he saw the intelligence operatives storm his building, he joked to himself: 'What if they came to arrest me?' But they had come to do exactly that. They ran up to him and barked: 'Are you Mutayyem Taweel?' 'Yes' he answered. They put his t-shirt over his head, zip-tied his wrists, and began beating him up all the way to the car. They drove him to the branch, stripped him and beat him; only once when they dumped him in the cell, did he begin to feel pain and see blood. He collapsed in a state of shock. As his first ever arrest and detention, he began to dissociate after two days: 'We call it *'fasalit'*: you're conscious, but you think you're somewhere else. I stood for two days and then snapped: 'Alright guys, I'm bored of this cell, I'm going home.' I became nervous, imagined that I needed to attend a meeting at my job, daydreaming, hallucinating. The other detainees tried to wake me up, slap me: 'Mutayyem wake up!'".[50]

•   ## Excerpt from a psychologist's report on a former detainee, 28 December 1994:

In general, the person concerned makes a resentful impression. He comes across as somewhat morose and compulsive. He seems very religious, carrying certain prescribed principles (prayer, body cleanliness) far into his daily life. On the one hand, there is some level of affect. On the other hand, there are periods when he tells his story with great emotion and busy gesticulating, especially when it comes to his current situation and also when it concerns his own family. During the very penetrating torture-anamnesis in which he is asked, for example, to show how and in what body position he would have been tortured, there are briefly some tears in his eyes. Also noteworthy are the jeering responses to what appear to him to be 'stupid' questions about the conditions under which he was imprisoned. An emotionality coloured by anger overshadows the whole psychic picture. The anger is fueled by feelings of injustice.

Excerpt from a physician's report on a former detainee, 18 November 1998

Summary of physio-therapeutic findings:

- Disorders: sharp pain attachments gastrocnemius, both sides; stretching dorsal vessel/nerve cord very painful, both sides.
- Limitations: walking more than 50 metres produces pain in back of the knee, both sides, radiating downward; pain in lower back, both inactive and active.
- Handicap: walking or standing work not possible due to pain in backside of legs.
- Condition: damage of attachments m. gastrocnemius, damaged vessel/nerve cord at back of knee resulting from maltreatment (beatings with stick in the back of the knee, 10/1997).
- Causal mechanism condition: trauma.[51]

Excerpt from a physician's report on a former detainee, 28 September 1992

During the medical intake, the gentleman explains that he spent a long time in prison in Syria, where he was subjected to much torture. He was repeatedly beaten, immersed in water, lived in poor sanitary conditions, given little and poor food. He was also sexually assaulted, by blows to genitalia. As a result, there was bleeding and infection in his scrotum, which had to be treated surgically. Furthermore, he was tortured psychologically by threatening to harm family members. During the same intake, he complains of sleep disturbances, feeling tense and crying a lot. On physical examination, the physician finds acne in beard area, on chest and back, impaired vision, and on the lower abdomen on the left a scar. His scrotum on the left is very sensitive and painful on examination. It is agreed with him to go to the optician, to institute treatment for his skin abnormality, and to discuss his psychological problems if necessary. He explains that his nose was broken in prison because people stepped on his head while he was lying face down on the floor. At the beginning of August 1992, he presents with the same psychological complaints and headaches and nightmares appear to be present. In Syria he was already given Valium, which he is now prescribed again, along with painkillers for the headaches. Summarizing, I conclude that we are dealing with a young man who in the past was subjected to many and prolonged physical and psychological tortures. Since then there have been several chronic complaints, both psychological (nervositas, sleep disorder, nightmares) and physical (back pain and headaches).[52]

Ranim Maatouq[53] arrested on 30 June 2014, says:

I was placed in a cell on the ground floor. I think it was a detention place for women. The basement prison seemed to me like a terrifying world. I moved between two cells. In the second one there were six of us. The cell was about one and a half metres by two metres. We had scabies and lice and food scarcity; sleeping became impossible. I used to peek through the air vent, a window in the door of the solitary cell, onto the evacuation of dead bodies. I started counting their numbers daily, for no particular reason. I was called again for interrogation, and the interrogator threatened to arrest my mother and brother. I went back to the cell, shaken and shocked. I don't remember the details of what happened, but I know I started hallucinating and seeing yellow cabs crossing the branch. One of the girls knocked on the door for help, she yelled to the guards: 'She switched off', referring to me. The detective in charge of my file came and slapped me several times, but I didn't respond. My mind remained busy looking for a cab to go home and arguing with the driver about the fare, and after reaching an agreement I tried to hop into the taxi. The detective placed me under running water in the bathroom. The irony is that when I came to my senses, I saw a strange look of fear in the detective's eyes.

The testimonies of Maatouq and Jaamour concur that there was worse medical negligence towards men. Jaamour says: 'We suffered scabies and asthma. Others of course had chronic diseases such as diabetes and hypertension. The doctor came once a week and gave medicine only to those who answered his question: 'Who's sick among you, you animals?' He would just give a pill.' Starvation was used as a method of torture as well as sexual torture in the District Branch. Jaamour says: 'They intentionally hit us on the genitals saying 'we don't want to see your offspring'. In addition, food and water deprivation for two or more days was practiced as a sort of punishment during interrogation.'

Rape with a bottle

After my interrogation ended, during which the torture was limited to beating, punching and kicking, I went on a hunger strike hoping to improve the situation in the cell, or even being transferred to a civilian prison. The prison chief called me and brought a girl prisoner who was still undergoing interrogation. He looked at me and said: 'I will not punish you, but...' and he ordered one of his operatives to strip the girl standing in front of me of her clothes. He undressed her and sat her on an empty bottle, which penetrated her. I will never forget this situation until the day I die ... Physically, the girl didn't seem to have been harmed, but she's definitely been hurt psychologically, and she won't forget what happened her whole life.

Branch 293

At the start the Syrian uprising a number of branches of Military Intelligence emerged strongly on the domestic scene for the first time in the division's history. For example, in the capital Damascus, the Officers' Affairs Branch, known as 293, came to the fore as a detention authority. The branch was previously known for spying on military officers. It holds evaluation, monitoring and follow-up files for all army officers, and plays a key role in the promotion, removal, transfer and appointment of army officers to or from their posts. The head of this branch has direct access to the President and can submit reports to him. For these reasons, Hafez al-Assad kept a close eye on the branch, under the management of Brigadier Ahmed Abboud. He was head of the branch for over 25 years before being demoted, along with General Ali Douba, just before Bashar al-Assad came to power.[54]

A former officer in the Syrian army, Khaldoun Mansour says:

On Saturday 5 November 2011, a patrol of Branch 293 arrested me. They took me from my service station in the 78th Brigade – tanks in the Qatana area in rural Damascus. They presented their warrant and declared their identities. They said it was just a chat over a cup of coffee. I stayed in the branch for 59 days and was then transferred to the Military Investigation Branch, then to Saydnaya, from which I was released in June 2014.' Mansour's charge was sympathizing with the people of the area where he served as a labour officer. He was charged with transporting weapons from al-Qusayr in rural Homs on the Lebanese border to rural Damascus. Mansour says: 'The interrogation was very bad. The head of the branch, Brigadier Rafiq Shahadah, addressed me aggressively saying: 'Have some respect for your job.' I answered that I knew nothing and had nothing to do with any opposition movement. Then a young civilian from the opposition group I was collaborating with was brought in. The young man had confessed everything after 12 days of torture. I denied knowing the guy. Brigadier Shahadah said: 'No problem. Now, downstairs, you will speak.' The bell rang, summoning someone to handcuff and blindfold me and take me down to the basement. We went down to the basement and there they took off my chevron and the torturer placed me in a car wheel. I could distinguish the voices of five people who all started hitting me from all directions. Someone came in, stopped the beating, and asked me if I was willing to confess. I kept denying, so he used a quad cable to hit me on the feet for about 15 minutes. Things were already known by them, so I decided to confess and stop the pain ... At that point they sent me back to Brigadier Shahadah to tell him all the details. He rang the bell and asked an assistant to hand me a white paper to write down what I confessed. He took the report and I stayed in the room until about 1:00 a.m. I was then taken into a room that had about ten *Shabbiha* (pro-Assad thugs). I waited there a little, then the warrant officer returned to tell me that the head of Military Intelligence division had sent a telegram for my arrest. He took my military coat and band, handcuffed, and blindfolded me, and then threw me down in front of the *Shabbiha* who started hitting me with their hands and feet ... After this 'party' they placed me in the elevator and took me down to the basement where they handed me to the guard saying: 'receive this customer'. That's when all the wardens started a new beating ceremony that lasted about half an hour. I was then sent down to solitary confinement where I stayed for two weeks. Then I was transferred to a dormitory with about 35 other civilians and military detainees. I stayed there until I finished 59 days.

Branch 291

Branch 291 came to the fore as an arresting authority under Military Intelligence. It is the administrative branch, also known as the Personnel Branch. It is responsible for a number of administrative functions as well as personnel and HR affairs, and monitors performance within the system to prevent any loopholes. The assessment it provides plays a support role in promoting, removing or transferring staff within the system. The functional role of the branch is to accept, examine and dispatch volunteers as either operatives or warrant officers.[55]

Mohammed Qannas says this about the Personnel branch:

We were transferred from the Badia branch in Palmyra to Branch 291 in August 2012. The moment we arrived we were told to lie on the ground, face down, in pairs. The soldiers started beating and squashing us. I was removed from this party because of a leg injury. After about 15 minutes of beating, operatives ordered us to stand up. They pulled us, without handcuffs or blindfolds, through a long corridor with exits on its right and left sides. They placed each four of us in a solitary cell. The name of the cell I occupied was 6-3-Left, which meant the 6th cell in the 3rd cluster, on the left side of the corridor. The sounds of torture reached us in that cell. In time, we learned that four detainees in a solitary cell was a blessing. The customary numbers at the time were 8–10 detainees in one solitary cell.

The solitary cells in here differ from other Military Intelligence branches in that they contained a toilet hole and a water faucet. This branch shares the same numbering system for detainees as the Palestine branch.

Qannas and his companions were left in their solitary cell after they had placed their fingerprints on papers which carried the same confessions they were forced to give in the Military Intelligence branch in Palmyra. A month-and-a-half later, a strange incident took place:

One morning in October 2012, detainees started banging on the doors of the solitary cells chanting the slogan 'We sacrifice our souls and blood for you, Bashar!' The wardens went on maximum alert to silence the prisoners and regain control over the prison. The commotion in the prison continued until early evening, that was when the prisoners succumbed to fatigue. The torturers started their torture party that night, and no prisoner in the branch went to sleep that night without being beaten up. The first blow in the wheel paralyzes sensation. With the second you feel you are going to die. By the third you lose all sense of reality.

The extremely narrow space, lack of food and the complete lack of any medical care created a state of constant torture for detainees, resulting in hallucinations and 'switching off'. Qannas says:

> You have twenty centimetres in length and similar in width, this is your living space inside the solitary. With such narrow space, life becomes pure torment. Added to that is the absence of light and the continuous darkness on the door, the walls, the faces, and everything. We reached 8 in the cell which did not exceed two metres by one. This lasted for about a month. Anas, who came with me from the Palmyra Branch, was in the opposite cell. He became completely detached from reality. He started thinking he was an officer and acting like one. He started shouting military orders at his cell mates all night: 'Stand up ... jog in place ...'. Then he thought they were calling his name, so he started banging on the door. The warden came and Anas told him that the judge was asking for him, but they took his colleagues and left him behind. The warden replied: 'Sleep now for a couple of hours and tomorrow I'll take you out to the judge.' Then the warden ordered his colleagues to make room for him to sleep. That night Anas fell asleep to the sound of a young soldier from Hasakeh, who was my fellow inmate. His wounds were decaying, reeking a catastrophic stench. We decided to wash him with our hands under the water from the faucet in an attempt to save his life. The soldier started singing to his mother and crying ... we cried along.

Branch 215: the Raid and Incursion Force

During the Syrian revolution, the Raid and Incursion force, later known as Branch 215, had a major role in the suppression of the uprising. For many years before the revolution it was headed by Assef Shawkat, brother-in-law of Bashar al-Assad. The force consisted of approximately 4,000 highly trained operatives, who specialized in breaking and entering, kidnapping, assassination and the arrest of the 'most wanted' by all branches.[56]

According to a rights report, the force is located on Kafr Souseh, 6 May Street, known colloquially as 'Political Guidance Street',[57] in a building composed of seven floors, identical in design. The first floor is reserved for the reception of detainees, whose information is taken in a wide hall. The basement, eleven steps beneath the surface, is identical to the rest of the branch floors. Its cells are reserved for the temporary placement of new detainees until they are transferred to the upper floors for interrogation. The basement hall holds the detainees' confiscated personal belongings, such as computers and mobile phones. The second, third and fourth floors are reserved for detainees whose confessions have already been extracted. The fifth and sixth floors were used to interrogate detainees and obtain confessions.

The report states: 'The conditions of accommodation in Branch 215 are in and by themselves physical and spiritual torture. The space allocated to each detainee is that of one floor tile, that's where everything needs to happen, sleeping, eating, and sitting. Sleeping and sitting had to be squatting. In 'Hadid 4' dormitory for example, there were about 85 detainees. The food is similar to that of the Military Intelligence branches in terms of scarcity and quality. Visiting the toilet was a long trip of torture, repeated twice daily.'

The storyteller

Omar Jamal Al-Din was arrested on 15 December 2012 and says: 'After the humiliating inspection process, the wardens placed me in the basement of the branch, which is completely isolated from the rest of the world. There, time does not exist. You feel they control your life inside the prison, but also out of it. I occupied myself with daily details and keeping track of time. I pondered on them deeply after the passing of the first week, which was loaded with the pain of torture and the grief of thinking about my parents. I was placed in a dormitory called the 'Blanket Dormitory', which was four by three metres. We were more than 70 detainees almost glued to one another; if you stood up, you'd lose your sitting space. They took us out to the toilet three times a day for intervals that did not exceed the time it takes to count to ten … I was concerned with this and wondered what danger does urinating comfortably pose on national security.

The details of the place were plenty; they all indicated how much they controlled our fate. I thought of a solution to the deadly situation we were living. And when I say deadly I mean it literally, not metaphorically. The main cause of death was disease resulting from despair. Our colleague, Mustafa Malla, decided he didn't want to live anymore, so he refrained from eating, drinking, or going to the toilet. If you don't eat and drink, the others will immediately devour your share. It's more like living in a jungle in there. Malla died, and with his death, my fear grew.

One day they brought us lunch that smelled like petrol. The whole dormitory refrained from eating in fear of poisoning. Opposite me sat Ahmed, a young man no more than 16 years of age, hungry and desperate. Cancelling lunch was disastrous for him. I usually give him some of my food, but with the contaminated food incident, no one had any food to share.

I looked at Ahmed and said: 'How about I tell you a story?' He lifted his head off from his knees and his eyes glistened with joy. That's when I realized that I haven't really prepared any story to tell him! My thoughts started racing. I told him I'd tell him the story of Damascus. The presentation sparked his interest, and he was ready to hear the story and forgot about the food.

I started: 'Once upon a time, in the old times … Shaam [Damascus] was a kingdom with a large lake. Running this kingdom was a wise man raising his beautiful orphan daughter 'Badr al-Budoor'. The man grew weary of the responsibility, so he remarried, years after Badr al-Budoor's mother passed away. The new stepmother was cruel to the little princess. As soon as she had the chance, she decided to marry her to an old, ugly man. The Princess refused the stepmother's decision and ran away from the palace on her white horse. On her escape route she fell into the big lake. From the body of the horse and lake water, white jasmine trees were born. Apricot and peach trees carried fruit that borrowed their red and pink colours from the Princess's luscious cheeks . . ' I carried on, borrowing figures from my imagination. I linked Damascus to women, love, and beauty . . . The rest of the detainees started listening to the tale . . . We were dreaming of life and wishing for it. The story of Damascus was the way I survived death in despair, and perhaps the way Ahmed survived his fear and terror from that hell.

The situation of women in Branch 215 was not very different from that of the men. Rafif[58] who was arrested at her home in Damascus on 14 April 2014 says:

> They took me out of the patrol car the middle of the branch square near the statue of Hafez al-Assad. I was received by prison chief, Ahmed Al-Olaya (known as 'Gargamel'), who said: 'Welcome, whale'. Operatives took me to a big torture chamber on the ground floor. It looked like a parking lot. There were a lot of detainees, almost naked, looking awful, some suspended from the ceiling, others lying on the ground bleeding while dead bodies scattered here and there. They left me there, without a blindfold, to watch and see torture. Then they took me to hand in my personal belongings. Their interrogation began about two hours after my arrest and continued until late that night. They would take me into the interrogation room, ask some questions and then take me back to the hallway over and again. I stayed in the lounge until around 8:30 a.m. The morning light highlighted many of the hall's features. Its floor was blackened by the blood of the detainees.

Gargamel

His name is Ahmed al-Olaya, and he's the prison chief. He comes from the coastal city of Jableh but lives in Damascus; he's over 60 years old. He personally oversaw the inspection of the female detainees, which is more like a sexual harassment. He also oversaw the quantities of food. The female detainees who met him up close during the inspection called him Gargamel. Alaa, [59] arrested in November 2012, says:

> They took me to Gargamel. He took me into a room with so many personal belongings. He asked me to completely strip for inspection. I first refused so he started beating and slapping me, and then threatened to call in a number of operatives to force me to take my clothes off. I succumbed and took my clothes off. He searched them very closely and thoroughly inspected my body. I knew why he was nicknamed Gargamel. He's ugly and short with little white hair, his face conveyed his evil. During his thorough, ugly, curse loaded body inspection, you get the feeling that he's your big sister. He was diligent with his work, confiscating all items considered dangerous, such as jewelry, hair bands and pins.

The testimonies of most of the women detained in Branch 215 are consistent in their description of Gargamel; they differ, though, in the levels of interrogation and torture. Rafif was not tortured because the branch had obtained her intelligence file from another branch. They just threatened to rape her and arrest her parents. Alaa, on the other hand, was beaten, harassed and sexually assaulted.

Alaa says:

> After the inspection, Gargamel placed me behind a curtain covering one of the walls of the outside passage. Shortly afterwards, an operative in his fourth decade, wearing dark blue and red sweatpants came in. The operative took me into a room with another detective. They placed me between them and ordered me to unlock my cell phone. I refused so they started hitting me on the head to force me to open it. I didn't succumb but started crying. The guy in the sweatpants asked his colleague to leave. He started kissing my hand, but I jumped away. He put a chair against the wall of the room and ordered me to sit on it, my face against the wall and my legs spread out. He stuck himself to my body from behind and hit me with a stick on my leg. Every time the door opened, he moved away from me, annoyed, but kept the hitting. As soon as the door closed, he went back to sticking his body to mine and rubbing against it. Half an hour later, he seemed to have reached his orgasm. He sat behind his desk to continue the interrogation. The irony was that I wear a head scarf, and every time strands of my hair appeared, or parts of my body were exposed during the beating, he would cover me ... I think he was a psychopath.

Following that opening session, Alaa was transferred to cell 13 on the seventh floor. There she managed her fear and anxiety by sleeping. Three days later, a new interrogator named Abu Rawan called for her. She thought they responded to her complaint because she had told the warden about her assault. Alaa says: 'Ironically, the stories of harassment of women I heard in the branch were all starring Abu Rawan, but he never touched me.'

The above discussion concerned the central branches of Military Intelligence in Damascus, since and during the revolution of 2011. But what about the branches in Syria's other provinces? The branch in Homs offers a good insight into how Military Intelligence functioned in the regions.

Branch 261: Homs

The Military Intelligence branch in Homs partially disappeared from the Syrian domestic scene, after its head, Ghazi Kanaan, was transferred to the reconnaissance branch in Lebanon. However, it made a strong reappearance after 2011, as Homs was considered 'the capital of the Syrian Revolution'. The branch was led during this period by Brigadier Mohamed Zamrini. Rights reports talk about the brutality of torture in Homs by electrocution, suspension by the hands, the wheel (*dulab*), and the bastinado (*falaqa*), in addition to overcrowding, bad food and poor sanitary conditions.[60]

Alaa was forced to sign her confession papers in Branch 215. After that, she was transferred to the Homs branch. This process goes against the majority of the transfer movement from provinces to the capital. This process goes against the majority of the transfers which were mainly from the provinces to the capital. Alaa says:

> The Homs branch received me while watching a report on Al-Jazeera about snipers of the Free Syrian Army. The minute I walked in, someone said: 'This is the sniper.' He started hitting me along with his companions while I was telling them it's impossible, I am the same girl they just saw, but they hit me even harder. Then they took me into the branch. It was like an old Arabic house with a yard full of men in their underwear, suspended and bleeding. Their feet were blue from torture … It was terrifying. Then they put me in a cell that was two by two and a half metres and had six other women.

Alaa was called for interrogation the following day. Without any questions, she was suspended by the hands and then passed out. The suspension was repeated the next day, but for longer: 'The warden who suspended me looked just like Hafez al-Assad, but with a dark skin … When there were no operatives watching the torture, he would take me to his room to drink matte and smoke … He talked to me about his family and kids … He was a good person inside, and that's what I was going to know for a fact later.'

The branch head tried to pressure Alaa to confess, but she refused so she was called for interrogation again:

> The kind-hearted warden took me into the interrogation. He warned me about the new detective who called for me.... The detective started flipping through my pictures, then verbally harassed me, and then forced me into giving him oral pleasure. He grabbed my head from the back with one hand and with the other hand he grabbed my lower jaw and stuck his penis in my mouth until he reached orgasm … The story repeated again the next day, but this time there were two detectives … I tried to mislead them by claiming I had vaginal bleeding to stop them from raping me. The detective did what he did the previous day though … I tried the whole time and with all my might to keep my mouth closed, but I failed.

In Syria, the terror of being arrested afflicts civilians, military personnel and even operatives working in the Military Intelligence division. Bassel Rouhi Sounaib who was arrested by the Homs branch on 11 May 2012 says:

> The moment the detainee enters the branch they feel they stepped outside time and space. As if entering a world of endless nightmares, where the first thing they are ordered to do is to completely strip down in front of others. For the Syrian society this is considered extremely humiliating and degrading: for a man to be seen naked by others. After this the torturers unleash their hatred. The beating I saw during the Syrian revolution was not just for torture. It was clear from its methods and tools that it was meant to kill. Inside the cells, for me, the real torture was the air. Yes, oxygen. Breathing air in that place was the hardest thing.[61]

Branch 245: Deraa

With the Syrian Revolution officially breaking out in Deraa, the Military Intelligence branch, led by Louay al-Ali, had to counter the uprising. Rights reports noted the use of torture in this branch, just like others of the Military Intelligence. The detainees stayed there for short periods before their transfer to the capital.

Ibrahim al-Hariri who was arrested in March 2012 says:

> The Military Security detachment in the town of Izraa arrested me. I stayed there for two days without any food. Then, I was transferred to the Deraa branch, where I stayed for 16 days. We survived there on crumbs of dry bread and some boiled potatoes. The congestion was catastrophic. We were dozens of detainees in a dormitory that opens to the branch basement lobby. All the cells and dormitories were open to one other because of the massive numbers. It was a very surreal situation. No ventilators to circulate the air, and no light to brighten the darkness. We took off our clothes and put them under us as covers to sleep as there were no blankets or mattresses. The odor was catastrophic, with the stench of the rotting wounds of all the neglected tortured detainees. After this experience I had a hemothorax and severe anemia.[62]

Branch 221: Palmyra

The story of the Military Intelligence in the city of Palmyra is no different from the rest of the branches during the Syrian revolution. Led by Ali Safi, the branch suppressed the uprising that reached Palmyra which is geographically and socially close to Homs.

The crime: a dream

Mohammed Qannas, who was arrested by the Military Intelligence branch in Palmyra on August 20, 2012, says: 'The moment I arrived at the branch, and while I was handing over my personal belongings, the operatives slapped me over fifty times for no apparent reason. They blindfolded me and then led me to the branch's interrogation headquarters, which is a half-basement. At the stairs I tried to make up my way, so the operative pushed me, and I tumbled down the stairs. Downstairs, I was handled by a warden who completely stripped me down for inspection. He put me, blindfolded, in a room and ordered me not to talk, to not even let out a whisper. I started hearing soft sounds around me. I stayed like this from noon until evening. Dinner arrived, and that's when I found out I was in a room with other detainees. We were all blindfolded with our heads to the wall. The distance between one and the other was about a metre. We were about 40. At night we slept on blankets handed to us by the warden and collected back at 6:00 a.m. We went into the bathroom in threes, three times a day. That was my situation for three days.'

Then the interrogation started with Qannas: 'He called me for interrogation, Captain Qusay al-Jahni; I learned his name later. As soon as I walked into the room, he ordered me to lift the blindfold. He threatened me immediately that if I didn't cooperate, he will suspend me like the others in the lobby I was in when I arrived.' Qannas' torment was similar to those of other detainees, using cables, plastic water pipes and suspension. The torture caused a huge edema to his leg which required the intervention of the doctor who gave him some ointment. The subdermal congestion exploded. The doctor intervened again to cut the damaged skin without any anesthesia or proper medical environment.

Qannas says: 'The situation became unbearable, and torture intensified despite my injury. I asked the interrogator for water, so he brought hot water they use to prepare matte and poured it on my body burning my skin. That's when I told him I would confess to whatever he wanted. He said: 'You erected military checkpoint and detained army personnel, then killed them and threw their bodies in the al-Jabal well in the groves area of Palmyra.' I said: 'I confess', although the story was a dream that I had told my friends. I had dreamt that I detained one of the branch staff, killed him, and dumped his body in that well he mentioned. One of these friends wrote a report to the branch telling them of my dream so I was arrested.'

Arrangements in Military Intelligence branches in the other governorates are no different to those of Homs, Palmyra or Deraa. According to a rights report,[63] the estimated prison capacity of the Military Intelligence branch in Aleppo is about 400 detainees. They were all placed in the basement of the branch that forms the prison of that facility. The report estimated the capacity of the Military Intelligence branch in Idlib to be 200–300 detainees with about 20 solitary cells. All the cells were underground. It can be concluded from the study of the infrastructure of all branches of the Military Intelligence that they comprised a prison area, usually located in the basement. In some rare cases the prison, or prison area, was on the ground floor such as in the District Branch, or on every floor such as in the Raid Force – which was an exception.

2

The Air Force Intelligence

The Air Force Intelligence Department was created at the beginning of Hafez al-Assad's rule of Syria. It was managed by Mohammed al-Khouli, an officer close to Assad. This service is considered the most loyal to the regime: it garners highly qualified staff with advance technical qualifications and is considered one of the most sectarian intelligence departments, as it has the lowest percentage of non-Alawite operatives and officers compared to other services. It follows the Ministry of Defence administratively, financially and with armaments, however the Minister of Defence has no authority over it. The Department of Military Intelligence oversees the work of the Minister of Defence and has a say in his appointment. The primary mission of Air Force Intelligence is to protect the Syrian Air Force as well as the presidential plane and ensure the security of the President while abroad.[1] In reality, its power extends much more widely.

From 1963 to 1987, Major General al-Khouli was the head of the Department. He was used by Hafez al-Assad in the security operations against his opponents after he seized power in 1970. Al-Khouli arrested Salah Jadid's supporters in the Arab Socialist Baath Party, the army and government ministries. Hafez al-Assad gave him eight hours to carry out the mission; he did it in two.[2] After Al-Khouli, Major General Ibrahim Hawija was head of the Department and remained in office until 2002. He was followed by Major General Izzaddeen Ismail who was in charge until 2005. He was succeeded by Major General Abdel Fattah Qudsiyah until 2009; Major General Jamil al-Hassan until 2019, and finally by Major General Ghassan Jawdat Ismail, who is head of the Department today.

All these officers preserved the brutal image of Air Force Intelligence. The Department enjoyed wide powers since its inception, powers which became most evident during the years of the Syrian uprising. In addition to its authority over all military and civilian air facilities, it oversees air defence formations in Syria and, most importantly, it owns several secret detention centres. Of all these centres, a prison in the Fourth Division, the 555 Paratrooper Regiment in Sumeriya, on the outskirts of Damascus, became widely known.

Structure of the Air Force Intelligence

The Air Force Intelligence differs in structure from Military Intelligence. It divides Syria into five regions, and has a major branch in each. These regional head branches controls several sub-branches in the major cities of each region. In addition to the five

Figure 2.1 The first from the right – Ibrahim Hawija, from a pro-regime social media site.

Figure 2.2 Jamil Al-Hassan, from a pro-regime social media site.

Figure 2.3 Maps of Air Force Intelligence Amiriya, Google Maps.

regional branches, the Department has six branches in Damascus, including Aviation Command, the oldest Air Force Intelligence headquarters in Syria. It is safe to assume that each branch of Air Force Intelligence has its own detention centres. Each branch can determine how long they can hold detainees. Our research shows that the branches of the capital in addition to the branch of the southern region of Harasta, in the suburbs of Damascus, had the longest periods of detention.

In the capital, the Aviation Command is located in a building adjacent to the Syrian Army Staff Authority headquarters near Umayyad Square, where the Deputy Head of the Department sits. The Administration Branch is located near Tahrir Square close to Old Damascus. It contains a file on every employee within the Department, and monitors them within the Department to prevent any loopholes. It also plays a role in promoting, removing, or transferring staff within the system. It has a large detention centre of at least two floors underground.

Damascus also hosts the Technical Information branch. This is concerned with the general information of the Department and contains many different sections – including a section on religions and political parties. The branch monitors the activity of local and global printed and audio-visual media (including the internet). It also deals with those directly or indirectly, based on what is important to the work of the Department. It has a detention centre located near Abbasiyeen Square. Mezzeh airport also hosts the Studies Branch near the Investigation Branch, which serves as the main investigation body of the Department. It is considered one of the worst intelligence branches in terms of torture. The Airport Branch is located close to the Investigation Branch. It is responsible for the security of the presidential airport and the presidential plane. Dissident sources indicate that this branch is also responsible for intelligence tasks related to the personal security of the president during his travels abroad. The Operations Branch is also located at the airport. It runs the internal and external operations of the Department including matters relating to the air force and those which require external intelligence work. It coordinates with the Airport branch whilst performing external intelligence functions related to the security of the president during his movements abroad. Agents from this branch are spread across the offices of Syrian Airlines around the world.

The Department also includes the Special Tasks Branch. This well-equipped elite branch is widely spread over all Syrian governorates in the form of sections. It performs combat operations using air defence units, the air force, military and even civilian airfields.

Regional branches are as follows:

- The Southern Region branch covers the governorates of Deraa, Quneitra, Suwayda, Damascus and its countryside, and is based in Damascus.
- The Central Region branch covers Homs and Hama and is based in Homs.
- The Northern Region branch covers Aleppo and Idlib and is based in Aleppo.
- The Eastern Province branch covers Deir Ezzor, Raqqa and Hasakah and is based in the city of Deir Ezzor.
- The Coastal Region branch covers Latakia and Tartus and is based in the city of Latakia.

The Air Force Intelligence's responsibilities are not limited to providing intelligence for air defence. The reach of this Department extends to cover large sectors of public life in Syria. Air Force Intelligence took command of operations during the internal events of the 1970s and 1980s.[3] However, the violent and highly visible role of Air Force Intelligence accelerated during the Syrian uprising, when it adopted a policy of 'non-interference with small issues'. It does not burden its personnel by following minute details, but instead focuses on the big issues.

Aviation Command: 1970 – 2000

Hafez al-Assad was a highly skilled pilot, and it was no surprise that he built a strong network in the air force and its intelligence agency. Air Force Intelligence arrested opponents of late President Hafez al-Assad in the 1970s. It continued with these arrest s until the end of the 1970s but at limited levels; after that, it was not visible on the domestic political scene up until the turn of the millennium, when it oversaw the arrest of most of Hizb al-Tahrir al-Islami's cadres in Syria. In 2005, Air Force Intelligence arrested a large number of jihadists returning from Iraq, the cadres of a liberal youth political group and, at the beginning of the Syrian Revolution, it carried out extensive arrest operations across all its branches. The Air Force Intelligence detainees were in the thousands, and dozens of them later appeared in Caesar's photos.[4]

The oldest arrest we were able to trace to Air Force Intelligence was in 1978. That experience confirmed that Air Force Intelligence was living up to its violent reputation from the beginning. Faraj Bayraqdar whose testimony, in itself, constitutes a micro-history of the Syrian intelligence, says:

Air Force Intelligence was not a standard of all Syria's intelligence at the time. I was arrested by them for a few months, during which I endured severe torture. The interrogation was led by Ali Mamlouk who was a Lieutenant Colonel in the Air Force Intelligence, and his assistant Jamil al-Hassan, who was a First Lieutenant. The Investigation branch at Mezzeh airport was not yet there. I was detained in the basement of the Aviation Command. I wish I'd been arrested by Political Security or General Intelligence. That experience was not comparable in terms of cruelty and torment to any other intelligence department's detention experience at that time.[5]

Torture with light

As well as the known types of beatings with cables, bamboo sticks and torture with electricity in the Aviation Command, there was torture using very bright light. How? The prisoner is thrown on his back in the middle of the large torture chamber. His hands and feet are tied with metal chains to rings in the floor of the room. The body becomes glued to the ground. The four extremities are tied firmly to the four corners . . . His eyes are forced open and a matchstick is placed between the eyelids to ensure the eyes cannot be closed and remain open. The prisoner is ordered to 'confess'. If he does not, the latter turns on a bright light (projector) and tells the prisoner: you will stay like this until tomorrow; and leaves the room. Whatever the prisoner's endurance, after two minutes he would start screaming and crying. The detective would be standing in an adjacent room listening to the screams, aware that the prisoner would not be able to endure this bright light. He would then come to him and say: confess. The prisoner says: 'Please turn off the light; I will confess to whatever you want'. The investigator insists that the confession is made before the light is turned off.[6]

Investigation Branch

The name of Air Force Intelligence did not come up much as an arrest and investigation department in the 1980s. The confrontation against the Muslim Brotherhood and the left-wing opposition parties at the time was spearheaded by both the Military Intelligence Division and the General Intelligence and Political Security Departments. However, Air Force Intelligence re-emerges as a detention and investigation department with far-reaching powers at the beginning of the millennium. In 1999, the department arrested the cadres of Hizb al-Tahrir al-Islami in Syria. Air Force Intelligence handled this independent from the rest of the security services. No other agency interfered with this file, neither in cooperation nor in conflict.

The name of the Investigation Branch of Air Force Intelligence, led by Ali Mamlouk, stands out in connection to the Tahrir arrests. Within a month, the Department arrested most of the party's members, leaders or individuals, civilians or military personnel. Mamlouk and Colonel Adnan Al-Ashi managed the investigation with the party's cadres, particularly with the military personnel. The mechanisms of arrest, search, and inspection (photo with the number) in Air Force Intelligence do not differ from those in Military Intelligence.

The detainee is fully stripped and is subjected to 'the Military Police inspection' after he has handed over his personal belongings, papers, money, etc. He keeps his clothes but without his belt and shoelaces. After those procedures, the prisoner is sent to their solitary cell and from that point on carries its number as his name. This is especially true for military personnel. Since then, the conditions of detention in Air Force Intelligence have been described as extremely difficult and cruel. The prison solitary cells have no toilets, and the food is scarce and of poor quality.

One eyewitness reports:

> The hunger was intense. Throughout the day, the detainee receives either two loaves of bread or one and a half, sometimes even one. Breakfast was three olives and one spoon of *labneh* [dried yogurt]. Lunch was *bulgur* or rice in very small quantities that amount to 1–3 spoons per person. Dinner was only a spoonful of yogurt. We have not seen boiled eggs, boiled potatoes, or any of the army allocation that we know. We only defecated once every three days an amount that equaled two olives. Hunger has caused diseases for some of us. Salt was forbidden and we begged for it for the ill among us.[7]

During the investigation period, which was between five to seven months, visits were completely forbidden. The clothes of the detainees were damaged after a while. No branch of Air Force Intelligence enforces a uniform for prisoners, as is the case with the District Branch of the Military Intelligence. After pressure and demands from detainees and their families outside, the prison administration decided to allow the purchase of some supplies. 'Four months after the arrest, the prison administration asked us if we had the money to buy us some underwear, pajamas, soap, towels, toiletries, a brush and toothpaste. The question was strange to us then. I knew after my release that there were activists who moved to improve our conditions in the same period that we got this offer to buy clothes, toiletries, etc.'[8]

The prison of the Investigation Branch of Air Force Intelligence, the old headquarters, is located above the ground. The left side of the building is shaped as an open box that consists of 14 solitary cells, toilets and bathrooms. The interrogation rooms are located on the same side; they have a special gate that leads to the outside of the building. The opposite right side houses four dormitories. The ventilation in the prison is very poor. Solitary cells are similar to those in Military Intelligence; they were no more than 2 metres by 1 metre, with only a blanket on the ground. 'We were placed in the solitary cells after the humiliating inspection. Solitary cells are all without bathrooms. They are only empty spaces with lice-ridden blankets. The detainees had numbers. Mine was no 2, which was the number of my cell. The solitary cell was above the ground and it had a window from which I could see the light.'[9] Dormitories in the Investigation prison have different measurements. More than 20 detainees were placed in a dormitory that was 185 cm wide and less than 3 metres long, for three months. Bathrooms and toilets were outside dormitories and solitary cells, one had to go out two to three times a day. Going to the toilet is no more than a few minutes for each dormitory, preventing any possibility of washing, cleaning, or even urinating or defecating normally.

TD, born in Damascus to an upper-middle-class family, was arrested by Air Force Intelligence on 6 January 1988 accused of being a member of the Muslim Brotherhood. He was arrested around 1pm by three men with AK-47s, placed in a Peugeot 504 station wagon, and beaten and insulted: 'You monkey, I'll have you forget your mother's milk', or 'I will show you God personally'. He spent 50 months and four days in Mezze prison, where he was tortured while asked questions such as: What do you think about our government? Why do you utter critique? Why do you want changes? What is wrong with this government? Most importantly, they were interested in mapping who his friends were and what they had spoken about during meetings. The torture consisted of the usual beatings, e.g. bastinado (*falaqa*) while folded into a car tyre (*dulab*). He was given an ointment after the beatings, which healed his soles within a day. There was also electrocution, drowning and the Magic Carpet. In every single room where he was not blindfolded, he saw photos of Hafez al-Assad on the walls, which looked like they had been pasted on with the blood of detainees. He heard from an older man that it was crucial to stay busy, so they played with olive pits, talked to each other, and gathered their thoughts. At first the torture sessions were every day but decreased in frequency over the months. Throughout the entire process, he never knew who was responsible for his imprisonment and torture. About three months before he was released, the prison regime improved, and he was allowed regular toilet visits, as well as showers. The day before his release, he was forced to sign a letter of gratitude to President Hafez al-Assad. They released him on 10 March 1992. Only later, did he hear from his father that Ali Mamlouk was in charge of the prison. During his imprisonment, his father had paid a fortune to gather any information about his whereabouts, and to secure lenient treatment. Well after he was released, officers' wives would walk into his family's clothing store and take the most expensive clothes for free, and to have alterations done for nothing. Due to the many beatings he received, his testicles were damaged so he was unable to have children. Worse still, his identity card was never returned, therefore he remained a non-person in the eyes of the law. That same year he fled to Europe.[10]

Overpopulated and underfed

After the end of the investigation I was transferred from solitary cell 2 to a dormitory. The dormitory lacks all the elements of life, it is devoid of air, and heat there is suffocating. Because of the bad storage inside the branch, where we were more than thirty detainees in an area of no more than 3 metres by 4; we got scabies. They took us out to grease us with kerosene and benzoate then they painted the dormitory with kerosene. Scabies was decreasing, however we got lice from the blankets of the new detainees transferred to us from their solitary cells. We started taking off our clothes and sitting under the blanket, searching for lice in our clothes.[11]

During the period of scabies they increased the amount of food. They doubled the amount of ghee in meals on doctor's orders to help detainees recover. Yet the day I arrived in Saydnaya, I learned I had lost 40 kilos in five months. My fat colleague lost more than half his weight, all because of malnutrition.[12]

Despite the prevalence of skin diseases such as scabies and allergies, detainees were faced with the lowest levels of health care. Detainees of the branch at that time agreed that the doctor was harsher than the investigating officers and 'more demeaning than them in treatment'. The doctor was called upon to attend to injuries resulting from torture such as fractures. Also, a health officer came in on a weekly basis to deal with any cases that required follow-up. 'I had joint pain during my arrest. Knowing that medical care is only a formality that does not exceed an aspirin pill, I didn't ask for the doctor. A doctor was available, and some have obtained medicines for chronic diseases.'[13] 'The greatest dependence in medical matters was on detainees who were doctors.'[14]

The investigation: methods and techniques

The methods of investigation at the end of 1999 do not differ from those used in Aviation Command since the beginning of the 1970s: extreme violence and unjustified torture, not only for the purpose of obtaining information, but also during their stay in the prison cells or dormitories. However, Air Force Intelligence relied heavily on some unconventional methods of torture.

Hunger, drowsiness, fatigue

I was placed in a solitary cell of two metres by a metre, that was almost completely empty. I was completely deprived of sleeping, sitting, and eating. I tried to sit on the second day of the punishment, but the guards were watching me through an opening in the door – the 'judas window', so I was punished. They allowed me only to drink water. The agony lasted for three days during which I lost my balance and control over myself. My feet swelled with all the trapped blood. I later learned that the Brigadier in charge of the investigation ordered this torment. I was called for interrogation directly afterwards. When I did not respond to the interrogator's questions, they took me to the usual torture chamber where I had my share of beatings with a bamboo stick. At the end of those three days, they started giving me a quarter of a meal on the first day and then a half on the second day and so on until the food portion, which was originally scarce, returned to the usual.[15]

Starvation, sleep deprivation and preventing the detainee from sitting or lying down was a much-adopted technique during that period. Homam Youssef says: 'It was used for days until the detainees confessed the requested information. A detainee in cell number 18 was deprived of food and sleep for about a week.'[16] The food ban was used to make the detainee physically weaker. 'It makes it easier to control you. I was tortured with deprivation for eight days in a row'.[17]

The interrogation ritual starts the moment the cell door opens. The warden starts insulting the detainee, who must turn his face to the wall. The hands are tied by plastic cable ties and the detainee is then dragged to the interrogation room on the same floor. The detainee is taken to the interrogation wearing only his underwear.

> 'The hands become numb because of the constraint, and you get severe pain in the shoulders. We remain naked; standing in a long corridor before they bring us into the interrogation room. After every question you receive a beating. Everything you say is a lie. Your feet are clutched together while you're laying on your stomach. You are hit with the wooden stick, then with an iron one. Toes get broken sometimes. They threatened to remove my nails or put electricity on my genitals. You sit on your knees during the continuous interrogation that is filled with swearing and insults. Torture sessions take place daily, and sometimes every other day. Torture sessions last an hour or two.'[18]

The use of traditional methods of torture was reported in Air Force Intelligence, such as the German chair, the Flying Carpet, suspension and electricity, in addition to the 'normal' methods of beating, whipping, and kicking, which caused broken ribs for some detainees. Omar al-Sayyed Youssef reminisces: 'The Aleppo Air Force Intelligence torture was harsher and more severe than the Investigation Branch. One of our fellow detainees, M.A., told us he was placed in the refrigerator for hours. After his release, he retired from public life and moved away from people.'[19]

None of the detainees were killed under torture. The general state of imprisonment and torture caused a series of psychological disorders. Some of those disorders appeared directly and publicly in prison. One of the detainees began singing, urinating, and defecating on himself. His condition exhausted the prisoners. They believed that this would eventually be their fate.

What's my name?!

I was very fatigued during the first period of the interrogation. That day I had a strange incident. I don't know until this day if I was asleep or awake then. Four wardens opened the door. Two of them went into the cell and started beating me immediately, as usual. Someone asked me: 'What's your name?' I replied: 'I forgot. . .'. He yelled at me: 'Bastard number 2, what's your name?', 'I swear I forgot,' I replied. This dialogue continued for a few seconds before he hit me on the face. I woke up to the wardens laughing before I could remember my name and tell them.[20]

Air Force Intelligence prisons must be considered as an environment alien to normal life; it is more like a special territory with its own values, subjective components, and unique daily routines. Homam Youssef again puts it well:

Inhumane overcrowding; feet swollen of torture that they look plastic. I sat squatting observing the feet of my colleagues, swollen from frequent beatings. Once, the foot of an elderly man burst and blood sprayed on the wall. You cannot but despise those who carry out such acts on other humans; a contempt mixed with pity. For they are manufactured by a methodical crushing machine from hell to which they are subjected to the point of wiping out all their human inclinations. They are Frankensteinian beings. A contrasting set of weird ingredients. For example, one of the particularly violent wardens had a beautiful voice. At night, he sang for his mother. Prisoners cried to his songs and reacted to them. Some wardens asked the doctors detained with us for consultations regarding their illnesses. While moments earlier they themselves were torturing this or that doctor.[21]

Regional branches

Prior to 2011, there were no large-scale arrests by regional Air Force Intelligence branches. Those branches conducted arrests based on orders from the administration in Damascus. They did not keep detainees in their custody for more than two days or a week at the latest. They sent the detainee to the central Investigation Branch which was the heart of the Department. The Central Region Branch, led by Brigadier Abdul Karim Nabhan, arrested Officer A.Kh. from his military base. The arrest order was executed by Colonel Jihad Dayoub who was later promoted to Brigadier and was put in charge of the Eastern Region branch. A.Kh. narrates:

They took me down to the branch prison in the basement. They removed the military insignia and took my belongings. They put me in a very small solitary cell, 120 cm long and 1 metre wide. I was placed there handcuffed. There was a lot of faeces in it. I stayed in it for hours. They called me for a preliminary investigation. From the onset I was beaten by hands accompanied with insults and threats, especially of rape. I stayed at the branch for two days and was then transferred to the Investigation Branch at Mezzeh military airport.[22]

The same experience befell an Air Force officer in Aleppo. He was arrested by the Air Force Intelligence Branch in the Northern Region under the command of Brigadier Mohammed Bakour at the end of 1999:

They took me down to the basement without a question or a word and start beating me immediately. They took me out of the basement to the first floor to meet the director of the Department, Major General Ibrahim Howaija. They took me back to the branch detention center, which is very small. I stayed there for two days, unaware of the date and the time, nor what was going on around me; all details were mixed. The toilet was outside the cell. The warden would drag me to the toilet while I remained blindfolded.[23]

Figure 2.4 Mezze Military Airport, Google Maps.

Figure 2.5 Map of Harasta Branch, Google Maps.

Southern Region Branch: Harasta

The Branch is located on the entrance to the Eastern Ghouta in rural Damascus. It oversaw the Southern Region of Syria as well as Damascus and its environs. The branch houses a large underground prison. According to one survivor, 'Harasta Branch looks like Syrian public schools in terms of construction and shape. Above ground were officers' offices, and underground was the prison.'[24]

Figure 2.6 Mohammad Rahmoun, from the Syrian Ministry of Interior website.

In 2006, the Branch was headed by Mohammed Rahmoun, who remained in charge until he became Minister of the Interior in 2018. In early 2006, the branch arrested a group of young liberal activists accused of setting up an opposition group, the first of whom was H.S., who was sent to the branch prison along with his colleague the day after they reported to the branch. 'After being searched by the Military Police they sent us to prison. Opposite the door was a corridor to the left of which were the assistants' room and the investigation room. Then came a narrow passage with three cages on the right and two cages on the left. Each cage had four solitary cells with a mesh ceiling. Bathrooms and toilets took place of where the third cage was supposed to be located on the left. The corridor ended with a wider space with four dormitories and a breathing space.'[25]

The branch prison was completely full. The second solitary was four metres long and three metres wide and had about 40 detainees. The dormitory had a toilet with only a wall separating the toilet pit and a sink from the dormitory. The food and medical situation in the Branch was quite similar to that of the Investigation Branch by the end of 1999, and the Aviation Command in 1978.

Website raid

The lead investigator of the case in the Branch, Captain Yarub al-Tawil, knew everything he wanted about our case since the day we were brought to the Branch. But the day after the arrest, they began beating us and expanding the investigation. The beating was to teach us a lesson, not to extract more information. A detective with the rank of soldier, poorly educated, came to us asking for the address of the website where we wrote. I tried to answer that the site was 'www...' but he immediately interrupted me with beating. He yelled at me: "I want the address of the website so that we can raid it." I tried to explain that it was a website with no physical headquarters. The more I explained, the more he hit me until my screams reached the office of the Captain who came and saved me from him.[26]

Detection and investigation

In 2006, six years after the arrest of Hizb al-Tahrir cadres, all cases were transferred to the Investigation Branch, which was then led by Adib Salameh. There the rounds of interrogation began to expand and with them the rounds of torture for the young liberals. The branch prison was overcrowded, with six to 14 detainees in one solitary cell (two metres by 1 metre). Heavy congestion meant the day was filled with tasks of food distribution which lasted from 5:30 until 8:30am. Then solitary cells were opened to take detainees to the toilet. Although the allowed duration is no longer than half a minute, because of the large number of detainees, the process took a long time. Lunch and dinner were distributed at 14:30, this took about three hours. 'These tasks consumed about seven to eight hours between the distribution of food and visiting the toilets, which pushed the interrogations and torture to the night.'[27]

The new upgrade to the interrogation in Air Force Intelligence was that torture operations were organized by a bell. If the detainee's answer was unhelpful to the investigator, the latter rang the bell and an assistant came. He takes the detainee to the torture chamber and starts beating him until the bell is heard again, when he returns the detainee to the interrogation room. 'There was a special room for bamboo sticks in the Branch. They kept them soaked in water to ensure they stay soft and hence more effective.'[28]

If none of the usual methods of torture worked, the investigator resorted to threatening the detainee with harming their parents. One of the detainees at the time of Al-Qaeda's proliferation did not confess despite a long torture session with bamboo sticks, the German chair, electricity, etc., so they brought his wife in. The moment he heard her voice telling him that she was in the Branch he confessed to everything they asked him.

Air Force Intelligence is effective at implementing a policy of keeping detainees preoccupied with the banalities of daily life. The hours it takes for the distribution of food, visiting the toilet for less than a minute, the scarcity of food and drinking water; all these factors kept the detainee constantly occupied with his need to defecate, the hunger that squeezes his stomach and his attempts to get rid of lice. Just as the day ends, the suffering of interrogation and torture starts. If not torture, then it is the pain of sleeping in another detainee's lap. All the detainee can do is try to preserve his mental abilities. The public order of the prison insists on breaking the relationship between the prisoner and the warden. The relationship cracks at the reception of a new detainee during which the warden beats the new arrival. The warden is prohibited from asking any questions or knowing any details about the detainee. Interaction is by numbers. The beginning and ending of a torture session is marked by ringing the bell, so the warden becomes part of a machine that works mindlessly.

Torture mechanisms and overcrowding in the Investigation Branch continued until 2010. In the spring of that year, there was a huge increase in numbers, similar to that which the branches of Air Force Intelligence would witness during the years of the Revolution. Akram al-Saud narrates:

> On 29 March 2010, I was placed in solitary cell no. 2 with an influential person. He was arrested on the background of corruption in the Customs Service. I learned from him that the Air Force received the dossier of combating smuggling following an order from the Office of National Security. After this the prison situation became unbearable. The cell, which was two metres long and one metre wide, held 17 of us. They gave us blankets, but they were full of lice. The situation became disastrous. We began to suffer from shortness of breath. Scabies and lice spread widely. We suffered a strange case where the body enters a boiling-like state, after which large pimples appear on the skin. You would feel like your body wants to explode.[29]

Congestion caused not only the spread of diseases, but visiting the toilet had to be faster than before. The detainees spent over three months without access to a shower which exacerbated hygiene problems and skin diseases. This difficult situation led to the spread of 'switching-off'. The situation remained unchanged until eight detainees died because of overcrowding. Al-Saud continues:

> 'That was a tense day in the prison. We could hear the sounds of military salutations. The door of our cell was opened, and its filthy air came out. By the door we saw a man in a blue suit. He covered his mouth and took a step back. He scolded the wardens harshly. We later learned that he was Major General Jamil al-Hassan. Under his orders, they placed eight of us in a cell. The next day they installed air extractors, opened the bottoms of the doors, and placed a metal mesh to improve ventilation.'[30]

Al-Saud, who was detained because of his political stance, was placed the next day with some of the detainees in the Information Branch prison, located at the same airport. The prison was more of an Arabic-style house with an open courtyard, covered by a net, encircled by guards in black uniforms with the inscription 'anti-terrorism'.

Overlooking the courtyard was the door of one dormitory, three solitary cells, a toilet, and a bathroom.

Air Force Intelligence after 2011

The functional role of Air Force Intelligence greatly expanded following the start of the Syrian Revolution in the Spring of 2011. The branches were converted into detention repositories, which brought into use other buildings belonging to the department or the military units cooperating with it. Aircraft hangars were used as prisons at Mezzeh airport. The Investigation Branch, led by Brigadier Abdul Salam Mahmoud, placed a large number of its detainees in the 555th Regiment of the Fourth Division. All of these numbers are in addition to those who were transferred to Saydnaya prison or died under torture or as a result of difficult conditions in detention. The Air Force Intelligence dispatched Brigadier Qusay Mayhoub to Deraa in the south of the country to quell demonstrations there. Brigadier Mayhoub managed the Deraa section of the Southern Region Branch for the next nine years. The branch arrested dozens of protesters and those on wanted lists such as lawyer and rights activist Thamer Al-Jahmani.[31]

Green badges

On 29 April 2011, operatives in military uniforms raided the house where I was hiding. All members of the security and military services dress the same, except that they put coloured insignia on the left forearm to distinguish their affiliation. Those who arrested me were wearing green badges. They tied my hands to the back and took me to the Omari Mosque. The mosque was completely empty and turned into a collection point for the detainees. The operatives beat me whenever they passed next to me. In about two hours, the remaining detainees including me, were transported in an armored personnel carrier to the old Deraa customs building, another collection point. The moment they got us off the wagon, we were attacked by operatives dressed in army uniforms; they beat us violently. I completely lost consciousness. Rainwater gathered on the ground woke me up. They then handed me over to the Air Force Intelligence Department in the Industrial Area of the city of Deraa. They collected dozens of detainees. Most were either injured or had fractures in the ribs, hands, or feet. Two days later I was transferred with a number of detainees to the Investigation Branch at Mezzeh airport.[32]

Air Force Intelligence used military airfields to transport detainees from distant provinces. Air Force helicopters transported detainees from Deir ez-Zor in the east of the country, Aleppo and Idlib in the North, and Latakia and Tartous on the

Mediterranean coast. The aircrafts delivered the detainees to Mezzeh airport, which, along with the rest of the branches in Damascus, was converted into a long-term detention facility. Muhannad Al-Ghobash[33] was flown from Aleppo's Al-Nayrab military airport with several detainees coming from Deir ez-Zor to Mezzeh airport:

> The aircraft landed in Mezzeh at night on 21 March 2012. Air Force Intelligence operatives climbed onto the plane and welcomed us with beating. We were taken to a bus where we remained for two hours doing nothing but receiving more strikes and blows. The bus moved for a few minutes then stopped. We offboarded the bus to a gravel ground. The strong lighting turned night into day. Then a security operative confronted me saying [in an Alawite accent]: 'Do you know where you are?' I said I didn't. He said: 'You're in hell . . . and we are the angels of torment.'[34]

After the outbreak of the Syrian Revolution, torture and beatings were a custom that accompanied the detainee from the moment they entered the Air Force Intelligence branches until the day they left. The number of detainees in solitary cells with identical dimensions, 2 metres by 1 metre, reached 14 and sometimes increased to 20. They slept in alternation and were taken to the toilet in fours, for intervals of no more than 30 seconds. Showering was cancelled, and wardens replaced it by extending a hose to the cell. They would suspend it from above the door into the cell and give detainees small pieces of soap to bathe. Then the forced labourer would clean and rinse the cell floor. Food was available in that period. Torture in the prison, began at night. The warden requested the names of newly arrived detainees to the branch. The hands of the new detainee would be tied with a plastic cable tie to the top of the cell door where he remained standing all night. If you passed through the corridor of the cells you could see hands tied to the upper sections of the doors of the solitary cells. Apart from tying the hands of the new arrivals, there were those punished by a decision from the investigator. The wardens took out those punished and suspended them on the walls of the corridor or in the investigation yard that was empty at night. The detainee must ask for drinking water every ten minutes so that the forced labourer would bring him a bucket of cold water and flush him with it. If he didn't ask for drinking water, he would receive beating as a punishment.

The 'Hitler of Mezzeh'

All punishments were nothing compared to those of the warden 'Hitler'. His colleagues gave him that nickname. The punishment of this warden was a game he played with his colleagues. He called upon the punished detainees and divided them into teams. Each warden had a team. They would agree on the types of animals they want to have and train and carried out that training on the detainees. For example, Hitler wants a fierce dog and a calm one, so he would order one of the

> detainees to play the role of a fierce dog to battle with the fierce dog raised by his fellow warden. If you're a nice dog, you have to kneel near Hitler's feet and howl gently and endearingly. At times they ordered detainees to be cats, chickens or any animal that comes to mind and the game continues all night. If a detainee objects or violates the rules of the game, they shall be punished by extinguishing cigarette butts or the charcoal of the hookah in their body. [35]

The new headquarters of the Investigation Branch entered service at the beginning of the Syrian Revolution. The new branch prison was underground, unlike the prison in the old headquarters. Officers from the Air Force, such as Captain Mohamed Khalil Bostaji, were detained there.[36]

> We reached the branch at 3 in the morning. We descended 20–25 stairs. After the inspection procedures were completed, I was transferred to cell No. 21. This solitary cell was two metres long and 120 cm wide. It had three detainees. They were all facing the wall opposite the door of the cell. The height of the cell was four metres. It had a small window looking up to the sky. They gave me the number 1801.

Numbers are usually given to detainees according to Air Force Intelligence measures. The number comes from the detainee's registration number in the prison registry. Most detainees arrested under the same dossier carry serial numbers. Detainees are forbidden from giving their real names. If a detainee with a number dies, and the warden asks for his name and receives a name (rather than a number) from the detainee in charge of the cell, that detainee receives a long punishment. But no one knows why detainees are given numbers instead of their names, which are easier to use among them. In Caesar's photos, these numbers later appeared on the foreheads of the detainees who perished in the intelligence branches.

The modernity of the new building of the Investigation Branch did not prevent the spread of bacterial infections resulting from rotten wounds of the detainees. A new detainee is usually shocked by the heat of the place and its repulsive smell which takes some time to get used to. All detainees had long hair and long beards as there was no regular grooming in the branch. A shower was allowed once a week outside the cell in the bathroom for no more than a minute. The same daily prison details of the old branch prison were transferred to the new one. By the end of 2012, the number of inmates in a solitary cell increased to an average of 16. The available area per detainee was one tile of only 40 x 40 cm. All of those arrested remained in their underwear after their clothes and blankets were collected in April 2012. The same tools of torture were used in the new headquarters.

The dream

The detainees shared a magical dream among them, as if a lucky charm. The dream was that the Syrian regime is building a great wall around Damascus. The wall was of great solidity, height, and size. The regime had almost finished construction. As the final moments of finishing the wall and placement of the last stone approaches, the wall collapses completely, and behind it mount Qassiyon appears, completely covered in greenery except for a small brown spot. Interpreters exchanged the dream and diligently analyzed it. They agreed that we will win, but only after the regime has almost regained total control of the ground and is about to declare the end of the Revolution. The Revolution will then return and win all Syrian ground except for a small part.[37]

On the ground, the treatment of Air Force Intelligence does not differentiate between military personnel and civilians. The former receives stronger punishment. The same methods of torture were used for men and women alike, although women are threatened more with sexual assault. S.A., like many, was subjected to sexual harassment and assault during her detention in the Air Force Intelligence.[38]

> They took me to a torture chamber. A place full of torture tools from cables to bamboo sticks and wheels. They completely stripped me down. I was tied from my hands and feet to metal rings fixed to the floor of the room. In the room stood the detective in charge of my file, and a big torturer who later left the room. The detective raped me several times, then poured hot water over my body. I was burned in more than one location. He extinguished his cigarettes in my body at the wrist, above the ankle and in the sensitive area.

Subjecting women more than men to sexual torture does not mean that the practice did not happen to men. The difference is in the method of torture. Women are harassed or raped. Men are often beaten or electrocuted on the penis, or have their penises tied. They are rarely raped. M.H.[39] was arrested at the beginning of March 2012 by Air Force Intelligence, where he remained for a year and a half. 'I refused to [falsely] confess to carrying weapons and killing, for I am a civilian activist. The detective ordered me to take all my clothes off. The warden brough a wrench like tool. He inserted my penis into its opening and started shrinking the hole. The pain was unbearable, but they continued to tighten it and threatened to cut off my penis if I didn't confess.'

M.H. and many detainees of that period were transferred between several buildings. He was initially placed in the Information and Studies Branch building at the airport. He was then transferred with others to the Aircraft Security building where he stayed for about two months in a classroom designated for Air Force cadets. It was a large hall 11 metres long and 6 metres wide that housed more than 180 detainees. He was then transferred to the new Investigation building and placed in a solitary cell of 2 metre by

1 metre along with 14 other detainees. After the interrogation was completed, he was transferred to a hangar with about 700 detainees. 'Every day one or two detainees died of suffocation due to congestion and poor ventilation.'[40] How many times someone could be transferred is demonstrated by the example of Mohammed Abu Hajar from Tartous. He was arrested on 14 March 2012 and held for two months in total: first at the police station, then at Political Security, then Criminal Security, then at the court, then to the civil prison, then to Balouneh prison in Homs, then to Adra, and finally to an underground prison he did not recognize. His detention came to an end when they took him, blindfolded and handcuffed, to a square and dumped him on the street.[41]

Congestion not only happened in the planes' hangars. The dormitories of the modern headquarters of the Investigation Branch were overflowing with detainees. Abu Zeid[42] was placed in the fifth dormitory with more than 97 detainees. 'Each detainee gets the space of only one tile to sit and sleep in a tandem shape. Three detainees slept in the toilet to make room for the rest. I was hoping to sleep in the toilet as there was some oxygen there.' The days in the dormitory are similar, from waking up to breakfast, interrogation, lunch, interrogation again, dinner and trying to sleep. Detainees are forbidden to sleep or place their backs against the wall during the day. Cases of mental trauma 'switching off', are frequent due to overcrowding, malnutrition, lack of sleep, constant torment, and anxiety. These harsh conditions did not affect every detainee. Akram al-Saud was arrested in 2011 by the Air Force Intelligence in a Damascus internet café on suspicion of opposition activity. It was his second detention, so he knew what to expect. At Mezze airport he was crammed into a cell that quickly became overcrowded due to the influx of demonstrators:

I saw two young men who were wounded in their faces, so I thought it was because of beatings at the branch. I wiggled my way over to them and asked them about the investigation, but apparently, they had only arrived that day. 'Where's the beatings from then?', I asked. Well, their fellow dentistry students at the university had beaten them up and handed them over. They were second-year students, from rich neighbourhoods in Damascus. I thought, 'they'll never make it: too soft, too sweet, too civilized'. After two weeks, they died of course.[43]

During 2018 and 2019, Air Force Intelligence experienced something of a transformation. The number of detainees decreased, and the security situation came more under regime control than before. Sarah Al-Abdullah[44] was transferred to the Investigation Branch at Mezzeh airport in mid-2018 having been released from Damascus central prison.

They brought me into the old prison at the Investigation Branch at Mezzeh airport. The whole prison is monitored by cameras. I was searched by one of the female guards overseeing the women section of the prison. She asked me if I was taking any medications.' These procedures were un-heard of in Air Force Intelligence. This was coupled with the talk of possibly increasing exercise time for detainees to more than once a week. 'We felt that something had changed. I later learned that there were committees overseeing these prisons. Former female detainees said they were placed underground.' Female wardens started working at the Branch since the end of 2017. They moved female detainees from the basement to cells above the ground.[45]

Imprisonment as violence against the family

Imprisonment is a form of violence that affects not only the victim himself, but also the families of detainees, who suffer, both during their loved one's detention and after. In fact, even subsequent generations suffer the consequences of a parent's detention. During a loved one's detention, family members will frantically search for information on their arrested family member, worry about scraping together money to pay off the intelligence, and attempt to bribe intelligence officers who can help them gain any information or slightly better treatment for their family member. Thus, detention as a system was as much a repressive tool as it was a lucrative business for the officers in the Mukhabarat. R.A.S. was a young Kurdish singer from Qamishli, who was arrested every time he played the *tembûr*, the Kurdish lute, and sang Kurdish songs during a wedding or a secret Newroz celebration. Intelligence officers broke his *tembûr* and arrested him in a white Peugeot 504. He suffered the usual torture and maltreatment, fled the country upon release, and applied for asylum in the Netherlands. But flight sometimes complicated events even more: detainees who left Syria after being released feared for their family members, as they were often intimidated, threatened, arrested, and tortured.[46] Two of R.A.S's documents demonstrate these pressures on the family:

From a plea brief of his lawyer to the court in The Hague, 26 May 1992:

> That it has remained with short-lived arrests S. owes to his father. Each time he was able to buy S.'s freedom. He did this through intermediaries, who managed to bring the ransom or bribes (about 300 dollars each time) to the intended location. This was each time a race against time, for should S. have confessed as a result of the beatings, whatever the accusation, or should his file have been forwarded to the higher echelons in the organization of the security service, the bribes would have been of no avail.[47]

From a letter from his father to R.A.S., 11 February 1992:

> My dear son,
>   Warmest greetings. I beg for mercy and blessing from the Almighty. I pray that you will always be healthy and out of the dangers that wanted to end your life.
>   My dear son,
>   We are very happy that you arrived safely there and are no longer in danger. We always prayed that you would not fall into their traps. I hope that this letter will end up in your hands ... We heard from your brother, ..., that you finally arrived there safe and sound. I am very glad that you are safe where you are now.

Don't ask me how the situation here is right now. You know very well. It is even worse. They come into our house whenever they want to. When I am not home, then they look for me at the neighbors to take me to their branch in the neighborhood. There the interrogation starts. For hours they insult me without showing even a grain of respect for my age. I simply have to calmly accept everything. There is no other way. Still I am happy that you and your brother... are out of their reach. They can do whatever they want. I don't care, I am old enough and they know it.

Your mother misses you very much and wishes you the best. She thinks and worries a lot and therefore does not feel well. It is not easy for her to allow two of her children to be in exile and far away and that she is harassed by the authorities every day. She prays to see you again safe and sound.[48]

The Southern Region Branch after 2011

The Southern Region Branch recorded a significant shift in the way it dealt with detainees after the start of the Syrian Revolution. The branch prison was filled to the brim, including its four dormitories and the outside space. The four dormitories are underground 'basement' rooms with an average area of 3 metres by 4 metres. The numbers of detainees placed there exceed three to four times its maximum capacity. In addition to these dormitories, there were 20 solitary cells spread over five cages, four solitaries per cage, each solitary cell being 2 metres by 1.5 metres. The outside space was also underground. It had an open ceiling roofed with a metal mesh. The area was 96 square metres, but very crowded. It housed about 340 detainees. A small trench-like passage, 30 cm wide and 30 cm deep, passes through. It was used as a toilet. 'We used to relieve ourselves, publicly, in that trench during breathing time. You would find one detainee eating right next to another who is defecating.'[49]

The conditions of everyday life in the Harasta Branch were similar to those in the Investigation Branch. Toilets and bathrooms were strictly regulated. Various forms and methods of torture prevailed. The lack of any form of hygiene such as showering, and the complete absence of medical care produced many serious diseases. The doctor only attended torture sessions to prevent the detainee from dying.[50]

Fish scales

Our protest in dormitory no. 2 succeeded. That was about 15 days after my arrest. We protested because of the unbelievable congestion we were living where most of us slept standing. It was also because of the liquid that covered the floor of the dormitory, up to 10 cm high. The liquid was formed from water dripping from the roof and the sweat of the detainees. I was transferred with some detainees to the breathing space. I was struck by the daylight coming from the mesh ceiling of the breathing space. In the dormitory we lived in red light all the time. My eyes were initially harmed. Then the journey of diseases started. The trench in which we urinated and defecated often overflowed, and we would drown in dirty water. We rarely had the chance to shower. The contaminated water and congestion produced a disease that we called 'Fish Scales'. I started scratching my skin, like with scabies. I kept scratching my skin until it bled. The wound dried out, however keeping under the coagulated blood a lot of mucor, germs and pus. Then I started scratching another area, activating the same chain reaction. This often happened on the buttocks and the back of the thighs. The thickness of the coagulated blood would reach 1–2 cm. The disease took a shape similar to fish scales and covered large areas extending from the buttocks to the knees. Those boils harden and ossify and start extending deeper into the body. They stunk. I decided to treat myself, so I asked one of the detainees to use his long nails to peel the coagulated layer. I bit on a cloth in my mouth so I wouldn't scream but to no avail. My colleague took that layer off. I screamed in pain. The wardens came and whipped me in punishment.[51]

Former detainees in the same branch believe that these diseases were the result of poor hygiene and medical care. The policy of starvation played a prominent role and produced an additional type of disease: the 'Hunger Disease'. The detainee turns into a being who eats without stopping and does not feel any form of satiety. Their ultimate

Figure 2.7 Ahmad Hammadeh after his release, from his collection.

dream becomes an increase in the portions of bread, a spoonful of sugar or a heap of jam. Ahmad al-Hamada continues his powerful testimony:

> Once I went to the head of the dormitory and asked to join the forced labour in exchange for half a loaf. Forced labourers are those who pump excrement and urine from the ditch of the breathing space, place it in a barrel and empty it in the toilet of the nearby dormitory. The harshest torment is illness and hunger. When you're hungry, you are humiliated. You would agree to anything in exchange for food. Some detainees became skeletons. It was a massive famine in the Branch. One time they brought pieces of cucumber with the food. They caused us severe diarrhoea. A young man from the room died of diarrhoea. We started defecating in our eating bowls. When it was time for next mean they banged on the doors to hand in our bowls. I emptied my bowl from the feces on the floor and handed it over. We ate from the very same bowls.[52]

All these harsh conditions were combined with a clear presence of the prison administration inside the dormitory through the *Shawish* [literally the 'Officer']. This prisoner is appointed as the head of the dormitory by the wardens. His charge is often not political.

> The Shawish is a real criminal, usually a thief or a gangster used to kidnapping and looting, unlike the other political detainees. The wardens appoint him as the head of the dormitory to implement their instructions, and he does it with pleasure. He is assisted by members of his gang or others like him if they are placed in the same dormitory. He and his group occupy a large area of the dormitory and squeeze the rest of the detainees in the remaining space. About 2 metres by one for him and his group in the first dormitory, and the remaining 3 metres x 3 metres for the rest of the detainees. The Shawish is the strike force of the wardens inside the dormitory and sometimes he would act worse than them.[53]

A military offensive by Jabhat al-Nusra

One day in October 2012, we heard a loud explosion. Ahmad Hamada and I were in the bathroom inside the dormitory. The bathroom window overlooked a narrow street within the branch with a guard tower. The first explosion occurred in the beginning of the night. Shortly afterwards an ambulance arrived. We could glimpse it red lights from the window. The ambulance exploded and went in big flames. All the things we put on the windowsill overlooking the outer square fell to the ground. Immediately afterwards shooting started. The wardens walked in to check on us. They came in to calm the detainees who started screaming. The power went out and chaos ensued. We were screaming in fear and panic, while the artillery stationed on the roof of the branch was firing shells and the guns were firing.[54]

In a unique experiment in the history of Syrian intelligence, the Air Force Intelligence Branch in Harasta began a new form of punishment. Old detainees in the branch were used for hard labour: digging and building at nearby military sites, uninterrupted hard labour as a continuation of torture and abuse. If a prisoner completely lost his physical abilities, he was tortured to death in the field. The details of these events were recorded at the headquarters of a military checkpoint run by the Fourth Division, which has a close affiliation with Air Force Intelligence. 'Around 1 am the warden called out our names: Wael Saraqbi, Ghassan Ballor, Mohammed Al-Khatib, Fawaz Badran and me. They chained us to each other. Before we were taken out of the branch, we were met by a Lieutenant Colonel named Ma'an. He was short, bearded and was nicknamed the Father of Death (*abu al-moot*). When he saw us, he said: "How are you guys?" We said: "Alhamdullilah". He said: "I would like to introduce myself. I am Azrael [the angel of death], or I own Azrael, I am God. With me you will go to the afterlife. But since I am God, I will prolong your lives by a few days." He took us to a small pick-up car, a Suzuki. We climbed on and set off into the unknown.'[55] The first batch of detainees was transferred in July 2013. They took them to the headquarters of the checkpoint stationed on the South Mutahaleq bridge, about one kilometre from the Branch. The checkpoint is an advanced defence point for the Branch, manned by about 60 soldiers and four officers, two of them Captains, and a First Lieutenant. All were under the command of the Lieutenant Colonel.

Ahmad al-Hamada narrates:

> We arrived at the checkpoint around 2 am. Operatives welcomed us with a beating using wooden sticks, batons and chains. They burned us with hot water and melted nylon bags. They kept beating us until the morning. They then took us to the edge of the bridge to work on digging trenches about two metres deep. We worked to remove the tiles of sidewalks to form barricades to protect them from the bullets of opposition snipers on the opposite side. Each stone weighed more than 100 kilos, and we were exhausted after everything we had lived through in the Branch. We could barely carry ourselves, but they forced us to work. Hard and continuous work without sleep. If we wanted to drink water, we had to kiss the boot of Lieutenant Colonel "Father of Death" and he could choose whether to allow or refuse it. The beating continued all the time, and the soldiers had the authority to do anything they wanted to us.[56]

A few days later they brought more detainees to the checkpoint. They brought Mohammed Khair al-Nadaf and Abdulmoeen al-Shalit, who was already battling to stay alive. Although Al-Shalit was in a worse condition than the rest, no-one's health allowed for hard work. All available information strongly suggests that the goal of this hard labour was to kill, by investing whatever capacity is left of the detainees before liquidating them in different ways. 'Al-Shalit survived for only six hours on the checkpoint, during which he was subjected to the most severe torture, from burning with melted nylon bags, to burning with gunpowder. They wrote the name Bashar al-Assad on his chest with gunpowder and lit it. He died after that. That's when we became certain that we will all meet the same fate.'[57]

The killings on this checkpoint were repeated in different ways. When a detainee is killed or dies, the Lieutenant Colonel asks for a replacement from the Branch and returns the dead bodies. This led the remaining detainees to consider fleeing. Escape was more of a suicide considering that every two detainees were chained together by the hands and the legs, and the fact that they were all kept under constant guard 24/7. Hamada narrates:

> Around midnight, the guards changed shifts. At the time we were digging the deep trench. I used the drill to break the chain tying me to my colleague Louay Ballor. It was pitch black as it was a moonless night, which helped us. We came closer to each other to discuss the next step. We broke the chains of the rest of the colleagues. We expected death, so we considered it a suicide operation. The guarding soldier sat about 15 metres away from us. He opened his cell phone and we saw the light reflected in his eyes. That's when we decided to run towards the Free Syrian Army point. We agreed that if we crossed the road, we could help anyone who falls from us, but before that we should not stop for any reason. We started running. We only crossed few metres when the operatives of the checkpoint opened their fire. More than 50 guns were firing at us. After about three minutes, the Free Army returned fire, shooting at us too. They thought we were members of the regime army trying to break in. We miraculously survived. Some sustained minor injuries. We reached the checkpoint for the Free Syrian Army and introduced ourselves, briefly telling our story. We were taken to the medical point in the town of Irbin. People gathered around us. That day I had a sudden episode of crying and screaming. An old man took me to my town of Saqba. I entered the mosque; people were praying there as it was the occasion of Lailat al-Qadr.[58]

The other regional branches

Like other branches of the central Air Force Intelligence service, the work and roles of regional branches expanded after the start of the Syrian Revolution. Air Force Intelligence headquarters in the provinces became the source of terror and panic for the people because of the brutal torture they carried out on their detainees. Even those small branches played a role in detention and torture but maintained the system of short arrests before the detainee was transferred to the central branches. Before the uprising, these branches used to hold detainees for a day or two and then transfer them to the centre, in particular to the Investigation Branch at Mezzeh airport. After 2011, the detention period before transfer became longer. Imad Abu Ras was arrested on 19 December 2012 at Basel al-Assad airport, which later became Hmeimim military base in Latakia province. He was transferred to the headquarters of the Air Force Intelligence Branch in the coastal city of Latakia. He was then transferred to Damascus, the first in a long line of transfers.

> Latakia was the worst branch of all the branches I have seen. Those days events were heated in the cities of Jableh and Banyas and the situation was very difficult.

The branch was very small, with only nine solitary cells and two dormitories, but the numbers of detainees were very large. They opened the doors of the solitaries to accommodate the detainees. Many of the detainees were in poor condition. The majority suffered fractures and serious wounds. They were arrested from the demonstrations and were brutally tortured. Some had broken feet for over a month, so they became swollen and blue. The wounds were infected and rotting. The torture there was very bad. The tools used for torture in Latakia were very different to those in any other branch. They used equipment used for construction work, such as metal pipes and rods. Obviously, the goal of the torture was either killing, paralyzing, or crushing bones. I stayed there for nine days and they were disastrous.[59]

Abu Ras was transferred to the headquarters of the Air Force Intelligence Branch in city of Homs. During the reception torture he lost 14 teeth. The detention prison in Homs is bigger than that in Latakia. It had at least 30 solitary cells and a number of group dormitories. 'You go down to a separate cellar outside the building where you hand in your belongings. Then they hand you over to the slaughtering branch operatives who would beat you everywhere and in any manner. Torture is only stopped during the actual interrogation. There is no professionalism in beating or torture. It was all random, contrary to what I later learned in the Investigation Branch at Mezzeh airport.'[60]

What applies to the branches of Latakia and Homs also applies to the branch of the Northern Region, based in the city of Aleppo. The branch headquarters is large and modern compared to the Latakia Branch. The use of various methods of torture was reported in this branch. Muhannad al-Ghobash narrates:

After more than 24 hours of torture, my first hours in the Branch, I was transferred to the third dormitory. It was two and a half metres by almost four and a half metres. There we were about 30 detainees. The number reached 60 as days passed. I stayed in Aleppo for 95 days, during which time I saw wardens and investigators use the silicone rod for torture. This was a long, thin, and lightweight rod that the torturer wraps around his fist, keeping about one and a half metres for beating. The rod wraps around the detainee's body and overreaches several points causing inexplicable pain. Just a small wave by the torturer results in a hard blow to your body. After 50 to 60 blows, the stings become flaming, where they wound and burn at the same time. This is apart from the usual instruments such as the high-amp electric sticks, batons, wooden sticks, and water pipes. What was even worse was food and sleep deprivation for three days which happened to me.[61]

The Administration Branch

The Administration Branch is located near Tahrir Square close to Old Damascus. It had a large detention centre of at least two floors underground. The prison was L-shaped, with three dormitory cages and 42 solitary cells divided into three cages with

14 solitary cells each. The only ventilation was through air extractors. The prison of this Branch was assigned to officers suspected of being members of Hizb al-Tahrir al-Islami at the end of 1999 and during 2000.

After 2011, the branch emerged again as a custodial prison for the Investigation Branch. Former detainee Abu Zeid remembers:

> They dropped us at an iron door, then we descended about seventy steps to a cellar. We entered the dormitory. It was assigned to the sick. We found the people crammed in its far end, opposite the door. It was six metres by about ten metres and had a small light. It also had a toilet, two showers and above the bathroom four extractor hoods. Detainees in the Administration suffered an aggravated condition of scabies and herpes. Of the 170 detainees in the dormitory, only five were not infected with scabies; those included the cell officer and night supervisor. Among the injured were 25 detainees battling death. Scabies opens the skin and eats the body. Some of the images that later emerged of open legs and the eaten flesh are the same scenes I saw in the first dormitory of the Air Force Intelligence.[62]

These difficult health conditions affected daily life in the dormitory. Abu Zeid continues:

> We woke up at five in the morning. The warden opens the 'judas window' and screams 'wake up' and we would immediately stand up. The life cycle begins with standing in line to go to the toilet. Then we rinsed the floor to wash the residues of scabies and boils off the floor. We collected the skin lying on the floor and threw it in the garbage. We collected over a kilogram of torn skin every day. After breakfast we re-rinsed the dormitory floor as per the orders of the doctor Lieutenant, who was the health officer in the Administration. They gave us soap, medicine, and shampoo. They were trying to improve our figures which became worse than a dead mummy. They gave us benzoate. If used by those with festering skin they would cry in pain for hours.[63]

All this everyday horror was better than being transferred to the solitary cells. The detainees believed that transfer to the solitaries in the Administration meant certain death. There were no lights in those cells. Each cell hosted five to seven detainees. One survivor recalls:

> On 17 April, they brought us some chicken pieces. Since I was an Army pilot, I knew that they boiled chicken with English Salt to have it cook quickly. That day I forgot about this and started eating the chicken. In only a few hours I developed a severe diarrohea. I started sweating heavily and couldn't hold myself. If I asked to go to the toilet, I'll receive a hundred lashes. A colleague instructed me to relieve myself it in the empty water bottle that we usually use to urinate. I initially refused but after the situation got worse, I went deep into the solitary cell. My colleagues turned their backs, and I relieved myself crying. I cried so hard. That plastic water bottle turned into a toilet for all of us. We all suffered from diarrohea. After hours

of asking to go out to the toilet and complaining of diarrohea they brought all of us in the solitary cells dry tea leaves to chew with the aim of fighting the problem! Some died as a result of the diarrhoea. We'd see them take out the dead. They threw them on military blankets in the corridor for hours before the doctor examined them and the forced labourer took them somewhere.[64]

The return of Aviation Command

Returning to the oldest of the Air Force branches and the most prominent in Syria, we see that it regained its role in arrest and investigation after 2011. The branch prison became so overcrowded that corridors were used as accommodation spaces for detainees. One survivor recalls:

I stayed there for about 45 days, thrown in a corridor in the Branch. The moment I entered, the interrogation and torture began using electrical rods and suspension. All the time I was trying to observe what was going on, but it was difficult. Torture sessions lasted about three hours followed by a break, then they started again, and so on. Wardens had shifts. Beating was with the green pipes. There was one investigator, but up to six torturers, with 12-hour shifts. I spent 45 days in the corridor. I sat under a blanket and slept in this position, no more than ten minutes, for the moment they noticed the wardens woke me up. They didn't allow me to rest.[65]

3

The State Security or General Intelligence

Civilian security sectors in Syria do not differ from those of the military in terms of affiliation. The General Intelligence Department is known as a civilian security service; however, its employees are divided into three categories. The first is military personnel who volunteered to work for the Department. Their records are kept in the General Headquarters of the Army and Armed Forces. If they are ever expelled from the Department, they return to the army. The rest of the military personnel in the Department are seconded from the Ministry of Defence. The second is personnel seconded from the Ministry of Interior. The third is civilians who volunteered to work in the Department. Those are subject to the uniform Labor Code of the Syrian Arab Republic.[1]

Since its establishment by Legislative Decree No 14, issued on 25 January 1969, the General Intelligence Department has been known as the State Security Department. The Decree stipulates in Article 16, that no personnel from the Department may be prosecuted for crimes they commit during the execution of the specific tasks assigned to them or while carrying out such tasks, except under a prosecution order issued by the Director of the Department. Article 30, the last article of the Decree, stipulates that it shall not be published and shall be in force as of the date of its promulgation.[2] This effectively means that all employees of the State Security are above the law while conducting their tasks, and that, for decades, the department as a whole has operated

مرسوم تشريعي رقم ١٠
تاريخ ٢٦/٤/١٩٧١
تعديل تسمية ادارة امن الدولة وتصبح ادارة المخابرات العامة

رئيس الجمهورية
بناء على احكام الدستور الموقت

يرسم ما يلي :

مادة ١ ــ تعدل تسمية (ادارة امن الدولة) اينما وردت في التشريعات والقرارات والانظمة والصكوك الاخرى
وتصبح (ادارة المخابرات العامة) .
مادة ٢ ــ ينشر هذا المرسوم التشريعي في الجريدة الرسمية ويعتبر نافذا من تاريخ صدوره .
دمشق في ١/٣/١٣٩١ و ٢٦/٤/١٩٧١

رئيس الجمهورية
الفريق حافظ الاسد

Image of Legislative Decree No 10.

Figure 3.1 Ali Mamlouk, from IRNA, the Iranian news agency.

with impunity. Following the arrival of Hafez al-Assad to the presidency of the Syrian Republic, Legislative Decree No 10 was issued on 26 April 1971 under the title 'Amending the Name of the State Security Department into General Intelligence Department'.

The General Intelligence Department was headed by Adnan Dabbagh from 1970 to 1976. He was succeeded by Ali Hamdani until 1979, Nazih Zrair until 1984, Fouad al-Absi until 1987, Majid Said until 1994, Bashir Najjar until 1998, Ali Houri until 2001, Ali Hammoud for only two months from October to December 2001, Major General Hisham Ikhtiyar until 2005, Major General Ali Mamlouk until 2010, Major General Zuhair Al-Hamad as Acting Director until 2012, Major General Mohammed Deeb Zaytoun as Head of the Department until 2019 and Major General Husam Louqa who is still in place today.

This Department reports directly to the President under the name 'Unit 1114' without going through any agency or ministry, except in coordination with the Office of National Security (*al-amn al-watani*), formerly called the Office of National Security (*al-amn al-qawmi*). The Department has twelve central branches as well as operational branches in all governorates. It also includes the Higher Institute for Security Sciences, which was established in 2007 as an academy for instructing new personnel in the art of intelligence and security.[3]

Structure of the General Intelligence Department

The director of the Department and his assistants are appointed by presidential decree. The Director has more than one assistant, whose powers, functions, rights, and duties are determined by him. In addition to hosting the headquarters of the Department, the capital Damascus, has ten other branches:

- Information Branch 255, whose mission is to obtain all political, economic, and social information and follow up on the religious, party, and media sectors. All information received from the other central and provincial branches and from other sources come into this Branch.
- Investigation Branch 285, investigates information communicated by security branches or certain sources or agents. Most detainees arrested in the provincial branches are referred to this Branch after initial interrogation in these respective branches.
- Counter-Terrorism Branch 295, known as Najha Branch, teaches military and security sciences to graduating batches of volunteers who will work for the Department, as well as training Department operatives (especially those from the military).
- Spy Branch 300 tracks foreigners and those suspected of dealing with external parties. It monitors government and private institutions dealing with entities outside Syria. It tracks the work and relations of political parties and figures and has a functional relationship with the Technical Branch and the Telecommunication Police.
- Foreign Branch 279 manages foreign intelligence stations in embassies and consulates in countries around the world. It investigates all information related to the Ministry of Foreign Affairs, or ministries that send missions and secondees abroad. It also monitors expatriate Syrian citizens.
- Technical Branch 280 specializes in eavesdropping, interference, and technical surveillance. It provides technical support and supplies to all branches. It carries out all the engineering and mechanical works of the Department and its branches. Its most important sections are wired communication, wireless communication, computer intelligence, postal monitoring, coding, internet, the top-secret 'al-Ghadeer' wiretapping project, and the space interference project.
- Internal Branch 251, the Department's branch in Damascus, is also responsible for counter-intelligence inside Syria, especially in Damascus and its surrounding countryside.[4] It intervenes in the appointment of government officials, heads of trade unions, chambers of commerce and universities, general directors, secretaries of party branches and all major departments of the state. Mohamed Nassif, Bahjat Suleiman, Tawfiq Younis and Ahmed Deeb were the most prominent heads of this Branch. It includes a section known as al-Arba'een Section [literally the Forty Section], which is considered a separate department based on its authority and conduct. For a long time, its management was assigned to Hafez Makhlouf, a relative of President Bashar al-Assad.[5]
- The capital also houses the Training Branch or Ghouta 290, Economic Branch 260 and Branch 111, which is tasked with the Office of the Head of the Department. The Department also has a Branch in each Syrian governorate.[6]

Figure 3.2 General Directorate and Investigation Branch 285, Google Maps.

Beginnings

The apparent presence of the General Intelligence on the domestic scene began in 1973. One of the earliest eyewitnesses is Ahmed Maatouq, who remembers:

> I participated in demonstrations against the secession of Syria from Egypt in 1961, and I was 13 years old. We were arrested by Riot Police. During my participation in the 1968 demonstrations demanding the return of the Golan occupied by Israel after the Six-Day War, I was also arrested by Riot Police. In 1974, while participating in demonstrations demanding the continuation of the war against Israel and the liberation of the occupied territories, I was detained by the General Intelligence for only a few days. It was the beginning of the presence of the General Intelligence on the domestic scene.[7]

During the 1970s, the General Intelligence carried out the orders of the Central Security Committee in Mezzeh prison. The Committee was led by senior Syrian intelligence officers under the supervision of the Office of National Security. The Department arrested one of the most prominent figures of the Muslim Brotherhood in Syria in 1973. Said Hawa documented his arrest in his memoirs: 'I was arrested by the Idlib Intelligence in Ma'arat al-Numan, then transferred to Idlib and from there to Aleppo and then Damascus where I stayed for a few hours in the Intelligence building in al-Halbouni neighborhood. I was then transferred to Mezzeh military prison and remained there until I was discharged.'[8] Hawa's experience in the General Intelligence is similar to Marwan Hadid's in Military Intelligence. They were both interrogated at Mezzeh Military prison. However, after his release from prison, Hawa was transferred to the Aviation Command under the Air Force Intelligence, where he met the Director of the National Security Office, Naji Jamil, the Head of Military Intelligence, Ali Douba, and other officers. The method of investigation, a joint security committee, can be read as the Syrian intelligence forces uniting in the face of internal opposition. This unity would fail by the end of 1978, with Naji Jamil being forcibly retired in March of the same year. His place in the National Security Office was taken by Major General Mohammed al-Khouli, who was the Head of Air Force Intelligence at the same time.[9] Following these radical shifts in the upper layers of security services, these services started a very noticeable expansion during the 1980s and 1990s. They came strongly to the fore during the years of the Syrian Revolution.

The joint work of security services during the 1970s did not stop these Departments from carrying out independent, long-term arrests; arresting opponents and putting them in detention centres for months or even years. For example, Mohammed Adel Faris was arrested on 6 April 1973, accused of being a member of the Muslim Brotherhood. He remained in General Intelligence detention centres between Aleppo and Damascus until 6 October 1975, after which he was transferred to Aleppo Central Prison, where he remained until 7 April 1977.

Branch 322: Aleppo

In Aleppo, the General Intelligence took over the Nablus school building to use as its HQ. this had previously been the mansion of the wealthy Al-Addas family, which had been confiscated by the government. It is located opposite the Governor's Palace. The Branch was managed in the early 1970s by Captain Mohamed Khair Diab, and his Deputy, Lieutenant Mohamed Said Bakhaitan. Its most prominent investigator during that period was Abdelkader Haiza.[10]

The Branch detention centre was in the basement, about 20 steps underground. The way the prison, torture and food were managed was no different to other Military Intelligence branches. During the 1970s, torture tools were limited to bamboo sticks, the wheel, and the electric dynamo. Faris narrates: 'They moved me continuously between the torture chamber and the interrogation room. They stripped me of my clothes, except for the underwear. They subjected me to horrible torture by beating me with bamboo sticks all over my body and with the terrible electrical shocks. Bamboo stings hurt like ironing with fire. A number of bamboo sticks broke on my body . . . I bled from different places as a result of severe beating. Some of the blows were so strong that they left dark streaks and spots that remained visible on my legs and back for over a year.' Electrocution was administered by the officer in charge of the interrogation with the help of one of the torturers.[11]

Concluding the interrogation does not mean the torture stops. Investigators often subjected detainees to sleep deprivation in the solitary cells. Faris writes: 'I had to stand on one foot and carry the torture wheel, on my head and shoulders.' The warden keeps watch during this punishment to ensure good execution. 'He would pass by the cell irregularly: every two minutes, or every quarter of an hour. He would open the Judas window to check if I'm still holding the position, or he would just hit the metal door very hard to startle me.'[12]

The food in the branches of General Intelligence came from the nearest military barracks. The Aleppo Branch received daily meals from the Hanano barracks, which came from the Syrian army's allocations. Until the spring of 1973, the quality of food was different. The prison provided only two meals a day, consisting of halwa, fava beans, chickpeas and falafel – food not usually offered in military allocations. After May 1973, the prison started providing three meals, all of which consisted of the known military food allocations. However, food was also subject to the hierarchy, with the officers receiving the largest rations of good food items, particularly meat and chicken. The prisoner's shared what was left: 'One day our breakfast was tea and olives. There were five of us in one room; the room's allocation was 4 olives!'[13]

According to the testimonies of detainees who passed through the Branch in 1979, Lieutenant Colonel Ali Saad al-Din became the head of the Branch, while Major Aleef Wazzah became the Head of the Investigation Department. Other changes to the methods of interrogation, torture and arrest took place. Blindfolding was introduced, which was absent from 1973 until 1975, according to the memoirs of Mohammed Adel Faris. This seems normal compared to other Syrian security services, which introduced blindfolding around 1976. Interrogation processes retained their reliance on sleep deprivation as a torture tool in addition to beating, but added sexual torture, such as inserting a wooden stick in the anus. The interrogation technique depended on having two officers playing the 'good-cop-bad-cop' shtick. The Branch also started documenting the detainees by taking their names and photos. 'The black prison door opened onto a small hall in a basement beneath the beautiful building, standing opposite the Governor's Palace. . . . The photographer came and took some front and side (memorial) pictures.'[14]

A matter of national liberation

Abdelkader Nasser, the cousin of the then Minister of Interior, Major General Nasser al-Din Nasser, had a natural sense of humor and a fun side. He was a soothing oasis in the harsh deserts of the dungeon. His good manners gained him the love of all prisoners. The fact that his cousin was the Minister of the Interior did not save him from torture. He would scream and beg without anyone caring. During one of the torture sessions they were stinging him with electricity. He was naked, so they put the wires in the place they always preferred. He started screaming in pain: "Ouch . . . Ouch. . . Let it be, it's the only one I have!" Detective Aleef laughed and said: "And who in the world has two?" The prisoners joked with Abdelkader asking him: "Why were they choosing that place to electrocute you?" "For matters of national liberation," he answered wittingly. And when they asked: "And what about sticking the stick in the bottoms?!" He answered: "It's the message of the leading party!".[15]

In 1980, the Branch was headed by Brigadier General Omar Hamida. During this period, the levels of violence increased dramatically, because of the armed confrontations between the regime and the Militant Vanguard. The number of detainees increased, so

Figure 3.3 Omar Hamida, from a pro-regime social media site.

they crammed more than five detainees in one solitary cell of about 2 x 1 metres. Congestion, malnutrition, and lack of medical care caused the spread of diseases such as scabies, lice, and diarrhoea. 'Medical treatment in case of illness was excessively brutal that it even fell below the level of treating cattle. We only saw the doctors when one of the detainees died and they came to call the time of death.'[16]

Detainees of the detention centre in the Branch during this period reported several methods of torture. The first was psychological, by playing the sounds of torture for about 15 days to add to the smell of blood and the stench of pus and rotten flesh. Beating on the way in and out of the toilets. Beating during the distribution of food as well as indiscriminate forms of beating and constant torture. The interrogation relied on tools for torture, namely the wheel, the German chair, suspension, the Magic Carpet, electrocution, extinguishing cigarettes in the scalp, and pouring boiling water to the point of severely burning the victim. These methods of torture have been documented as being used by the various intelligence services in Syria. However, the testimonies also spoke of 'burning the skin with heated metal bars, placing the detainee's chest in front of an electric heater until his skin burns and fat melts, and using the back of an axe to break arms and legs'.[17] These methods are exclusive to some of the exceptionally perverse behaviors in military prisons such as the desert prison of Tadmor (Palmyra). However, their use was documented for the first time in interrogations in the General Intelligence during the 1980s. These violent methods became standard during the years of the Revolution and were practiced by different intelligence branches, albeit in different forms; still, they remain fairly alien to the general line of violence of the Syrian intelligence.

The General Intelligence Branch in Aleppo followed the approach of starving the prisoners, placing them in a small solitary cell and withholding water and food, forcing some detainees to drink their urine. However, they did expand their use of sexual torture. In addition to the previous methods reported, they resorted to raping detainees by inserting beer bottles into the anus, or hitting them severely on the penis and testicles. Some detainees died because of this torture. Sexual torture also amounted to 'raping sisters, wives or daughters in front of some detainees to force them to confess'.[18]

Hamad's tile

The following night, we were to witness a long interrogation. A torture that will prevent all detainees in the Investigation Branch from sleeping, despite severe fatigue and stress. The corridors were buzzing with the stomping feet of the operatives as they dragged one prisoner from one room to another. The prisoner apparently did not respond with the investigator's desired confessions. They took turns whipping and electrocuting him, as evidenced by the way he screamed throughout every hour of that unforgettable night. We were squatting, while horror chewed the remanent of our humanity... More than an hour later, one of the detectives shouted: 'Hand me the brick!' We thought he was going to crush his head with it. It was only a few minutes and the brick was in the hands of the detective, who ordered his torturers to pin this unresponsive victim. Between the shouts of the torturers, and the screams of the prisoner who was resisting something we didn't know, we heard a loud thud of a rock, and a great cry followed by tomb silence that fell over the whole place. In few moments we heard the sound of the dead body being dragged on the floor of the corridors between the rooms... The torturer explained to his new colleague that Captain Hamad, who was one of the harshest and most aggressive in torture, slammed the brick against the testicles of the prisoner, killing him almost instantly.[19]

The Aleppo Branch used a special section of the city's Central Prison to house its detainees after the investigation, which lasted at least two weeks. The transfer came because of the congestion of the Branch detention centre within a short period of time. The General Intelligence placed its own guards in this section of the civilian prison. A security detachment and a military one oversaw the prisoners' affairs.

A.M. was born into a middle-class Yazidi family from Qîbar village in Afrin. Had it not been for his Yazidi and Kurdish background, he would have worked as a woodworker in a furniture workshop until retirement, but a lifetime of discrimination led him to political activity in the Kurdish opposition to the Assad regime. During Newroz 1988, he performed in a theater piece about Kawa, the epic figure in Iranian and Kurdish mythology who led a popular uprising against the autocrat Zahak, a thinly veiled critique of Hafez al-Assad. Two days later, he was arrested for the first time by State Security. During this arrest, he was questioned by two plain-clothes officers with thick Alawite accents about his suspected involvement in Kurdish politics. He was subjected to the traditional *dulab* and *falaqa*, followed by being hung by his ankles from a ceiling fan, which rotated as he was beaten and whipped. A big roughneck called Abu Hussein swore at him with a thick Latakia accent: 'I know which tribe you are from. I know this is a dirty tribe. You are known to us. You are a son of a bitch. You understand only two things: our boots and sticks on your heads.' He then slapped A.M. so hard on his ears he suffered from tinnitus for the rest of his life. Insults about his Yazidi faith were accompanied by allusions to the Sunni Kurds' alleged hatred of Yazidis, meant to sow discord and doubt. He was released after two months and returned to his job but was fired because his boss was terrified that the workshop would be associated with opposition politics and draw the attention of the intelligence. Like many other detainees, A.M. became a pariah; even his friends stopped greeting him in the street.

His second arrest, on 31 October 1988, occurred in the middle of the night, when plain-clothes officers of the State Security dragged him out of bed and took him to their Aleppo headquarters, across from the provincial capitol building. Again, they began interrogating him gently, trying to cajole him into cooperating. But when cigarettes, coffee, and flattery about his 'kind and civilized family' did not yield the required result, they stuffed him into the *dulab* and beat him until he was unconscious. The blood vessels in the soles of his feet were so badly damaged that he was unable to stand for long periods. He was released on 4 February 1989 and had to report once a week to the Military Security branch in Aleppo's Suryaan neighbourhood. Like many other families, his father paid serious bribes to Mustafa al-Tajer, the notorious head of the Military Security in Aleppo and later head of the Palestine Branch in Damascus, including a sum of 200,000 Syrian Lira, construction materials from his factory, fifteen cans of olive oil (each weighing 18 kilos), honey, and other produce. Well after his second release, his father continued to pay bribes to Mustafa al-Tajer. By that time, A.M. had snuck across the Syrian-Turkish border and paid a human trafficker to smuggle him to Europe.[20]

The situation in other provincial branches was similar during the 1970s and 1980s. However, their roles were limited to the preliminary interrogation, as, after about two weeks, the detainee was transferred to the Central Investigation Branch. One survivor remembered: 'We were transferred days later from Homs to Damascus, where we were met by a committee led by the Head of the Investigation Branch and his deputy. The torture stopped and we were interrogated politely and respectfully. We were about twenty young men from the largest families of Homs. The outcome of the investigation underscored our innocence, so it was decided to return us to Branch 318 Homs. However, days later, a presidential decision was issued ordering the transfer of everyone to Palmyra, and so it was on Wednesday 11 February 1981.'[21]

However, some branches in the provinces did not have military allocations to feed their detainees. They also kept detainees for longer periods in the 1990s. Yaqoub Bahi narrates: 'I was arrested in June 1993 by the General Intelligence Branch 330 in Hasakah on charges of belonging to the Arab Revolutionary Workers Party. I stayed at the Branch HQ in Qamishli for three months before being sent to the administration in Damascus. All three months I spent in the Branch's underground prison, I ate at my own expense. I was spending my money on my food and drink, to be afterward beaten and tortured violently and threatened with the arrest of my wife and family on top of all that. They suspended me upside down until my eyes were red and the ringing in my ears almost got me deaf.'[22]

Branch 285: Investigation

The General Intelligence Department requires all its branches in Damascus and the governorates to refer their detainees to Central Investigation Branch 285 – the heart of the General Intelligence Department. Its old HQ was in the House of Syria's first president, Taj al-Din al-Husseini, located in the Halbouni neighbourhood in the centre of Damascus. Since 1976, it has been based in the Kafr Sousa area of the capitol. It specializes in interrogating detainees, as well as auditing information received from security branches, certain sources or agents. The Branch included two detention prisons, the first was underground with mostly solitary cells and at least one dormitory. The second one was above ground and comprised four lined-up dormitories. They were separated from the spacious courtyard by a two-metre high wall that stands about 2.5 metres away from the dormitory windows. They had no bathrooms or toilets.

At the beginning of the 1970s, the Branch was headed by Major Arif Nasr. Faris remembered him as 'a mysterious figure, who ran things from behind a wall. We remained his 'guests' for more than fourteen months, yet never met him'.[23] Late in 1974, Major Mohammed Ahmed Fathallah took over from Nasr and made several changes. Food was supervised, so it improved. Detainees were able to go outside for half an hour every day instead of ten minutes a week. He worked on transferring detainees to civilian prisons, which started at the beginning of 1975. Major Fathallah remained in charge of the branch for just one year.[24]

The escape

In the autumn of 1974, the first dormitory of the prison of the Halbouni Branch was occupied by eight detainees from different political backgrounds and nationalities. One of them was a German, another was from Gaza, and another was a Syrian Circassian. They were all between 25 and 40 years of age. The eight prisoners were in the room that had a wall on the street. This wall had no window or opening. Some of those prisoners thought of a scheme for survival: digging a hole in the wall opening onto the street. That was not easy, because from where would they get tools to dig? Where would they dispose of the rubble? How could they go about this operation without drawing the warden's attention?

They spent 20 days of vigilant work lest the prison administration notice and crush the project. Prisoners carefully acquired spoons with pointed tips made of chrome and with a wheat spike engraved on the handle. They gradually dug out the cement layer covering the building blocks on the inner face of the wall, in the area where they decided the exit would be, at the bottom of the wall. During the digging one of the prisoners stood watch by the door. When they were not digging, they put blankets in front of the excavated place, and sat next to it, so that everything looked normal. They sneaked the rubble out gradually, with the garbage. They then proceeded to remove the cement around the block from which they would exit. The exit opened in front of them after midnight. They sneaked out one by one, until the seven prisoners had escaped. The eighth prisoner, the German, did not see the point in escaping since his re-arrest was inevitable, as he didn't speak Arabic, did not know the streets of the city and his passport was held by the prison administration.

At seven o'clock in the morning, the warden came to give the signal of permission for the detainees to go to the toilet. He looked into the room and found only the German, and shouted: 'Where are your colleagues?!' The German did not understand what the warden said, but realized he was asking him about his colleagues, so he pointed his index finger repeatedly at the hole from which they had escaped and made the following sound: 'Fist, fist, fist' to explain that they had sneaked out one by one.[25]

In al-Halbouni food was served three times a day. The food came from the first HQ near the Officers' Club in Damascus, so it came out of military allocations. Following mealtimes, detainees were allowed to use the toilet using the term 'the line', i.e. going out to relieve oneself. Bathing, though, was not regulated. The interval between showers could be one week, ten days, two weeks, or three. The water might be hot, or cold but the bath or shower had to be done in a short window of time. Usually, the prisoner was given no more than ten minutes. Detainees therefore resorted to using the water from the sink to keep clean. Also, shaving did not follow a specific schedule, but it was mandatory to shave off any hair on the head and beards. In terms of accommodation in the branch prison, the cells were small and narrow, and the dormitories were flooded with prisoners. There was no heating. The prisoner was placed in a naked room which had nothing. They slept on the floor, without any mattress, blanket, or pillow, especially during the first interrogation period. After two or three days, things would start to change; the prisoners were given a blanket or two. In the dormitories, the situation was slightly better. Each prisoner's was entitled to four blankets. The available space was often small. The dormitories were only 40cm wide and prisoners could not lie down without folding their legs. As numbers increased, prisoners were forced to take it in turns to sleep?.[26]

In al-Halbouni they distinguished between the terms a 'visit' and an 'interview'. A 'visit' meant that some of the detainees' relatives could come to the door of the Halbouni Branch and deliver some items; the detainee was also informed of this. This was always available. An 'interview' meant a meeting for about quarter of an hour between the detainee and their family, in the presence of intelligence operatives.[27]

Branch 285: new headquarters

The construction of the new General Intelligence HQ in Kafr Sousa began in 1972 and was completed in 1976, amidst a broader urban transformation of Damascus. The writer and former political detainee, Mufeed Najm, participated in its construction during his teenage years. Almost ten years later he was detained in the same place.

> The northern prison of Branch 285 was designed in a L shape and consisted of two parts, one for dormitories which extended on both the right and left sides as you entered, and which began with the interrogation room, followed by two dormitories which usually hosted double their capacity of detainees, followed by the women's dormitory, the kitchen and bathrooms. The second section, which was to the left of the entrance, and which formed the short leg of the L, consisted of nine cells and the northern long dormitory which was located directly opposite the kitchen. The northern dormitory which was the largest of the dormitories was where they placed us, after having distributed the first group over the dormitories of the southern section. They placed the three women in the women's dormitory, which was located almost opposite ours.'[28]

The second prison was located under the administration building and included only solitary cells, 'paired' cells (those slightly larger than the solitary cell and meant for two people) and some outside space. Najm's memories are particularly insightful on this prison:

> It never occurred to us that it will become a terrible prison, and that all detainees of State Security branches in Syria would end up in it, on their way onto Syria's many prisons. When they brought us in, I was surprised by the number of corridors and doors we had to pass through inside the Branch and the administration ... I was surprised by the number of solitary cells and dormitories which were built at later stages. It was a scary place that makes you terrified. As you walk through all those gates you are followed by insults and stings of black whips and you stand blindfolded facing the inner walls of the prison corridors.[29]

The torture did not end there:

> The investigator spared no means of torture to compel the prisoner to confess to what he expected he's hiding, be it the Magic Carpet, foot whipping, electrocution in a wet-floor room, suspension for long hours or hanging like a rotisserie chicken by tying the prisoners' arms and legs with a chain or rope and hanging him horizontally to a metal rod. Throughout the fifteen days that we stayed there, the evening interrogation hours were no different to those in the morning.[30]

The Second Escape

Things were starting to get exciting. The plan was meticulously drawn up, ready for execution and every prisoner knew his specific role. On Monday evening, Sergeant Tahir Houry sat in front of the prison door with the four wardens: Abu Mohammed,

Abu Shihab, Sa'adoun and Fawaz. He made a jug of chocolate milk, put the drug in it and presented it to them to celebrate his engagement, as he claimed. Fawaz refused to drink which raised concern. Half an hour of anxiety and bewilderment passed. It was an unresolvable problem. At sunset, Fawaz came asking for one of us, Dr. Malik, to give him a painkiller for headache. The doctor stuffed the anesthetic into a regular medicine capsule and gave it to Fawaz ... At ten o'clock at night, the warden Abu Mohammed, who also did not drink the chocolate milk, was sneaking out of the prison to his home. The other three wardens, Fawaz, Sa'adoun and Abu Shihab, fell into a deep sleep. At midnight, the execution of the plan started. Sergeant Tahir called the Al-Halbouni Branch, the old headquarters, to report a prisoner in a critical condition. After emphasizing that the patient's condition was bad and he might die, they sent a car to take him to the hospital. Half an hour later the Jeep passed the main gate of the building and parked in front of the prison door. Tahir asked the two operatives to help him carry the prisoner to the car. Both operatives entered cautiously and hesitantly. They walked through the narrow corridor that ends at the door of the third dormitory where the patient lay. Meanwhile, three prisoners came sneaking behind them, coming from the opposite dormitory in pajamas, pretending to be curious intruders. Two prisoners swooped on the two operatives, detained, and handcuffed them, then placed them in the dormitory and injected them with the anesthetic. The prisoners changed their clothes and emerged out of the prison door in order, as if they were being taken to a requested interrogation. The vehicle, carrying twice its load, set off towards the main gate. Sergeant Tahir's well-known face was what made them open the gate for the car to get out. They did not have time to note that the operatives who went in did not come out. Instead, two prisoners came out, one driving the car and the other next to him, while Tahir sat to the right next to the window. Fifteen prisoners were stacked in the closed rear compartment.[31]

The treatment of female detainees did not differ to that of males held in the General Intelligence. In 1981, Hiba al-Dabbagh was taken hostage in place of her brother, an Islamist political activist, and remained in prison for nine years. Similar to male prisoners, Al-Dabbagh was inspected but by a female employee of the General Intelligence. Torture sessions immediately began, using the Magic Carpet and electricity. But they also used a kind of psychological torture. They told Al-Dabbagh that they would transfer her to the desert prison of Tadmor. She writes in her gripping memoir: 'An operative dragged me from the torture chamber through the corridors and stairs again to a car parked at the door. I was surprised to see my friend Magda already in it guarded by another operative. The car went off in a theatrical move until it reached the outside door. The operative asked me again: "Still refuse to talk?" I felt like all my tensed nerves screaming with me when I said: "I don't have anything to tell. I have nothing to do with anyone. Do you want me to lie to you?' The car stopped, and the driver took us back to the building".[32]

The women's room at the detention centre of the Investigation Branch 285 was 'a medium-sized room with a bathroom to the left of the entrance, and a shower head on top but no door. The bathroom also had an electric heater which was exclusive to the women's dormitory. The men's dormitories had no bathrooms, no heaters, not even water taps. Our room had no outlet except for an opening at the top of the wall close to the ceiling covered by iron bars, and two layers of nets that would not allow even the air to pass and blocked any rays of light.' [33] Life in the branch prison was monotonous, especially after the end of the interrogation. It was also characterized by ill treatment and medical negligence, difficult psychological conditions and the separation of the detainee from reality.

Prison or monastery?

I still remember the moment the warden Ibrahim opened the door while he grabbed her by the shoulder and called on me: 'Hiba... Come, receive, she's your job.' He pushed inside the girl whom I was watching through the peephole when she was in the solitary cell. Her clothes were dirty; they obviously haven't been washed since God knows when. We waited a minute for her to move, but she didn't leave the spot the warden pushed her to ... We all approached her and asked gently: 'What's your name? Where are you from?' But she didn't answer. She stayed there motionless as if wedged to the floor until after midnight. When we tried to move her, she was stiff like a nail hammered into the ground. Our complaints to the wardens did not work. They were convinced she was faking this to avoid interrogation. The day Hala spoke she asked if this was a monastery or a prison? Hala's veil and clothes when she came were so dirty. As the days went on, they grew dirtier and stunk worse. Whenever one of us tried to approach her or touch her clothes, she curled on herself more and kept her from getting close. She remained like this for eight months, not talking, not eating, not drinking, not going out to the bathroom. We forced her to drink water and had to squeeze food into her mouth where she would chew it slowly over an hour. [34]

Branch 251: Al-Khatib

Branch 251, also known as al-Khatib branch (after the area in which it is located), can be considered among the most important and central branches of the General Intelligence service. The branch has sections scattered in and around Damascus. The most famous is the Al-Arbaeen section near the headquarters of the French Embassy in central Damascus. Branch 251 has extensive powers and offices concerned with religious affairs, the economy, parties, media, universities, and communications, as well as the investigation section. The HQ of the Branch in the Al-Khatib neighbourhood contains at least three buildings and one prison. The area of the prison is 190 to 200

Figure 3.4 Mohammad Naseef, from a pro-regime social media site.

square metres. It has four large dormitories and 25 solitary cells. Some of these solitary cells have been under video surveillance since at least 2000. Surveillance equipment is planted invisibly next to lighting fixtures. The investigation rooms of the branch, the prison administration, the inspection room, and the private belongings area have surveillance cameras wired to the Office of the Head of the Branch on the third floor.[35]

The most prominent of the former branch heads is Mohammed Nassif Kheirbek, an exceptionally powerful and nefarious confidant of Hafez al-Assad, who was considered the real director of General Intelligence during the 1980s. He was succeeded by Brigadier Mueen Ismail and later by Bahjat Suleiman, who was transferred from the Spy Branch 300. The Branch was managed by Fouad Nassif and Tawfiq Younis and is currently managed by Ahmed Deeb. One of the most prominent officers of the Branch is Investigator Turki Alamuddin, and the long-standing Director of the Al-Arbaeen section, Hafez Makhlouf.

The mechanism of arrest in the Internal Branch does not differ from other branches of the Department where the director of the responsible office issues a memo with brief outcomes of the interrogation, a short biography of the detainee and his demeanor,

Figure 3.5 Internal Branch 251 (Al-Khatib), Google Maps.

Figure 3.6 Bahjat Suleiman, from a pro-regime social media site.

with a recommendation to the Head of the Branch. The Head of the Branch refers this to the administration requesting either a release or arrest based on his conviction and the attached recommendation of the branch investigation section. This correspondence takes at least 15 days, during which time the detainee remains in custody. The Head of the Branch can make an arrest without returning to or coordinating with the administration outside the bureaucratic process. He can order the arrest of the detainee without noting him down in the records of the Branch. 'Such situations occurred often' said a former director of the prison, interviewed for this book. Apart from these cases, since 1991 no detainee has remained in Branch 251 for more than six months.[36] Observations during the hearings of the case of Anwar Raslan at the Koblenz court in Germany confirm this modus operandi.[37]

From its early years, the branch adopted torture as a way of obtaining information from detainees, using whipping, suspension, electricity, and sexual torture. Branch investigators enforced sleep food and drink deprivation as penalties. During the 1970s, detective Haitham al-Shama'a was known for his cruelty. The cleanness of the prison and the quality of the food in the prison then were much better than in the following years. The prison administration allowed the detainees the opportunity to meet their needs by requesting an 'invoice'.[38] It also provided detainees with a small radio. The overall state of the prison in terms of meals and medical care has deteriorated severely over time and has reached catastrophic levels in the past ten years.

The illusion of falling

Two wardens pulled me out of my cell. They dragged me on a long journey in the Branch building up and down. We passed through doors, and exited others. I came to realize this from the surrounding sounds. They ensured I was fully blindfolded so I didn't know where they were moving me to. They stopped on the roof of the building. I felt the air had changed. They told me not to move at all or I would fall into the building's skylight. They stood right behind me to prevent me from retreating, while I stood on the edge of the skylight as they told me. I almost lost balance and passed out. I stayed like that for several minutes during which my heart almost stopped. They did the experiment a second time and my fear was accumulating and increasing. My mind had no explanation for what was going on and what was the purpose of it. In the second time they placed me in the same place after the same journey. Two minutes later I decided to move forward and face whatever comes my way. That's when I found out that there was no skylight in front of me. To this day, 44 years later, I still do not know the purpose of that experiment or the punishment or what they actually wanted from me.[39]

Prior to the proliferation of small cameras and their easy implantation in interrogation rooms and cells, surveillance was carried out via internal telephone. Mufeed Najm confirms this:

While interrogating us at Al-Khatib Branch, the Head of the Branch could press the button of the intercom placed on his desk to listen to any interrogation carried out by the investigating officer with the detainee. He could even interfere with the interrogation in some cases. Everyone was watching everyone in the republic of fear and tyranny, and that's what made the regime last for decades.[40]

After 2008, the prison administration of Branch 251 began distributing uniforms to detainees. Mahmoud Hilal states:

> I was transferred from the Nabk Section to the Khatib Branch. There, the general approach changed towards violence. An operative started issuing orders and mocking us: 'Put your head down. Congrats on the glasses', referring to the blindfold. They had me standing facing a wall with a map of the city of Damascus divided in different colour-coded sectors. The map's title was Branch 251. I was searched in the manner of Military Police, fully nude and performing security moves. They put my personal belongings in a bag with my clothes and gave me a blue suit, like the one nurses wear in hospitals. I was placed in solitary cell no. 23.[41]

During the first decade after 2000, the meals and hygiene situation in the prison were better compared to previous and subsequent years. The prison allocations according to the testimonies were sufficient and the quality of food was acceptable. They were the same as the Syrian army allocations. Hygiene practices were reported such as washing and sterilizing the extra set of uniforms and punishing the residents of dirty solitary cells.

Torture continued during the interrogation sessions, but in a different way. The beginning of the interrogation took a gentle and patriarchal character, still with the eyes blindfolded. Gentle interrogation is repeated twice or thrice, then the journey of violence begins. Hilal remembers:

> They brought me to the interrogation room for the fourth time. They began hitting me with the quadruple cable. The detective got tired from the beatings and so he brought one of the torturers to beat me. Interrogation and torture sessions were sporadic, one day I was interrogated and tortured six times. The torture tools were limited to the quad cable, which caused me a problem in my left knee. I lost my ability to walk, and I started crawling on my stomach. They called for the doctor who asked the torturer if I confessed or not yet? He negated. The doctor stood me against the wall with my blood congested in my legs as a result of the beating.[42]

The situation in Branch 251 was reversed with the start of the Syrian Revolution in the spring of 2011. The Branch is responsible for Damascus and its countryside within the General Intelligence Department. Its operatives arrested the first protesters in Al-Hamidiya market in the centre of the capital. The levels of violence increased during the investigation and reception. Yahya Hakoum recalls his arrest:

> The moment we reached the Branch, a new round of beating started on top of the one we received during the arrest. A large number of Branch operatives gathered

in an open courtyard, where they dropped us from the car. In beating us, they used everything they could grab: belts, pipes, sticks and even their own hands. After about a quarter of an hour they took us inside the building, then to the basement after covering our heads with the shirts we were wearing. We arrived at a metal door under the constant blows and strikes. They brought us into a room and immediately began questioning us and asking why they were protesting. After brief answers, they took us out to the corridor and ordered us to hand over our clothes. We stayed in our underwear. I entered the investigation office again but this time I was handcuffed to the back and blindfolded. They placed me on my stomach and before answering their questions they started beating me again. I woke up in cell number 16, the number of which replaced my name by force. The warden asked me again about my name. When I replied 'Yahya', he beat me and reminded me of my new name: no. 16.[43]

'Take him away, and make him remember . . .'

The operative, who took me to the investigation the next day, did the military salute the moment he entered the investigation room, which meant there was someone with a high rank. The blindfold didn't cover my eyes well, so I got the chance to observe the room. There was a small desk to my left with a computer on top. Behind the table sat a bald short man and to his left stood two men in civilian suits. The computer user started asking why I was participating in the demonstration. I denied the confessions of the first day. I started weaving a different story trying to deny the protesting accusation. The investigator paused a video of the demonstration on a take showing the faces of its participants. He asked me about them one by one with me among them. The moment he heard the word 'no' he started hitting me. I refused to confess anything. Then, a person I later learned was Colonel Anwar Raslan, ordered the investigator: "Abdullah take him, make him remember . . ." Abdullah growled: "Yes Sir!" I was dragged into the torture chamber where the hands of more than three operatives handled me and started beating me everywhere. The investigation and torture continued daily.[44]

With the rising levels of violence and torture and increasing numbers of detainees, health conditions became catastrophic accompanied by a deterioration in the quality and quantity of food provided to the detainees.

In Al-Khatib Branch there was a problem with food. On the day I entered they served 3 meals, that went down to 2 with very small quantities. I was in a dormitory called Al-Tutiyah. We were over 200 people there, while the dormitory's capacity was fifty. It had a toilet with a wooden door that does not close. Relieving yourself takes no longer than half a minute. Due to congestion and lack of hygiene, skin diseases such as scabies and boils spread. Some people had dead limbs due to torture and lack of medical attention. These limbs had disintegrated and reached catastrophic levels. One of the detainees in my dormitory 'switched off' due to hunger and extreme pressure and started eating the flesh off his wound. They didn't bring us any doctors. Knocking on the door is forbidden unless one of us dies. Every day two or three of the detainees died from their wounds.[45]

Things in the rest of the dormitories were not any better. The detainees were given a space measuring less than 30 square centimetres in which to sit and sleep. Those circumstances prompted the detainees to take some strange and sudden actions against each other, especially when one 'switched off'. 'One of the men from our cell was killed in Al-Khatib Branch. He didn't die under torture, but because of his switching off. We put him near the toilet, as is customary in Al-Tutiyeh dormitory. We assigned this place to those battling death or who have switched off. We tried to feed him, but he suddenly stood up and started jumping over us. Our colleagues in the dormitory tried to stop him but to no avail. So, the Shawish, who is close to the wardens, stood up and ordered his group to beat him until he died and his voice was silenced.'[46]

Torture tools evolved compared to previous periods and became more cruel. Long hours of suspension by the hands and legs, electricity, targeting sensitive areas with indiscriminate beating and sleep and food deprivation in the solitary cells. As the number of detainees increased and the burdens of Branch 251 intensified, Al-Arbaeen Section started taking a central role in the arrests for the Branch. Dozens of detainees were arriving daily.[47]

Returning to the role of the Al-Arbaeen Section, known to detainees as the Raid and Counterterrorism Section. The Section's prison is not designed to hold detainees long-term, but for preliminary investigation before transfer to Branch 251. The prison has a large dormitory for men and at least one solitary cell for women. One survivor recalls: 'At some point it accommodated 12 women. It was only about 1.5 x 1.5 metres. The toilet was in the men's dormitory. For us to use the toilet, men were crammed into the corner of their large dormitory. There were no food allocations in Al-Arbaeen Section. You can only buy sandwiches.'[48]

Dealing with women in the Branch was no different from men in terms of severity and cruelty. The scarcity of food and medical care was the same, with the difference in the large numbers of men compared to women. Women were subjected to sexual harassment, humiliating searches in front of surveillance cameras, and sometimes even rape. In some cases, women were also arrested with their children. The children stayed with their mothers for months or even years. After the investigation was over, they were transferred to the Central Prison. A telling example is that of a Kurdish woman from Qamishli, from a family known for political activism across different generations, who was studying at Aleppo University when she was arrested. Due to a childhood accident, one of her legs had been amputated. She was arrested for Kurdish activism, which could be anything from speaking Kurdish to celebrating Newroz to discussing the legal status of undocumented Kurds in Syria. During her interrogation at the State Security branch in Aleppo, the officers pulled her hair, beat her, kicked her, and had no respect for her disability. She was simply subjected to *falaqa* under her one foot.[49]

Televised investigation

One spring day in 2014, a month after my arrest, I was called upon to meet the Head of Branch 251. It wasn't to talk to him about facts; they took me to receive more threats. He ordered me to respond to what they would ask, or he would torture my children in front of my eyes. I nodded my head silently and left. At the door, the detective asked me to adjust my clothes and hair in front of the big mirror in the corridor. I didn't respond to him, he walked me up to the second floor where I entered a starkly lit room. He untied me and sat me down in front of a familiar TV reporter. I didn't remember his name, and I can't recall it now. The reporter smiled and told me to speak easy and without fear. My thoughts were racing: What should I talk about? What do they want? Many Syrian detainees have lived through this experience before me. Months after their arrest, they appeared on Syrian television to tell strange stories about betrayal and conspiracy. It was a method to further brainwash regime loyalists that the country is under cosmic war. The detective, sorry, the reporter started asking questions about the details of my work in documenting the chemical massacre I told you about. I told him the tale that I confessed under torture. A few minutes later he stopped me, objecting to the story. I knew from him that my statement on the papers was different. There, there was a different narrative that tells the story of 'a young Damascene woman, manipulated by "terrorists" in eastern Ghouta, where the massacre took place. They sent her pictures and she discovered through her high knowledge of the arts of photography and Photoshop that they were fake. She threatened to expose the story, and that's what she's doing.' I felt the marks of the handcuffs on my hands and I remembered my son's cries the moment he was arrested and I started repeating what the reporter wanted like a parrot. I don't know where and when they used this confession.[50]

Branch 285 after 2011

Branch 285 maintained its toughness and prominent presence after 2000, firstly for being the final destination for all detainees arrested for the General Intelligence; secondly, for being the central investigative body that re-expands the investigation of incoming detainees. The Branch adopted a process of violent welcome of detainees to create a state of panic and build an immediate barrier between the warden and the detainee. Breaking any such supposed relationship is a policy adopted by most Syrian Security Services. Mahmoud Hilal noted:

We were greeted by the wardens of Branch 285 with an hour-long torture session after which we were lined against the walls, standing on our feet, for two hours. The object of this practice is humiliation. Then they brought us into what they call 'the double cell', which is 190 cm wide and 3.5 meters long. The only air vent there was small holes in the ceiling. They took us to the toilet twice a day. We kept an empty plastic water bottle to pee in. Sleeping in the Branch prison was at 23:00 and waking up was at 06:00.[51]

The levels of violence in the Branch increased after the first days of the revolution. Yahya Hakoum narrates how he ran the gauntlet:

We were dropped off in a yard and there were operatives waiting for us on both sides. We ran towards a black door that led to a staircase. Halfway through the staircase, there was another door leading to a wide square yard, 10 meters by 10, and covered by a roof over 10 meters high. All along the way leading to this yard, operatives formed a human wall on both sides. They used sticks and batons to beat us. They ordered us to strip completely in the yard. The clothes were piled up. They gave us a paper called the 'information brief' in which we filled out all our personal and family information. Then we each received one hundred foot whips in the middle of the yard, after which we were taken into the dormitory. We were called the 15 March Group. We were placed in a solitary cell, 180 cm by 70 cm. We were nine men. The whole time we remained standing, in rows, facing the wall. The Judas window was always open but moving your head to look outside was strictly forbidden. The interrogation began, and the torture was more severe than in Branch 251.[52]

Medical care was completely absent from the Branch, and food allocations to detainees dropped into unprecedented levels. This was accompanied by constant torture inside the prison. Hakoum continues:

Food was almost non-existent. Only olives in the morning with two loaves of bread for seven detainees, and a similar amount of food for lunch. A liter of drinking water all day for everyone. Going out to the bathroom was once a day. The door opens with operatives lining the walls on both sides, sometimes wearing metal fists on their hands. We received strikes on our way out and back. Toilet time was ten seconds, which the warden counts for you. I remained in the Investigation Branch for 41 days. The interrogation stopped after about a month, but the routine torture sessions continued. Every once in a while, they took us out into the yard to be tortured then returned us to the cells.[53]

The testimonies of survivors from the Investigation Branch are consistent in terms of torture instruments, lack of medical attention and lack of food. Testimonies confirm the use of sexual torture and harassment by placing a stick in the detainee's buttocks and threatening to rape him with it. Interrogators, operatives, and wardens also practiced various forms of torture, such as the electrical stick; extraction of nails especially from the hands; indiscriminate beatings on the face, chest, and head; extinguishing cigarette butts on the detainee's body, especially on the hands and the back; beatings with a bat or power cables, using the city's power grid for torture in some cases; suspension by the hands; deprivation of food and sleep; deprivation of medicines and health care; deprivation of soap and bathing; depriving female detainees of sanitary pads; burning detainees with hot water; the Magic Carpet, and other tools and modes.[54]

Branch 320: Hama

It is clear from these testimonies that there is no difference in the treatment of women and men in the General Intelligence branches. The General Intelligence Branch in Hama recorded a special experience dealing with female detainees during the summer of 2012. The Branch launched a raid and arrest campaign in the neighbourhoods of the city of Hama targeting female family members of fighters in the Free Syrian Army. In addition to interrogation and torture, they were all subject to consecutive rape sessions. Maria Kh., born in Hama, and the mother of three children, recounts:

> My torture continued for three days, incessantly and violently. The interrogations lasted from two o'clock until eight in the evening. Every day they took two of the female detainees to the office of Lieutenant Colonel Suleiman Juma. The office had an attached bedroom containing two beds, and a bathroom. On the fourth day of the arrest, after the interrogation, which was accompanied by beating and insults, at around 9 p.m., I was taken to the Lieutenant Colonel's office. I had another female detainee with me. As soon as we walked into the office, we noticed two people laughing, which later turned out to be friends of the Lieutenant Colonel. The Lieutenant Colonel ordered one of his female operatives to take off our clothes, we tried to resist, but to no avail. The episode of gang rape began. The Lieutenant Colonel, along with two of his friends took turns in raping me. I don't think they were officers working in the Branch. After that day, I was repeatedly raped, along with the six other ladies arrested with me, several times throughout my 24-day detention at the Branch.[55]

The General Intelligence branches in the provinces did not differ in terms of violence and cruelty in treatment. The usual lack of the minimum levels of health care. The usual lack of food and ill-treatment in detention centres. It was reported that children were arrested in 2012 at the General Intelligence Branch in Latakia and were subjected to various types of torture, not limited to electrocution and indiscriminate beating. What applies to the Latakia Branch applies to the Aleppo Branch, which also arrested children and used in their torture the 'blanco' (suspension from the ceiling with their hands tied behind their back) in addition to the methods previously mentioned. Suspension from the ceiling was reported a lot in the Idlib Branch, in addition to nail extraction. The situation was similar in other branches of the General Intelligence in Syria during the uprising.[56]

4

The Political Security Division

The Political Security Division, established in 1947 by Legislative Decree No 77, falls under the Syrian Ministry of Interior. The Division is legally a unit of the Ministry of Interior. The Head of the Division is appointed by decree of the President; submits his security reports directly to the Office of National Security or to the President himself; and appoints the leaders of the central branches and governorate branches following approval from the Presidential Palace without taking advice from the Minister of Interior. The head of the Division has direct and exclusive authority over all officers and operatives of the Division.

The Political Security Division monitors the work of the Ministry of Interior, from the Minister all the way down to the most junior operative. Operatives of the Division fall functionally under the Ministry of the Interior, and there are officers seconded from the Army to the Division. All employees of the Division are members of the ruling Arab Socialist Baath Party. Only a Baathist may be affiliated with the Army or the Ministry of Interior. Article 40 of the Police Internal Code states: 'Police officers are prohibited from being members of political parties, bodies, associations or organizations other than the Arab Socialist Baath Party. They are also prohibited from expressing political and party related views that oppose principles of the Baath Party.'[1] In other words, the Political Security division is an explicitly politicized strike force that works in service of the party and the regime, not the state.

The Division is considered the security apparatus that has the most infiltration in society, and is the most widespread as it covers the entire country. Many civil transactions or business and enterprise license applications require the approval of the Political Security Division. The Division is the Syrian regime's information reservoir. However, it is considered a third-tier security apparatus in comparison to Military Intelligence or the General Intelligence departments.[2] Hafez al-Assad strengthened it by transferring military officers from the army and Military Intelligence to lead it. In 1987, Major General Adnan Badr al-Hassan, was transferred from the Syrian Army Infantry Corps to be the Division's Head.

The officers and operatives of the Division are selected from the personnel of the Ministry of Interior with the exception of the head of the Division who is appointed by Presidential Decree. The most prominent Head was Major General Adnan Badr al-Hassan, who succeeded Ahmed Saeed al-Saleh in 1987. He was succeeded in 2002 by Major General Ghazi Kanaan who came from Military Intelligence, who was replaced in 2004 by Major General Mohammed Mansoura, for many years the Head of the

Figure 4.1 Ghazi Kanaan, from a pro-regime social media site.

Figure 4.2 Political Security Branch – Damascus (Al-Maysaat), Google Maps.

Military Intelligence Branch in the province of Hasakeh. He was succeeded in 2009 by Major General Mohammed Deeb Zeitoun from the General Intelligence Department. He was succeeded in 2012 by Major General Rustom Ghazaleh from the Military Intelligence Division and Head of the District Branch 227. He was succeeded in 2015 by Major General Nazih Hassoun from Air Force Intelligence. He was

Figure 4.3 Rustom Ghazaleh, from a pro-regime social media site.

Figure 4.4 Hossam Luqa, from a pro-regime social media site.

Figure 4.5 Nasser Al-Ali, from a pro-regime social media site.

succeeded in 2017 by Major General Mohammed Khaled Rahmon who for years had managed the Southern Region Branch of Air Force Intelligence. He was succeeded in 2018 by Major General Hossam Luqa, who remained in power until 2019, when the management of the Division was taken over by Major General Nasser Al-Ali, who remains in power.

Structure of the organization

Similar to the rest of the Syrian security and intelligence services, the Political Security Division has a headquarters and central branches in Damascus. Damascus harbors the following branches: Police Security, Information, Patrols and Surveillance, Parties and Bodies, Economic Security, Personnel Affairs, Arab and Foreign Affairs, Administrative Affairs, Signal, Vehicles, and the Investigation Branch, to which all detainees from the governorates and other central branches are referred. This is in addition to the governorate branches, which are present in all governorates except for Quneitra, which is covered from Damascus.[3]

Even in the 1970s and 1980s it was clear to any observer that the Political Security was omnipresent. Seale noticed:

A traveller in the Syrian provinces would have discovered three men of importance in each provincial capital: first in terms of protocol was the party secretary who, at the apex of the local party organization, was the instrument of the Regional Command and hence of Asad, its secretary-general; second came the governor who, like a French préfet, was the representative of the central government and hence of the president; and third was the head of political security, as often as not an 'Alawi colonel, whose role was to uncover and deal with any seditious activity and whose chain of command also led ultimately to Asad.[4]

Each branch of Political Security in the governorates includes the segregation of the Division in the form of offices for all previous departments. All branches of the Division have detention centres and use civilian prisons in the governorates to help hold detainees. Each civilian prison includes a special Political Security wing operated by the governorate's Political Security Branch.

Hama

The role of the Political Security Division emerged as the confrontation between the Muslim Brotherhood and the Syrian regime started. The conflict intensified at the turn of the 1980s and the city of Hama was the centre of this political and military confrontation. Security branches in Hama were engaged in security operations under what were called 'joint patrols'. These began extensive arrest campaigns among the city's youth. A survivor of that repressive period, Mahmoud Ashour, recalls:

In 1980, the city of Hama was cordoned off several times to carry out arrests. On 7 October of the same year, I was arrested during one of those campaigns. An hour before dawn, an armed patrol raided our house. In those days, inspection raids were a norm. However, this time they asked me to go down to the street. They stole money, jewelry and all valuables from the house and beat my mother and sister. I was immediately blindfolded and handcuffed and didn't know what was going on. It was a giant joint patrol and all the detainees were children like me, the oldest among us was 17 years old. I was arrested by the Political Security Branch which was headed then by Walid Abaza.[5]

The Political Security Branch cooperated with Military Intelligence during that campaign, which involved arresting about fifteen young men. They collaborated to link them to the organized Militant Vanguard that had Islamist tendencies. The usual violent interrogation tools were used throughout the 33 days during which detainees were transferred between the two branches. Along with the young men, some of their fathers were arrested for pressure and to blackmail them into providing their confessions. Ashour testifies:

Figure 4.6 Walid Abaza, from a pro-regime social media site.

When they finished designing the investigation report to the outcome they wanted, they started preparing to transfer us to prison. With charred matches I drew gallows on the wall of the solitary cell and wrote my initials under it: M. A. Back then, the law criminalizing and executing the Muslim Brotherhood was passed, so that was the fate I expected. They called us by our names. We were taken straight into a minibus. They sat us there like ordinary passengers, but shackled, until we passed through Hama. On the outskirts of the city, they blindfolded us, lowered our heads to the seats and proceeded to Tadmor prison, where I remained for 25 years.[6]

Aleppo

The relative weakness of Political Security did not prevent competition with the General Intelligence on the domestic scene. Osama al-Askari narrates:

I was arrested at a joint security checkpoint in the city of Qamishli on 25 May 1982. One of the operatives at the checkpoint from the General Intelligence recognized me, he used to be a classmate. I was transferred to the State Security Branch in Qamishli. They interrogated me very violently to find out my political affiliation and my charges. They started from the Muslim Brotherhood and moved all the way to the 'Rightist Baath' (those close to the Iraqi Baathists). They knew I was wanted by Political Security but they didn't know what for. They tried to achieve a security victory in their favour by pushing me to confess. I lost hearing in one of my ears as a result of the violent beating. I was tortured with electricity, suspension, and whipping. Three days later they handed me over to the Political Security in

Qamishli who confirmed the incident in a medical report at the city's government hospital. The treatment differed in Political Security, not because they were kinder but because what they would have wanted to do was already done by public intelligence operatives. Three days later, interrogating me became useless as all the appointments I had that they might have benefited from were canceled; that was as per the arrest tactics of the Communist Labour party. We used to change appointments exactly 24 hours after one of the comrades was arrested.[7]

Political Security is known to use the Magic Carpet as a torture tool, adopted in all its branches. After tying the blindfolded detainee to the Magic Carpet, he is hit with a bamboo stick. 'Every now and then, the torturer rubbed the bottom of the feet with the bamboo, this hurt more than the beating. This method was adopted in the Qamishli and Aleppo Political Security Branches.'[8] Similar to other security and intelligence branches, Political Security adopted a method of isolating the detainee from the outside world. The new detainee is kept separate to deprive him of knowledge about the details of the prison and the interrogation. This isolation period lasts until the interrogation is concluded and perpetuates the fear of the unknown in the detainee.

The Magic Carpet is not the only tool used for torture by Political Security. The Aleppo Branch used sleep deprivation throughout the duration of the interrogation. They also used sexual torture on some of the detainees. Al-Askari remembers: 'One of the comrades who arrived to the prison coming from the Political Security Branch in Aleppo, was subjected to sexual torture by inserting a broken Coca Cola bottle into his anus. His anus was lacerated and his health condition deteriorated.'

Ghosts of the victims

By the beginning of the 1990s, we were in Damascus central prison. The investigator of the Political Security Branch in Aleppo, Lieutenant Mohammed Jouma, was arrested. The political wing was packed with detainees from Tadmor and Aleppo prisons, all awaiting the end of the trials. Jouma identified many of his victims among us, dozens of whom he unjustly sent to Tadmor prison. He tortured them, forcibly extracted their confessions, and then sent them to death under torture in that terrible desert prison. He experiencing a deterioration in his mental health and became dysfunctional. He banged the door of the ward every day hysterically asking for help, claiming that the ghosts of the prisoners wanted to kill him. In fact, prisoners tried to look after him and help him, but to no avail. Jouma completely lost his mind. After years of wealth, money, and power as the Branch's Chief Investigator, he made one fatal mistake and was arrested. He sent an intelligence report to the Head of the Division in Damascus complaining about the corruption of the Head of the Political Security Branch in Aleppo. As a result, he was arrested and charged with corruption and taking bribes to free detainees. He was later transferred to Tadmor prison.[9]

Detention periods at the Political Security Branch in Aleppo did not last long. The detainee was then transferred to the Political Security wing in the city's Central Prison. However, these periods of detention, which could last up to a month, lacked all forms of care. Bakr Sidki recalls:

> During my arrest in the Branch, I was in a solitary cell. They fed me at my own expense. They brought us falafel sandwiches twice a day, bought from the money they took when we handed in our personal belongings. Although Political Security was less violent than other security agencies, the tools they used for torture were harmful and harsh. Torture on the Magic Carpet caused feet to swell and skin to peel. The health officer in the branch came to try to sterilize the wound, but his procedure was a second torture, more severe than the beating.[10]

Damascus: al-Maysaat

The capital Branch, al-Maysaat, the most famous branch of the Political Security Division, did not record any differences in torture and interrogation methods from the other branches of the Division in the governorates. The Branch, which was under the leadership of Amin Al-Ali, renewed its stack of bamboo sticks used for torture in 1983 during the campaign launched against members of the Communist Labour Party and in which the Political Security Division participated. He ensured the Division was protected from the charge of 'murder under torture' by all available means. Jalal Noufal narrates:

> As soon as I entered the Branch, they began the interrogation which was accompanied with beating. Every time they hit me with a bamboo stick, it broke. They brought a new batch of bamboo sticks. These had a disastrous impact on the feet. The marks remained on the feet for more than three years. After the end of the interrogation, which was going on day and night, I was deprived of sleep. I fell asleep and woke up to the sound of Captain Ali al-Hamwi, the officer in charge of the investigation. He ordered the wardens: 'Bring him medicine and disinfectants, I do not want him to die and be regarded a martyr of my ass.' And indeed, they brought disinfectants and anti-inflammatory pills.[11]

A narrow staircase connected the detainee to the Branch prison in the basement. The prison had at least 11 solitary cells and several dormitories. Survivor of the prison, Rateb Shabo, wrote in his memoir-novel:

> The solitary cell in Political Security is 180 by about 120 cm. It had a bench with blankets on it, as well as a toilet and a water tap. I found this different to the conditions of detention that our colleagues who passed through the branches of Military Intelligence told us about. Even food was acceptable, in comparison to what we've heard. It was cooked food and quantities were acceptable.[12]

The relatively 'positive' setting compared to the Military Intelligence or state security branches did not diminish the poor psychological state the detainee suffered when stepping down into the branch prison. Shabo again:

For the first time you find yourself in a basement. For the first time. Your skin feels the smell of a tyrant's torture. You feel your blood escaping to the most vital places, leaving you pale, dizzy and taken by an overwhelming desire to vomit. Just picture this: a long, narrow basement lit by tens of neon lights fixed to the ceiling ... stenching with a heavy musty smell ... and in one corner of the glossy floor you see the rubber frame of a medium-sized car wheel ... you can keep imagining, adding to the picture a water tap emerging from one of the walls, attached to it a relatively long hose ... add to the image the silhouettes of the torturers: young operatives whose words are curses and orders, and whose touches are shoves and beating. Then tell me, after the picture is complete in your mind: didn't you feel the smell of torture through your skin?[13]

Growth of the senses

In security prisons ... Especially during the interrogation, latent senses are activated, ones you did not realize before. In great adversity, you feel the senses become exceptionally symbiotic. For example, the skin can smell and hear, and the ears can see (the soles of the feet could feel and hear the slamming of the doors and the detective's ringing bell before the ears). In adversity, the sleeping inner senses are mobilized, but unfortunately the only benefit they offer is telling their owner of the gravity of what awaits them, as if the final hope of the soul, as if to send the alert brain extreme distress messages to do whatever it can to survive.[14]

The levels of violence at the Political Security in Damascus increased at the beginning of the 1990s. The tools of torture evolved, and the Branch began to use electrocution. It also used the German Chair and long torture sessions in the presence of a health official. Mahmoud Issa, a survivor of the prison, writes in his memoir:

The torture lasted for a month. On the first day it was constant torture, from 10:30 p.m. until 2:30 a.m. the next morning. Four torture sessions that lasted hours. There were forms of sexual torture. Three to five security personnel attended torture and interrogation sessions. The doctor also attended these sessions to check whether the health state of detainee allowed further torture. The torture caused a fracture in my right wrist and pinkie due to the German Chair. The last round of torture was attended by the Head of the Branch, Brigadier General Mahmoud Abdul Wahab. The Head of the Branch asked that I call him 'Sir', but I said: 'I'm not a military staff under you, my dear!' The phrase 'my dear' (*azizi*) aggravated all his brutal, killing instincts. He understood it as ill as his manners!

The operatives started beating me with boots as I lay on the Magic Carpet. I screamed: 'There's nothing manly in beating a tied-up person.' The Head of the Branch ordered them to electrocute me. My senses are split between the wires, the incoming charge, and the shock. His heavy foot kicks me in the stomach just as a brutal electric current creeps through my loins. My cries shatter the quiet and darkness of the night. Silence return, and with it a new quiet and cold water. My lips shiver and the words stumbled as they leave my trembling teeth. . .[15]

As the level of violence during interrogation increased, the quality of daily life in the Branch prison deteriorated. The medical care was limited to monitoring the detainee's condition during torture. The usual diseases such as scabies, lice, and skin diseases spread due to overcrowding in the dormitories and spaced-out showers for detainees in solitary cells. Duha al-Askari narrates:

The place was cramped and there was no ventilation nor good hygiene. I could hear them taking the detainees out into the corridor and spraying pesticides, but to no avail. You were never given enough opportunity to bathe well. I suffered skin abrasion because I stayed in the same clothes for so long. I stayed in the Branch for three months. I tried to hide my new pregnancy from the detectives, so I stayed in my clothes all the time. I asked for the doctor, but they didn't call him, so I asked them to buy me some disinfectant and baby powder to deal with what happened to my skin; they did.[16]

The absence of health care was accompanied by the deterioration of food allocations for detainees. Al-Askari continues:

We had three meals a day, but they were useless. I was asking them for eggs, for I was pregnant, and I knew I needed good nutrition, but they didn't respond. Breakfast was very bad olives, although Syria produces good quality olives, and a loaf of bread. Friday was the exception where they swapped olives with a piece of cheese. There was a lot of jam for breakfast. Lunch was tomato broth with some pasta, peas, or vegetables in a very small amount. Dinner was badly boiled potatoes, or they were of poor quality, or horribly cooked lentil soup. There were no fruits or vegetables and exclusively on Friday they served spring onions.[17]

Methods of arrest used by the Political Security did not change according to the gender of the detainee. Munir al-Hariri, a defected intelligence officer, said in an interview: 'Arrests were made in brutal ways. The moment the news arrives about a wanted person, the whole neighbourhood, street and house are encircled and the wanted person is extracted in any way and in any form.' However, the method used to arrest Duha Ashour al-Askari was slightly different, as she notes: 'We received a tip from an informant that Duha was in front of the Maysaloun library in central Damascus opposite the Al-Sham hotel. I was commissioned with her arrest. I took a small patrol in my own car. We followed the target in the streets of the city. We managed to arrest her in a nearby yard. She was aggressive and strong and attacked me. After some effort we managed to put her in the car. She caused people on the street to react against us. When we put her in the car she fainted.'[18]

The methods of interrogation also did not differ. The detainee is isolated from the outside world as soon as they enter the Branch. The interrogation starts immediately, and they are deprived rest or sleep. 'They deprived me of sleep for a whole week. They took turns interrogating me all the time, day and night. They only gave me half an hour per day for lunch. I used it to sleep, but the moment I closed my eyes they called for me. The interrogation was intensive and was done in the presence of two officers at the rank of Major. The first was the 'good cop' while the other exerted great pressure on me.'[19]

Psychological pressure or torture is not just used to extract information but also carried the characteristics of education, rehabilitation, or retaliation. Ahmed Maatouq remembers: 'Atef Najib interrogated me in 1992. He would come drunk at night to interrogate detainees. He was always spiteful and violent. One of the colleagues was arrested with us the same year. He directly confessed all the details of his party work. However, he received worse torture than any of us.'This torture party is a reminder that you were arrested by Political Security', Najib told him.'[20]

The arrival of the Baath party to power was linked to the increased levels of violence in the Syrian security and intelligence services. Maatouq remembers the period: 'The violence used has never been eradicated, however its modes and methods were upgraded. Torture methods increased in severity between 1961 and 2011. On top, they introduced electrocution, suspension, the German Chair, the Magic Carpet and many other methods that increase the levels of pain caused by torture.'[21]

At no point did any torturer explain to any of his victims why he was being tortured. M.S.I., born in Qamishli as a stateless Kurd, took great pains to study architecture at the University of Damascus. He was arrested by Political Security at the end of May 1989 for swearing against Hafez al-Assad on the streets, during an argument. A Peugeot with a white license plate drove him to the Qamishli branch. Upon arrival they sat him on a chair and began beating him. He implored them: 'Why are you beating me?' The torturers answered: 'You do not need to know this. Neither do we. It is our job.' M.S.I. was subjected to the usual torture methods, but also had to chew on his shoes – a particularly degrading form of humiliation in Syrian culture. After two hours of torture, he was thrown in a cell and soon joined by a corpulent man, who was planted there to extract information from him. After 10 days he was released. His life in Syria ruined, like many others he fled across the northern border to Turkey, and then onward to Europe.[22]

Damascus: countryside

The role of Political Security was not limited to raids and the arrest of members of leftist parties or the Muslim Brotherhood. The Division monitored student and university activities as well as religious activity in all its forms. Through its operatives it monitored mosques, churches, all schools, and religious groups. It summoned those suspected for an interrogation that might lead to an arrest. Mohiddeen Kanaan recalls:

We were called, about 16 young men, through the Political Security detachment in Al-Qutaifah area. Upon arrival at the Damascus Countryside Branch, we were immediately arrested on account of our religious activity. The interrogation lasted four months with torture using foot whipping, stripping clothes off and cold and hot water. They also practiced psychological torture. We were left in the dark and cold solitary cells without calling us for interrogation, as if we were forgotten. In those cells, we could hear the screams of tortured detainees, which increased our fear and anticipation. They also insulted us by shaving off our hair and beards. During shaving they played with our hair by drawing funny shapes and laughing at them.[23]

With the spread of the internet, the Political Security Division began monitoring this sector as well, and many Syrians were arrested for their online activities, such as Ibrahim al-Olabi: 'I was arrested from an internet cafe because I browsed the Muslim Brotherhood website. They took me to the Jaramana detachment in Damascus countryside and then I was transferred to the Rif Branch in the Mezzeh area. The Branch prison had only two dormitories; the rest were all solitary cells.'[24] The Division branches maintained low levels of health care which was accompanied by malnutrition. The only thing that was plentiful was the levels of violence and torture. Ayat Ahmed recounts: 'They started beating me hard as I was strapped to the Magic Carpet. They beat me with their hands, legs, and bamboo sticks. They broke my foot. I wasn't taken to the hospital until days later, which caused me a problem that I still suffer from to this day.'[25]

Investigation Branch: al-Fayhaa

After 2000, the Central Investigation Branch in the Fayhaa area of Damascus took on a larger role, as those arrested by the Political Security were transferred there. However, like the Division, it remained weak compared to the rest of the intelligence services, which could call upon any of its detainees for interrogation.

New Year's Eve rape

After 28 days of violent interrogation in the Rif Damascus Branch of Political Security, I was transferred with my colleagues to the Investigation Branch in the Fayhaa area. New Year's Eve 2010 was very cold. The solitary cell had a blanket on the floor and a second to cover ourselves. I knocked on the door along with my colleague, a young Kurdish woman arrested for her PKK affiliation; we knocked the door asking for more blankets. No one responded to us, but we asked several times. Two drunk wardens came and opened the door. They were celebrating the New Year. They took my colleague, stripped her off completely, and then put her in the rubber frame of a car wheel. They began brutally raping her. She was still a virgin and she bled a lot. I couldn't do anything. My colleague was shocked and silenced, so was I. As a result of this silence, I was taken to the hospital. The first time I spoke afterwards, I told Brigadier General Mahmoud Al-Khatib, Head of the Branch, the details of the incident. His was shocked and said it was an individual act that cannot be tolerated, so they put the wardens in jail for a few days but then they returned to their work. My colleague had venereal infections and suffered a high temperature. They took her to the hospital. She went and never returned to the solitary cell.[26]

The violence of the torture in the Investigation Branch reached the point of murder. Al-Olabi recalls a critical moment:

They transferred an employee of the Bemo Saudi-French Bank in Damascus, from the Criminal Security Branch to the Al-Fayhaa Branch. All ongoing interrogation with us stopped. They all were freed up to torture him brutally. Once I counted the cable blows on his feet, they reached 500, then stopped. I was scared of keeping count. On the third day of the interrogation with the employee, the Branch prison witnessed a strange commotion. We later learned that the employee died under torture. The wardens told us the details of the incident. Detectives and torturers tortured him with suspension and burning for the previous three days. The torture of all detainees ceased. They started a daily inspection of prisoners' health. This lasted a month after which torture gradually returned to the interrogation sessions as if nothing had happened.[27]

Figure 4.7 Investigation Branch – Al-Fayhaa, Google Maps.

Hasakeh

The Political Security Division, together with the rest of the Syrian intelligence and security services, contributed to the implementation of the orders of the national security office. Extensive arrests were carried out in the 1980s and later during the 2004 Kurdish uprising. A feud over a football match between the teams of the governorates of Deir ez-Zor and Hasakeh turned into a rebellion against the regime. A security committee was immediately formed, comprising the Governor of Hasakeh, the heads of the security branches and the Police Commander in the governorate. The post of Head of the Political Security Branch in the province was vacant, so Brigadier Munir Al-Hariri sent a representative of the Division to the Committee, which also included Assistant Head of the Political Security Division, Mohamed Mansoura, due to his considerable experience in the region. The committee was based in the district directorate. Al-Hariri recalls: 'We arrested many Kurds and Arabs. They were placed in Hasakeh Central Prison. A committee came to investigate those. It was led by Colonel Jalal Al-Hayek of the Military Intelligence Division.'[28]

After 2011

The 2011 uprising created an historic challenge to the capacity of Political Security. Overcrowding and levels of violence increased in its prisons, and its employees worked overtime to 'process' the masses coming through its system. Osama al-Askari had already experienced arrest before this period, but he now witnessed a completely different era:

> After the revolution, Syrian security entered a state of general defilement of society. 80 people breathing through a small hole in the cell door. Congestion prevented you from sleeping. Scabies reached catastrophic levels. Going out to the toilet was a grave issue. A month and a half in Aleppo's Political Security was as harsh as my previous sixteen years of detention. Rising levels of regime violence aimed at tearing the social fabric apart. The Political Security Division participated in this task with all its branches.[29]

The situation in the Aleppo Branch, for example, applied just as much to the branches of the capital. There was a staggering rise in levels of violence and torture. Electrocution and suspension were used, in addition to the Division's trademark, the Magic Carpet. Overcrowding reached unprecedented levels, causing the spread of prison diseases. Those arrested for the first time were shocked by the violence and depredations, such as A.B.: 'Scabies spread widely in the Damascus Branch and Investigation Branch. It reached a level where skin would break open, pus would come out, then dry and become black. The smell that came from this condition were catastrophic. We also had diarrhoea.'[30] Similar conditions reigned in the prison of the Political Security Branch in Idlib, which included five dormitories and several solitary cells in addition to an interrogation room in its basement. The situation of the Branch in terms of torture, medical care and food was no different to the other branches of Political Security in Damascus and the governorates.[31]

The increased levels of torture and violence were accompanied by a near-total absence of healthcare. Rising numbers of detainees reduced food allocations to the lowest levels. Branch prisons were flooded with hundreds of detainees under similar conditions in terms of medical care, food, and unprecedented levels of violence. The Political Security Division started moving some of its detainees to Saydnaya military prison by transferring them to the custody of Military Police. This development was indicative of a change in the policy of the Office of National Security during the Revolution. The Political Security Division and some military and civilian security branches initially transferred their detainees to civilian prisons in the governorates prior to this shift. They were clearly overworked.

Ghaith Faris was arrested by the Homs branch and recalls his torment:

I was arrested by the Political Security Branch in Homs in the summer of 2016. I remained in its prison for 27 days. I was on the solitary cell no 6 which was close to the solitaries 7 and 8 assigned for women. Branch wardens walked into their cells every day and they started screaming and crying. I think they were raping them one by one. On top of all the psychological pain, I was beaten even though they didn't treat my two bullet wounds during my arrest. The sounds of torture filled the Branch prison, which included nine solitary cells and some dormitories, as well as an investigation room and a torture chamber.[32]

Those who survived the prisons of the Political Security were left with trauma and deep scars. Mohammed Abu Hajar (1987) from Tartous was severely tortured in the Tartous Political Security branch. He survived, fled Syria, first to Italy and then to Germany, where he started a rap group and rapped about his captivity:

I am fed up, after one jail there will be only another one /
a minute is an hour for me, for you a second /
every morning, they wake you up like a dog for a count /
yet, torture is heavier today than yesterday /
the torturer laughs: "yesterday was a joke, today is real" /
you stand up, naked, while it is too cold /
continuous rounds of torture and *shabah* and electrical shocks /
a new detainee has joined – welcome brother![33]

5

The Military Police

The Military Police in Syria is one of the military departments of the Syrian Army General Staff Authority in the Ministry of Defence. It is the executive arm of Military Judiciary. It is based in the Al-Qaboun area of Damascus and has brigades in city centres and governorates, especially in the border areas. The most prominent of these are Al-Balouni in Homs, which is a large Military Police centre and Hanano in Aleppo. Some of the most prominent leaders of this Department have been Ali al-Madani,[1] who was succeeded by Rasmi al-Eid, previously the Director of the Mezzeh military prison who remained the Head of the Military Police Department for about 15 years.[2] Since 2018, the department has been led by Major General Riad Habib Abbas.

The structure and functions of the Military Police

The tasks of the Military Police in 'peacetime' are limited to maintaining military discipline and punishing military personnel. The Military Police is the executive apparatus of the Military Judiciary, so they bring those wanted for military prosecution and execute the orders of the Judiciary. The unit investigates all crimes committed in military sectors, even issuing traffic tickets if any military personnel are involved. The Military Police is the guarding brigade of important military sectors such as the General Military Staff Authority, the Military Judiciary, and other important individuals. It operates military prisons and detention centres for military personnel or civilians convicted in cases that touch on 'state security'. It carries out the sentences of Military Judiciary, against military personnel or civilians be that imprisonment or execution.[3]

To clarify the role of the Military Police, a map of arrests and detention in Syria must be drawn. When a security department carries out an order to arrest a person from the street, their house, workplace, a demonstration or a battlefield, that person undergoes an investigation in a similar manner to that which has been explained and described in the previous sections. The transfer of any political security detainee to Military Judiciary must be done through via the Military Police, or by transferring the detainee for re-investigation in a branch of the Military Intelligence, then following one of the routes such as detention in a military prison, death under torture, poor prison conditions or medical negligence. After their arrest, the person will be subjected to one of the following scenarios:

Figure 5.1 Military Police insignia, from the Syrian Ministry of Defence website.

Figure 5.2 Map of Al-Qaboun Headquarters of Military Police, Google Maps.

Scenario 1

Arrest. Branch detention centre. Interrogation, during which torture is often used. Injury as a result of torture or poor conditions in the Branch. Medical negligence. Death. The person is then given a number. Transported to a military hospital. The number of the branch from which they came is added to their number. Contact

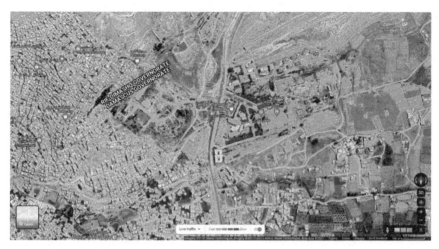

Figure 5.3 Hospital 607 Teshrin, Google Maps.

Figure 5.4 Military Hospital 601, Google Maps.

the Military Police to complete the burial procedure. The body is documented by the Evidence Office of the Military Police. They are given a Coroner's report number. Transport to the designated burial place. The burial is carried out in coordination with the Mortuary Office in the governorate, this is often Damascus. The burials are accompanied by joint patrols from the four intelligence departments. Some of the most familiar cemeteries used by the Military Police as per intelligence orders are:

- Najha cemetery. The cemetery is located in rural Damascus, in the al-Husseiniya area, and covers an area of about 750 m². Before 2011, this was no more than 105 m², according to local residents. Satellite images show a big expansion in trenches dug in the cemetery between 2012 and the end of 2014.
- Tabukiya cemetery, located near the HQ of the Third Division, located in the Qalamoun mountains in the northern countryside of Damascus covers an area of about 15,000 m². It is hard to locate this accurately as it is inside a military area so civilians are not allowed.
- Al-Bahdaliya cemetery (known as the City's Southern Cemetery) located in rural Damascus in the Al-Husseiniya area.[4]

Inform the Civil Registry of the death of the detainee based on the causes listed by the coroner's report, which are often sudden cardiac arrest or the cessation of the vital functions of the detainee.[5]

Scenario 2

Arrest. Branch detention centre. Interrogation, during which torture is often used. Injury as a result of torture or poor conditions in the Branch. Medical negligence. Deterioration of the health condition. They are then given a number. Transfer to a military hospital 'for treatment'. The Branch number is added to the detainee's number. Return to the branch after completing treatment. Interrogation ends. Transfer to the Military Police headquarters. Transfer to a military prison, often Saydnaya. Papers transferred to the Military Judiciary, the individual judge, or a field court, which is the most likely option. Carry out the sentence issued against them: imprisonment or execution. Military Police enforces discipline regulations and sanctions against military prison inmates as and when instructed. In the case of execution, this is documented, and a report of the case is written. Notify the Civil Registry of the death of the detainee. These last actions are often delayed or not carried out, creating a state of confusion and false hope that the detainee is still alive.

Scenario 3

Arrest. Branch detention centre. Interrogation, during which torture is often used. Injury as a result of torture or poor conditions in the Branch. Medical negligence. Deterioration of the individual's condition. Give them a number instead of their name. Transfer to the military hospital 'for treatment'. Add the number of the branch from which they came next to their number. Death in hospital as a result of torture or poor care. Request the Military Police to complete the burial procedures. Documentation by the Evidence Office of the Military Police. Given a Coroner's report number. Transport to the designated burial place. Inform the Civil Registry of the death of the detainee based on the reasons listed in the report of the Coroner.

Scenario 4

Arrest. Branch detention centre. Interrogation, during which torture is often used. Injury as a result of torture or poor conditions in the Branch. Medical negligence.

Figure 5.5 Photo of Najha, Google Maps.

Avoiding death or being transferred to a military hospital. Interrogation ends. Transfer to the Military Police headquarters, then the detainee is transferred into the jurisdiction of the Terrorism Court. Transport through the Military Police to the nearest civilian police cordon. The Civilian Police transfer the detainee to the central civilian prison in the governorate. The Political Security Division does not need the Military Police to transfer its detainees to the civilian prison. The Division has its own wing of the prison, which it oversees and manages directly, therefore it transfers its detainees once they are routed to the Judiciary.

Why does the regime document its victims?

Based on previous scenarios, it is apparent that the transport and guard brigades of the Military Police are widely involved in the completion of security work in Syria. The Evidence Office of the Criminal Investigation section of the Military Police also exercises its bureaucratic functions within the broader system and oversees the completion of burials of detainees. This process came to light after the defection of a Military Police officer who carried the alias 'Caesar'. In one of Caesar's interviews, he stated:

At first the name of the deceased was plastered on their body. But within a short period of time the bodies no longer had names, but only numbers. When we arrived at the military hospital there were two numbers on the bodies, either written on adhesive tape or written by a pen on the skin, on the forehead or chest. The adhesive tape was of poor quality, so it often fell off. The first number belongs to the detainee, and the second to the intelligence branch in which they were detained. The Coroner who arrived early in the morning gave a third number for the medical report. The last figure was the most important in our records ... The Coroner recorded the medical report number on a piece of cardboard. He or an intelligence operative placed it near the body or held it in their hand when we took the picture. The hands you see on the pictures I leaked belong to one of them. Sometimes you can see the feet of the coroner or intelligence operative near the body.[6]

This documentation process is managed by the coroners. They were, Caesar stated:

our superiors and we had no right to speak, especially to ask questions. And when one of them gave us an order, we had to obey. He would tell us for example: take pictures of bodies from number one to thirty and then you're dismissed. We had to take more than one picture of the body, so we could quickly identify it in the files. A picture of the face, a picture of the whole body, a side picture, a picture of the chest and the legs. Bodies were grouped by branches, for example, there was a special coroner for Branch 215 of Military Intelligence and another one for the Air Force Intelligence branches. It made it easier for us to take pictures and then classify them later.[7]

According to the functions of the Military Police, especially the Judicial Evidence section, evidence must be collected in 'photographs and writing. These have been documented in the usual documentation methods used by the state and its institutes as a routine act under the responsibility of the Ministry of Defense, which documents all criminal offences under its authority; including persons killed in military actions of both sides, as well as cases of death under torture in prisons and military detention centres'.[8]

Regarding the burial of the bodies, some documents obtained by the Syrian Association for Missing and Conscience Detainees reveal that:

orders from Branch 227 were sent to the Damascus Military Police Branch requesting it to bury the bodies of some of the detainees in a known location in coordination with the Mortuary Office, pursuant to the Decision of the National Security Office ... dated 22/2/2012. Other documents show that the Military Police Branch in Damascus addressed Branch 227 that the necessary action had been taken and sent an annex to the correspondence that insinuate this.[9]

A total of 26,948 photographs of 6,627 detainees imprisoned in 24 detention centres in Damascus were counted. Most of them were from the Military Intelligence branches Raid Brigade 215 and District Branch 227. All the bodies in the photos published by Ceasar were numbered. Of these numbers, one part was to distinguish the detainee, another was the branch number and a third was 'given by the Coroner, who had these numbers serialized in his notebook, one body after the other, from 1 to 5000, after which he moved to the second series of numbers 1/B, 2/B, 3/B, until it reaches 5000/B, then he started with the third series 1/D [Tha'a]. This documentation mechanism omits the third letter of the Arabic alphabet – the T [Ta'a]. He moved to the D without knowing the rationale behind omitting the C. Why does the list contain 5,000 numbers only? Maybe it's all mere routine, nothing more'.[10]

It is clear that the Military Police is responsible for officially photographing the victims. 'It is the responsibility the Military Police to preserve the body in the hospital, although it is not the entity responsible for the torture, except for those detained in its prisons.'[11]

Memory loss and hallucinations

We were transferred from the Southern Region Branch of the Air Force Intelligence (Harasta) to the Military Judiciary, and from it to the Military Police HQ in Al-Qaboun. A month after our arrival, they brought wardens from Saydnaya military prison. Those people applied their discipline methods and punishments to the life in the Branch. The place turned into a miniature and disastrous version of Saydnaya prison. They had no mercy on the ailing or those coming from the Military Police Branch in Homs, Al-Balouni, most of whom suffered severe burns as a result of throwing boiling water or hot oil at them there.

They put us in dormitories above the ground. We reached them through a long corridor that led to a second corridor leading to a new building, as the old detainees explained to us. The new prison had at least 13 dormitories for various cases and crimes. Among them was at least a dormitory designated for those transferred to the Field Military court. The rooms were of different sizes, on average were 6 x 4 metres, similar to our room, no 5.

A strange disease spread among us. I lost the ability to eat, like the others who were infected. If I forced myself to eat, I immediately threw up. Then I entered a state of loss of memory and hallucinations. I was asking myself about tahini, how it's manufactured, and the raw material used in this industry. I struggled to remove this thought from my head, but only to be replaced by a question about the number of the members of my family. I put them on a list, but then I immediately lost focus and forgot where I started. My temperature rose, my colleagues supported me and tried to lower my temperature but to no avail. Days later, the wardens called upon all those ill in our dormitory and sent us underground to a prison with a very large iron room, 9 x 8 metres. Its floor was covered with blankets. The warden threw us over those blankets as if we were dead bodies. They threw us in a terrible way. The head of the dormitory with his gang had a role to play similar to the situation in the Air Force Branch. He dealt with us as a warden and torturer inside the dormitory. After this transfer, they brought us a lot of food, but it was useless as we couldn't eat. Food was already bad and disgusting. At night they brought in dinner and forced us to eat it even if we vomited. Some patients died, including an elderly man from Homs whom the head of the dormitory grabbed and shouted to his face: 'Die . . . die. . . just die!' We were in a long line awaiting death.[12]

In addition to the well-known Military Police detention centres in Al-Qaboun near Damascus, Al-Balouni in Homs and Hanano in Aleppo and others in the rest of the governorates, the Military Police managed prisons under the Ministry of Defense. The details of this management are discussed in the next chapter. However, Military Police are also responsible for the execution of death sentences issued by military courts, the field court, and the war field court. It also undertakes burying bodies of the executed after documenting the execution and completion of the sentence. All this shows that the Military Police is a giant information repository containing thousands of files of those who died under torture, on the gallows or from the bullets of military death squads. All in all, this means that the Military Police represents a crucial dimension of the Syrian security system.

Part One Conclusion

In 2016, a former detainee was invited to give a guest lecture at a Dutch university about his experiences of arrest and detention in Syria. He explained that, in 2011, three plain clothes intelligence operatives arrested him near his university campus, pushed him into the trunk of a car, drove him to an underground dungeon and tortured him for two months. He was never officially charged, never allowed to consult a lawyer, and never found out the identities of the men who had arrested and tortured him. Consequently, he argued, he suffered great physical and psychological scars from his arrest. A full classroom of almost 100 students listened breathlessly for about an hour. When he finished and it was time for a question-and-answer session, a young woman raised her hand and asked: 'But why didn't you go to the police?'

What may sound like a naïve question by an uninformed layperson in fact touches upon the vital issue of the almost unlimited powers that the intelligence agencies enjoyed over any other government agency in Syria. The main function of all the Syrian security and intelligence agencies since 1970 has been to protect the Assad regime from internal danger. All these formations and services are strictly subject to the individual authority of the Commander-in-Chief of the Army and the Armed Forces, the President of the Republic – until 2000 Hafez al-Assad, who was then succeeded by Bashar al-Assad – and subject to his sovereign power until today. Indeed, the power of these services transcend those of the state and the law. The security services can use the infrastructure of all government institutions, from military facilities to schools, to meet their needs, be it as prisons, branches, temporary detention centres or military headquarters. They can undermine the state and reconfigure it to suit their own requirements and objectives. The only red line these powers cannot cross is the position of the President.

These services, in addition to their obvious functional role, have a competitive relationship that contributes to protecting the hard core of the regime from any danger that may emanate from one of these military and security formations or any party thereof. The special forces were on the front lines, together with the Military Intelligence and the Republican Guard, to face Rifaat al-Assad and expel him from Syria to preserve the regime.

Based on this clear role, these formations and services have full authority to decide how to manage any confrontation with the opposition as they see fit. Since 1970, exceptionally high levels of violence have been recorded in most Syrian security and intelligence branches. This violence increases in frequency and intensity during open confrontations with the opposition, for example, what happened between 1976 and 1982, and after the Syrian revolution in 2011. The extreme violence gave these services a horrific reputation among the Syrians and beyond – after all, the Syrian intelligence services have also targeted people of different nationalities, such as Palestinians, Lebanese, Jordanians, Iraqis, and Turks.

It is undeniable that the military security formations and the intelligence services in Syria are disproportionately staffed by Alawites. It seems that there is an unmistakable sectarian-clientelist policy that governs these services, not only by privileging Alawites to enter these agencies, but also by limiting individuals from other sects from entering certain formations – such as the Republican Guard, the Fourth Armoured Brigade, and the Defence Brigades. Military Intelligence is a case in point: it hovers above all other intelligence agencies, and its heads and senior staff since 1974 have all been Alawites. This has also been the case in the Air Force Intelligence. As for the rest of the state institutions, the regime used a deputization mechanism from the army to ensure that its most loyal officers controlled the management of the Political Security Division and the General Intelligence Department. These intelligence services managed to turn Syria into one large prison.

This part of the book has also looked at the role of the Military Police, an often-overlooked agency in Assad's apparatus of violence. The Military Police can be considered the engine oil of the Syrian security and intelligence system. It manages all the central military prisons in Syria, as well as the temporary detention facilities such as Al-Qaboun and Al-Balouni in Homs. Comparing the experiences of the 1980s, in Palmyra and Saydnaya after 2011 it can be confirmed that the Military Police is an institution that preserves its own memory and passes it along. The same levels of violence perpetrated by the Military Police in Palmyra were fully applied in Saydnaya prison after 2011. The Military Police have their own traditions in the management of military prisons: some for times of peace, and others for times of war. Similar to the rest of the services loyal to the Assad regime, the Military Police has turned into a sectarian institution at the management level. With the exception of the Director of Mezze prison from the beginning of the 1970s until 1976 (Rasmi al-Eid), the prison was run by a succession of Alawite loyalist Military Police officers. All administration levels of Palmyra prison were from the Alawite sect, which is also true for Saydnaya prison from its foundation to the present day. The secrecy and sensitivity of the tasks in these prisons prompts the regime to select its operatives only from among its most loyal base.

Poem in Morse Code

In April 1987, a poem was written on the wall of a cell in the Palestine Division prison. Syrian poet Faraj Bayraqdar passed it on to his colleague Akram al-Bunni in the adjoining cell, using the Morse language the prisoners had developed amongst themselves. A whole language with its own origins, complexities and methods, and al-Bunni and Bayraqdar were well versed in it. Bayraqdar tapped on the cell wall that separated him from his colleague Al-Bunni, eleven ticks associated with the letter 'qaaf' (ق) in Arabic. Then he continued tapping, 'Once upon a time ... "Zaman bin Zaman" told me. The fire is proof.'

Bayraqdar went on to recount the poem that he had written in his head after years of hiatus in poetry. Bayraqdar ended the recitation of his long poem by tapping on the wall. Al-Bunni quickly expressed his admiration, but the poet replied with coldness, 'Don't compliment me and give me your real opinion'. Al-Bunni recited the same poem to him by tapping on the wall to assure him of his admiration. However, he made a mistake with one letter and Bayraqdar corrected the mistake by tapping. And they laughed for a long time, wiping the blood of torment from their faces, while Bayraqdar concluded his poem, the title of which was 'A Story':

Master Despair
Inform your master the Sultan
The cell is not narrower than his grave
The cell is not shorter than his age.[1]

Part Two

The Prisons

Introduction

In addition to the prisons run by the intelligence services, the Assad regime's individual prisons are a second core pillar of the Syrian Gulag. The intelligence services act as a vacuum cleaner in society by arresting, torturing, and temporarily detaining people with the intention of eventually channelling them into the individual prisons, which then serve as their final destination. There are three categories of separate prisons: military, civilian, and secret. The military prisons of Mezze, Tadmor, and Saydnaya can then be seen more as camps than prisons, the civilian prisons are a final, milder stage of imprisonment before release, while the secret prisons are above the law.

The military prisons of the Assad regime fall under different umbrellas: those under the Ministry of Defence are the most notable. Although these prisons were actually exclusively for military personnel, the detention centres were always used to punish the Syrian opposition. Many politicians were often detained here for countless years, without any form of trial. The Syrian justice system is not comparable to that in Europe or elsewhere in the world, but has a character all its own. These detention centres were managed by the Military Police of the army and armed forces, specialists in punishment. The Military Police managed both the Mezze military prison, the western and eastern buildings of the Tadmor prison, and to this day manages both the red and white buildings of Saydnaya military prison.

Civilian prisons are in sharp contrast to military prisons. Not only do the collective experiences of detainees differ like night and day: there is almost no torture, fairly reasonable food, and bedding and clothing are much better quality than those in intelligence or military prisons. Prisoners can exercise outside, read books and communicate with each other. There are even cultural activities such as music, poetry, and lectures. This huge difference is mainly because civilian prisons fall under the Ministry of Interior.

Chapter 4 takes a closer look at several civilian prisons: the Citadel Prison, Karakon al-Sheikh Hassan, the Central Prison of Aleppo, the Central Prison of Damascus, the prison in Adra, and the women's prisons of Qatana and Douma.

Chapter 5 offers an overview of the secret prisons, some of which have existed since Hafez al-Assad's 1970 coup, but most of which have mushroomed since the 2011 uprising. Due to prison overcrowding (or, as the regime cynically described it, 'undercapacity'), newly formed militias and elite forces had to take their detainees elsewhere. They solved this problem by setting up ad hoc prisons in makeshift facilities such as farms, apartments, abandoned farms, or simply in the basements of their own private homes. The fundamental problem in studying these prisons speaks for itself: they are secret. How many secret prisons exist in Syria is unclear. This chapter will therefore describe the best-known cases.

This set-up does not prevent the overlap of security and judicial powers. There have been dozens of cases of detainees coming from Military Intelligence departments and undergoing military trials yet being held in a civilian prison. The opposite, however, has not been recorded. A prisoner of a military prison cannot be under the authority of a civilian judiciary in any way. This situation is explained by the overriding jurisdiction of the twin military intelligence agencies (the Military Intelligence and the Air Force Intelligence) over all other state security agencies. It is also justified by the massive power of the Military Judiciary which is considered the highest legal authority in the country.

6

Mezze Military Prison

In 1949, the Mezze military prison was first used as a detention facility for politicians overthrown by Hosni al-Zaim. The prison became a symbol of all coup operations until the united republic with Egypt in 1958, where the name of Syrian intelligence man, Abdelhamid al-Sarraj, came to the fore. During the Sarraj period, Mezze prison became the symbol of suffering and political conflict in the country. The Baath party's assumption of power increased the severity and aggression of the prison. However, its detention periods remained short compared to those that were later recorded when Hafez al-Assad ascended to the presidency. The prison maintained its punitive and political role until its closure in September 2000.

Figure 6.1 General Hosni al-Zaim, from a private collection.

Set-up and management

Between 1923 and 1924, the French army in Syria rehabilitated an old Ottoman fortress into a military headquarters for its soldiers. It used this military HQ as an observation point overlooking the capital Damascus as well as a prison for militants fighting the French occupation of Syria. With the military entering politics a few years after Syria's independence, the military HQ was turned into a political prison. The Mezze prison gained its infamous reputation as the prison of the country's elite, the political and intellectual classes. Suad Jarrous describes Mezze as follows: 'The prison was located at the top of the hill which starts from the Mezze vegetable market and extends upwards to where that building stood. It deserved its reputation as the prison of the elite. Most of those who entered it represented the ruling and educated elites, officers, party members and politicians, over decades of political volatility.'[1]

Barbed wire surrounds the prison's hill, forming three barriers. 'The structure consisted of two blocks, each with two floors. The two blocks were separated by the prison's internal yard. The first block overlooked Damascus and the outer yard of the prison.'[2] Like other military prisons, this one had no heating in the dormitories or the cells. All food allocations and other prison supplies came from the Army and the Armed Forces. The prison administration used military prisoners, 'men absconding military service', as service operatives. These soldiers were forced to distribute food

Figure 6.2 Map of Mezze Prison, Google Maps.

allocations to inmates under the supervision of prison wardens. Considered 'forced labour', they worked continuously to keep the prison corridors and yards clean. They could also be used for other work such as coordinating the days of baths or shaving for political prisoners, transporting the bodies of the executed to ambulances or any work demanded of them.

In 2000, Lebanese newspaper *al-Nahar* published an elaborate description of the prison:

> After passing the outer gate you come to an inner courtyard. On the side of the outer building ran a dark corridor that served the solitary cells, which were 1.5 by 1 m. Those were added to the building at a later stage. In the opposite direction rose a two-floor block. In the lower floor, on the side of the inner yard, were the rooms of the assistant director, the storage room, visiting rooms and investigation rooms. In the middle of this block stood the double iron door that led to the inner section of the prison. The internal section had 6 dormitories and 10 solitary and double cells in its ground-level. Those were called 'the smelly halls'. They were considered the most terrible in the prison. These cells were usually 3 by 2m and each had a mouldy, open toilet and a concrete bench used as a bed. They didn't have any window for ventilation or light. They often hosted those sentenced to death. That level had an internal breathing space of 10 by 8 m. It also had the prison kitchen and bathroom. The upper layer contained six dormitories and a breathing space of 8 by 6 m. It also contained 14 solitary cells and five rooms with beds for 20 people, each of which was 3 by 3 m. The upper and lower dormitories could theoretically accommodate 25 people each, but often held more than 60 people.[3]

The prison had 24 solitary cells, 12 large dormitories and six small ones. One of the cells was called 'Tombo' ('The Tomb') and was designed to hold one person. The cell was designed like an ancient grave, 2 metres long, 80 centimetres wide and 4 metres high. It didn't have a toilet or any other type of services.[4] From 1970 until its closure in September 2000, the prison was headed by three officers. From before the 1970s until 1976, Mezze prison was managed by Colonel Rasmi al-Eid, who was later transferred to head the Military Police Department. He was succeeded by Colonel Bahjat al-Saleh, who continued to manage the prison until 1991, and then by Colonel Barakat al-Osh until the prison's closure in 2000.

The period 1970–2000

Mezze prison had a large presence in Syria's history since the first military coup in 1949 mostly due to the constant political upheaval in the country. The prison became a symbol of coups and power struggles and remained a temporary residence for its inmates. After the Baath Party came to power, however, there was a significant shift as political struggles became intense at both national and Party levels. With this transformation, the prison and other security HQs became spaces to settle accounts;

nevertheless, the prison remained a temporary residence. President Hafez al-Assad came to power in a coup in 1970 and brought with him several variants of the concept of imprisonment. Mezze became a permanent, or at least a prolonged, retreat for political and military opponents from inside and outside the Party.

Ironically, Hafez al-Assad and several of his leaders were inmates in Mezze after the secession coup in 1961. They were arrested together with officers and politicians of Arab Nationalist and Unitarian orientation. Al-Assad and his later Defence Minister, Mustafa Tlass, and Director of the General Intelligence Department, Adnan Dabbagh, were inmates of the fourth dormitory at Mezze prison.[5] This was also the prison into which Hafez Al-Assad threw then President Dr Noureddine Al-Atassi for 22 years on 12 November 1970. Towards the end, Atassi developed cancer and was released two months before his death. Assad also imprisoned the Assistant Secretary General of the Baath Arab Socialist Party, Major General Salah Jadid, who died after 23 years in prison, without ever having faced a trial. They were accompanied by Prime Minister Dr Youssef Zoayn, who was released after 10 years because he was suffering from a terminal illness. He later left the country for Hungary.[6]

These periods of detention were not only the longest Mezze prison witnessed during Assad's reign, they were also the most extensive. The years of Hafez al-Assad's rule saw the imprisonment of large numbers of political prisoners from diverse affiliations: communists, Muslim Brothers, Baathists, and other Syrian opposition political currents, in addition to large numbers of Lebanese and Palestinians. In fact, Mezze was ironically the one Syrian prison in which both Palestinians and Israelis could be found. When one

Figure 6.3 From left to right: Atassi, Assad, Jadeed, 1968, from a private collection.

of Hafez al-Assad's Palestinian clients was killed in May 1966 in Damascus, Assad blamed Yasser Arafat and wanted him sentenced to death. Chief of Staff Salah Jadid disagreed, but Arafat still spent 51 days in solitary confinement in Mezze, and never forgave Assad for it.[7] Israelis, too, were detained in Mezze, especially after the 1973 Yom Kippur War when dozens of prisoners of war were captured. Noah Hertz was a fighter pilot when his airplane was shot down by the Syrian air defence five days into the war. He was mistreated in the Syrian military hospital, where his leg was amputated, and ended up in Mezze, where he became increasingly religious and was finally released after a decade. Not everyone was as lucky. Avraham Lanir (1940–1973) was a Lieutenant Colonel in the Israel Air Force flying a reconnaissance mission in Syrian air space, when his airplane was shot down. The Syrian intelligence immediately picked him up and, after a short hospital stay, moved him to Mezze prison, where he was tortured to death. His wife received his mutilated body on 6 June 1974.[8] The highly acclaimed Israeli drama series 'Prisoners of War' (*Khatufim*; חטופים) depicts three Israeli soldiers captured by the Syrian army in Lebanon in the 1980s and held in Mezze prison. In one of the very first filmic representations of the Syrian intelligence and prison system, the series shows physical and psychological torture with evocative power.[9]

The prominent Turkish socialist Mihri Belli (1915–2011) was forced into exile due to the military coup on 12 March 1971. He fled to Syria by liaising with the Palestinian Liberation Organization but, on 20 September of that year, Military Intelligence arrested him together with his driver and his local guide. In his memoirs, he paints a bleak picture of his 100-day imprisonment, laced with disappointment about expecting to find a socialist government in Syria but ending up in a horrific prison with other socialists:

> The *fedai* ward was a concrete place of 15–20 metres on all sides. We were lying on concrete bunk beds on the right and left, and on the floor in the middle passage, nearly 100 humans were lined up like in fish cans. It was winter. The hill on which Mezze was founded was the highest point of Damascus Plateau. It was almost always under snow. We were trying to protect ourselves from the cold with the old blankets given by the administration.

To pass the days, he played chess with kneaded pieces of bread dough, because there was never anything to read in Mezze. When the prisoners went on hunger strike to protest about their conditions, Belli became the spokesperson for dormitory and castigated the warden:

> You took over this building from the French. You use it as a prison like them. Forget about the building, but you follow the French regulations as it is. At the time of the French, those who were kept here were Arab patriots, the guards were French. Nowadays who is kept inside is Arab, and so are his guards. This is the only difference. The aim of those who wrote that regulation implemented by the French was to crush and suppress Arab patriots and to break their will to fight. If you try to apply the same regulations to the Palestinian fighters today, this man will not go and fight Zionism. Is this what you want? Probably not.

The warden laughed and left without saying a word. Nothing changed in Mezze prison. Mihri Belli was released on New Year's 1972; he left Syria and never returned.[10]

Until the end of 1979, the Mezze military prison was characterized by being an investigation centre in addition to being a central prison. The wanted person was arrested by one of the Military Security or the General Intelligence services. These Departments, through their branches, conducted a preliminary interrogation of the detainee using their usual methods. The detainee would be then transferred to Mezze prison for further interrogation by a high-level security committee. The committee included the commanders of military, Air Force and General Intelligence, as well as the official in charge of the National Security Office, the prison director, and sometimes the commander of the Military Police. Under the management of this committee worked lower-ranking officers and torture operatives. Former detainee, Said Hawa, narrates:

'The Director of the National Security Office Naji Jamil, the Head of Military Intelligence Hikmat al-Shihabi,[11] the Director of the General Intelligence Department Adnan Al-Dabbagh, the Military Intelligence Officer Ali Douba, the Commander of the Military Police Ali Madani, the Director of the prison Rasmi al-Eid, the Director of Air Force Intelligence Mohammed al-Khuli and others cooperated in interrogating me . . . .'[12]

Figure 6.4 Naji Jamil – behind Al Assad- Damascus University 1978, from a private collection.

Figure 6.5 Marwan Hadid, from a private collection.

This Committee interrogated many politicians and leaders opposed to the Assad regime. One of the most prominent was the Islamic leader Marwan Hadid. Abu Ibrahim, one of his followers, narrates:

> Sheikh Marwan was severely tortured in Mezze prison. He was placed in the second solitary cell, and I was in the first one, so I knew what was going on with him in detail. He went on hunger strike in protest of ill-treatment. He became emaciated and his weight dropped drastically, from about 100 kgs to about 50. He was transferred to military hospital 601 where he died in June 1976, one year after his arrest.[13]

Hadid's death as a result of torture and lack of any healthcare did not change the reality for the rest of the detainees in Mezze. The prison maintained its aggression from the beginning of the 1970s until the end of the 1990s, with cases of 'switching-off' of some detainees recorded at the beginning of 1973. Former detainee Jerios Hames writes:

In the corner of a cell in Mezze prison, there were iron chains to which the detainee would be restrained with his head fixed inside Iron pliers. Then from a pipe in the ceiling water drops would continuously drop on his head until he passed out. At night the power was cut off. A giant torturer, specifically selected for the task, opened the cell door. He wore horns on his head and a scary mask on his face. He would shout at the bleeding face of a detainee exhausted from all the torture. I recall that two of the detainees lost their minds in this brutal practice. The torturer who did this job was about 190cm tall, he was Abdullah Al-Herek from Al-Salamiyeh.[14]

Madness and Israelis in Mezze

My cell was no 8, it was internal and overlooked the entrance of the prison. They apparently put me in it to ensure I was under the direct supervision of the prison administration. But from it I could see the newcomers to Mezze prison. On bathing day, I could see all the inmates ... Some of the dungeon dwellers suffered sudden episodes; we could hear their screams when these episodes occurred ... The war of October 1973 started while we were in the solitary cell. The Mezze prison was bombed but the rocket deviated and landed close ... They took us out of the solitary cells because they needed them to hold the Jewish prisoners. Otherwise, we would have stayed in those cells for years. That's how I ended up in a dormitory with Nasserists imprisoned following the tension over the Constitution and subsequent events ....[15]

Whether through direct arrest or transfer from a security branch, the moment the detainee arrived at the prison, they underwent a series of procedures. The process began with the documentation of their personal information and arresting authority in the prison registry. He was then subjected to a reception torture session, followed by the inspection ritual of the Military Police 'completely stripped down and performing safety movements'. All personal belongings: money, watch, rings, chains, belt, etc. were taken and placed in the deposits area. They were then moved to a solitary cell, to keep them isolated from the world and other prisoners.

The day following their arrival, or a few days later, the detainee would be taken to the interrogation committee. Former detainee Mahmoud Tarjuman writes:

I passed through the iron gate and led directly towards the storage room where the delivery of detainees is processed. I signed my name on the 'honor' register, and that's where the role of the arrest patrol ended ... I was transferred to cell no 8, which could barely accommodate one person. The cell was devoid of everything, except from the red spots scattered on its walls and door in a surreal artistic way ... The next morning, complete calm ... Suddenly, a loud call on no 8, along with the rest of the numbers ... The battle began. The interrogation committee is ready and excited. My turn came, and I was forced out of my cell at gun point ... as well as beating, punches, and insults ... This interrogation committee gained great fame in the country. Its members were all high-ranking officers ... There, in the centre of the interrogation room, which was an infamous as its lords, sat the Chair of the committee like a God. In front of him lay a dish filled with all types of fruits and vegetables: lettuce hearts, apples, grapes, pomegranates... He enjoyed eating as much as he enjoyed torture ... The act of the play began!! Questioning and beating, questioning and insults, a question after a question ... They wanted names, just names, even if they did not belong to anyone, even if they were not in the civil register. The more names the committee extracted the more it was successful, proved its loyalty and gained more stars on the shoulders ... An hour or more later the Chair of the committee uttered his favourite phrase, the one he loved the most: 'take him', that is, to the storage room. There begins the second act of the play and the most prominent, a real human tragedy. Torturers on the one hand, and the 'arrested human' on the other. Some of them whipping, others beating and kicking, others splashing cold water while others are tying wires or ropes around necks. Between them all lay the 'arrested human' screaming in pain, grunting, and begging, shedding tears and dripping blood ... I spent the first phase of my first arrest moving between cell no 8, the interrogation room, and the storage room.[16]

The torture chamber known as the 'storage room' included tools such as the wheel, different types of whips, and a wooden ladder in addition to devices used for electric torture.

The letter that one detainee, who spent nine years in Mezze military prison, sent his daughter summarizes the reality of the prison from 1976 to 1985. He wrote the letter using a nail he found in the solitary cell, memorized it, and then published it after his release from prison.

I don't know if this pen (nail) I hold in my hand is able to paint the picture with all its blackness, thorns and blood ... How can my pen convey to you, my daughter, my feelings? Days rolled. Torturers rotated. The day was darker than the night ... Another one is asking me for more information. I was put for the sixth time in the wheel: that whip is ruthless, my dear daughter. The torturer does not understand Arabic, he does not believe in God nor in man ... There I found a friend of mine hanging between the earth and the sky, bleeding from his nose, head and sides ... What happened had happened, then the prison doctor came to me to treat the wounds. He asked me about my name and number and the reasons. He left just as he entered out of fear of the warden ... I was called upon once ... I don't remember the count exactly, for things got mixed after a day or two. I heard the guard screaming my apartment number, sorry, my cell number in the ground floor ... The warden and the torturer were occupied away from me so I managed to peek through a small hole in the door to see a new convoy arriving to its resting place, blindfolded, handcuffed, some elderly, some disabled, others children ... They were directed into the storage room; the festive reception area. The convoy went in there and came out an hour or two later. Their features, looks and even colours have changed from torture . . . The cells are full and the corridors and yards are teeming with hundreds. There was a 'housing crisis' everywhere so this group was taken to the bathroom. There, the man stood naked for a day or more until a permanent cell or place is arranged for him . . . The days rolled slowly. Minutes were like hours. We woke up and went to sleep to torture and torment . . . I was moved between cells, all to the whims of the warden. What I saw was chilling. Swollen hands, feet so electrocuted they became paralyzed, as if they don't belong to the human body. Another lost his mind so started praying to God in language that no other human could understand. Another remembered his wife and daughter, and asked God to help them cope with his absence. Bodies here, bodies there, all motionless, all without souls . . . Until the next letter.[17]

Bread chess and a butterfly

I was transferred to solitary cell no 6 on the top floor. A small pretty cell, innocent as a child. The best thing about it was a small round window in its wall, allowing sunlight and air to enter. I took off what was left of my bloody, coloured undershirt. I stood there, exposing my body to the rays of the sun . . . I started arranging my apartment . . . For the stay may be long. I tried to make chess pawns from the stone-hard loaf of bread I received every morning. I painted the squares on the floor, and started playing against myself. I would move a pawn here then sit on the other side and move another pawn there, and so on until one of us won . . . The Chief Warden came to me one day as I was playing chess, and said: 'Whom are you playing with?' I said: 'With the person sitting in front of me'. He said: 'But I don't see anyone!' I said: 'And this is the ultimate calamity'. In the second or third week, a butterfly flew in through the net. I thought, at first glance, that she lost her way and the wind forced her into the prison cells . . . She wandered around in the air of the room as she pleased for an hour or so. She landed on the ground after hardships, and laid her first egg, the size of a pinhead . . . Fatigued, she died. I cried warm tears for her . . .[18]

Disciplinary regulations for Mezze

In addition to the reception and inspection rituals at Mezze prison, its inmates underwent a list of strict instructions and disciplinary procedures. The administration conducted surprise inspections of the dormitories. Former detainee Mufid Najm narrates:

One of the horrors we experienced in this prison on regular basis was the inspection campaigns that the prison administration carried out almost every two weeks. These were more like a real terror party for prisoners. These campaigns were surprising and only took place at night. The door would suddenly open, and before we knew it a large group of prison operatives broke into the dormitory screaming, cursing and stinging our bodies with their whips. We had to quickly gather over one of the two cement benches, as ordered. We had to sit in a squat position, with our backs turned to them, and our heads bent until they almost touched our knees. The operatives of the prison would then immediately begin searching everything, throwing everything wherever and however, including the covers that we used as mattresses.[19]

Discipline regulations also included the daily roll call of prisoners. The process took place at 14.00, in preparation for the change of the guards. Najm paints a bleak picture:

The procedure entailed that we had to scramble to sit on both sides at maximum speed, in straight lines of three persons. Bending our heads until they almost touch our knees. The stench of the dormitory, as a result of lack of ventilation and overcrowding, disturbed the operatives so they often rushed through the procedure. As a result, we spent less time in this demeaning position, which represents their constant desire to humiliate us.[20]

These regulations forbade growing head or facial hair. Najm remembers the humiliation:

They forced us, almost every two months, to insure we had the price of manual shaving tools for the head. However, the fact was that they only bought one or two machines, and then moved them from one dormitory to the other ... The machine would break down and start plucking the hair causing pain for the prisoners ... We were trying to overcome those pains and suffering by turning this tragic scene into a comic one, where the groans and moans mixed with laughter and sarcastic comments.[21]

The central bathroom in Mezze, located on the lower floor, was communal and bathing happened at night. Mufid Najm continues:

We were gathered by the stinging whips, semi-naked, in the outdoor bathroom. They placed every two prisoners under a shower head ... Before we could remove the soap from our bodies, the prison operatives would start yelling at us to turn off the water taps and put on our underwear. If one is a little late in removing soap off their body, they would pull him out from under the shower by the stings of their whips. The duration of the bath did not exceed three minutes; rarely five. They weren't keen on ensuring the hygiene of the prisoner. With the large numbers of prisoners, they were not concerned with what diseases could affect prisoners' health.[22]

In addition to roll calls, inspections and bathing, the health care in Mezze was limited to tetanus shots, pain killers and anti-inflammatory drugs. Those prisoners in critical condition were taken to military hospital 601. Prison food was limited to military allocations – the same as food used by Military Intelligence branches. However, they allowed the procurement of food from outside the prison. Prices inside the prison could be up to three or four times the market price.

Tarjuman recounts:

> Food was a disaster, fatal starvation and unbelievable thirst. We raised our voices and wrote petitions, asking for improved conditions relating to the quantity and quality of food. The management ignored our requests for a long period of time. In the end, they came up with a system they called the 'invoice' which was a money-making mechanism for them. They allowed us to prepare weekly lists of the food items we needed. They placed themselves as intermediaries between us and a greedy merchant in the local market.[23]

The list of disciplinary instructions also determined the mechanism and time of exercise. Tarjuman notes: 'One day the guard opened the door and said: "Now you are allowed to breathe. Five minutes a day in the morning, but pay attention, the commands are strict: it is forbidden to run. It is forbidden to stop, even to drink water. You have to go around the yard calmly." I went out early in the morning to the small yard next door. There I spent the most beautiful five minutes in my life. . . .'[24] This mechanism was not binding on VIP detainees, who received special treatment. The doors of their rooms remained open, they could exit to the yard at any time, exercised and listened to the radio.

The disciplinary regulations did not neglect the visits. Those took place in two forms: either inside a small room with a chair and an office table behind which sat one of the guards. Or standing at the prison's inner gate which consists of two opposite doors of iron bars and overlooks the yard. Those two doors were 1 metre apart. Two Military Police operatives stood inside this space between the two doors, while the prisoner stood behind the interior door with his family on the opposite side behind the exterior door. Tarjuman writes:

> Suddenly we learned we could have a visit: 20 minutes, once or twice every month or two, depending on the prison conditions and the will of the administration. I was preparing a list of questions and answers ... My turn came and I rushed towards the place of the visit next to the storage room, the 'Reception Room'. I stood behind the inner iron bars, my family stood behind the outer bars, and between us the guard, his weapon and his watch ... Children's smiles become invisible and words get lost across the bars; questions mix with the answers. Big crowd and so much noise that you think you may need a speaker next time. Only moments later, our faithful guard points to his watch ... and the twenty minutes end before they even begin.[25]

A dream in Mezze

When we were in Mezze Prison I dreamed that the doors of our cells were opened – as if there was a divine power in the dream – and we started to come out of our cells. The prison guards were looking at us without saying anything. When we reached the prison yard ... the guards started shooting at us from above. But the strange thing was that they fired and no bullets came out. The prison was full, and there were lots of us. We all came out as if we were in a demonstration. The guards ran toward us. They encircled us and started shooting, and no bullets came out. So, they attacked us physically and started beating us. Out of excruciating pain and hunger, I woke up. I looked around me and found that I was still in the prison cell. The doors were closed, and people were asleep.[26]

Life in Mezze

The long list of disciplinary regulations, the changing conditions and numbers of detainees after 1980, produced a much harsher prison system. Major overcrowding saw more than 100 detainees crammed into dormitories which were only 12 m by 6 m. Prisoners often had to wait up to two hours to use the toilet. Overcrowding naturally reduced the sleeping space, which was often a bench only 34 or 35 cm wide in the dormitory or the corridor. This forced the prisoners to sleep 'head-to-toe'.

The door of the dormitory opened onto a long corridor separating two concrete benches half a metre high and 180 cm wide on both sides of the dormitory; at the end of the corridor was the toilet. The prison administration filled these spaces entirely. Old detainees occupied their own spots on one of the benches, while new detainees slept in the corridor. The air in the dormitory came from a single opening located at the top of its rear wall. A small window of only 30 by 20 cm made it almost impossible to ventilate the dormitory. Najm lamented: 'We were breathing the air coming out of each other's lungs. That small, high window was our only connection with the outside world in addition to one local newspaper, which the prisoners who had some money paid for, and which we had to return it the next day, without a scratch nor a word written on.'[27]

All this was incorporated into a system designed to catch any lapses of the detainees and punish them. Najm wrote:

After the lights were turned off by the prison officers at 21.00, we are obliged to refrain from any movement for any reason, even if to go to the toilet and even if you were ill. Whoever was caught during the successive raids, carried out by the prison guards, through the Judas window, which the warden opened in conjunction with turning the lights on in the dormitory, was immediately identified by the chief of the dormitory. He got his share of punishment early the next morning. They were looking for any way to practice violence against us, because often, it was enough for the warden to notice that you were moving in your sleep during those raids, to teach you to 'stick to your location', which would keep you up all night stressed and anxious, waiting for the punishment of the morning . . . It was enough for any operative of the prison to open that window in the morning or evening and see you walk in your place for him to take you to the yard and give you the punishment you deserve. If you are caught doing any sort of exercise, God's wrath came upon you, and you must expect anything.[28]

These conditions, as well as the lack of hygiene and ventilation, caused the spread of diseases, especially skin diseases:

It was normal for lice and scabies to spread rapidly among prisoners, especially with barely any washing of the clothes. This forced the prison administration to try to stop its spread among us, by isolating the infected in special cells for treatment until they recovered, then return them to their dormitories. Everything was awful there, far worse than any imagination. This pushed the vast majority of the prisoners to worshiping the divine, even those who did not practice religious rituals outside the prison, hoping for God to grant them salvation and a nearby release.[29]

All these conditions overlapped with the different backgrounds of the detainees in the same dormitory. Some were members of the military who were punished for looting, especially members of the Defence Brigades, while others had Islamic, pro-Iraq-Baathists or communist backgrounds. Some prisoners were accused of smuggling or non-political crimes. This wide diversity of political and cultural affiliations created a kind of conflict. Some became affiliated with the prison management who used them to play the role of wardens inside their dormitories. They relayed information to the administration, which inflicted torture and punishment based on the news that was relayed, thus decreasing the free spaces political detainees had even in their dormitories. Political conversations took place in whispers for fear of those harmful 'informants'.

One category of detainees at Mezze were Kurds accused of Kurdish nationalism. For the Syrian Kurds, Newroz was not only an annual celebration of the beginning of spring, but also an annual ritual for arrest, torture, and trauma. M.S.H., an Arabized Kurd from the Ruknaddin neighbourhood in Damascus, was arrested the day after Newroz 1987 for singing songs in Kurdish at an illegal meeting. Plain clothes Mukhabarat officers nabbed him, smashed his guitar on his head, and drove him blindfolded to a prison, which only five months later he found out was Mezze. He was interrogated by a brute speaking with a distinct Alawite accent. After the usual *dulab, falaqa*, electrocution, whipping, threats of sexual violence, and endless insults, he was sent off and stayed in prison for two years. On Newroz 1989, he was kicked out of a car at Umayyad Square. Blinded by the sunlight, it took him two hours to get to his house in Ruknaddin, where his mother fainted when she saw him at the door. M.S.H. had lost 20 kilos, continued to suffer from stomach pains, and soon fled Syria, never to return.[30]

The hospitality of the rats

My sleeping space was at the end of the corridor which ran between two half-metre high benches. My space was next to the dormitory sink that erected at the front of the toilet; part of the drain between the two was exposed. The dormitory was filled with dozens of prisoners, whom we later learned were either detained on charges of corruption or embezzlement, or were members of the Defence Brigades accused of robbery and rape at gun point. There were no political prisoners among them ... I folded the blanket in two folds, so it served as both a mattress and a cover. The prisoner next to me advised me to cover my head with the blanket while sleeping. That was to prevent the rats that came out at night from the sewers when the lights went off, from jumping on my face during their night tour ... We had to adapt to the new reality of the prison, and to keep its strict rules, for when the warden opened the judas window, we were forbidden from looking, or even glancing towards the door. If the door opened fully, however, we all had to immediately squat wherever we were, bowing our heads to the point where they would almost touch our thighs, so that we could not see anything of what was happening around us, or the identity of the operatives who entered. If anyone tried to sneak a peek and was caught by the warden, he had to bear the consequences, where the wheel in the yard outside will be waiting for him, with a severe punishment that would leave him with bleeding feet.[31]

All of the above divided the prison into three levels of detainees. The veterans, detained from the beginning of the 1970s until 1979, enjoyed a kind of quiet residence. The post-1980 detainees were divided into two sections: the first were those settled in the prison after a trial. The second were the temporary inmates awaiting field trial, then transfer to other prisons. Those two sections were treated similar to branch detainees and were subject to strict and harsh discipline regulations, reduced or increased depending on the political situation outside the prison. These two groups came from different political affiliations: Communists from the Labour League or politburo, pro-Iraq Baathists, and Muslim Brothers. All were classified as opposition to the Assad regime. The third level of detainees were the ruling political elite, the former leadership, who had been arrested at the end of 1970, and were known in prison as 'chamber detainees'.

They were isolated from the two other types of detainees. They are about 10 detainees who occupied the top level. There was a patio bordering a number of small rooms with a bed or two. Their doors were always open and they had freedom of movement. Their stay in prison was closer to house arrest. They were assigned special Military Police operatives to deal with and had a direct relationship with the administration. We were in the school dormitory which overlooked their yard and we could see them walking, exercising or listening to the small radio.[32]

Infiltrating Mezze

MSI, a young Kurdish man who had sympathies with the Kurdistan Democratic Party (KDP), in the 1980s was studying architecture at the University of Damascus, where he befriended Moawiya al-Deiri, son of Ishaq al-Deiri, the director of Political Security prisons. He also befriended Nasrin al-Khouli, the daughter of Mohammed al-Khouli, the infamous head of Air Force Intelligence. For one of his assignments in the third year of his Architecture degree, these high-level contacts allowed him to choose any building in Damascus for architectural examination. He suggested to Moawiya that he study prisons, as a pretext so he could bear witness to the conditions of the detainees. Any plan to gain access to these top-security prisons, which would have been impossible for ordinary citizens, was easy due to Ishaq al-Deiri's position. They were granted written permission to study Mezze and Saydnaya (which was still under construction). The text below is an account of MSI's visit to Mezze in 1983.

MSI's visit to Mezze 1983

Mouawya and MSI received written information about two prisons of Damascus:

- the prison of Mezza, located on a mountain;
- the prison of Saydnaya.

The information included details about the construction period and the layout of the prisons. They also asked for the prison drawings which were provided to them. MSI told Mouawya's father that they also wanted to take photos and visit. However, taking pictures was prohibited.

An excursion was organized to Mezza. A military jeep came to pick them up. Only Mouawya and MSI went. They had a map of the prison. On the way, the driver had to stop often on MSI's instructions. He also wanted to take a good look at the surroundings, a prohibited area. They arrived at a sign 'forbidden entry, for anyone'. This was the first checkpoint. The driver had to identify himself. They had to drive down into a cave. At a depth of 30 metres, the jeep was left behind. There a system of corridors began. Walking they went in there. They entered the second corridor. They were stopped by two sturdy men. The driver stayed behind with the men. He and Mouawya each received an emblem, square, round with a diagonal line after the two policemen had verified them by telephone. One of the policemen accompanied them.

They arrived at a door in a corridor 3 metres wide and 5 metres high. Many old chains were hanging at the door. There was an old-fashioned lock. They passed this door and saw policemen sitting behind three or four desks. They were taken to a cell gallery. They measured out a cell. There were no windows. Only a small air hole. No electricity. Black walls. There were scary faces painted on the wall. There were

---

holes in the floor with dirty sewage. It stank. They couldn't measure it properly because it was dirty. MSI agreed with Mouawya that for reasons of time they would each measure a part of the prison. His intention was to see if there were any friends of the Party there. He asked the policeman to open some closed doors because he wanted to measure the rooms. He was measuring in Kurdish so that the prisoners present could hear him. It was a gallery with cells on either side. This gallery opened onto a central square. Star-shaped galleries open onto this. In the cells he saw Arabs, people from India, but also two Kurdish friends.

The two Kurdish friends recognized him and were shocked. They thought, he was a prisoner. He said in Kurdish, 'The Party sent me.' They knew that he was an engineer by training. When he mentioned the agreed code word (Rok = first sunshine) they immediately started talking to him. These friends were Djuan and Hussein. They said: 'We have been severely tortured here. They wanted the names of our party members. We did not give them.' They had no fingers left. They were cut off. They showed their feet. These were blue from the chains. Their bodies were burned. They had received electric shocks. They looked like corpses. They were psychologically broken. They were extremely emaciated. They cried during the conversation. He said to them: 'Maybe I will come back.' They asked him to pass on to their families that they were alive, that they were being interrogated and tortured, that they were receiving medical treatment, and that the food was inedible. They had no shoes. They had long beards and mustaches and wore dirty clothes. He could no longer talk to them in Kurdish. He had to go to another room.

If there were no Kurds in a cell, he stayed for a few minutes. In another cell was an Arab. This one asked him who he was. He said he was a journalist. The Arab said that he was had been accused of being a member of the Al Amal Al Shouai (Communist Party). He asked him if he could write an article about the conditions in the prison so that a human rights delegation could come to investigate. He complained about the food. He could not see all the cells. He saw 20 of the approximately 80 cells in this gallery. He did not see the other corridors. He also met other prisoners, one of whom showed his one blind eye. Yet another showed the scar where his penis had been removed. Another showed scars all over his body. He was able to provoke reactions by telling Arabic-speaking prisoners that he was a journalist. Mouawya and Issa saw each other again in the square. They asked each other how they were going to get back out. He told Mouawya that their work was not complete and that they should make another appointment to come back. However, this second appointment did not happen because of a failed attack on Hafez al-Assad in 1983 by the Aghwan Al Muslimin. Assad suffered a knee injury during the attack . In response, Rifat Al-Assad bulldozed Tatmour (Palmira) prison and prohibited anyone from visiting prisons. As a result of this official decision, he was unable to complete the project.[33]

Changes in prison life

With the renewal of the presidential term of President Hafez al-Assad in 1985, the detainees expected the usual amnesty. Nothing was issued, but the prison administration decided to improve the conditions of the detainees. Najm describes these changes:

> The blankets that were covering the windows on the outside corridor were taken down to ventilate the dormitory in which we were suffocating; we had been asking for this for a long time. They also allowed us, for the first time, to bring in some books and those who could afford it could buy a small radio. Since the vast majority of prisoners had no money, because they were forbidden from receiving visitors or communicating with their families in any way, only two inmates could afford a radio. They became the source of news for everyone in that turbulent period, when the fronts of the Iraq–Iran war and the civil war in Lebanon were raging. This entailed that everyone gathered around the radio eagerly to hear the news from London Radio or Monte Carlo, which were our sources of news every day. Two weeks after that they let us out for exercise for the first time. It was for 15 minutes.[34]

The following year, 1986, however, came loaded with misery. It was one of the worst and harshest years of imprisonment. During that time, the Syrian regime was suffering from a severe and suffocating economic crisis. Sanctions had been imposed by most neighbouring countries and world powers. Food was scarce for all Syrians. This was reflected in the lives of prisoners in Mezze. Najm offers a vivid description:

> We were offered small amounts of bread and food ... both were of poor quality. The bread was stale and smelled bad because of its age and poor storage ... The miserable amount of meat that was served to us twice a week required two people, or one volunteer from amongst us, to strip it off the bone, stack it and then distribute it in quantities proportional to the number of prisoners, often over eighty, very accurately ... The prisoner's daily allowance was no more than two loaves of military bread. The fruit consisted of grapes or dates, not exceeding five ... While our daily lunch always consisted of poorly cooked rice and bulgur, along with cooked cauliflower or eggplant broth. Because we were served the same food over the years, we would lose any appetite for food when we smelled it, despite our hunger.[35]

Presidential candidate in Mezze

One morning, a prisoner nicknamed Ba'boud Al-Hayat, stood suddenly on the edge of the high bench of the dormitory. He looked stressed and emotional as he asked everyone to be silent and listen to what he was about to say, which surprised everyone. He remained quiet for a few moments as he pondered the faces of the prisoners around him. He then announced in a strong and tense voice that the national leadership of the Arab Socialist Baath Party, following the president's illness, had nominated him to be the president. Applause and expressions of support broke immediately, despite the state of astonishment and bewilderment that followed this sudden and strange behavior. This sudden phenomenon was a strange and funny event that took everyone in the dormitory by surprise, breaking the monotony and inertia of life. It had awakened their sense of humor and bitter irony, after everyone realized that the devastating consequences of imprisonment had begun to take their toll. This scene repeated almost daily for more than two weeks amidst fun and humorous comments, but at different times, until, one day, the commotion of the prisoners reached the guards. They hurried to open the door of the dormitory to see what was happening . . . Our presidential candidate returned, with his feet swollen from the beatings, cursing those who implicated him in running for the presidency of the State . . . .[36]

Like other military prisons, Mezze has seen military field trials, as well as executions. The process was carried out by transferring those sentenced to death to solitary cells. Najm writes:

They would force us to sleep early, and then the successive checks on the dormitory doors would begin, to make sure that there was no movement among the prisoners, and that everyone had taken to sleep. As our dormitory overlooked the inner courtyard of the prison, where the executions were carried out, we could hear the sounds of iron pipes being erected in preparation for the executions . . . The first thing that Military Police officers did when they opened the cell door was to handcuff the detainee after confirming his name, and then another operative put duct tape on his mouth, after which they took him to the place of execution.[37]

Execution was a direct and quick way to end the life of any opponents. Another way, however, was adopted for sideline opponents: leaving them in prison until they died. The previous leadership that Assad put in prison at the end of 1970 was not the only example of this. The story of the Officer Akl Qurban is a perfect example of how Hafez al-Assad retaliated against his enemies.[38] Qurban was kidnapped from Lebanon after fleeing there following Assad's rise to power. He was put in a solitary prison cell in Mezze. Najm explains:

His crime was that during a security meeting in the mid-1960s, he got into a heated disagreement with Hafez al-Assad, and eventually spat on him in contempt. Assad did not forget that insult, so when he became in the supreme position of power, he took his evil revenge, and put him in this worst cell and ordered him to receive the worst treatment for the rest of his life. Every day, with each meal he received his share of beating, which led him to breakdown and go crazy. He died inside that terrifying cell, in which he spent ten continuous years.[39]

Prison conditions did not change during the 1990s. Levels of violence decreased compared to previous years. However, the methods and allowed duration for toilets and showering remained the same.[40] The same food and the same quality remained despite the reduction in the number of inmates because large numbers of them had been transferred to Saydnaya military prison, which opened in 1987.

Those who witnessed the closure of the Mezze military prison in 2000 confirmed that the situation remained the same, with some improvements. Exercise was allowed twice a day, for about half an hour each time. However, the prison administration maintained discipline and daily procedures. An 'Invoice' was issued every two weeks to buy vegetables and a general invoice, once a month, covered the rest of the prisoners' needs.

> Ironically, purchasing from outside was allowed, but we had no money, nor did we receive visits. The Prison Director however sent us some military uniforms in replacement of our damaged clothes. The prison administration facilitated many services for those who had money, such as bringing food from outside the prison, however they forbade cooking utensils in the prison.[41]

This purchase system and provisions of services for money did not affect the prison's general system. The administration banned communication between dormitories. As one former detainee narrated, 'if we spoke we got punished … During the inspection, we all had to sit on one bench in the dormitory, each 3 on a mattress and in lines to make it easier to count us. During the inspection, the prison drowned in complete silence'.[42] The time of the roll call changed from 14:00 to once in the morning and again in the evening. The roll call began with an instruction to 'inspect' and ended with an instruction to 'release'. The instruction also applied to the bathroom: 'We entered the showers together. We had 5 minutes. It started with the opening of the water and ended with the instruction "wash yourself"… Life inside the prison was run with instructions only.[43]

Mezze prison maintained the quality of its own bread, the *samoun*, from its opening until its closure. As one detainee remembered: 'They handed out two pieces of French bread [*samoun*] a day to each detainee. We thought it was a good thing, but then found out that when it cooled it became as hard as a rock. The food was generally of good quality but came in small quantities.[44] Improvement in food quality was accompanied by an improvement in health care, as the administration started asking for a weekly list of patients. The head of the dormitory then handed these over to the sergeant in charge and some health care was provided.

Secret Election room in Mezze

On the day of Bashar al-Assad's first election, they asked us to vote. We went down to the ground floor in our dirty ragged clothes, most of us barefoot. Brigadier-General Barakat Al-Osh ordered his operatives to bring us some khaki military suits instead of our clothes, along with plastic slippers. He then explained to us the mechanism for free elections and informed us that there was a secret room isolated with a small blanket, which we can us to cast our votes. He said that we were free to vote positively or negatively and explained this to us using the election paper. He affirmed that we had the right to vote since we received no sentence yet. Days after those elections, Mezze prison was closed in September 2000, and we were transferred to Saydnaya military prison.[45]

The closure of the Mezze prison did not end the chapter of military–political prisons. The Saydnaya military prison has maintained its penal work since it opened in 1987.

7

Palmyra (Tadmor) Military Prison

High fences of tenacious cold cement . . .
Control towers . . .
Minefields . . .
Barriers and check points . . .
Fortifications and highly trained military units . . .
Lastly, so many examples of pure national horror
O, names of God!
Even if the whole of Syria falls,
This prison . . . is impossible to fall.
==
Has it ever occurred to any artist
To paint a flawless blue sky
Wearing a scarf of barbed wire?
Whomever once stood in one of the courtyards of Palmyra prison
and peeked up,
would have seen this unfortunate painting,
and would have realized what genius nurtured our reality and our dreams![1]

Introduction

Palmyra is considered the most famous military prison in Syria. It gained that reputation from its harsh and deadly arrest conditions. The prison fell under the Army and the Armed Forces, was managed by the Military Police and was built in three stages. The first section was built during the French occupation and was used as a military outpost and desert penal colony in the Syrian desert. Later, that same military point was named the Zenobia barracks. The second section of the prison was built in the 1960s to be used as a prison for judicial military offenses, deserters of military service, or any other legal violations committed by military personnel. The third section of the prison was built at the end of the 1970s and the beginning of the 1980s in preparation for transferring detainees of the Muslim Brotherhood and other opposition parties from security branches, civil prisons and Mezze prison to Palmyra. The prison underwent a series of expansions and renovations until the closure of its political section in 2001.

Figure 7.1 Faraj Bereqdar, from his collection.

Palmyra was first used as a political prison in 1966. Some leaders of the Muslim Brotherhood and Hizb al-Tahrir al-Islami were detained there, among them Abdel Fattah Abu Gheddeh and Marwan Hadid, who died in Mezze prison in 1976. One of those arrested in Palmyra at the time was the nonviolent thinker Jawdat Said. They were all released following the Six-Day War, the 'Naksa' of June 1967. After that, Palmyra was absent from the political scene until 1980. Abdullah al-Naji explains why:

> Events escalated in the early months of 1980, especially following the escape of some Muslim Brotherhood detainees from the General Intelligence prison in Kafr Sousseh on 25 May. The Palmyra project came to light even before its new sections were completed. Military and judicial prisoners were released from Palmyra on a presidential amnesty decree in preparation for the transfer of political detainees to it.[2]

Since its official launch in May 1980, the political prison in Palmyra has been run by Faisal Ghanem, who was close to Rifat Al-Assad, the brother of Hafez Al-Assad and the commander of the Defence Brigades strike force. Ghanem was removed from Palmyra's prison management after the rift between President Assad and his brother Rifat. He was succeeded in 1984 by Ghazi Al-Juhani, who continued to manage it until 1996 when he was succeeded by Ghazi Dayoub who was arrested for archaeological

Figure 7.2 Map of Tadmor Prison, Google Maps.

Figure 7.3 Faisal Al-Ghanem, from a pro-regime social media site.

excavation in Palmyra. He was succeeded in 1998 by Talaat Mahfouz, who remained in charge until the prison closed in the summer of 2001.

It is believed that the regime re-used Palmyra prison after the outbreak of the Syrian Revolution in 2011, specifically to detain dissident military personnel. At the end of May 2015, ISIS destroyed large sections of the Eastern Wing, the military section of

Figure 7.4 Ghazi Al-Juhani, from a pro-regime social media site.

Figure 7.5 Talaat Mahfouz, from a pro-regime social media site.

the prison. Before razing the prison in a carefully planned demolition, a video clip by ISIS' media channel 'Amaaq shows militants walking around in the prison yard, opening the doors of isolation cells, and commenting on the cruelty of the regime. This was the only footage of Palmyra prison. Mohammed al-Tadmori, who had inside knowledge of this operation narrates:

ISIS had detailed information about the prison; the presence of about 90 Military Police operatives to guard the prison, as well as some military clusters around the prison leading to the nearby military airport of Palmyra. The plan was to take over the airport, decommission it by heavy fires to be able to make way to the prison. The group that executed the raid was a highly trained group called the "Army of the Caliphate". The majority of the group members were from Chechnya, with two Arabs for translation purposes, one of them was a Saudi national, the other a Palestinian-Danish.[3]

The military prison had been evacuated, according to al-Tadmori:

The Regime had transferred prison detainees to security branches or others prisons 3 days before ISIS offensive on the prison. 14 members of ISIS were the executing force, attacking the prison from the North side. After controlling the airport by heavy fires, they climbed over a high structure and attacked the prison guards. The operation lasted approximately 4 hours after which the prison fell under IS control. The prison didn't have any detainees. Four days later I entered the prison myself and saw tens of files on former detainees. There was a designated room for task management and personnel, and it contained files of all allocations to prisoners and other such details, in addition to personal information of detainees and the fate of each. I tried along with a Syrian member of ISIS to collect these files and preserve them, but the princes of ISIS prevented us from taking them out. It must be noted that the part of the prison that was destroyed was the military section only. I placed all the papers and archives in that section; later it was bombed. It was then that I started doubting that ISIS had ties with the Syrian regime.[4]

Since the regime regained control, no one has managed to obtain any confirmed information about the fate of the prison or its reality today.

Former detainee Yassin al-Haj Saleh wrote extensively about his experiences in Assad's prisons, including a year in Palmyra.[5] He recalls the moment when he saw that ISIS destroyed the prison: 'I felt terrible and orphaned, because I dreamt about one day going there with my friends and entering, touring, reminiscing, and then walking out by our own free will to a restaurant. Palmyra prison was the holiest place in Syria because the suffering and torture, the emotional history of Syria is preserved there.[6] Many others, such as the Palestinian writer Salamah Kaileh (1955–2020), who spent two years in Palmyra, felt the same, as nowhere else in his experience of imprisonment had he witnessed such cruelty.[7] The destruction of Palmyra was an assault on the collective memory of its former detainees.

Internal structure

When it was closed, Palmyra prison contained eight courtyards with 45 dormitories, of which 38 were numbered while the rest were given names according to their previous or current use or function, such as the Clinic dormitory, or a name derived from the construction of the dormitory, such as New 3. In addition to these dormitories, there was an unknown number of solitary cells contained in the fifth courtyard, which was considered the black hole of this prison. The courtyards were separated by corridors, most of which ended with iron doors that were always locked. The ground in these courtyards was covered with corroded asphalt and contained many pits.

The oldest courtyard of the prison is the first, containing seven dormitories, the fifth and sixth of which were connected to each other. This double dormitory was particularly humid and dark. It is believed that the fourth dormitory was in the past a cinema or theater lounge based on its interior design.[8] The second courtyard contained three dormitories in addition to the prison's central bathrooms. The third consisted of eight dormitories, two of which had different names, the Warehouse dormitory and New 3 dormitory, which was built after the courtyard and carried its number. The third courtyard included several solitary cells. The fourth courtyard had eight dormitories. At its centre stood a dirt basin used by the wardens to grow vegetables. The fifth was considered the most mysterious and secretive in Palmyra prison. It was known for its solitary cells and 'those who were punished were taken there'. The sixth courtyard was the largest, containing eleven dormitories, it was 'where executions were carried out'. The seventh courtyard housed four dormitories, built in 1981.[9] The eighth was not named as such, but was known as the Clinic courtyard. It contained two numbered dormitories and the women's Clinic dormitory.[10]

Most sections of Palmyra prison were old, with thick walls built of stone. The ceilings of the dormitories were low and had large iron doors, closed from the outside with a thick iron bar at the end of which a lock was placed. Each dormitory had only a toilet and a faucet. These dormitories were lit with an electrical lamp or two, controlled by the prison administration. The prison did not have any form of heating in winter or cooling in summer. The surrounding Syrian desert is known for its low temperatures in winter and soaring heat in summer.

These dormitories and their inmates were subject to a strict and heavy guard regime. The prison is located in the middle of a military barracks so, as one survivor said, 'it was surrounded from the outside by a number of special units' battalions permanently and continuously. This was known to us by the sounds of their training that we could hear. Their presence around us was considered the first security line of the prison'. Permanent guard shifts around the prison walls and above the roof of the dormitories represented the second line of security. The third line was the closest to the prisoners, and that was the wardens and torturers working inside the prison, their numbers were estimated by tens. In terms of construction, the prison is surrounded by a trench 'dug around the prison from all sides. In addition, the fence is more than 7 metres high, which no one can climb. On top of that, the prison's open courtyards were roofed with barbed wire to the East and West'.[11] The tight guard procedures did not end with the architecture and guards. Prisoners were periodically moved between different dormitories to ensure the breaking of any personal relationships that might lead to any action against the prison administration. The dormitories were subject to monthly inspection raids in which the wardens inspected the floor of the dormitory, to check for any digging. Added to all that was the constant torture, whether by beating, starvation or medical negligence, which impacted the detainees' physical and psychological abilities.

After being opened, the transfer of detainees from the intelligence branches to Palmyra began, and three groups arrived. The first came from the Qala'a prison in Damascus: the detainees from different branches of the General Intelligence and Political Security. The second group came from the Military Police prison, Al-Balouni, in Homs, sent by a decision of the Military Intelligence branch there. The third group came from the Military Intelligence branches in various Syrian governorates. These three groups arrived in Palmyra prison before 27 June 1980. The make-up of the detainees was varied. In addition to the Muslim Brotherhood detainees, the prison held a number of Iraqi Baathist detainees and others on various other charges.

The Palmyra massacre

The 1980 Palmyra prison massacre was one of the biggest single-day massacres in Syrian and modern Middle Eastern history. It earned the prison its bad reputation for cruelty, which lasted throughout its twenty-one years and reverberated in Syrian collective memory. Most former detainees and human rights organizations estimate that at least 800 to 900 detainees were killed. All were accused of belonging to the Muslim Brotherhood, since detainees with other charges were segregated.[12]

On the morning of Friday, 27 June 1980, the day following the assassination attempt on President Hafez Al-Assad, two units of the Defence Brigade, in full combat uniform, led by major Moeen Nassif, the deputy of Rifat Al-Assad and his son-in-law, were airlifted by helicopter from Mezze airport to Palmyra. At 06.30, half of the force, about 60 men, drove to the desert prison with orders to kill every last person. They were divided into six or seven groups. At least 500 detainees were killed. In an attempt to cast a legal veil over the massacre, it was later reported that the prisoners were sentenced to death by a field court with exceptional powers.

---

26 survivors

They opened the door of our dormitory on the morning of Friday 27 June 1980 for the roll call. We were 26 detainees in the dormitory and all of us were accused of belonging to the Iraqi Baath, the 'suspicious right', as it was referred to in the intelligence circles. A few minutes later, a large group of Military Police entered, accompanied by the assistant of the Prison Director, whom we had met previously, in addition to an officer dressed in a Defence Brigade uniform with a notebook in his hand. The Defence Brigade officer asked us: 'Are you all from the suspicious right?' We confirmed. They went out and locked the door without saying a word.

We thought that an order had come to move us from Palmyra. We started wearing our good clothes in preparation for the transfer.

A few minutes before 9:00, a large number of soldiers entered the prison. Their military boots made a loud noise as they banged the ground. They lined up on the wall of our dormitory overlooking the third courtyard awaiting orders. Loading weapons started; there were too many rifles. We exchanged looks in the room, but no one dared to utter a word. Usually, bringing weapons into the courtyards of the prison was forbidden. We were consumed by fear, but no one was able to ask or inquire. At 9:00 sharp they threw grenades into the fifth and sixth dormitories, which were packed with detainees. Bombs were thrown from the open window by the roof, the vent. Detainees started shouting 'Allahu Akbar'. The soldiers slammed open the doors of the dormitories, except for ours, and opened heavy fire on everyone. The voices of the detainees slowly faded under the wheezing of bullets and cries of death.

We lined the walls of our dormitory with our backs to the dormitory door. One of our colleagues suggested moving to an area closer to the door, for death there would be faster and less painful. We fought to stand there, each wanting to be the first to die. We asked each other for forgiveness awaiting the bullets to harvest us. On the other side of the door of our dormitory, stood a sergeant who kept opening the Judas window and closing it. It made sounds similar to reloading weapons. Every time we thought he was opening the door to start shooting at us. He just opened the window, looked at us, and then closed. The shooting lasted three hours, until midday. After that, we sat down, each to his own, in complete stillness, waiting for what might happen next. We were not able to say anything. Blood leaked out from under the doors of the rest of the dormitories.

We had no water, food, or light due to the power outage, until the evening. The prison administration extended an electricity cable with a lamp at its end to illuminate the third courtyard over which our dormitory overlooked. We peeked onto the yard where one of the wardens, Adjutant Ahmed Kassibi, whom we called Abu Jahl, sat on a bench in the middle of it. More than 100 'municipal workers', judicial prisoners from the personnel of the army, were forced to transport the bodies. They placed each body onto a cover in front of Abu Jahl. Abu Jahl then inserted a thin iron skewer into the corpse to make sure it was dead. They discovered some who were still alive among the bodies. They were shot dead. Those transfers continued all night.[13]

In February 1981, less than a year after the Palmyra massacre, Jordanian intelligence arrested Sergeant Issa Fayyad and Corporal Akram Bishani of the Defence Brigades due to their involvement in a failed attempt to assassinate former Jordanian Prime Minister Modhar Badran. In their (likely forced) confessions on Jordanian state television, they recounted details of the massacre they took part in a year earlier: 'At

Figure 7.6 Khaled Al-Aqleh, from the author's collection.

3:30am that day, two groups from the Defence Brigades were called for a meeting in full combat uniform. The first group was from the 40th brigade, led by Rifat al-Assad's son-in-law, Major Mo'een Nassif. The second group was from the 138th brigade, led by Lieutenant Colonel Ali Deeb.[14]

Major Nassif met with members of the 40th brigade in the brigade's cinema hall. He addressed them saying: 'You will attack the biggest Muslim Brotherhood den, the Palmyra prison.' The two groups met at the old Mezze airport. Soldiers and officers from both groups were transported on board of 10 helicopters to Palmyra. Heading the operation was the Chief of Staff of the 138th brigade, Lieutenant Colonel Suleiman Mustafa. Lieutenant Yasser Bakir, Lieutenant Munir Darwish, and Lieutenant Raif Abdullah also participated.

At around 6:00am, the helicopters landed at Palmyra airport, loaded with operatives, officers, and non-commissioned officers. Members of the Defence Brigades were invited to a meeting in which they were divided into three groups. The first was made up of eighty men. Their mission was to enter the prison. They were called the Raid Group. The second was made up of twenty men and was tasked with protecting the helicopters. The third remained at the airport as a reserve group. The Raid Group was transferred to the desert prison where it was divided into small teams each led by an officer.

The mass execution was organized into two batches. The first covered rooms overlooking the first, second and third courtyards. The second covered rooms overlooking the fourth, fifth and sixth courtyards. The soldiers took out the inmates of the fifth and sixth dormitories in the first courtyard and grouped them in the northeast corner of the courtyard. They also took out the inmates of the eighth, ninth and tenth dormitories in the second courtyard and grouped them in the western corner of the courtyard opposite the eighth dormitory. The inmates of the dormitories 12, 13, 16 and 17 were grouped in the southeastern corner of the third courtyard in front of dormitory 12.

After these preparations, the start signal was given. Within a few minutes it was all over in those yards. After that the soldiers went off to the other three courtyards. Officers decided to enter the dormitories and kill detainees there. Six groups of soldiers rushed into the three dormitories in the fourth courtyard. The doors opened, the head of each dormitory duly presented the dormitory. The soldiers went in and asked them to move away from the door. They threw two defence bombs at one of the dormitories, before they stormed the place. They started firing machine guns. Detainees fell to the ground some dead, others wounded. Groups of soldiers set off to the fifth and sixth courtyard. They spread over the remaining five dormitories, killing everyone there. In the bathroom of one of the fifth courtyard dormitories, one of the detainees hid. When the soldiers entered and opened fire, he pounced on Sergeant Iskandar Ahmed and took his weapon. He killed the Sergeant and wounded two others before he was shot dead by the soldiers.[15]

The period 1980–2001

Thus the beginnings of Palmyra prisons left us with only one option, which is to preserve our mental, psychological and physical strengths with minimal losses! We had to temporarily lose any memory of the past, to not feel sorry for what has passed, to cheat the looming ghosts of death. We took refuge in despair every time the knifes of doom wounded us; we shielded ourselves with silence and suppressed our fury to avoid provoking their killing instincts. We weaved ourselves a different path, thus cutting the time in half, one for them and one for us, to be able to find spaces that took us a little far from the grim daily scenes. We did this to restore some of our balance amid this dysfunctional world which forces you to remain half awake, half hungry, half envious, half crazy, half skeptical, half dead and half blind. We tried to collect the other halves to be able to form new bonds with life.[16]

From its early days, Palmyra formed a special context that existed outside the human sphere. The written and oral testimonies of survivors confirm the existence of a well-defined system through which the prison administration controlled the lives of detainees from the very moment of their arrival. A system that orchestrated the finer details of their daily lives and reshaped their human needs according to its way, which we will call the 'Palmyran approach'. This 'meant a number of key events in the life of the Palmyran inmates, as well as others specific to each individual.

The 'reception ceremony', according to the Palmyran terminology, represents the first meeting between the torturer and the victim. The role of the torturer here is played by the warden in a blatant functional merge and overlap. Violence is the most obvious feature of this noisy concert. This opening act often claimed its victims from among the newcomers. Some lost their sight or hearing, limbs or ribs were broken, not to mention the bleeding that turned the torture area into a red pool. Suleiman Abu al-Khair writes:

> Time loses any meaning here. We didn't know anything about what's coming. We were always expecting the worst. In the midst of this, we were ordered to leave our stuff aside, and then they called on us one by one to move to the opposite room. By the door of the room stood a bunch of torturers, who beat us with their terrible whips, and with a stick over 6 inches thick. I saw the torturer holding it with both hands and striking down the person who passed before me. I couldn't believe my eyes until it was my turn. I received his blow, and I no longer remember how I regained my breath which was almost gone . . . I barely managed to pick myself up and then I ran. That was their process to direct us to Personal Information section.[17]

Violence accompanied the administrative procedure of writing down the name of the new detainee and by which authority he was captured. The charge was also noted down in this record, which included documenting the personal belongings of the new inmate at Palmyra prison. After that, the official reception ceremony began. Guests were stripped down to their underpants. They were then asked to perform the Military Police inspection procedures which entails performing safety movements in complete nudity to ensure that there is nothing in the detainee's anus. Immediately after that, the torture session began. Abu al-Khair continues:

> In only a few moments you lose your sense of space and time. Your voice starts fading down until it becomes a rattle before it's completely gone and you drown in silence. You get into a state of hebetude, as if your nerve sensors have malfunctioned or died . . . They ran towards me, and with their heavy boots, and big bodies they jumped on my back. I lay on the ground with my feet in the air, receiving their whips. I was submissive, I didn't even have the energy to scream or moan. Who would have believed that after this massacre, I could jump on my feet and start running, groping my path between two rows of torturers, guiding us again with their whips, to carry the clothes that we have taken off earlier and go towards the dormitory. Lacerated flesh and blood pools were the main characters of the place.[18]

The reception was managed by the Adjutant on duty most of the times, accompanied by a large number of Military Police officers.

> The column stood in front of an Adjutant . . . With him, over a hundred Military Police operatives hovered around us. All prisoners avoided looking directly at any of them. Our heads were facing down. Our shoulders were sagging. We stood in humility, obedience and abasement. How did all the prisoners simultaneously strike the same pose as if we had rehearsed it before? I don't know. It was as if each one of us was trying to hide inside himself . . . The inspection was over; conducted with a professional meticulousness. Every fold in every piece of garment was searched. They confiscated all the money and papers, anything metal, belts and

shoelaces ... Zahi told me that I remained unconscious and stuck between life and death. Salt was the only sterile substance available. I was treated with salt by Sheikh Zahir, as he liked to be called, willingly abandoning the title of Doctor. He would give me water and jam diluted in water ... He told me, after explaining my health situation, about the information they received from other dormitories. The information said that the number of our batch was 19 people, 3 of whom were killed in the first courtyard during the reception. These were not taken into the dormitories. 10 others died while I was unconscious from their wounds and severe injuries. Two of the batch were permanently paralyzed as a result of severe spinal damage, and one lost his sight after a blow of a whip gouged his eyes out ....[19]

Moving to the dormitory did not mean the agony was over. The detainee's day in Palmyra was divided into only two parts. Twelve hours of compulsory sleep and twelve hours of compulsory sitting. The detainee's sleeping area represented his final space inside this place. He would only leave his space to go to the toilet inside the dormitory or to execute external functions such as bathing, roll call or exercise. 'Each prisoner was given three military blankets only. He would fold one of them and use as a mattress on the floor and use the other two to cover himself. If anyone had excess clothing, he would fold them into a pillow, or use his shoes as a pillow.'[20] This space, mostly narrow, also had its laws. Movement was forbidden during the twelve-hour sleep. So, in fear of punishment, the subconscious of the detainee worked to prevent him from moving during sleep. If he moved and was caught by the roof guard through the observation window in the roof of the dormitory, he received a horrible punishment the next day. This violator, in Palmyran vocabulary, is then known as the 'marked'. The next day, the police would call out all the 'marked' inmates for punishment, which was 50–100 foot whips with a cable.

In addition to forbidding movement during sleep or crowding in the dormitory during the day, silence was imposed by force. It was forbidden to speak in a loud voice; more accurately, speech was strictly forbidden. In many cases, inmates whispered or used hand gestures to communicate. They created a series of special signals, symbolizing names, daily events or emergencies. For example, a hand gesture to the right indicated the presence of Military Police operatives in the courtyard opposite the dormitory.

A day in the life of Palmyra

Every detail of every day in Palmyra was run by commands of the Military Police. The first half of the day began at 06.00. The command came from the roof guard: 'wake up you ...'. The command was accompanied by a series of insults. Detainees woke up quickly under any circumstances, for fear of punishment if they were seconds late. They collected their 'mattresses' and blankets, and each sat in his space motionless waiting for the roof guard to move away from the window. The head of the dormitory worked, along with his 'administrative staff' to coordinate toilet visits and maintain calm and order. Some dormitories had more than 250 inmates, so detainees had to wait an hour or two before entering the toilet. 'Prisoners lined up sitting behind one another.

Here it was necessary to control matters and coordinate people's access to the toilet with discipline so that chaos did not bring punishment for everyone.[21] The detainee had a short time in the toilet, no more than a minute. He invested his minutes in relieving himself, washing his face and returning to his spot to wait for breakfast.

Bringing in breakfast was the first confrontation between the detainees and the Military Police. Detainees with an Islamist background called it Ghazwa [an old Arabic term used in Islam's early days to refer to battles] because one side of the confrontation is armed, while the other is completely defenceless. The command came, announcing breakfast had arrived. The inmates of the dormitory stood with their faces to the wall and their hands behind their backs. The door opened, and the head of the dormitory offered respect to the Sergeant as required. The command to bring the food in followed. Three men would 'sacrifice' themselves and go out to bring two large plastic bowls into the dormitory. The first contained cold tea, and the second held breakfast provisions for the day.

The process seems easy, but carried a great deal of risk. As soon as 'the three young men came out of the door and grabbed the bowls, they started receiving whips, punches and kicks from every side. The aim was to make them stumble so one of them dropped some tea on the floor. That's when disaster struck, as new men had to be called to clean. So rather than one being tortured and kicked, we ended up with 2 or 3, until the guard finally yelled to let them go inside. Some brothers would go out to carry the injured back in, but they became injured themselves and could not work before a while.'[22]

The amount of food allocated per person was extremely scarce. It didn't exceed 10 grams of the substance intended for daily breakfast, a dried yogurt, jam, halva, cheese, or few olives or one-fifth of a boiled egg with a loaf of military bread and some tea. These scarce quantities forced the dormitory administration to divide its members into even numbered food groups (6, 8 or 10) to make the distribution easier. Initially, food was divided to the groups, in reusable plastic bowls. Then the head of each group distributed food among the members of his group. These groups created their own methods of distributing hard-to-divide food items such as eggs. One of which was braiding a plastic thread to be used by the head of the group to divide the egg into five or six parts, then one of the members of the group closed his eyes and answered the question from the head of the group 'whom is this piece for?'. These same quantities were applied regardless of the type of substance, for both lunch and dinner. Prisoners in Palmyra weighed between 45 to 70 kg, with the vast majority weighing 60 kg or less.[23]

Dirty Food

The food came three times a day. With it came the torturers who competed in their creativity to humiliate us. One would put his military boots, full of dirt and animal waste, in our food bowls, before opening the door to bring them in, especially when the food is liquid … We brought the food in under their kicks and whips as they laughed hysterically. If his boots were clean and he was in a hurry, he would grab a hand full of sand from the courtyard which over the days mixed with our blood and threw it over rice or bulgur. It happened more than once that one of them urinated over the food amid hysterical laughs from his colleagues. These actions reached the Prison Director who recorded them as positive points. The detainee watching the door would refrain from telling us what he saw. Perhaps he would refrain from eating this meal and make various excuses, but there is no way he would deprive the rest of their meal that barely kept them alive.[24]

'Breathing'

Exercise was run similar to everything in the Palmyran day, a process that began with a command of the sergeant of the Military Police. He hit the door of the dormitory with whatever torture device he had in his hand, a stick, a cable or a metal pipe, and shouted: 'Dormitory! To breathing!' He opened the door, shouting: 'Everybody out!' Morning 'breathing' in Palmyra took place between 9:00 and 13:00. Evening 'breathing' was after 16:00. It was cancelled in winter from October until March of each year. Morning and evening 'breathing' did not last more than an hour, and it was an open torture session. The 'breathing' breaks were combined with some strange practices by the Military Police sergeants. The police took the inmates of each dormitory individually to the courtyard to prevent inmates of dormitories in the same courtyard from mixing with each other. The small number of inmates in the yard gave Military Police officers more opportunity to practice torture for longer periods.

'Breathing' time was associated with torture and humiliation for most Palmyra inmates. As one survivor narrated:

When the hour of breathing approached and we could hear the sounds of the Military Police in our yard, our hearts started beating fast. Our organs trembled. Our faces went pale. Eyes stopped blinking as if awaiting the arrival of the angel of death. We sat still, motionless, not a word, not a whisper, not a blink. Silence and stillness reigned, and panic filled the air of the dormitory. Hearing the sound of the key in the door lock was worse that hearing whizzing bullets. The head of the dormitory presented the dormitory. Everyone stood in military preparedness. Their eyes closed. Their heads down. Their hands behind their backs in preparation to go out.[25]

Military Police cables struck detainees leaving the dormitory to the 'breathing' yard. Mohammed Berro narrates:

We would start running out of the dormitory, as they stood waiting for their preys. As soon as the last of us got out, the sergeant entered and did an inspection to ensure no one stayed inside, and then locked the door. We ran in circles, each one of us clutching the back of the person in front of him. Whips had their gypsy dance on our backs and heads. The sergeant threw in his commands, so uncoordinated like a cacophonic musical note: "Face down to the ground ... on your knees ...

continue jogging ... lay down ... on your knees ... face down to the ground ... continue crawling." He would go on, in a fast, breath-taking rhythm. If one of us misunderstood the command and did something else, one of the awaiting torturers picked him up voraciously. He would strike him with a blow to the head then order him to step aside from the ring, and lay on the ground face down to receive what the fate had in store for him.[26]

Circular running was not the only form of exercise in Palmyra. Sometimes it was just sitting or walking. When sitting, prisoners were often topless, especially in the summer. Detainees were crammed into one corner of the yard. Their heads down, hands behind their backs, and eyes closed. Palmyra inmates from left-wing parties were partially exempt as they were allowed to raise their heads and open their eyes in the 'breathing' yard. However, the torment of this daily process did not end with beating during the exit and torture during the break. The sergeants devised their own methods. Torture was by asking impossible questions, such as calling on whomever had ears. If any prisoner responded, he was punished, and if no one did, the sergeant punished someone of his choice. Torment during 'breathing' fell heavier on those with distinct features, tall, short, fat, gray haired, bald, etc. The unlucky holder of such characteristics became the focus of amusement for the supervising sergeant.

This 'breathing' hour resulted in dozens of injuries of varying severity among the inmates. Detainees eagerly awaited the sergeant's command: 'To the dormitory!' They crammed by the door to return to their less harsh and safer space. The trip back to the dormitory was also accompanied by police cables. The trip concluded by presenting the dormitory in the military style by the head of the dormitory: 'Stand prepared! As you were! The class is done with the inspection, sergeant.[27]

'It's water, Sir!'

Yes, in this mini hell, we had glimpses of hope and love for life, but they were bitter and short lived. Those moments soon faded away by the torture rounds. The most deadly and ferocious of which were those supervised by the Discipline Adjutant personally. He would enter our yard at breathing times waddling like a prince. With a cigarette dangling from the tip of his lip, and a metal rod with a pointed head in his hand. If he wanted to talk to a prisoner, he would just stick the rod into his body, and ask the prisoner next to him to take it out. Blood poured out and the stabbed inmate was dragged back to the dormitory. Then the Adjutant would ask: 'What is this?!', pointing to the blood. The prisoner should answer: 'It's water, Sir!' The Adjutant would reply: 'Well done. Drink it then.' As soon as the poor man kneeled down to obey the order, he received the same fate and followed his predecessor. At the end of the 'breathing' session, someone else would come and ask the head of the dormitory: 'How many injuries do you have?' The head of the dormitory would answer: 'Twenty, Sergeant!' The latter would reply: 'Only 20 ...?!'[28]

The guards' shift ended around 14:00, but in order to complete the hand-over between the two shifts, a roll call took place to check the number of detainees. From the beginning of September 1980 until the beginning of April 1981, the police maintained the roll call process inside the dormitory. The non-commissioned officer in charge would give his command to the dormitory: 'Roll-call!' Detainees would stand in a row in the middle of the dormitory, with heads down and eyes closed. The non-commissioned officer and a number of operatives would enter the dormitory. The head of the dormitory issued the military command: 'As you were … stand prepared. Dormitory is ready for inspection, Sergeant.' As the number of detainees increased, they began to stand in a double row, then triple, then quintuple. However, after the outbreak of cholera among the detainees in April 1981, the roll call took place in the courtyard outside the dormitory. The same commands remained, but this time the detainees were counted in the yard, to stop the police becoming infected. Inside or outside the dormitory, torment still accompanied the roll call. Police officers beat detainees from the moment they opened the door until they closed it, this was also accompanied by a series of insults, derogatory words, and humiliation. 'If anyone was given the choice to go out to the roll call or engage in combat in a battle, they would gladly accept the latter; but never to go out for the roll call. Because in a battle you would have a weapon to defend yourself and your brothers. But in the roll call you were defenceless; you had nothing. Stripped from everything, even your sight and hands, and put to face an evil, malevolent adversary.'[29]

The routine did not end with the roll call. After this came lunch, which was similar to breakfast; the 'sacrificers'[30] went out to bring it in. After lunch came evening exercise; a torture hour not dissimilar to that of the morning. Then, at the end of the day, came dinner with its accompanying torment, insults, and slurs. At 18:00 the Palmyran day ended. Blankets were spread out again and the prisoners stayed in their places with closed eyes in stone stillness. It was time to go to bed, and with it began the Palmyran programme for the night.

The sleeping period formed half of the Palmyran day. It came with its own torture. The dormitory administration created a 'night guard' function, rotated on several detainees throughout each night. Each shift lasted two hours. The night guard's task was to stand ready near the kitchen space in the dormitory. It was located directly under the monitoring eye of the Military Police operative roaming the roof of the dormitory. He received orders from him, if any detainee moved during his sleep, he would say 'marked', meaning he should be punished the next day. The function of the guard in these situations was to identify those 'marked' who were to be taken out for punishment during breakfast distribution.

The violence was most intense during the 'days of torture' – the five months following the 1980 massacre. Abdullah al-Naji offers a striking description:

> In October of that year they started torturing us in a new way. They asked us to stand on one foot all night, with both arms up, because that was more painful. Most dormitories had large openings in the ceiling that enabled the guard to monitor prisoners, so we were forced to keep on standing until the morning. When breakfast distribution started, everyone sat in anticipation of a new Palmyran daytime programme. Once they asked the detainees to collect their blankets and clothes

under the opening in the ceiling, and the torturers poured water on them. Sometimes they poured cold water on prisoners while they slept.[31]

Those were winter days, the dormitories had no heating facilities and the windows had no glass. Prisoners suffered from extreme cold combined with water punishments until the end of 1980.

Besides heat and cold, nature was used in a different way to torture prisoners. M.A., a Kurdish man from Rukneddin, was arrested during the infamous Newroz celebration of 1986. Initially, he was taken by Political Security and tortured for two days, but when the officers found out he was officially in military service, he was transferred to Palmyra. After a long ride through the desert, he arrived in 'a hellish place underground', with guards from the Military Police who wore black boots, beige uniforms, and red berets with an eagle emblem on it. The Homs Military Court sentenced him to two years' imprisonment for disturbing the public order. In Palmyra, he suffered the worst torture ever. One summer day, he was tied to a metal pole outside in the scorching heat and smeared with jam. All kinds of insects and wasps attacked him and stung him. After two years of misery, he was remanded to the army and had to complete his military service. M.A.'s life story also demonstrates how entire families were targeted by the Assad regime. Because of his imprisonment, his younger brother K., as well as older brothers Y. and M. were also arrested and tortured.[32]

Far from direct torture, which varied depending on the period and the mood of the roof guard, sleeping in those crowded dormitories was a punishment.

> Your space for sleeping was only a span and two fingers. A dormitory that was 18m long and 5m wide hosted 200 people … Each 3 people slept on the space of one sheet, which was 180cm by 80cm. If one person put his head on one end, the other must put his head on the other side. Sleeping position had to be on the side because of the tight space but also because sleeping on the back was forbidden, as that indicated that you are comfortable in your sleep, and this was not the prison's principles or its system![33]

Side sleeping did not negate wearing blindfolds during sleep. Added to the regulations of sleeping, was the complete prohibition of any movement, under penalty. The prisoner was forbidden to go to the toilet, even in cases of illness. If any violation occurred and was picked up by the roof guard, he would order the night guard to punish the violator inside the dormitory and remember him for additional punishment the next morning in the courtyard.

A prisoner and a torturer

One of the brothers moved in his sleep unintentionally which caused him to fall prey in the hands of a powerful and unjust warden. The guard asked the night guard to wake him up and bring him to the kitchen area. The guard ordered the young man who moved to take his clothes off and lie down in the soiled kitchen floor. It was January, the cold and snowy month. The kitchen floor which was covered in water was frozen, however the command must by executed, and that brother gave in. The guard didn't stop there. He ordered him to put in his mouth an old slipper that was too disgusting to look at, let alone put in your mouth . . . But the order cannot be disobeyed. But the guard didn't stop there either. He ordered the night guard to pour on the young man buckets of ice water. He ordered him to pour a bucket every ten minutes. The torment continued until the shift of the roof guard ended. We thought the punishment was over and a new guard will come who will not know what his colleague had done. The young man got up, got dressed and went to his blankets, hoping to regain some warmth. We were surprised that the new guard asked about the punished young man when he did not find him. The disaster occurred again, as the first guard seemed to have asked his colleague to continue the punishment. The young man ran back to the kitchen area but this time he didn't pour water on him, instead the guard ordered the night guard to hit him with slippers. This continued until 6am, the time to wake up. His body became blackish blue like an eggplant. He almost froze; his lips and all body parts were trembling continuously. He got dressed and sat in his place awaiting the rest of the punishment at breakfast![34]

This was the traditional daily routine in Palmyra. There were many exceptions such as trial days, executions, periods of illness, and many more. However, the Palmyran approach had weekly, monthly, and annual mileposts. The prison had a central bathroom in its second courtyard. The bathroom remained in operation until late August 1984, when the then Acting Director of the prison, Barakat al-Osh, informed some prisoners that bathing had been officially cancelled.[35] The central bathroom returned to the life of Palmyran prisoners for a few months in 1989.[36] The veteran chronicler of Assad's prison system, Mustafa Khalifa, wrote: 'It was cancelled shortly afterwards due to overcrowding, and the bathroom was converted into a dormitory where Communist detainees were placed.'[37]

Military police officers took detainees to the bath once a week. 'Bathing in the Palmyra prison system was a real disaster from which there was no escape in any way. It was a bloodbath made from bodies that barely had any blood left to survive . . . If bathing is mentioned or referred to by the police to a dormitory, many of its inmates developed diarrhoea in fear of what was awaiting them minutes later. Imagine over 200 people standing naked with their eyes closed, heads down and hands behind their backs, surrounded by torturers with whips designated to eat the flesh of the backs.'[38]

The bathroom was organized for each dormitory separately. The command was given: 'Everybody in shorts within 10 seconds!' Detainees were ready, with only their underwear on, for the journey to the bathroom, which might be far away depending on the location of the dormitory in relation to the second courtyard. The police waited for the detainees at the door of the dormitory and accompanied them with beatings and insults until they reached the bathroom courtyard. Detainees had to cross several

Figure 7.7 Mustafa Khalifa, from a private collection.

Figure 7.8 Office in Tadmor Prison, from the ISIS film about destroying the prison.

courtyards on their journey, where they faced more torment as they passed by police officers or sergeants, all of whom participated in beating the moving naked group. Crossing the gates of the courtyards meant guaranteed torment for the detainees. 'The double door of the courtyard was 1.5 metres wide. One of its sides was closed, which left it 75 cm wide. It could only be crossed by one person at a time.' The individual trickling of prisoners enabled the guard standing in front of the door to freely hit the prisoner. If the officer missed one detainee, his colleague waiting on the other side of the door would not fail to. 'Imagine how many booby-trapped courtyards you had to cross until you reached the bathroom courtyard, exhausted by running before the police.'[39]

Military police officers divided the detainees of each dormitory into two groups in the bathroom courtyard. One entered the bathroom compartments whose 'gloomy antique look suggested they belonged to centuries ago; they were more like stone age baths. Rusty metal pipes hung from the ceilings of the compartments. They poured either boiling or cold water'.[40] The second group of detainees waited in the courtyard, at the mercy of Military Police cables. The military command would come that detainees in the showers had only two minutes. 'They often walked in on us with their whips, the stings of which mixed with the scalding boiling water, or blood freezing cold water. Between this and that, you only came out with your back battered in all colours of torment.' The first group replaced the second, and received the torment in the courtyard, while the second group replaced the first, and received the torment in the bathroom compartments. A painful sequence of events, where the only losers were the detainees. 'As soon as we arrived at the dormitory and the door was closed, we looked at each other's injuries and consoled each other in this ordeal'.[41]

The irony was that bathing cost every detainee 5 Syrian Lira at that time, equivalent to about 11 Euro cents. It was not a large amount, but most detainees did not have any money, because they could not receive any visitors. Whoever had money, donated the bathing fee for the rest of the detainees, as bathing and its fee were mandatory and no one was exempt, not even the sick. Shaving facial hair was also a mandatory weekly procedure; again, no one was exempt. Weekly shaving sessions were similar to the bathing day in terms of torture. The weekly shaving continued from the summer of 1980 until April 1986. Head shaving also took place outside the dormitory once every three weeks. But the poor medical conditions prevented shaving too, as Mohammed Hammad wrote: 'Jaundice spread, and that was a disaster that eliminated the disaster of shaving!'.[42] Acting Prison Director Barakat al-Osh cancelled the shaving process. During that time, the official prison director Ghazi al-Juhani attended a Military Staff Course. Baraa al-Sarraj explains that 'shaving was then done by hand shavers that hung from the window above the dormitory door. We returned them when we were done ... We then bought manual shavers with medicine. They allowed us two head shavers'.[43]

Prior to its cancellation, the shaving process required the prison administration to call upon six 'municipal workers' from the military prison, three for foaming and three for shaving. The first 'foamer' covered the detainee's face with shaving soap, his two colleagues finished the task until the barber arrived. The latter drew maps of shaving wounds on the faces of the detainees. One survivor noted:

> The detainee would silently endure dozens of wounds on his face in fear of punishment ... No one was exempted from this shaving, even young men with no facial hair yet, which is what happened to us. We were imprisoned when we were 17, and we didn't have any facial hair back then. We were being slaughtered, however we had to go out for shaving and pass under the hands of the 'foamers', then the barbers, then the wounds and blood, followed by the whips, kicks and punches ... Those were like the 'happy shaving!' wishes.[44]

The same scene was repeated every three weeks.

As soon as you finished that head shave, went back into the dormitory and looked at the others, you were taken aback by those distorted faces and plucked heads that now looked like shiny pumpkin beads. You would laugh spontaneously on these strange shapes. Soon they became completely familiar to you, in fact any others would look foreign.[45]

We still need to mention the monthly inspection and the annual sterilization. The first was where the police order the head of the dormitory that detainees must place their belongings and all the items in the dormitory in the middle of it after which detainees were taken out to the yard and crammed into one of its corners. The whips continued torturing the bodies of the detainees while they waited for the other police officers to inspect the floor and walls of the dormitory. They made sure that there was no digging, even though they were quite sure that no one would attempt to escape.

During the annual sterilization, the Military Police ordered detainees to strip completely. As one survivor narrated: 'The command also included that each detainee wrapped his body in a blanket after he collected all his belongings, clothes and dormitory items and took them out into the courtyard. They took them to a place we didn't know, claiming that they were sterilizing them there. During that time, we stayed in the yard, each with a blanket wrapping his body.'[46] This was the last of the Palmyran routine mileposts. Daily life was full of repeated torment to a degree that it became normal. Yet the tales of Palmyra's prison did not end there, and to paint the whole Palmyran picture, we must look at the routine, diseases, trials, executions, cultural life and hope.

Palmyra's 'academy'

We went through many events during which our needs and priorities were evolving. It was about each of us making what made him feel his individual and collective presence. We exchanged our experiences and knowledge. We conversed a lot. We reviewed our political experiences at every stop. We put forward our critical opinions about those experiences. We ran oral courses in presentation, poetry, languages, economics, and engineering. We learned how to improve food and behavior. We created means of entertainment: theater, pantomime, charades of folk proverbs, chess games, cast table, barjis (a traditional board game). We nicknamed each other: 'the one who carries the ladder crosswise, the thread head, the storyteller, the dreamer'. We shared the specialties: embroideries, darning and sewing, nylon threads, primitive ink which was a strange chemical mixture made of onion and pomegranate husks, tea residues and anti-inflammatory pill capsules which we melted under the light bulb that hung from the ceiling ... Towards the end of the late twentieth century, we lived the primitive ages of the human being. In the era of nylon, which came with the arrival of bread into the dormitories in nylon bags, we discovered the way to spin threads thanks to those who preceded us to the place and who left this information on the wall. We used them, as they did, in making kitchen shelves, laundry cords, sandals, mini rugs and mesh bags which our wives will use for shopping years later . . . During the cartoon era, we made tablecloths, tables from cardboard dough, notebook covers made from wastepaper and cigarette box covers that we kept, playing cards and paintings for drawing . . . Sometimes the same human experience is repeated. The difference is the accumulation of experiences, efficiency, and coincidences. Our ancestors in the Palmyra prison performed simple and medium surgical operations with tools made out of bone and wood as well as metal chips from ointment tubes and steel strips they cut out from the bottom of the corroded iron door. They polished them with rubbing . . . They used vinegar and salt for sterilization. They ate bone powder and eggshells to compensate for the lack of calcium. They made water tanks from nylon bags and adhesive to survive the near absence of running water. They bathed using five litres of water. They used magic boards to write. Many of them memorized the Quran by recitation from others . . . They communicated with Morse signals through the walls.[47]

Diseases

The reality and conditions of the prison contributed to the spread of diseases, epidemics and serious injuries; physical and psychological torment; severe congestion and unsanitary conditions in most prison dormitories. The absence of health care; lack of clothes and blankets and total lack of heating sources in winter. The side dormitory windows were open as well as those on the roof. The wide spread of dirt and insects such as cockroaches, flies as well as rats. Poor quality food and small portions. Extreme summer heat made the dormitories suffocating. Severe water scarcity throughout the summer. The toilets and kitchen, where washing dishes and clothes took place, were in the middle of each dormitory, which drowned the place with unpleasant odors. Al-Naji notes that 'the smell of the dormitory was similar to public toilets or barns'.[48]

These circumstances were combined with physical injuries resulting from torture. Some detainees arrived in prison paralyzed or with a permanent disability as a result of the interrogation methods used in the various security branches. Old injuries, or those resulting from Palmyran torture, in time developed into lifelong disabilities. The most prominent injuries suffered by detainees in Palmyra prison were bone fractures and joint dislocation as a result metal or wooden tools being used for torture. Injuries were also caused by police officers or sergeants jumping on the body of the detainee lying on the ground, causing fractures to the rib cage or spine. Faraj Bayraqdar noted grimly:

At the head of the courtyard, two soldiers held a prisoner by the hands and legs. . . They swung him with an upward pendulum motion, and then threw him into the air. . . As soon as his body hit the ground, they grabbed him again by the hands and legs, and repeated the game . . . three, four and five times, after which the dead body is left to rest at its leisure.[49]

Indiscriminate torture cost some detainees their hearing or sight to varying degrees. Torture injuries, wounds or fractures often turned septic causing death. The total lack of healthcare not only caused the death of detainees due to complications from torture injuries, but also contributed to the spread of epidemics. Abu al-Khair remembers:

> Diseases never stopped; we had the two types of lice, including pubic lice. The only way to get rid of the first type was to inspect the clothes, kill the insect and crush its eggs. Fungi of all kinds spread among us. Teeth and gum diseases. Kidney disease accompanied me for many years; I suffered so much of them, to the point of crying. I could do nothing but patience and prayer. Later, cholera spread ... Not to mention the other diseases which were difficult to diagnose due to lack of means.[50]

Attempts by Palmyran detainees to eliminate lice by inspection and killing the insects using nails failed. When yet more detainees arrived from security branches carrying with them lice and nits, the prison administration decided to intervene. Al-Naji testifies:

> The torturers began spraying the dormitories with insecticides mixed with fuel (kerosene and diesel). They used automatic spray machines which covered dormitories with pesticide spray and vapor. They pushed us into the middle of the dormitory and closed it down completely, while we inhaled the poison ... Many prisoners fainted ... That was catastrophic for the elderly and people with chronic diseases such as asthma and heart and lung illnesses.[51]

That was the method to beat regular lice. However, detainees tackled pubic lice by shaving or burning their body hair to get rid of it.

In April 1981, Palmyra prison was hit by an epidemic of cholera. The aggression and spread of the disease prompted the prison administration to swiftly fight it, fearing that Military Police personnel would contract it. Mohammed Hammad witnessed one of these scenes:

> We woke up one morning to the sounds of vomiting and muffled pain cries in the dormitory ... We found that many of us were suffering severe diarrhoea. The infection spread day by day, causing the brothers to drop due to fatigue inside the dormitory or breathing time. Cholera aggressively spread ... The prison doctor Mohammed Yunus al-Ali stopped by the dormitories to record the number of the infected. Two or three hours later, the police returned and asked the head of the dormitory to get all the infected out. They were moved to dormitory 13 in the third courtyard. They opened it for the infected. About 40 people came out of our dormitory alone ... The prison administration at the time provided them with immediate treatment in fear of spreading the disease to the police officers and wardens.[52]

Most of those who contracted cholera were cured; some died. Some Palmyra detainees believe that the speed with which the administration addressed the cholera was because they feared the disease could be transmitted by sewage. The prison's sewage system flowed into Palmyra's system which was sometimes used to irrigate the surrounding farms. This meant that the disease could have been transmitted to the city of Palmyra, and from there to the rest of the country.

The Cholera epidemic was over by the end of 1981; however the prison detainees were then hit by scabies. The prison entered a severe water shortage crisis – there was no running water for over a month.

> We had to share it by the cup. The dormitory's share of water was several buckets for a day and a night ... We would give each detainee one small cup before sleeping, and another for private use in the toilet ... This made our situation in the prison difficult, even dire. Unpleasant odors and filth spread that we could not get rid of. They were a direct cause for a new guest to invade us, spread widely among us and violate our bodies more than its predecessor. It was the scabies that found the right and nutritious environment, which was everything it asked for and wanted.[53]

Scabies reached severe stages. Abscesses filled with pus and blood that soiled the clothes, but with the lack of alternative clothing, pus remained adjacent to the detainee's body. The wide spread of scabies and the prison administration's fear that police officers would contract it, led them to commission detained doctors to manage the crisis. They provided them with benzoates that were used in such cases. Mustafa Khalifa notes:

> I heard a conversation between Dr. Ghassan and a group of dormitory doctors ... After counting the types of scabies, he came to conclude that there has never been, throughout the history of medicine, recorded cases similar to the ones seen here. He mentioned that the most severe type of scabies was reported to have 300 pustules, while cases have been recorded here containing more than 3,000 pustules covering the entire body, which resulted in scabies causing deaths.[54]

Brucellosis arrived in Palmyra prison during the truce year, 1983, when the treatment of prisoners by the administration changed slightly. Visits were permitted for those who had connections. These were later known in the Palmyran dictionary as 'gold visits'. The mother of the detainee visited the mother of the Prison Director at the time, Faisal Ghanem, carrying a quantity of gold sometimes as much as 1 kilogramme. She gave it to the Director's mother as a gift and in return received a paper, through the Military Police, to visit her son.

The "golden era"

"The year 1983, saw the start of a more relaxed treatment. The debates and analysis for the reasons behind this were huge. Some were optimistic, others pessimistic. It was – as we later found out – a plan to extort money from the prisoners' families.

An impromptu mini-market was opened in the prison selling tea, some vegetables and stolen clothes. This was made by an agreement between the then Prison Director, Lieutenant Colonel Faisal Ghanem, and Adjutant Mohammed Khazem, from one side, and a prisoner in our dormitory 26 named Khalid Awad Al-Salem, nicknamed 'Abu Awad'. During their visits, parents brought money and other items to their sons. The Prison Director confiscated 90 per cent of them, and put them in the mini-market for Abu Awad to sell to prisoners at exorbitant prices. Prisoners bought them, knowing that those were items which their families had brought . . . But we could do nothing about this. Money was manipulated out of the prisoners by all means, but people experienced a level of comfort.

It is fair that I mention the positives of that period, which we called the 'golden era'. Some of the beatings and torture were lifted. We were also able to raise our heads and open our eyes during 'breathing' and in front of the police. You were able to laugh if we couldn't hold it, which was forbidden before. Detainees with money were identified and indirectly gathered in the dormitory of Abu Awad, which later became known as the 'dormitory of the connected'. They had available more than they needed. This era also reflected on the overall treatment in the prison. We were able to know the news of our brothers in the other dormitories. We knew who was going to be executed and how many there were at each execution 'party'.

Then friction happened between the pillars of the regime. This resulted in the overthrow of the prison administration, which was replaced by a new administration eagerly seeking revenge. 'They became more creative in modes of torment than before . . . Abu Awad became eternally punished . . . Which meant his blood was permitted at any time, and by any guard. He was exhausted, his body collapsed, and he reached a point where he could not stand to hear a guard's voice even from afar. The prison situation became worse and harsher than it was before. The frequent beatings, the lack of food, and the abundance of everything that disturbed daily life were back. The diseases that used to nail us from time to time came back, and that year we had brucellosis.[55]

The golden year ended with the arrival of brucellosis, which killed a number of Palmyra detainees even the 18–25 year olds. One survivor writes: 'I was then one of the two most severe cases that were expected to die of the severe disease that afflicted us. Three months after a horrible fight with the disease, my colleague died . . . I survived the disease with a skeleton body and a yellow face as if I had just risen from the dead. My hair stopped growing completely.'[56]

All these details about everyday life in prison made certain diseases a permanent guest in the life of detainees. Constant severe diarrhoea was caused by contaminated and spoiled food and as a result of intense stress and severe cold in winter. 'Most of Palmyra's prisoners suffered severe diarrhoea most days of the year, which led to constant overcrowding in front of the toilets. Despite that, the prison administration did not care.'[57] In addition to severe diarrhoea, typhoid, dysentery, fungal and skin diseases spread due to lack of hygiene. The greatest suffering of the prisoners was from the tuberculosis which accompanied them from the very beginning of their stay in prison. Due to the lack of resources among detained doctors, tuberculosis remained a strange, incomprehensible event. 'We were surprised by the illness of some ... Their bodies emaciated and they appeared to suffer some painful symptoms. The disease consumed their bodies until they reached the stage of bleeding, making it difficult to treat them. It was only in 1987 that we were able to diagnose this deadly disease.'[58]

The prisoners of Palmyra prison fell prey to tuberculosis of all kinds: lung, bone, intestine, meninges. The spread of the disease began from the double dormitory 5 and 6 due to its high levels of damp and poor ventilation. It also spread to dormitory 24 in the fourth courtyard and dormitory 13 in the third courtyard for the same reasons. The disease then moved through the rest of the dormitories to accompany the detainees for many years. The prison administration allocated a few dormitories for those who were ill, isolating them from the rest of the detainees. One survivor remembers:

> I found myself isolated with the rest of the detainees in dormitories that showed no special provisions that might have helped the ill overcome the disease. If they gave us medicine for 10 days, they cut it the following five, forcing the prisoners to undergo re-treatment; the relapse of the disease was more difficult. You would see in these dormitories people in severe pain from their serious illness; others coughing blood from their lungs; others spitting bloody mucus into a nylon bag or a small dish he designated for this; others wriggling from the severity of the pain with meningeal tuberculosis which consumed their bodies until they lost the ability to balance.[59]

More than half of the prison population contracted tuberculosis in 1987. By 1989 the percentage had risen to about 75 per cent. 'Post-1991 quarantine procedures proved useless. It was decided to abolish all isolation procedures and consider all prisoners in Palmyra prison infected with tuberculosis.'[60]

The grim health reality in Palmyra prison led the doctors among its inmates to invent their own methods and tools.

> They were led by the saying that necessity is the mother of invention. They collected grapes in a nylon bag and left them to ferment to use them later in disinfecting wounds. They put cigarette ash on the wounds to form an insulating layer over them to protect them from rotting.[61]

They used any available metal tools as surgical tools to burst abscesses and boils. Abu al-Khair recounts a painful memory:

> Nizar had an internal abscess. Two doctors in the dormitory tried to perform a cleaning operation. Due to the lack of means, they inserted a nail after they heated it on fire - to kill the bacteria on it - without the possibility of any kind of anesthesia. The nail lost its way to the abscess in the first try. Doctors repeated the operation for the second time also without anesthesia. Nizar did not live long after the operation. They called his name; and when he couldn't walk anymore, they dragged him to the gallows in the sixth courtyard.[62]

This also applied to developing dentistry tools in the prison. The dentists among us gained extensive experience by practicing on the teeth of detainees. However, the only remedy for incurable dental injuries was extraction. Aa Ali Abu al-Dihn experienced:

It was my misfortune that I developed an abscess under my tooth that reached a point where I could no longer move my jaw. Even opening my mouth to breathe air caused me pain ... Among us in the dormitory was a prisoner with experience in teeth extraction ... He looked inside my mouth he asked me to come back once the swelling was gone ... I went prepared. I took an old cotton shirt and tore it into small pieces after washing it with soap ... I braided a rope about 120 cm long from a nylon thread from an old sock ... I opened my mouth and closed my eyes with the blind fold as per the orders of the specialist. I felt a piece of metal in my mouth. It was the hand of a small pair of scissors that had been smoothed against the wall until it became like a scalpel to separate the gum from the molar. I dried the blood with a piece of the cotton shirt. The doctor continued to try to separate the gums. He wiped the blood over and again so he could see what he was doing. The expert wrapped the rope inside my mouth around the molar and started wiggling it forward and backward. He wiped the blood again. 'Open your mouth well'. He put his legs on my shoulder and pulled the rope again. A sharp cry of pain came out of me despite my panic. I saw the rotten molar with its three roots. All this happened without any anesthesia.[63]

Trials and executions

In those centres of arbitrariness, the judge, looking like a laughing mummy, recites his judgment on you. The warden whips you as he giggles, forcing you to keep count. If your miss a number as your brain battles to deal with the pain, the warden resets and takes you back to the beginning, in a true representation of extreme power when it is evacuated from any sense of humanity.[64]

The role of the torturer was clear: weeding out and destroying any resistance among detainees by any means. This task was supported by military field courts. These courts specialized in Muslim Brotherhood cases. They tried detainees accused of espionage or dealing with foreign actors and others accused of belonging to Iraqi Baath, also known as the 'suspicious right'. However, the largest share of cases of a political or security nature were those of members of the Muslim Brotherhood in Palmyra.

The first and second field tribunals were launched during July 1980. The first was headed by Suleiman al-Khatib and was based at the Military Police barracks in Homs, Al-Balouni. The second was headed by Hassan al-Qa'qaa and was based in Damascus, in Mezze military prison. In the beginnings of Palmyra prison, detainees were transferred to Homs to be tried there before being sent back to prison. Mohammed Berro narrates:

A military ZiL truck was waiting for us. We were blindfolded and our hands cuffed behind our backs in metal shackles. They tied us all to one chain making it impossible to move individually. We piled up on top of each other on the floor of the truck. We were about 24 prisoners. The truck, which we used to call 'the meat car', took off. We arrived at the Military Intelligence branch in Homs. An hour passed without anything happening. An officer came forward and informed us that we would be individually brought before a military court. A small square room, not more than 4m in width and length. The lighting was poor. In the room stood a medium sized wooden table, on which two stacks of papers were scattered. The honorable court did not sit for more than one hour. All the sentences handed down were the death penalty.[65]

During December 1980, the number of detainees arriving at Palmyra prison increased. It became more difficult to transfer large numbers to Homs for trial, so it was decided to send the court to the prison twice a week. On each visit to Palmyra, the court was presented with about 60 detainees. Detainees were crammed into the Pen courtyard, where the court was held. They sat them on the ground with closed eyes and heads to the ground, under the rain in winter and the desert sun in summer. Mustafa Khalifa writes:

When we heard the sound of the helicopter everyone in the prison trembled. Even the police and municipal workers became stressed. Some called it the death plane, or the angel of death descending from the sky ... The field court members arrived in the plane, on Mondays and Thursdays. The court handed two lists of names. The first included the names of those who would be tried on this day. The second was the list of those who will be executed by hanging on the same day.[66]

Those sentenced to death were set for execution on the death lists approximately one and a half months after their trial day. The execution was carried out through a command, which became known to the convicts. Their names were called out from the doors of the dormitories. Names of fathers were also mentioned to confirm the identity of the detainee. Whoever heard his name prepared himself to execute the guard's order: 'Pack your things and break your connection with the dormitory.' He would change into old, shabby clothes so that his fellow detainees could use his good ones. The detainee left the dormitory with cries of 'Allahu Akbar' or by repeating identifying phrases between him and his colleagues in other dormitories. That call was to make them aware of his fate. It was also his self-declaration of resistance and acceptance of his fate. These aspects later disappeared, as Khalifa knew: 'Now I know the secret: after the sentenced inmates left the dormitory, the policemen closed the door and shut the convicts' mouths with duct tape.'[67] The hands of those sentenced to death were handcuffed, their eyes blindfolded, and they were transported to the Workshop dormitory in the sixth courtyard where executions took place.

The Head of the court walked up to the detainees in the Workshop dormitory and informed them of the decision to carry out the death sentence. Municipal workers and police officers set up the gallows. One survivor remembered:

I once peeped out of the judas window and saw the gallows set up in the courtyard and the bodies of the brothers hung on them. Police officers pulled hanging bodies down to make sure the execution is complete and that their souls had left their bodies. They were accompanied on this mission by the prison doctor Mohammed Yunus al-Ali. Then they dropped them to the ground and dragged them to a collection place. I saw them with my own eyes dancing on the dead bodies with joy and pleasure. Then the outside door of the yard opened to allow a large military truck in. They threw the bodies in it in an unimaginably brutal way. Two guard grabbed the hands and legs of the executed brother and swung him and threw the body like a cement bag. The sound of the body crashing into the floor of the truck could be heard by most people around the yard.[68]

Executions continued from 1980 to 1992 at different monthly rates. Sometimes they stopped altogether. Internal political events in Syria played a role in the rising numbers of the executed, especially after the battle of Hama early 1982.

In the first period of prison, 1980, we were used to executions being carried out once every two weeks. In 1982, they drastically increased, and executions were held two or three times a week. The number of executed detainees increased, starting with a minimum of 50 and sometimes ending in hundreds, as was the case on 23/5/1984 where the court executed 390 people.[69]

Unsteady gallows

They were not like the ordinary gallows to which the sentenced person climbed. These gallows descended to the convict. The municipal workers tilted down the gallows until the rope reached the neck of the convict. They fixed it well around the neck and then pulled the gallows from behind. This caused the convict to rise with his legs hanging in the air. They brought him back down after he died. The second batch came, then the third. Most of the people I watched get executed were calm. I also saw many cases in which the love of life and human weakness appeared. Some lost control of their bladder and bowls. Policemen, in those cases got very upset because the smell was unbearable, so they cursed the person and beat him. Some prisoners would cry, trying to speak and beg, but the duct tape prevented them. Once a young prisoner managed to escape from their hands and started running in the sixth courtyard which was a very large square with two branches. But escaping it was impossible. Policemen and municipal workers had to run after him for minutes until they finally caught him. They stood him under the gallows, but he sat on the ground. Two municipal workers lifted him up and inserted his neck into the loop. Minutes later his legs were kicking the air.[70]

The microcosm of Palmyra

Amid the Syrian desert lies Palmyra and its prison, which plunged its inmates into suffering, oppression, execution and torment. In the heart of this burning desert prison tales of resistance and life were created. During the second half of 1982, the wave of violence and executions eased slightly. According to Suleiman Abu al-Khair:

> [n]one of us could claim then they knew the reason. The severity of torture, which had doubled in quantity and quality during and after the events of Hama, receded. The wretched prisoners showed some signs of relief. After roll call periods, and the police retreating to the shade, the detainees directed several plays. Of these I remember the play 'Bilal al-Habashi's conversion to Islam'. I played the role of the victim. It was as successful as the possible means allowed. They also directed some plays that told the reality of social and political life in Syria.[71]

After getting used to all aspects of Palmyran life, detainees started to build social alliances, creating a world parallel to that of the outside. They started educational sessions in various sciences. They also memorized the Quran, Sunnah and Islamic jurisprudence; there were lessons in Arabic, English and French; lessons in history, geography, and chemistry. These sessions got everyone busy learning. It did not rely on books or papers, but on a memory capable of storing oral information. These dormitories were filled with hundreds of university students and holders of higher education degrees in various specialties, which prompted the rest of the detainees to take advantage of their knowledge as much as possible. Some became experts in various forms of medical and scientific knowledge, at least at the theoretical level. These sessions and reviews produced a series of philosophical debates and arguments. Modern religious currents were born in prison. Some considered Islam to be the Qur'an only, looking at Sunnah as a historical tale. Those became known as the 'Qur'anists'. Abbas Abbas adds: 'In captivity we were able to steal a laugh from the dire situation. We indulged in the abundance of time to our liking. We argued just to break the silence. We competed in poetry, chess, dice and physical exercises.'[72]

The games were not just for fun but also to develop skills and experiences and create an integrated life in the heart of the Palmyran death machine. Mohammed Berro, a most astute observer, narrates:

> The 'secret' theatrical work was the closest activity we could practice. Upon urgent need, talents bloomed, innovations competed, and experiences abounded. One of us pointed out that we could burn the black rubber that was in our underwear, then dilute the resulting ash in the water and use it as an eyeliner and for drawing mustaches and beards. Its most important properties were the speed of its dissolution with water and ease of removal. Those of us who were good in sewing went on collecting colourful clothes and other things to use as a cloak here or a turban there. The training and rehearsals were in full swing throughout the week, only interrupted by our exit to torture, roll calls, and bringing food in. To complete these acts, which were a violation of the daily regime of Palmyra, the detainees

assigned people from among them to watch out from the police. They followed every detail of their movements and changing of their locations. As long as these observers remained still, it was safe. As soon as we saw or felt the slightest movement from one of them, we would all freeze, as if in a wax museum, until a signal is received to explain or instruct a change in the set-up.[73]

All previous experiences show that inside the dormitory there was a highly structured institutional system. In addition to the head of the dormitory, the 'Emir of the dormitory', the 'Shawish', the prisoners elected his deputy. After them, the dormitory had its government that catered for, and regulated, the needs of detainees. The 'Bakhsheh' officer, in charge of the toilet. The Sleep officer regulated sleeping places. The Food officer oversaw the distribution of food rations to food groups. The Health officer managed medical files inside the dormitory and was responsible for these before the police. The finance committee kept all the monies of the detainees in the dormitory, to manage and spend it as needed. The night watchman was a job that all detainees served in two-hours shifts while the rest were asleep. 'The most extended responsibility throughout the day was the Sound officer.'[74] It was also a function which six detainees rotated for 12 hours a day. The task was to walk among the detainees and warn those whose voices were raised above the limit. Talking was forbidden in Palmyra, so any conversation had to be whispered.

Voting and elections

Despite the fact that conversation was forbidden in daily Palmyran life, detainees were required to express their support for President Hafez al-Assad. The expression of support took place at all events of the ruling party, re-electing Assad, and any 'national' event. Bara'a al-Sarraj narrates: 'On 10 March 1985, they took us out of the courtyard to perform a parade, carrying each other on the shoulders to celebrate the re-election of President Hafez al-Assad. The election of the president halted executions for more than 6 months. On 4 May 1985, executions resumed.'[75] The prison radio broadcast patriotic songs; prisoners were forced to cheer and sing for the beloved commander. Mustafa Khalifa narrates:

> On 16 November noise from speakers filled the air. Patriotic and national chants and songs praising the head of state were broadcast throughout the prison and around it. The songs and chants described him as wise and courageous. They gave him many descriptions: he was the one we sacrifice our lives for, the great leader, the teacher, the inspiration, his profound graces over the people were countless: without him, the sun would not have even risen. It was he who gave us the air to breathe and the water to drink. All prisoners stood in arranged lines in the courtyards. They allowed us stand in the yard with our eyes open for the first time since I arrived here. They gave one of the prisoners a sheet of paper, he would read the chants and cheer, and we cheered behind him: We sacrifice our souls, our blood, for our beloved and worshiped president.[76]

The end of 1986 was the beginning of a further deterioration in prison conditions. The amount of food declined drastically. There was just one loaf of bread for every three prisoners. It can be said that 1987 was a year of famine in Palmyra. This period was called 'Black September' due the severity of the hunger that afflicted detainees. Hunger was a major cause of tuberculosis among detainees. It consumed hundreds, even thousands, who became bedridden. Food was not the only thing to become scarce. Any medicine that had been previously provided also disappeared. 'During the same year they began transferring a number of prisoners to Saydnaya military prison, the ones with Communist charges during September. Then prisoners of the Iraqi Baath charges during October. After them, batches of Muslim Brotherhood detainees were transferred, but at the same time many Lebanese prisoners started arriving in Palmyra in batches. About 1,000 brothers were transferred to Saydnaya and replaced by about 1,500 Lebanese in Palmyra.'[77]

The conditions of the Palmyra prisoners continued to deteriorate, to the extent that the administration was forced to distribute military uniforms to detainees to replace their completely worn-out clothes. 'I learned later that about 100 died that summer due to malnutrition and lack of food.'[78] The harsh days in Palmyra rolled on, as Ali Abu al-Dihn experienced: 'The year 1989 was called the year of death in Palmyra because of severe torture and beating to death deliberately and in a very cold blood.'[79] At the beginning of 1991, a large number of detainees were released. Mohammed Hammad recalls: 'About 2,000 people were released. Day after day, we started feeling lonelier, as many dormitories became empty. There were moments of quiet that felt like the end of the world.' By the end of March 2000, new release lists arrived in Palmyra. '540 prisoners were released. Our joy for them was equal to our grief for ourselves. In November, about 500 people were released.'[80] After that, prison conditions became relatively calm: 'During that period we began to notice a relative improvement in food.'[81]

Palmyra prison solitary cells

Only a few of the detainees who entered Palmyra prison solitary cells escaped death by torture or execution. These were called called the *saloul* and were similar to those in Mezze prison. Mahmoud Issa spent time in the *saloul* and described them as having 'a deck, at the end of which was a broken water faucet, wrapped together with threads, dripping, next to it a soap bar and a sponge. Opposite to it an operative roamed the roof of the opposite solitary, with a gun and a bottle of water. He didn't care about us, nor did he mean anything to us. Little by little, darkness spread its shadows upon us and brought along deep silence.'[82] These solitary cells remained one of the secrets of Palmyra prison. Abbas Abbas was also locked in solitary:

I did not know that I had spent 5 years in cell No. 6 until I was transferred to a dormitory. Every morning I sneaked some light from under the door to celebrate daylight. In winter, when the liquid stuff came hot, such as tea and soup, I would warm myself with the bowl of food. I put it in my lap and surrounded it with my hands. The seasons of the year for me were divided by crops seasons: carrots two months, beans one month and potatoes three months, and so on... I went crazy five times, and completely regained my sanity twice, I suppose. The three other times it came back fragmented, confused and unreliable.[83]

The guests of the solitary cell tried as hard and as much as possible to close the toilet hole for fear of rats coming out of it. Some of them used a dough of bread, dirt and some clothes to create a plug that would clog that hole as safely as possible.

Female inmates of Palmyra

A group of women came out of Palmyra in 1984 and came to us. It was like a miracle. Soon we were told that the reason for bringing them to us was the spread of tuberculosis and scabies there. In this context, the women were transferred to Qatana prison and rounded up in the same place. Five women arrived to us in Douma prison in one go. There, in Palmyra, they could see the processions of detainees being led to execution. But Salwa was due to give birth without having any means to deliver her or even clothes for the coming baby. They had a detained a midwife from Hama. When Salwa got in labour they hid the news and kept quiet, suppressing her screams along the way, fearing that it would cause them punishment. After she gave birth one of the guards on the roof heard the cry of the newborn. When he asked, they told him. This young man, whose humanity hadn't completely died, gave them an empty tin can and matches. They lit some of their clothes on fire to heat water in which they bathed the newborn. The mother herself recounted that they cut her umbilical cord with a piece of tin.[84]

The tale goes that a 12-year-old boy named Abdul Majid was later transferred from the women's dormitory to the men's dormitory. Abdul Majid stood before the writer Mahmoud Qadi Al-Qala'a in Palmyra. Al-Qala'a was in tears over his uncle, who perished during his reception in Palmyra. The boy told him: 'Here, uncle, men do not cry.' Al-Qala'a wiped his tears with the sleeve of his shirt and asked the boy: 'If men here do not cry, what do they do then?' The little one's response came direct and spontaneous: 'They die; they just die ... and they die silently.'[85]

The transition from Palmyra to Saydnaya was chronological, as Saydnaya was established later. But it was also biographical, as Saydnaya absorbed many prisoners from Palmyra. Many prisoners were unfortunate enough to experience both prisons. Raed al-Nakshibandi was arrested in April 1982 for sympathizing with the Democratic Socialist Baath Party and was transferred to Palmyra in May 1983: 'I received my first visit after two and a half years of incarceration, then once every three months. I still hadn't received any information about my file, a state of emergency having been declared, the authorities didn't have to justify their arrests. We languished ... At the end of 1987, I was taken to the more modern Saydnaya Military Prison, in a suburb of Damascus.'[86] Nobody had heard of Saydnaya, but it was about to match Palmyra's brutal reputation.

8

Saydnaya Military Prison

On a hill adjacent to the Damascus – Saydnaya highway, 30 km north of the capital, between the towns of Telfita and Tel Menin – stands Saydnaya Military Prison. It consists of two buildings: the first occupies a space of over 1km². It is constructed in the shape of a three-pronged star, similar to the famous Mercedes emblem; the second is a white L-shaped building. Both buildings are surrounded by multiple military defences and fortifications. They start with the outer wall, then there are two minefields, then a second wall, then several military barracks and machinery. The third wall is the prison's direct inner wall.

The prison is under the command of the Syrian Ministry of Defence and is managed by the Military Police. It differs from Palmyra prison in that the latter was designed as a military prison in the mid-1960s and then expanded in the early 1980s to include politicians, dissidents, and security detainees. Saydnaya's red building opened in 1987 as a prison for politicians and security detainees. The white building was built between 1998 and 1999 as a prison for the military judiciary. Some of the detainees under this military category perform forced labour duties in prison, similar to the 'municipal workers' in Palmyra.

Figure 8.1 Satellite image of Saydnaya, Google Maps.

The main watchtower in the red building, the hexagon tower, is the meeting point of its three blocks. These blocks are known per the alphabet letters (A - B - C). Three floors of these blocks are above ground and two are underground. According to the main design of the prison, each floor above ground includes a wing named as per the block and the floor, for example: A-1, B-1, C-1. The old design of the wing included a U-shaped corridor with two large gates at both ends. The inner space of the letter represented the 20 dormitories which are separated by walls. All doors opened to the corridor. At the end of the letter U stood dormitory no. 11, an open space connecting the two corridors. After 1993, the two sides of the wing were separated by a wall that split dormitory 11 into two parts.[1] After this split, the names of the wings were adapted, for example 'A-1 right', meaning wing A, on the right side, first floor. The prison has kept this set-up until the present day.[2]

After the last modification, each wing consisted of 11 rooms, or 'dormitories', including rooms with large metal doors numbered from 1 to 10. These detainees' dormitories completely overlook a corridor that is three metres wide and 60 metres long. Room 11, located at the end of the corridor, had no doors. This served as the wing's enclosed space and was used by the detainees to exercise or to watch television during the day.

Following the prison mutiny in 2008, this room was converted into the main bathroom for the whole wing. An additional change in the shape of the wing after the restoration was the extension of the wing walls to become adjacent to the hexagon watchtower, thus isolating it from the rest of the wings on the floor. These modifications added to the wing a space known as 'space zero' – the space between the metal wing door and the control tower. Previously, this space was open, forming, along with the spaces from the other blocks, a circle surrounding the watchtower that was a landing space to which the doors of the wings opened. The new design turned the prison into a metal fortress. The walls between the wings and the rooms were metal-coated, and the toilet and bathroom windows inside the dormitories were sealed with thick metal sheets containing very small holes. The prison rooms were more like tightly sealed metal boxes.[3]

All dormitories have an identical design. Each dormitory is over 6 metres deep, and almost 5 metres wide, with a dedicated space for cooking, a toilet and bathroom at the far end. The prison basement in block A includes ground rooms and solitary cells. Block B contains 100 solitary cells in the basement. The basement of the red building also houses the communal bathrooms, which were decommissioned shortly after the prison opened, and a canteen, which was never used. Attached to the prison's red block is a small building housing administrative offices, which overlook the highway opposite the prison. The kitchen and bakery are located in the basement of the hexagon watchtower.

The white building, which falls under the same administration, consists of 42 dormitories spread over three floors. Its basement houses central baths and solitary cells on the second floor underground. Most of the executions of detainees following the uprising in Syria in 2011 took place there.[4] This prison was used to hold political prisoners after the prison mutiny in 2008. Some of its spaces were used to hold security detainees from 2011 until at least 2015.[5]

Saydnaya prison stands out from other Syrian prisons for several reasons. First of all, there are no photos or videos of the prison (unlike Palmyra, due to the ISIS takeover), therefore satellite images are as close as one can get to it. The Association of the Detainees and the Missing in Saydnaya Prison has digitally followed some guards who were foolish enough to take selfies and post them on their Facebook pages.[6] Second, Saydnaya has held a wide variety of detainees, from the later head of the Salafi militant groups such as Zahran Alloush (1971–2015), to moderate liberals such as Diab Serriya, even some pro-Assad militia members.[7] In that regard, it was indeed the contemporary counterpart of Palmyra prison, which had hosted political groups not just diverging but roundly hostile to each other, such as Communists and Islamists. Most importantly, the Assad regime's policies in Saydnaya moved from a carceral universe to a genocidal universe: from 2011 onwards, Saydnaya can no longer be considered a prison, but a concentration camp, indeed perhaps an extermination camp.

Prison managers

After it opened in 1987, Saydnaya was run by Colonel Barakat al-Osh, previously the Deputy Director of Palmyra prison. He was succeeded in 1991 by Colonel Mohiyaddin Mohammed, who was succeeded in September 2003 by Colonel Louay Youssef, who was dismissed over the escape of a judicial military prisoner. He was succeeded in August 2006 by Colonel Ali Kheirbek, who was removed from office on the morning of the mutiny. He was succeeded on 5 July 2008 by Brigadier General Talaat Mahfouz, who was killed in a Free Syrian Army ambush on 5 May 2013, after which Colonel Ibrahim Hassan took over the management of the prison until the end of 2013. He was

Figure 8.2 Talaat Mahfouz, from a pro-regime social media site.

Figure 8.3 Wasim Hassan, from a pro-regime social media site.

succeeded by Colonel Adib Esmandar, who was the Head of the Military Police in Latakia Province. At the beginning of 2014, Colonel Mahmoud Maatouq took over; he was killed by Syrian opposition forces near the city of Harasta in rural Damascus. 'Most of the starvation, extermination, brutal torture to death and extrajudicial killings took place during his time managing the prison.'[8] He was succeeded in January 2018 by Colonel Hassan Mohammed, then, in September 2019, by Colonel Wasim Hassan who remained in office until June 2020. No information is available on the exact date of his dismissal.[9] He was succeeded by Colonel Saleh Marhaj who remains in position today.

Detainees: numbers and profiles

The transfer of detainees to Saydnaya began in September 1987. The first detainees mostly arrived from Palmyra prison, but there were some from the security branches and the Mezze military prison. 'Saydnaya was completely filled in 1990. That year, it was estimated that 3,200 to 3,500 inmates were detained there.'[10] With the great amnesty in 1991, more than half of the Saydnaya prison detainees were released. However, new prisoners from Palmyra and Mezze prisons arrived in Saydnaya during the 1990s. At the end of 1999, a large batch of Hizb al-Tahrir al-Islami members arrived in Saydnaya. The party's militants had been imprisoned in Mezze and were later transferred to Saydnaya after its closure.

The prison included detainees from various backgrounds, the Muslim Brotherhood, Hizb al-Tahrir al-Islami, communists from the Political Bureau or the Labour League

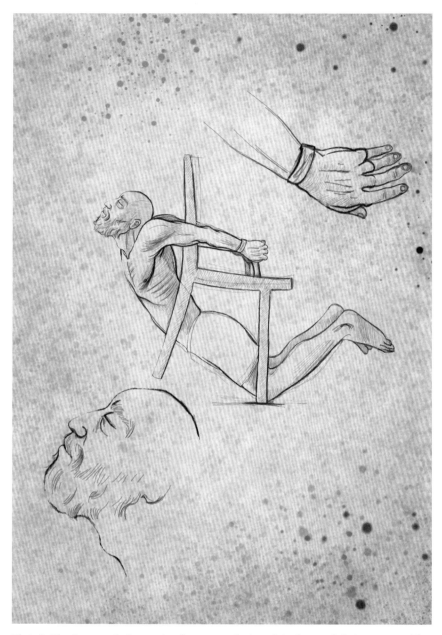

Plate 1 *The German chair*: a tool and torture technique. It is the usual chair structure. The detainee lays face down on the floor, the backrest of the chair is placed on the detainee's back and his hands are shackled to the back wedging the backrest between the detainees back and the shackled hands. The torturer slowly returns the chair to its normal position. This raises the backrest of the chair, tilting with it the detainee's back backwards gradually. The metal of the chair presses against the bottom of the detainee's back while the chair's feet gradually reach the ground. This method often causes fractures in the spine, which can cause paralysis of the detainee. At best, the detainee is temporarily paralyzed, not to mention the the severe pain caused by this method of torture.

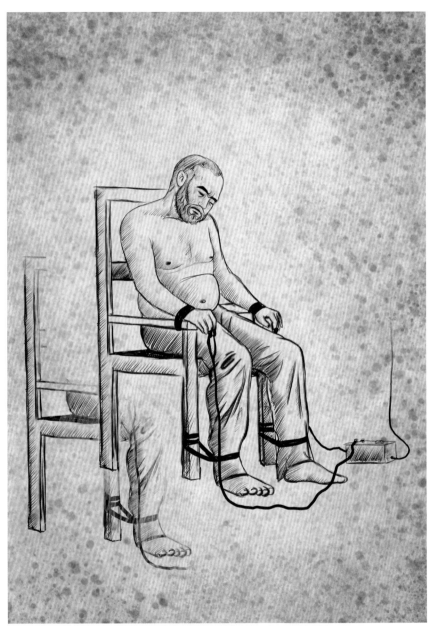

Plate 2 *The Dynamo*: a tool and torture technique. It is a small-sized generator that resembles an old military phone. The torturer quickly turns the axis of the Dynamo after connecting its wires to sensitive areas in the detainee's body. With the rotation of the Dynamo axis, the electric current runs through the body of the detainee, causing great pain.

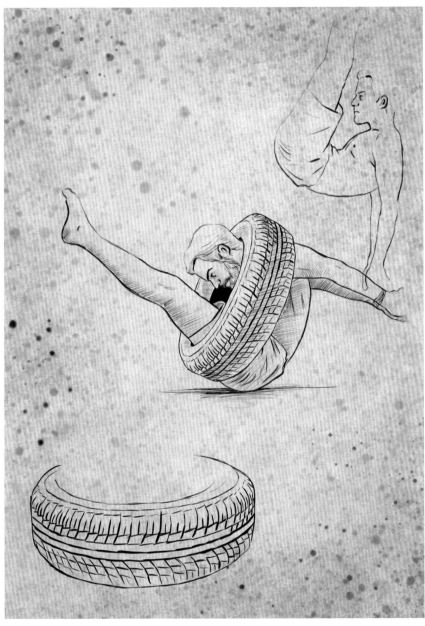

Plate 3 *The Wheel*: external frame of a car wheel, used as a torture tool. There are two ways to use the wheel. The most common one is to tuck the prisoner's legs and head inside the wheel, and then place the prisoner on their back, allowing the torturer to whip them easily. The second method is to push the prisoner's knees inside the wheel and when they appear from the opposite end, the torturer places a metal rod called the "Al-Qares [the biter]" under the detainee's knees and then place the detainee on their face. This method was used in Saydnaya prison after 2011.

Plate 4 *The blindfold*: a blindfold, mostly made of rubber or a piece of cloth. Its function is to shut the prisoner's eyes and prevent them from seeing. Theses are widely used in all security branches, in military prisons and in Saydnaya after 2011. They do not exist in civilian prisons.

Plate 5 *The whip*: is a cable usually used for electrical wiring in buildings, however used in prisons for torture and whipping. It is known as a "quadruple cable", that is a cable that comprises four thick metal wires wrapped inside a thick plastic casing.

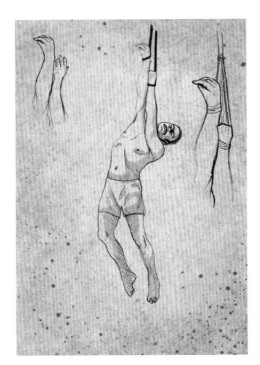

Plate 6 *Front suspension*: a torture technique. The detainee's hands are tied to a metal pipe over 2.5 meters above the ground, so that the prisoner maintains minimal contact with the ground via the tips of their toes. The commonly used term for this in Arabic is "Shabeh", used to refer to hanging the the body weight of the prisoner on their hands.

Plate 7 *The back suspension, the Blanco*: a torture technique in which a fixed lever often suspended from the ceiling is used. The detainee is handcuffed to the back then his hands are tied to the lever, lifting his body from their hands.

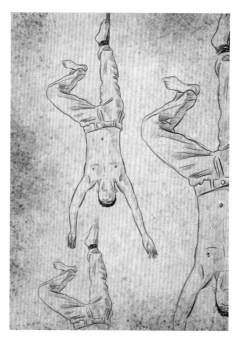

Plate 8 *Suspension by the feet*: a torture technique in which a prisoner is suspended upside down by tying one of, or both their feet to a pipe in the ceiling, a Blanco or directly to the ceiling, leaving the weight of the body on both feet or on one of them.

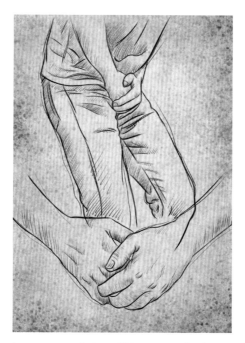

Plate 9 *Tying the penis*: a torture technique. This prevents the detainee from urinating. The detainee's penis is tied either by using a type of plastic thread, as was used in Military Intelligence in the 1980s, or by using a small metal clamp applied to the penis, as is used in Air Force Intelligence since 2011. The penis is released only after the required confession is extracted from the detainee. This technique causes health problems in the kidneys, ureter or penis that can persist throughout the detainee's life.

Plate 10 *The illusion of execution*: a torture technique. Used in different periods in Syrian branches and prisons. It is to convince the prisoner that they have been sentenced to death and that the sentence is about to be executed, or to place the prisoner's head into a noose and swing the chair or table on which they stand, or to convince the prisoners that they are being transferred to the firing field where they will be executed by a firing squad while they are in fact being transferred to another prison.

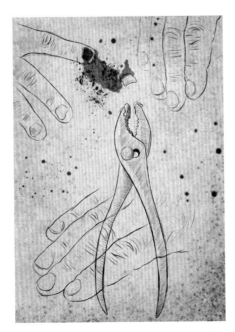

Plate 11 *Nail extraction*: a torture technique. Uses a special metal tool to extract the nails, to cause as much pain as possible to the detainee and push them to confess. A different method of nail extraction appeared in the history of Syrian prisons, especially after 2011. The method is to violently hit the nail bed with electrical cables causing the nails to fall off or causing blood congestion under the nails thus causing them to fall off over time.

Plate 12 *Lakhdar Brahimi*: a torture tool that spread after 2011. It is a thick plastic green water pipe commonly used in fresh water pipes in households. Intelligence operatives gave it that name in mockery of the UN envoy to Syria, Algerian diplomat Lakhdar Brahimi.

Plate 13 *The electric stick*: a torture tool. Some of its types are used for self-defense or by anti-riot police. It is battery operated, with two electrodes that emit an electric charge that distracts the target person. In prisons and intelligence branches, the electric stick was modified to release a higher electric charge, thus leading to fainting and, in some cases, burning the skin of the tortured detainee.

Plate 14 *The bamboo stick*: a tool of torture. A wooden stick made from bamboo. It's been widely used by Political Security Division branches.

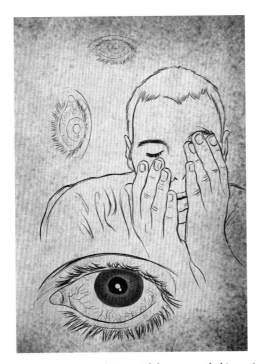

Plate 15 *Sleep deprivation*: a torture technique. It's been recorded in various periods in the history of Syrian prisons. This method is based on preventing the prisoner by all available means from falling asleep, like placing them in a very cold or flooded solitary cell, or have the guards rotate to ensure the prisoner is prevented from falling asleep. The detainee during this punishment is often forced to remain standing, to make easier to monitor them.

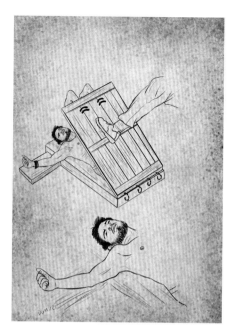

Plate 16 *The magic carpet*: a tool and torture technique. The prisoner is tied from their four limbs to a wooden board that moves from the middle. The lower part of the prisoner's body is lifted up by moving the lower section of the board. The board is fixed in a right angle while the prisoner is on their back. The jailer can beat the detainee all over their body, especially on the soles of their feet.

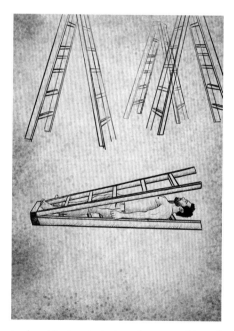

Plate 17 *The ladder*: a tool and torture technique. It was used in Military Intelligence during the 1980s. It is a metal ladder with two sides that meet at the top. The detainee is placed between the two sides and the ladder is closed with him inside. The ladder is then laid on the ground and one of the torturers walks over it with all his body weight squeezing the detainee's body. This technique often causes fractures to the bones of the legs, ribs or other bones of the detainee's body. The use of this technique was recorded again after 2011 in Deir Shmeil prison.

Plate 18 *Burning with cigarette butts or hookah charcoal*: a torture technique. Recorded at various periods in the history of Syrian prisons. Used extensively on women, particularly women who have been raped or sexually assaulted. The torturers systemically extinguish their cigarettes in sensitive areas of women's bodies after assaulting them. Burning with flaming hookah charcoal is used similar to the cigarettes on the bodies of detainees. However the flaming charcoal is more painful and harmful.

Plate 19 *Burning with hot water*: a technique and tool of torture. Hot, boiling water is poured over the body of the detainee, causing burns of different severity. The use of this method has also been recorded frequently on women who have been sexually assaulted.

Plate 20 *Cold water*: a technique and tool of torture. The torturers splash cold water on the body of the detainee after being severely whipped, and place them in a cold area such as an open yard in winter or in a wet and very damp solitary cell for maximum torment.

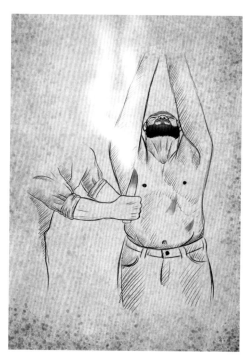

Plate 21 *Burning-ironing*: a technique and tool of torture. It involves burning parts or areas of the detainee's body using heated metal bars or liquefying nylon or plastic onto the detainee's body, leaving scars of varying intensity and impact.

Plate 22 *The parachute*: a torture technique. The detainee is placed on their back, then the torturers, or forced laborers as ordered by the torturers, lift the detainee by the limbs and waist up and down several times, accompanied by counting from one to three where at three they leave them to fall violently to the ground.

Plate 23 *The Pyramid pose*: a torture technique. The detainee is forced to lay on their stomach and their colleagues are then forced to lay on top of him/her one over the other, centering all the weight on the first prisoner. This method causes fractures in the ribs of the punished prisoner and may lead to their death. This method was used in Palmyra prison.

Plate 24 *Crucifying*: a technique and tool torture. The body of the detainee is fixed to a wooden cross and they are whipped. The use of this method was recorded in Deir Shmeil prison.

Plate 25 *Rape*: a torture technique. Used on both men and women, either by direct sexual assault from the torturer himself, or by using tools such as bottles or sticks. The use of these methods was recorded in different periods in the history of Syrian prisons.

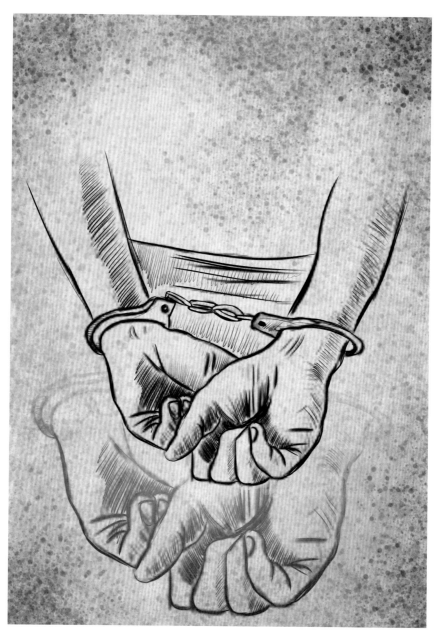

Plate 26 *Shackles*: the traditional metal shackle used by the police to restrain detainees. After 2011, the use of a different type of shackles known as "the tie" or "the gatherer" became common. It is a a plastic tie typically used to gather metal rods or electrical cables closer together. They were extensively used by the Syrian intelligence services because of the extremely large numbers of detainees.

or the Arab Communist Organization, as well as those accused of affiliation with the Democratic Baath or the Iraqi Baath, in addition to those accused of espionage, and then, after 2003, jihadists. The size of the prison and the separation of its wings helped in distributing detainees based on their charges in designated wings. From 2005 to 2008, the prison became the place of detention for jihadists and Islamists of all doctrines. The members of several Kurdish parties were also detained in Saydnaya following the Qamishli riots in the spring of 2004. 'The prison population reached over 1,200 prisoners, including more than 900 Islamists, before the prison mutiny.'[11]

With the start of the Syrian Revolution, the prison was completely emptied during the summer of 2011. It was being prepared to be the last stop for detainees of the security services against the background of revolutionary activity. During the years of the revolution, the prison turned into a state similar to that of Palmyra's in terms of the ferocity of torture and killing. Various human rights organizations and the United Nations later confirmed that the Syrian regime carried out thousands of executions in Saydnaya prison, amounting to a policy of 'extermination'.[12]

The timeline of Saydnaya prison can be divided into three phases: the first stretches from 1987 to 2007. Then the prison mutiny during 2008, until early 2011. Then the exterminatory phase from 2011 until 2020. Prisoners of the first phase describe their time there as a comfortable and much better place than the rest of the military prisons in Syria. The prison mutiny by security and political detainees that took place in Saydnaya was the largest in the history of Syrian military prisons. It lasted throughout 2008 and was followed by radical changes in the construction and management of the prison. The most violent phase in the history of Saydnaya prison is that stretching from the outbreak of Syrian Revolution until the present.

1987–2007

'Between Palmyra and Saydnaya prisons lay a few hundred kilometres, a dream and some longed-for freedom. The distance between them is abundant with content, yet void of any chance of true freedom; and both are a continuation of the experience.'[13]

The different conditions of detention between the desert prison of Palmyra and Saydnaya did not negate the military administration of the prison. The same Military Police operated both prisons, however with different the instructions on methods of treatment. Former detainee Mohammed al-Saleh noted: 'The instructions on the approach of prison management and processes come from the Office of National Security. The Prison Director can allow the best of the permissible limits, or the worst of the available conditions.'[14] Saydnaya prison was considered the dream and destination for Palmyra detainees. Mohammed Berro, one of the most astute observers of the prison system, confirmed: 'Going to Saydnaya was considered more than half a release. You can't begin to compare the two prisons in terms of the conditions of detention. Can Paradise be compared to hell?'[15]

Throughout the period from the opening of the prison in 1987 until 2007, the method of receiving detainees was based on an intelligence recommendation given by the head of the patrol to the adjutant on duty at the prison. Most of the detainees who came from Palmyra were not tortured with the usual 'reception party'. Some detainees coming from security branches were subjected to such sessions with varying levels of severity. Pierre Yohanna, for example, narrated:

> We were a large group coming from the Military Investigation Branch 248. We arrived at Saydnaya at 12 noon. They took our belongings, detailed personal information, and information about the detaining authority. We were then transferred to the reception wing, which we called the slaughterhouse. It was wing 'C-left, first'. There was a torture space there. The first six dormitories in the wing were removed and became the torture space. Inspection was carried out by the Military Police method, which is complete nudity and security movements. Then it was time to be beaten using the wheel which we were introduced to in the security branches. More than 20 police officers went on beating us. We remained under torture until 16:00. Military Police was accompanied by some 'municipal workers' which really hurt us, for they were prisoners like us, but they were more aggressive than the police.[16]

After completing the 'reception' procedures, inspecting the detainees, obtaining their personal data and listing them in prison records, they were transferred to the punishment wing or solitary cells. Some detainees spent an initial period in these places to be later transferred to the normal wings of the prison: 'The day I arrived I was placed in the black door, which was the punishment wing. I stayed there for a few days and then was transferred to "C-left second"'.[17] The black door wing 'B-right third', was intended for the punished or newcomers to the prison.

The prison administration resorted to punishing those inmates in 'C-left third' wing, instead of putting them in the punishment wing because they were all accused of affiliation with Hizb al-Tahrir al-Islami. As one detainee remembers: 'Our reception in Saydnaya was long. The torture lasted about three weeks. All dormitory doors remained closed throughout this period. We were severely beaten at every occasion such as food distribution, inspection and others'.[18] The ferocious handling of Hizb al-Tahrir al-Islami inmates came from a recommendation of Air Intelligence, the department that was responsible for their files. In addition to that recommendation, the prison administration spread among its staff that the inmates of that wing were dangerous. Remarkably, the detainees were discriminated based on their education, as Hammam al-Youssef recalls:

> Treatment in Saydnaya was unfair and devoid of any constraints. Torture came from a justifying mentality by Military Police, on the basis that they were dealing with "traitors". From the onset they ask about the level of education among detainees; those educated received more intense torture. I told them I was a tailor to protect myself from the increased dose of torture, as has happened with doctors, engineers, and other academics.[19]

The pattern of the selective reception, i.e. the torture of some and the placement of others directly in their wings, continued until 2005. By the end of that year, the distinction between the newcomers to Saydnaya and the old convicts in the prison became clear. The newcomers had a reception party, then were placed in the solitaries above the ground, i.e. 'B-right first' wing, until they were summoned by the court for a hearing. After the solitary, new detainees were confined to isolation wards until their sentences were handed down, or the prison administration changed their status. One detainee described his ordeal as follows:

> We were isolated in wing 'B-right third', that is the punished wing, until we were sentenced by the State Security Court. Our day started at 06:00. Food was distributed twice a day. The first was between 05:00 and 07:00. The second was lunch time, around 14:00. The latter included portions for lunch and dinner. The beating was not continuous or permanent. Their goal of the beating was to remind us that we were being punished. After a while they got used to us, and life took a peaceful course.

Added to the intermittent beatings was the fact that dormitory doors remained closed throughout the day. The prison administration provided running water to inmates of isolation wards only once a week.

> The arrival of water was an opportunity to bathe and wash dirty clothes. The duration of available water on that day was not enough for all the dormitories, especially as some of them contained more than 30 detainees. Not to mention the duty to fill the dormitory tank which we used for drinking, toilet, and normal daily uses for a week. A 300-litre tank was expected to suffice for all detainees in the dormitory, which meant only 10 litres of water per week for each detainee.[20]

The list of prohibitions for isolated wings included prohibiting 'breathing' time and 'the invoice', which allowed the detainees to buy food or other items from outside the prison. They were later allowed to buy only medicine. They were not allowed to have small food cookers or mattresses, 'Sleeping was only on blankets and the insulator. There were few blankets, so the prisoners used to spread them all to form a communal sleeping space in search of warmth in the extremely cold Saydnaya area. There was no heating inside the prison. The radiators were installed but they were cosmetic; they were never turned on. The prisoner had only two blankets and shared the cover with his fellow inmate.'[21] The detainee's stay in the punishment wing ended when he received his sentence. He was thereafter transferred to a different ward.

The punishments in Saydnaya Prison between 1987 and 2007 were not limited to placing the detainee in isolation. One of the penalties was to take the detainee down to the solitary cells, or transfer him to other wards with political, ideological or religious convictions that clashed with his. In 1989, the head of the Communist Party's Labour Wing, Ali Rahmoun, was sent to the solitaries. Rahmoun stopped one of the prison sergeants from beating him, so the sergeant punished him by taking him to one of the prison's solitary cells on the second floor underground. That punishment resulted in an incident that became known as the 'yogurt uprising', which had drastic consequences for all detainees.

The Yogurt Uprising

Following the release of the military prisoners 'municipal workers' from Saydnaya Prison, political and security detainees had to receive their own food allocations from the prison kitchen. On Sunday 23 April 1989, Sergeant Th. K. asked the head of our wing, Ali Rahmoun, to go down to the kitchen with him to receive lunch allocations. The head of the wing arrived at the kitchen along with others to carry lunch back to the wing. The meal consisted of a large bowl of bulgur and a bucket of yogurt. The head of the wing opened the lid of the bucket to find that it contained less than a quarter of what it was supposed to be. He asked the sergeant: 'Where is the yogurt? With this amount, a person can only get 10 grams, while the allocation for each person is 150 grams.' We knew the allocations for each prisoner. The Prison Director, Barakat al-Osh had already provided us with this information and asked us to inform him of any imbalance in these quantities.

An argument started between the head of the wing and the sergeant and then heated up to a degree where the sergeant tried to beat the head of the wing. The head of the wing reacted to the physical attack and refused to receive the yogurt. Military Police officers brought the head of the wing down to the solitaries. The rest of the group returned with the bulgur only but they left it outside the wing, which meant refusing food, and that was something that the prison administration did not tolerate. They put us in the dormitories and locked the doors. There was a commotion on the wing, and the adjutant on duty passed by each dormitory asking its residents: 'You don't want to eat?'. Our answer was: 'No.'

After a while we heard the door of the first dormitory open. The blows of the whip began falling on someone, but we didn't hear the usual torture screaming. Then we heard the whips fall on someone else. It is not known exactly who sparked the uprising, but a knock with a wooden stick on the door of one of the dormitories made the rest of the dormitories respond immediately. The wall of the dormitory from the side of the corridor was made entirely of thick metal tin, six metres wide and three metres high. The sounds of beating on this tin were terrifying. Cries united demanding the return of the head of the wing. The adjutant agreed to the request and within two minutes the head of the wing returned.

The prison administration did not let this pass by. The Prison Director Barakat al-Osh came and immediately ordered the transfer of inmates from the five dormitories to the wings of the Muslim Brotherhood. He thought he was punishing us with this transfer, but it was actually an opportunity to communicate and converse with them. We stayed in their wings about five months.[22]

Visits to most left-wing detainees in Saydnaya prison were allowed by the end of 1990. The rest of the inmates, however, were denied the right to receive visits, especially the Muslim Brotherhood prisoners. The inmates relied on the prison's food allocations.

Those who had money bought items to improve prison food which was limited to bulgur and rice with red gravy for lunch, olives, halva, jams and sometimes cheese for breakfast, while dinner consisted of potatoes and sometimes lentil soup.

The leftist wings adopted a socialist system within the prison. They established a common fund to purchase what everybody needed and distributed them equally eliminating any differences between prisoners who received visitors and those who did not. The same was the case in the wings of the Islamists, with some differences in the method and naming of the process. The method of providing food items was also applied to medicine and clothing. 'There was a prison kitchen, the food quantities were small and the quality was bad. It seemed like our sensitivity to food quality was getting higher. There was an opportunity to purchase food and other items via the invoice system. Once a week for vegetables, and once a month for other items. The wing committee used to purchase those needs in one centralized invoice.'[23]

The prison administration used this invoice system in a punitive manner at times, as Bassam Youssef notes:

It was a good source of income for the adjutants in charge of the prison. In the early 1990s, Saydnaya had more than 3,000 prisoners, so the total invoice of the prison could reach large sums. It was inevitable that the adjutant in charge benefited from it, either by doubling the price or by reducing the quantities. They made prison food even worse to force us to buy food from the outside through the invoice system.[24]

The general situation of Saydnaya allowed for everything to be purchased from outside the prison as long as prisoners had money, facilitated by the corruption of the Military Police there. Mohammed al-Saleh explains the extent of the corruption:

One of the heads of the wings, a prisoner from the Democratic Baath, had an excellent relationship with the sergeants and the police. He once said to the Prison Director: 'Don't withhold anything from us, we can buy them all [bribe] for 500 Syrian pounds (about $11 USD at the time) so we can get what we want. These conditions allowed us some luxury, so we made some alcoholic drinks like araq and wine. Some police officers drank from our araq and wine.'[25]

The state of corruption, or flexibility in treatment, allowed the detainees some gains such as a small transistor radio for each group or detainee. With time, buying books was allowed, so the leftists created a library that, by the early 2000s, held more than 4,000 titles. Most Saydnaya inmates considered the prison's wealth to be this library, which surpassed the central prison library, which housed some literary works and most of the books of the Arab Socialist Baath party. The library of communists, as it became known, included a wide range of books including those on heritage, psychology, international literature, politics, economics and a large number of Arab and international newspapers and magazines.

The local manufacturing in Saydnaya prison was not limited to alcoholic beverages. A number of crafts became popular among the prisoners such as carving bone, wood, olive or date pits, turning them into handicrafts such as photo frames, beads, necklaces and other small artifacts. Sometimes prisoners made musical instruments, such as the *oud*, as Baraa al-Sarraj fondly remembered: 'They made an oud out of fruit crates' wood. You couldn't tell that it was not made professionally outside the prison. They used to sing a folklore song. Whenever they started singing collectively, I used to say to my dormitory colleagues: the national anthem has started! and we smiled.'[26] Artifacts made of wood were later used to smuggle letters and literary works written by detainees to the outside. These were written in a very small font. They were then buried inside the woodwork, covered with sawdust and professionally processed to look like a uniform block of wood. Al-Sarraj gives an example: 'The detainees imprisoned on charges of Communism were moved to the second floor after a message they were trying to smuggle out was caught. It described the policemen as "bats of darkness" and us, the Islamists, as "comrades of the struggle".'[27]

Our children around the world

'Our dears, how are you doing abroad, tell us your news.' These were the opening words of the official song of the programme Our Children Around the World, which was broadcast every Saturday evening on the Syrian state radio 'Radio Damascus'. The voice of the Egyptian singer Najat Al-Sagheera came whispering through the small transistor radios hanging on the dormitory walls of the wings of the Saydnaya military prison. The intro is interrupted by the programme's presenter, Dr Amal al-Daqqaq, to announce a new episode. Detainees listened intently when the programme started receiving calls from families with members living abroad. The affectionate motherly voice of Umm Imran Msattet, from the Syrian city of Hama, comes weeping and deeply wounded, greeting Dr Amal. Umm Imran goes on, sending her love over the air to her firstborn son, Imran.

Umm Imran tells us a different story every time about her son's travels. One time he's in Germany studying medicine, another he's in Britain studying engineering, and a third he's in France working in a corporate. Umm Imran continues: 'My dear son, I sent you a wool shawl . . . It's cold, my son, please take care of yourself. May God protect you, save you from harm and clear your way.' Umm Imran stutters while praying for her son. The elderly mother breaks down in tears and the prison inmates share her tears in rivers. They all know he was executed years ago, but his mother doesn't know. The prison drowns in the silence of the weary. However, some rejoice to hear the news of their parents and loved ones through the programme's strange messages.

Former detainee Malik Dagestani believes that the beginnings of using Our Children Around the World to connect with parents, lay with the brothers Hassan and Hussein. They were two young men from the city of Homs, arrested young and spent most of their years in Palmyra prison, like many of those detained in the early 1980s. They were later transferred to Saydnaya prison at the end of the 1980s. Many years passed, not only without visits, but without any news about their family ... In Saydnaya, the two brothers met prisoners who were allowed monthly visits. It was during this period that many prisoners were able to smuggle radios into the prison. The brothers smuggled a letter through a leftist who received visits to reassure their family that they were still alive and that they were in Saydnaya prison. They concluded their letter by asking their mother to contact Our Children Around the World and to tell them during the call news about the family. This was the beginning, and the programme continued broadcasting the messages from families of the detainees in Saydnaya until the prison mutiny in 2008.[28]

Life in Saydnaya, within ordinary wings, followed a daily routine. Baraa al-Sarraj describes how the doors of the dormitories opened at '06:45 to take the garbage out and collect it in the floor's enclosed yard. At 09:00 "breathing" starts for an hour. Some people jogged, while others walked and talked or read books. The roll call was done every day at noon as we stood in a semi-circle facing the door of the dormitory. I used to avoid looking directly at the police as if I was still in Palmyra. It took me months to comprehend the new atmosphere. We would clean the corridors at noon, and then some would sit and talk while drinking matte and cracking some pumpkin seeds. In the evening, people visited each other. The last hour before the doors were closed, at sunset, the movement of people accelerated toing and froing along the corridors. People spoke hastily as if they were racing against time before the doors closed.'[29]

Life continued in this format, with some minor changes after the introduction of television to the wings. The TV was for the entire wing. During the day it was placed in dormitory 11, and then rotated every night to a different room. After 2005, detainees were allowed to buy televisions as well as radios. Metal beds were introduced. This was a strange, one-of-a-kind gesture in the world of Syrian military prisons, which at best provided military mattresses for detainees. However, all these features were withdrawn after the prison mutiny which destroyed most of the prison wings.

This settled routine contributed to the birth of some sort of cultural forms in prison. Poetry matches, foreign language lessons, acting plays. The latter was a daunting task especially in terms of providing the necessary equipment for the construction of the set. Participants tasked with this had to rely on the materials available in the wing. They made decorations representing buildings or walls from cardboard egg holders. Those cardboard dishes were kneaded and reshaped. Light reflectors were made from empty yogurt cans coated with the metallic foil of cigarette packs. Electric current for those lights was provided using wires pulled from central prison radio cables inside the wing. Costumes were made from old clothes, prison blankets or bed sheets that reached the prisoners through visits.[30]

These visits were difficult, with the visiting family suffering the most. Bassam Youssef spoke from experience:

The visit took place across two nets, the family on one and you on another. The distance between the two was about a metre. A Military Police operative stood between you and your family. He had the authority to reprimand you or your family if he believed you have exceeded the allowed visit time. He also had the power to cancel the visit and throw your family out. The visit was painful and humiliating for both you and your family. Yet we were punished by being deprived of it.[31]

The families had to make an extra effort to obtain approval for the visit from the Military Police headquarters in Qaboun. They could only ride to the main gate of the prison, and the road was uphill and difficult. The family had to carry any clothes and food they brought. The majority of visitors were elderly parents, therefore a visit was considered to be akin to cruel punishment to them. Yaqoub Bahi's family experienced this: 'The visit was disastrous for the family, we would spend hours waiting in the rain during which we would be subjected to insulting inspection and speech.'[32] There were some private visits which the detainee could get through connections or bribery; those allowed the detainee the opportunity to hug his parents and children. The duration of visits in all their different forms ranged from 10 minutes to half an hour, depending on the flexibility of the adjutant on duty.

During the first period of prison life, from 1987 until the opening of visits to most leftist detainees at the end of 1990, the movement of prisoners outside the wing was limited to breathing and the central bathrooms only. 'The prison was designed to conform with the specifications of correctional facilities, so it included a restaurant, a library and a central bathroom. All were in the basement.'[33] The bathrooms were a 'set of shower cubicles separated by concrete dividers 1.5 metres high. These compartments were located opposite the central kitchen which was under the watchtower.'[34] They were used regularly for the first three years of prison life, and later sporadically for some special cases. Bassam Youssef narrates:

Taking us to the central bathrooms was barbaric. Under the hexagon there was a kitchen that distributed [food] to prison canteens which made up half a wing under each block. The rest of the space is the central bathrooms of the wings of this block. At the end of the canteen, before reaching the bathrooms there was a staircase that took you down to the cells under each wing.[35]

Bathing was carried out using military commands. They the hot water was turned on the first batch of detainees were brought in, and then they brought the next batch. The second batch waited outside until the order was given to the first batch to end showering. When they came out, they were forbidden to look at each other:

When I was waiting for the batch in the bathrooms, a military policeman came and pushed me hard against the wall. He ordered me to move away so that I can't see who was inside. We had a verbal confrontation, and I was punished with 22 days in the solitary cells. They took me straight from the bathroom down to the solitaries. The solitary cells were very bad. They were located on the second floor underground. If anything happened to you and you screamed with all your might, no one would hear you. If you're punished, you'll suffer a torture session with every meal. You are under the mercy of the military operative there. There is no law that governs the relationship between you and him. There, I witnessed a military policeman toying with a detainee. He rode on his back and tortured him at the same time.[36]

During the end of the 1990s, the prison administration allowed a medical clinic, managed by Dr. Abdulaziz Khair, in the A-right first wing. This modest clinic received prison patients for examination. Before this clinic, detained doctors took care of their fellow prisoners. The presence of the military doctor under the prison management was a formality. Prisoners relied on fellow doctors to build their health system. 'We took care of ourselves. Our fellow detained doctors prescribed us medicines that we bought through a special invoice. The life of cooperation allowed us to have a central pharmacy that provided the necessary medical resources for us and the rest of the prison population. Our detained doctors were responsible for the patients in the rest of the wings.'[37] From 1987 to 2007, the prison administration transported emergency medical cases to the nearby Al-Tall military hospital. During the year of prison mutiny and post revolution, in 2011, these cases were transferred exclusively to Tishrin military hospital near Damascus.

The prison's relationship with the outside world was not limited to newcomers, radio, visits or release. There were a series of visits to the prison by security and health committees. After these visits, the regime released some detainees. The great amnesty in 1991 was followed by a series of mass releases. Baraa al-Sarraj remembered:

On Friday 26 November 1993, about 50 people were released from our wing hosting about 120 detainees. Most of those released were young men under 18 at the time of their arrest and years have passed since their sentences expired ... On Monday 27 December of the same year, the committee of officers returned again to interview those who remained, this time I was among them. Most of the conversation was with Major General Hassan Khalil. He was shouting, frothing, cursing and using foul language: 'Go away, bastard, we meet again next year', that was the last thing he shouted at me before I got out. I remained optimistic that there was a release for me being considered. But the death of Bassel al-Assad on 21 January 1994 stopped everything. Prisoners no longer dared to turn the radio up or even smile. A number of policemen stopped shaving their beards as a sign of grief.[38]

The security committee was absent from Saydnaya until 1995 and was headed by Major General Hassan Khalil and included Hisham Ikhtiyar. However, large batches of detainees were released in 1999, before all Hizb al-Tahrir al-Islami members were imprisoned in Saydnaya at the end of that year. 'In the same year, most of the Lebanese detainees were released following an agreement between the governments of the two countries.'[39]

The death of Bassel al-Assad halted the release of detainees for nearly a year. The death of President Hafez al-Assad on Saturday 10 June 2000, had a wider impact on the lives of prisoners at the time and afterwards. Omar al-Sayyed Youssef remembered the day well:

'The dormitories were closed. The prison suddenly went into a state of complete silence. We only heard the sound of reciting the Quran. We didn't know what was going on. Our torture that has been going on since we arrived in prison stopped. They started putting food bowls in front of the dormitory doors. We opened the door and pulled in the bowl without a word. We didn't know what was going on. We expected someone died. After almost 1.5 months the doors were opened for us to go out to the corridor of the wing. Life began to take a natural form. They brought us old newspapers after we insisted. We knew from the newspapers that Hafez al-Assad had died a month and a half ago.'[40]

From 1999 to 2007, the ideological and political composition of the Saydnaya detainees changed. However, prior to 2005, the prison was in poor condition. The electricity supply was poor and water and sewage pipes were damaged. These poor condition pushed prisoners to make up for the shortfalls in their own ways. They made power switches from the plastic parts of used injections. They designed refrigerators to preserve the vegetables they bought via the invoice. They tied four plastic boxes on top of each other, covered them in burlap bags, fixed them to the wall opposite the dormitory and placed a plastic box filled with water on top of them. Hanging from that box were plastic tubes commonly used to transport saline liquid to patients' veins. They kept it cool by dripping water on the burlap bag which had a moving flap in place of a fridge door. They made electric lanterns from some wood and yogurt or halva plastic boxes. They wired them to electricity using the same wires drawn from the central radio cables. They heated bathing water using heaters made from sardine can lids. They separated the two covers with plastic insulators and then connected them using thick cables they bought from police operatives.

After taking over the prison management at the end of 2003, Colonel Louay Youssef decided to rehabilitate the red building in Saydnaya prison. Pierre Yohanna was present at the period: 'After the visit of the commander of the Military Police, Major General Bassam Abdelmajid, to the prison in early 2004, they decided to fully rehabilitate the structure, the paint, electricity and bathrooms. Restoration lasted about a year.'[41] During that period, the prison administration moved prisoners from one wing to another, allowing prisoners from different ideological affiliations to mix with each other. The number of detainees with jihadi backgrounds in Saydnaya increased after 2004 and the prison became a major detention facility for those accused of belonging to the Salafi jihadist movement. A large number of Kurdish detainees arrived at the prison during the same period. 'Saydnaya became home for dozens of Islamist groups and some democratic detainees.'[42] The democrats, i.e. non-Islamists, along with a number of veterans detained on charges of espionage and treason also witnessed the prison renovation phase and subsequent events.

Death and escape

Before starting the restoration, the prison administration raised the levels of tension between prisoners. Prison director Louay Youssef asked Islamists to respect the 'spies' and lower the sound of the 'azan' [call for prayer] because it 'bothered them'. He asked the spies to turn down the TV or radio because the music 'disturbed' the 'Al-Qaeda' group. That process was accompanied by a series of incitement, lies and deceit by the prison management on both sides. When the detainees with intellectual and ideological differences met in the same ward, a murder took place. On Wednesday 7 December 2005, inmates of wing B-right second, the 'spy wing', were surprised by an attack by detainee Abu Said Al-Dahik on three veteran detainees at night. Al-Dahik attacked three of his colleagues with a metal water pipe with the intention of killing them for 'blasphemy'. The attack followed orders from a Sharia Court held by jihadi detainees. One prisoner was killed and the other two were wounded. Prison management practices were becoming more rigorous and stricter. However, the escape of one of the 'municipal workers', the judicial military detainees, in June of the same year was the final straw. There were two accounts of this incident, the first claimed he escaped by hiding between empty flour bags that were taken out after the load was emptied in the prison's bakery. The second claimed that he escaped during day visits, where he took advantage of the occupation of the Military Police, replaced the service suit given to him in prison with civilian clothes and fled with the visitors. The director of the prison, Louay Youssef, was sacked as a result of this incident and replaced by Ali Kheirbek Nassif, the nephew of the well-known intelligence man Mohammed Khairbek Nassif. A new phase started in Saydnaya.[43]

2008–2011: the mutiny and its aftermath

The prisoners of Saydnaya prison at that time agree that the prison mutiny was divided into three stages. The series of transformations and changes in the nature of the prison and the backgrounds of detainees within it paved the way for the biggest mutiny in the history of Syrian military prisons. The Salafi jihadist cohort had dominated the prison since 2006. The mass imprisonment of Salafi-jihadists was, according to former Salafi-jihadi Kheder Ramadan, 'an action designed to whitewash the Syrian regime's page with the United States of America. Most of those arrested on this charge, however, were simply people who had listened to audio tapes of Salafist sheikhs. Some of them were young men who attended jihadist sermons in mosques whose sheikhs were allowed by the regime to incite jihad against Americans in Iraq'.[44]

After the murder in wing B-right third, the prison administration imposed harsh treatment on all Salafis. Kheder Ramadan was one of those who suffered:

Healthcare had become a formality. In severe cases the prisoner was taken to the hospital. Food was from Army allocations. We were left in solitaries until the verdict was issued, after which we were transferred to one of the isolation wings. I remained there for more than a year, until the prison mutiny took place. The wing included detainees of various affiliations, including the perpetrators of the Takfiri murder. Block B on the third floor turned into isolation wings, and I was a resident of B-left third.[45]

The Kheirbek administration punished those wings by withdrawing benefits such as cooking gas, the invoice system, and 'breathing' time. They even cut the water. Another former Salafi-jihadi detainee noted:

The prison management cut off electricity from us for days before some young men came to a solution. They stole a soft line from outside the wing or returned the current by turning on the main power switch when the police were not looking. There were two different accounts of the incident, however they both meet in that a military policeman noticed the light, went in and quarreled with the prisoners. During the inspection the next day, 26 March 2008, a Sergeant Major named Ghadir insulted God. The detainees attacked the Sergeant Major, who escaped from the wing and called for help from the Adjutant on duty, especially after the detainees started banging on the metal doors. The Adjutant absorbed our anger by bringing back the power and running water to the wing.[46]

The first phase of the mutiny

The story of the Sergeant Major cursing God did not end there. The Prison Director came the next morning, 27 March, and immediately went up to wing B-left third.

The door of each dormitory was opened separately and its detainees were asked to take only a towel and go down to the ground floor. The first dormitory went down and its inmates did not return. They were being foot whipped and left in a dormitory there. The second group that came down realized the game so they beat the soldiers and went up to the wing immediately. They announced the details of what was going on and started shouting Allahu Akbar and cheering. The Director escaped immediately. The police closed the doors of the wing with detainees inside. It was 11:30 when the situation exploded. We dismantled the wing's door and the word immediately spread among the prisoners on the third floor. They broke the doors of their wings too. We went down to the second floor and we opened the doors of the wings there and then the rest of the wings of the prison, which housed more than 1,300 detainees.[47]

After opening the doors of the dormitories and wings, prisoners spread all over the prison. Some of them climbed onto the roof to burn blankets and wood to alert nearby villages that something was going on. Others tried to reach the administration building on the ground floor. It was at this point that the Prison Director asked the police to use the 'municipal workers' as a shield. They clashed with the detainees, causing injuries on both sides. Kheder Ramadan continues:

> The prison administration attacked us with tear gas. When we found a way to deal with gas, they opened live fire in the air to scare us. In light of this chaos, we asked Sheikh Samir al-Bahr to head the negotiating committee which was formed on the prison management's request to form a committee of 'elders'. Sheikh al-Bahr was a disabled man so we carried him to the park near the entrance to the prison and he was accompanied by his son and the human rights detainee Nizar Rustanawi. They were met by the Prison Director Ali Kheirbek, General Saeed Sammour and a number of senior officers in the military and military intelligence.[48]

The detainees submitted their demands to the regime committee and the prison management. These included the transfer of detainees' cases to civilian courts instead of military field courts or the State Security court; opening visits to those banned from receiving visitors, dealing respectfully with the families of detainees during visits and providing a vehicle to transport them from the prison gate to the building where visits took place; stop beating and torture in prison, reception party and isolation wings, and stop beating in security branches; abolish the penalty of solitary cells; improve the quality of food and health care and increase 'breathing' time. The regime committee promised to carry out those requests in exchange for ending the prison mutiny and reinforcing order in the prison. Kh.A. narrates:

> The prison mutiny ended on the same day. We went straight back to the dormitories. Some of the inmates in the wings refused to obey the decision. I helped bring them back to the dormitories, which helped end the problem. I stood in the wing corridor and took inventory of the damages in the dormitories. They asked for someone familiar with electrical wiring to assess the damages. Prison repairs lasted nearly a week. We asked for food because the day of prison mutiny came to an end without giving us any food. They handed us sandwiches instead of prison food. We were prevented from breathing due to repairs for almost a week. We asked them to return the gas stoves to the rooms, and they did. The next day the prison management returned to the hands of the Military Police. They conducted a roll call and closed the wings.[49]

The prison administration's treatment of detainees improved dramatically over the next three months. 'During that period it seemed that the Prison Director was frozen. Intelligence was constantly coming to the prison. The situation became very fluid. It reached a point where prisoners were not bothered when the adjutant or the sergeant came in for the roll call. Moving between wings became as spontaneous as prisoners desired without the permission of the management, an action that in previous times would have warranted punishment. Chaos started reigning in the prison. We did not know that all this was a prelude to what was coming. They told us that some good changes will happen in the seventh month.'[50] The prison management made every effort to monitor the actions of detainees without any deterrence or prevention. 'Some of the Islamist prisoners did not understand the situation and became arrogant. They thought they had triumphed over the regime. However, the prison management was reporting every detail to the Military Intelligence and the Office of National Security. We found copies of these reports later in the administration building during the second phase of prison mutiny. We also found the reports from prisoners who were informants to the management. We had identified them prior to that, but the reports confirmed our suspicions. They were monitoring all our movements, especially us with Islamist backgrounds, and reporting them to the security services.'[51]

The second phase

The prison management invested the state of disarray and chaos among the detainees to arrange for what led to the second phase of the prison mutiny. This stage can be called the 'revenge'. 'The Prison Director arranged for it by letting things go very awry. With time, this reflected on us. We must not forget that it was a military prison of a security nature.'[52]

Between 05:00 and 06:00 on Saturday 5 July 2008, the promised day came. The prison management spread a rumor that a fundamental shift would take place this month; prisoners expected a general amnesty or something. Kh. A. was present that fateful day and recalled: 'We began to hear cheering and Allahu Akbar shouts from the adjoining wings on the third floor. We expected that amnesty had arrived, but it was too early for such an action. It was about 06:00. We opened the radios to the BBC and Monte Carlo stations, as they would usually air such news. But there was no such news.' During those minutes dozens of Military Police operatives were storming the prison. They opened the doors of the first dormitories of our wings, and stormed them in full armor and with batons. 'They entered our dormitory with a number of officers. They tied the detainees up with plastic cable ties and started beating them.' Before starting the beating, they were pulling out all the gas stoves and metal beds out of the dormitories they opened. 'An officer and a Lieutenant Colonel walked in on us and asked me, being the wing head, to carry out those actions. I asked him about the reason behind this order and who issued it. He got angry and began to shout blasphemy, so the prisoners responded to him by shouting Allahu Akbar. They opened the door of the first dormitory, pulled out the beds and took out the gas stoves. They started tying some of its inmates with the plastic zip ties; the same happened to the rest of the wings. They restrained people based on their names which were on lists they were carrying. They obviously came carrying certain names.'[53]

The Prison Director asked for help to restore order to the facility, and he was given about 1,300 military personnel. Kheder Ramadan has profound memories of that day:

> They arrived at the prison the night before and were mostly new members who had just finished a course in the Military Police. They did not know where they were going nor what the task assigned to them was. They entered the prison with batons and instructions for a large-scale disciplinary process. They spread over the wings, a military policeman for a prisoner, as the number of prisoners was close to

the that of the attackers. The events were similar in all the wings on the third floor. My colleague Ahmed Hammadi tried to inquire about what was going on from one of the judicial prisoners, the 'municipal workers', who were helping the Military Police. He spoke to him through the ventilation holes of the dormitory under the iron door. That 'municipal worker' took advantage of Hammadi gazing from under the door and stabbed him with a wooden stick he was carrying gauging his eye. That was when we fully realized the gravity of the situation and started arming. The number of prisoners in each dormitory was about 16. That day I was in wing A-right third. As soon as the situation developed, we dismantled the beds to use their metal beams as weapons. The cries of Allahu Akbar began to grow louder inside the prison. The wardens and their companions were growing frightened and terrified. Cries of Allahu Akbar were accompanied by banging the metal dormitory doors. The sounds of banging and shouting caused the entire building to tremble. The sounds reached the rest of the dormitories on the rest of the floors. Everyone armed with pipes and started opening the walls between the dormitories and the wings. A large section of prisoners rushed to the tenth room of each wing. They opened the wall to dormitory 11, the rear space of the wing, and, together with the inmates of the first dormitory, surrounded the Military Police and officers in the middle of the corridor in each wing.[54]

Battles and captives

'We could picture the genocide that occurred in Palmyra in 1980, so we decided to fight until the end. Clashes between detainees, Military Police and 'municipal workers' began in the middle of the corridor of each wing. We hit some soldiers with the metal beams of the beds, causing them to bleed. They surrendered immediately. We took everything they had on them and pulled them out of the wing in their shorts. The same scenario occurred in the rest of the wings. When the situation exploded, most of the raiding officers fled and locked the doors of the wings on us with the policemen and the 'municipal workers' they left behind. We arrested 1,150 of them, including about 24 Officers and Commissioned Officers, Lieutenant Colonel, the Deputy Prison Director who was a Major, a Captain and two Lieutenants. I learned from the 'municipal workers', as I was handing them food, that Colonel Kheirbek gave them permission to do as they pleased in the prison. They allowed them, once our 'discipline' was over, to loot all our possessions: refrigerators, washing machines, televisions and any equipment we owned. The Military Police had to carry out the task of 'disciplining' using batons, some tear gas and protective gear.

A group of the detainees attacked the administration building, but the Prison Director shot Abdul Karim al-Haffar and Zakaria Afash. The first died after being transferred to Tishrin military hospital as a result of ill-treatment and torture there, while the second died on the spot. As the situation developed, the prison management decided to seek help from Damascus. A large group of Special Forces and Counter-Terrorism forces arrived. My brother was serving his military service in the latter. That force hit a tight cordon around the prison. During these developments we decided to occupy the roof to prevent any military landings. I took 350 of the captured operatives to the roof of the prison along with Kheder Alloush, who was later killed in the prison mutiny. We handcuffed them to the back and left them bare-chested. We stood them on the edge of the roof like a fence to prevent the forces besieging the prison from shooting at us. But they shot at them and us. One of the operatives we used as a human shield threw himself to the roof of the prison administration building and another to the ground of the breathing yard in fear of bullets.

The second goal of taking to the roof was to make a fuss and draw the attention of the people around us to prevent being massacred, or so we thought. We burned some mattresses and clothes to draw attention, knowing that we were going to die anyway, we had to do everything to defend ourselves.'[55]

Some of the detainees who went down to the ground floor reached the personal belongings room, where the prison administration kept the mobile phones confiscated from the detainees. Kheder Ramadan:

A man called BBC Radio to let them know the news and all the details. The journalist asked him about the accuracy of the information. She did not believe the number of the captured operatives, which she thought was exaggerated. He told her he could send her pictures of those captives. She refused the number, however the radio later broadcast reports of a mutiny in the prison and taking its guards hostages.' At this point, the regime resorted to disturbing the cell signal in the perimeter of the prison to prevent any contact with the outside. Further military reinforcements reached the perimeter of the prison, and the highway opposite to it was cut off. 'They started shooting at us and completely surrounded the prison with troops authorized to shoot live bullets at us.[56]

After the situation exploded, some detainees arrested informants among us to prevent them from communicating with the management. Kh.A. tells the story of these men:

We moved the informants to a ward that we assigned them. I interrogated all of them before Al-Qaeda group pulled them from my wing and formed a commission of inquiry and a Sharia court that subjected them to horrific forms of torture. At the same time on the ground floor, some discovered the bodies of six spies, no one knew who killed them.' The killings were not limited to the informants. Rights activist Nizar Rustanawi was killed during the chaos. Masked detainees took him to the ground floor where he was killed immediately and brutally. 'The day I went down to see the dead bodies, I could not distinguish Nizar's because of the magnitude of the injury he suffered. His head was smashed and his features gone. We identified him from his clothes. Everything went very fast; all these crimes took place on the first day of prison mutiny.

It is believed that al-Rastanawi was killed by the Takfiris, because of his cynical position on Islam.[57]

On the opposite side, the detainees took their captives down from the roof and placed them in the last dormitories of each wing. The old negotiating committee assigned some of the detainees to attend to those prisoners. They attended to the wounded among them as they did for their fellow wounded detainees. Through these arrangements, the forces surrounding the prison started throwing tear gas at them through the windows. There were cases of suffocation, some even died. Several deaths occurred among captured military personnel and detainees. Some were trampled underfoot because of large stampedes during clashes. 'The battles lasted until about 15:00. That's when regime forces spoke to us through loudspeakers to get the wounded out of both sides. They asked us to form a negotiating committee.'[58]

The first demands of the regime were to hand over its operatives and officers. At that point detainees were divided, some completely refused to hand over, while others considered them a bargaining chip to achieve their demands. Kh.A. continues:

We decided to hand over the captive officers days later in exchange for bringing food to the prison and stopping the shooting. In the early days, we relied on food stored in the prison, but it was not enough for us and the prisoners. As soon as we handed them the first batch of prisoners, they started shooting at us again. We remained trapped for several days, during which they threw tear gas at us and threatened to kill us and arrest our families. They placed cranes close to the corners of the prison so snipers could be stationed on them. Death became a daily status. They tried to raid the prison in cooperation with counter-terrorism forces but they failed. We arrested them, as they didn't know the prison plans. They entered one of the wings by mistake, so we locked them in it. They tried again, this time using a troop transporter. We stooped them by lighting up gas cylinders and throwing them on their wagon to explode. These battles lasted several days. We started fortifying the prison, especially the windows.[59]

Kheder Ramadan continues: 'Since I was a tailor, I made fortification bags from military mattress covers. We filled those bags with sand and broken tiles to block the windows and protect ourselves from sniper bullets. We stayed in a hit-and-run state for more than eight days during which we demanded a change in the prison management in order to return the prison to its normal state and forget about the blood.' Communication between the prison management and the detainees was being carried out via a negotiating committee headed by Sheikh Samir al-Bahr – the same committee which visited Tishrin military hospital to check on the wounded who did not return.

The detainees later discovered that several their wounded had died in the hospital. '25 wounded went to the hospital and only 19 returned. Some of those who died had minor injuries but doctors there killed them under torture. At that point, the prisoners demanded revenge for their fellow prisoners by killing the captives.'[60]

The regime spread a rumour that the director of Tishrin military hospital had been punished, and that they would meet the demands of the detainees. They returned drinking water to the prison and then provided the detainees with ready meals of excellent quality. This happened for 10 days, so the detainees handed over their remaining prisoners. Before all this happened, the prison administration had been taken over by the veteran Military Police Brigadier Talaat Mahfouz. Negotiations between the rebel detainees and the regime began. 'Mahfouz entered the prison and announced that he developed a reform plan and that the negotiations will happen directly with him. He was conversing with us like an old friend. He used a religious coating to gain our trust but did not stop the glorification of the President.'

The negotiations went beyond the Prison Director to senior leaders in Military Intelligence and the Syrian Army Authority. 'There was a representative of General Asef Shawkat taking orders directly from him. After that, the negotiating committee representing the detainees went to Damascus to meet Shawkat in person.'[61] At that point the regime negotiated taking over the administration building, the kitchen, and the bakery, on the pretext of improving the lives of the detainees. Ten days into the prison mutiny the new management regained the building. They then took over the ground floor including the bakery and the kitchen. The internal management of the prison remained under the control of the detainees, who demanded that workmen entered the prison under the supervision of outside officers. The repairs lasted more than a month and a half, during which the detainees suffered prolonged water and electricity cuts under the pretext of maintenance.

The water war

The new prison administration adopted a finger-biting policy. Our war with them was no longer limited to avoiding bullets from snipers stationed on the cranes near the windows of our wings or dealing with tear gas. The prison mutiny became protracted and we were exhausted by the constant state of alert due to continuous fake raid attempts. We were in a state of despair, especially with no gas and depending for food on some of the flour we had taken from the prison's bakery. We kneaded it with some water if available and baked it over a fire made of shoes or books. They fought us by preventing any form of medical care. Our field clinic, which we had set up in the A-right third wing was poorly equipped due to lack of resources.

All of the above was coupled with water cuts for long periods. However, winter came early and with the first rainfall we stored the rainwater that gathered on the roof of the prison. The regime noticed that so they brought fire trucks filled with sewage and flooded the roof of the prison with urine and feces. They pumped huge amounts of this dirty water on us, especially during the last confrontation. We drained that water and treated it to use it again. Especially since rainwater washed the surface again. It did not, however, wash away the taste of tear gas that did not stop throughout the last month of the mutiny.[62]

Military Police and army forces were controlling the perimeter of the prison, the administration building, the kitchen and the bakery. They had access to the ground floor to carry out repairs. The rest of the prison was managed by the prisoners under the supervision of the negotiating committee, which cooperated with the heads of the wings. Sector C on the second floor became the storage area for water and food, which was limited to some very small quantities of bulgur. The A-right third wing was converted into a battery-lit field hospital insulated from the outside with blankets that covered the windows. Everyday life was about being on high alert. H.M. one of the survivors of the uprising and massacre, noted:

I am Alawite and was arrested on democratic charges, so I was threatened by both Islamists and the regime at the same time. I had to provide my own food and water supplies and ration my consumption as much as possible. Like the rest of the prisoners, I was armed with a water pipe all the time. There was a military command for the prison, among them were Samir al-Bahr, Abu Huzayfah al-Urduni and others. They were the negotiating committee. They asked to meet with us, me and my fellow democrats, and discussed getting us out of prison if the regime gave them permission to get us out. My colleagues and I deliberated and refused to get out of prison. We wanted to stay with them come what may.[63]

About one-and-a-half months into the start of the second stage of the mutiny, the management announced the completion of works to the ground floor. The management asked the negotiating committee to take the floor over and start transferring prisoners. The detainees refused to go down to the first floor because, according to Kheder Ramadan, the management had 'coated the walls of the rooms with metal, blocked all ventilation outlets and had the bathrooms and toilets without doors. The water tank of each room was removed. In short, the dormitories were transformed into metal cans that cannot be lived in. They also installed surveillance cameras in the wings of the restored floor. The wings now had 3 sets of doors and became directly connected to the watchtower.'[64]

The management responded using further starvation, water and power cuts. The quantities of food fell to unprecedented levels in the history of the prison. H.M. remembers:

I lost about 30 kg of my weight during the prison mutiny due to lack of food and drink and because of the constant and long work. Most of the detainees I was with in the B-right second wing were elderly. I shouldered the tasks of fortification and protection of the wing. They worked on stitching the bags inside the dormitories, and yet some of them were killed by snipers. Snipers' bullets targeted everything that moved in the wing.[65]

As a result of the starvation and pressure exerted by the prison management on the detainees, disagreements, and conflicts between them began to emerge. All these new formations had a strong basis in the multiplicity of doctrines and tenets of the Salafi jihadist groups within the prison. Kheder Ramadan's observations would later prove prescient:

> There was now a prison Emir from the Al-Qaeda group running his group's affairs. A more militant current of al-Qaeda was born in prison, whose members later joined the Islamic State. It was this group that took control of the ground floor of the prison in the final confrontation. That group considered everyone infidels, even Salafi-jihadists and Al-Qaeda. The third group of the prisoners were the open-minded Salafists. They too had different factions that considered the others as infidels. The fourth group of the prisoners were the rest of the detainees, held on democratic backgrounds, or under espionage or political charges.[66]

The third phase of the mutiny: endgame

Tension ruled the atmosphere, and the volcano was about to erupt. Detainees were anticipating the day when regime forces would try to attack the prison and take back full control. On the morning of Saturday 6 December 2008, the final confrontation started. Kh.A. testifies:

> One of the jihadist groups on the third floor exchanged insults with an intelligence operative on the ground floor, through the watchtower. Shooting started from the ground floor to the top of the watchtower. Some prisoners were injured. Everyone thought we were being raided. The army and security forces got into full alert and began shooting at the prison. It was chaos again. We went back to the starting point. The cranes returned to the landscape, carrying snipers, food was completely cut off and the situation got much worse. Skirmishes between the prisoners and the operatives began. Regime forces tried to storm the prison for the third time using a troop carrier but failed. The number of prisoners killed by snipers started to increase. They asked us to surrender but we refused. They announced the arrival of a senior officer to negotiate.[67]

During that attack, the detainees regained control of the prison, the administration building, the kitchen and the bakery. During this confrontation, the regime had refused to receive the bodies of the dead detainees. So, after the floors of the solitary cells were dug up, they were buried in the basement. Twenty days after the confrontation, regime forces called for the negotiating committee to meet with a senior intelligence officer. Kh.A. continues:

They took them to the headquarters of the Military Intelligence Division for 48 hours. There they met General Asef Shawkat, who started his talk with threats. The Committee was blindfolded and handcuffed, but they knew who he was from the talks of the officers who transferred them to him. After the threats, he gave them four concessions on the condition that they carry out his orders. A pardon over what happened, opening visits a week after the agreement, moving us to another prison and speeding up court proceedings. The negotiating committee returned, but they kept them outside the prison. They announced the results of those negotiations through loudspeakers.[68]

Most prisoners agreed to the terms of the regime by surrendering. At this point, however, the confrontation peaked and they had to confront regime forces outside the prison while about 40 extremist detainees, who occupied the ground floor, prevented them from leaving. Kh.A. concludes:

These Takfiris were dreaming of liberating Syria from Saydnaya. I believe they took the decision of confrontation and armed action because they were the ones who committed murders inside the prison and the only way out for them was confrontation because to them the result was the same whether they surrendered or confronted. They negotiated an exit to Iraq with the regime forces. The regime forces agreed and lured them until the time of transferring prisoners from Saydnaya.[69]

The escape tunnel

'As the confrontation intensified, it became clear that death was waiting for us. Some men decided to seize the opportunity and dig a tunnel to escape prison. The owner of the idea Abu al-Tayeb al-Dirdar was a topographical engineer and had good knowledge of soil matters. We started digging the tunnel non/stop with arranged shifts; we were 120 detainees. We tried to dig under block A-right towards the outside, and the tunnel was supposed to take us out behind the army stations. Spies to the prison management leaked the news. The army dug a large and deep trench around the prison from the four sides. The trench was 6 metres deep which ruled out the success of any escape attempt through a tunnel.'[70]

A committee was formed within the prison to complete the transfers of detainees. The committee, which remained outside, was tasked with ensuring that prisoners were healthy and were delivered to other prisons safely. Kheder Ramadan was among them:

The detainees came out in 11 batches. They took the sick and elderly first and then the rest. The transfer lasted a few days. I was in the last batch. Exiting the prison door was through the administration building. The detainees crossed under a metal detector. Then to the tent to complete the inspections. We were allowed to take our clothes in just one bag. During our exit, the last batch, the detainees who remained in prison attacked the army members through a hole in the building near the inspection tent in the middle of the yard. The shooting started and two of us were killed erroneously. The inspection continued and we were transferred to Adra prison. I was very scared of both the army and security forces and of the Takfiris in prison who wanted to kill us so we wouldn't get out. They tried to kill the head of the internal committee.[71]

Most of the prisoners who were transferred to Adra prison were placed in the basement of the Drug Department there.

On Tuesday 13 January 2009, regime forces attacked the prison. They did a rooftop landing. They also attacked through a gate they opened in the prison wall. They killed all but three prisoners, including Nadim Baloch, the chief instigator of fighting regime forces during the prison mutiny. All three were taken wounded to Branch 293. This operation ended the mutiny, and an investigation was opened. Some were executed for murder, some were sentenced to life imprisonment by a legal committee headed by Faiz al-Nuri. Baloch himself got out three years before the end of his original term with a special pardon.[72] During the third stage of the prison mutiny and the last confrontation, 85 detainees were killed.

The Saydnaya uprising took place when smartphones and digital cameras had become increasingly widespread and sophisticated. There exists some grainy video footage from inside the uprising, as well as from its repression. Some video clips show the murdered detainees being buried in cells, there are clips of snipers lodged in cranes, clips showing the amassing of manpower outside the prison, or the digging of the tunnel. One of the most disturbing clips is the aftermath of the massacre: mutilated detainees are laying in a pile while intelligence operatives stand around victoriously. That clip ends with a shot of a slightly corpulent man in sweatpants, nonchalantly recording the corpses on his smartphone.[73] It is unclear whether it is indeed Maher al-Assad himself, but in any case, the scene inspired the famous pro-Assad song 'Ya Abu Shama', which includes the lyrics: 'Me and you, Abu Shama / Maher is still in his pijama.'[74]

Rebuilding Saydnaya

The prison management began repairs immediately after the final confrontation. The prison was remodelled in a completely different way. All the walls were now metal and there were no ventilation openings in the dormitory doors. The prison had been turned into a fortress, coated with metal from the inside. The wing now started at the watchtower, isolating it completely from the rest of the floor. Access to the wing was routed through a gate leading to space zero, and from that to the main gate of the wing. The change affected not only the prison but also the management methods. H.M. had survived the uprising and massacre to witness the changes:

We were back in prison after almost thirteen months. We were placed in wing C-left first. It had only five dormitories. After the prison mutiny, beating was strictly forbidden. All wardens were sergeants and trained to manage prisons. They addressed us respectfully. The invoice system was canceled, except for buying medicine. Radios, television, and newspapers were banned. Blankets were handed on request only. They played the card that it was an isolated security prison, where we had the right to have food and drink without any verbal or physical abuse, however everything else was canceled. Doors of the dormitories were never opened. There was no more breathing time. Bathrooms were in dormitory 11, and showering was twice a week, approximately 10 or 15 minutes long, with hot water. They took us there one dormitory at a time. The numbers inside the dormitories were small as they invested all available prison space and each room.[75]

The same modifications that were made by the regime on the ground floor and were rejected by the detainees during the prison mutiny became the reality of the prison as a whole. A large section of the inmates of the red building returned to the white building, such as Kh.M:

Two years after interrogating us in Branch 293 on the prison mutiny, we were transferred to the white building in October 2010. After a few months and many struggles with Talaat Mahfouz, visiting was allowed. Our visits took place on a special day where no other prisoners received visitors. These were much more securitized visits and only for close relatives. Receiving money directly was forbidden; money stayed in the prison's Personal Belongings department. Most of the items were not allowed in.

After that, the State Security Court started its functions on the prison mutiny.

We were three groups. The Court sentenced five of us to death and five others to life imprisonment. The third group received imprisonment sentences of varying periods. As the events of the Syrian Revolution intensified, the State Security Court was abolished and we were transferred to a military court to review our files. They wanted to empty the prison entirely. They distributed all its detainees to the provinces. I was transferred to Adra prison.[76]

On the eve of the Syrian Revolution, Saydnaya was converted into a heavily guarded and fortified prison. The White prison building became more like the backyard of the main prison. Ibrahim al-Olabi noted that 'it was better than the detention centres of the security and intelligence branches, but worse than the Civil Prison of Adra. There was no gas in Saydnaya prison for heating food or cooking. But we made a heater out of the sardine cans lids. This was a year into our stay in the white building. In the dormitory there, there were two toilet and bathroom spaces. The white building had three floors above the ground. It also had a basement and underground floor. They both had large bathroom spaces. Showering was compulsory and the duration was no more than 1 minute. In the white building there were only floors, no wing divisions. Each floor had numbered dormitories. Medical care was a formality, and those who provided it knew nothing about medicine. They treated people with great superiority. The only prescription was the painkiller 'Brufen'. If the detainee argued his illness with the prison doctor, the latter got angry and started shouting. There was no breathing in Saydnaya and visits opened almost two months later. Talaat Mahfouz announced the opening of visits and allowed us to inform our families through the visitors of others. At first, they took us out to the visit blindfolded and shackled; these rituals were later cancelled. An operative stood between you and your family, that is, between the two nets.'[77]

After 2011: the human slaughterhouse

Following the outbreak of the Syrian Revolution in the spring of 2011, the Syrian regime emptied the red building of the Saydnaya Military Prison. Since July 2011, the prison has become the final destination for a new generation of detainees who have been subjected to the crime of 'extermination'. It was specifically the Assad regime's treatment of detainees in Saydnaya that prompted the UN and human rights organizations to use the qualification of 'extermination': deliberately imposing conditions of life on the detainees with the intention of bringing them to their demise.[78]

No one has a definitive count of the number of prison inmates during this period. The numbers changed rapidly and dynamically as a result of executions or death due to catastrophic prison conditions or as a result of the arrival of new batches of detainees in Saydnaya. The only entity with the exact number is the Military Police Administration under the Syrian Army. However, the approximate figure ranges between 10 and 20,000, according to reliable human rights organizations who have kept track of the figures. The prison administration started carrying out executions in September 2011:

> For the first four months, it was usual for between seven and 20 people to be executed every 10–15 days. For the following 11 months, between 20 and 50 people were executed once a week, usually on Monday nights. For the subsequent six months, groups of between 20 and 50 people were executed once or twice a week, usually on Monday and/or Wednesday nights. Witness testimony from detainees suggests that the executions were conducted at a similar – or even higher – rate at least until December 2015. Assuming that the death rate remained the same as the preceding period, Amnesty International estimates that between 5,000 and 13,000 people were extrajudicially executed at Saydnaya between September 2011 and December 2015.[79]

The process for carrying out executions in Saydnaya began at 15:00 in accordance with the commands specific to Saydnaya post-revolution. Abu Ras was imprisoned in this period and remembered: 'The sergeant would shout at the wing's door: 'Pay attention to your name!', meaning they want to take out detainees. He read a list of about 40–50 detainees. Whoever heard his name announced his presence through the head of the dormitory. Seven to eight detainees came out of each wing. They stood behind one another in a train formation.'[80] This position meant detainees stood one behind the other, half bent over and holding the person in front of them. They had to keep their eyes closed and move according to the sergeant's instructions. Muneer al-Faqeer too, survived this period:

> They gathered these detainees in a dormitory that we used to call the '*tasfir*' [forced travel] dormitory. It was in our wing, C-left first. We thought they were transferring them to another prison. The wardens gave them some reassurance that they were awaiting release or transfer to a civilian prison. We believed everything the wardens said. They took them at night and the brutal beatings began. They brought them back to the room after they have inked their fingerprints on some papers. Sometimes they put 300 detainees in this room. We would ask those being taken to call our parents from the civil prison or from his home if he is released to tell them where he was, and they in turn, in an agreed manner during the visit, tell us where he was. We never heard from those who went out to the *tasfir* room.[81]

There was another room for collecting detainees to be executed in the ground floor solitaries wing, B-right first, which was 3.5 x 5 metres. Detainees transferred to this room received severe beatings between 22:00 and midnight. They were blindfolded and handcuffed from the back. They were 'brutally transported to the white building close to us. One car transported them in batches'.[82] This operation was supervised by five to six guards from the red building.[83]

Once orders arrived at the prison with the names of those to be executed, the sergeants began preparing them and transporting them to the designated place. They were all stripped and dressed in a blue uniform. They were later transferred to the white building where they waited until 3:00 the next day until the committee supervising the execution arrived. The Committee included 'the Director of Saydnaya, the Military Prosecutor of the Military Field Court, a representative from the intelligence agencies – usually Military Intelligence, the Brigade Commander of the Southern Front, an officer from the Military Medical Services at Tishreen Hospital, and the head doctor at Saydnaya. Most members of the panel are usually accompanied by one or two assistants or bodyguards'.[84]

The Committee entered the execution section in the southeast corner of the white building, a section that was expanded in June 2012 to allow for the execution of more detainees at one go. The execution process was as follows:

> What is commonly described by guards and officials as the "execution room" in fact comprises an open area containing three cells and two smaller rooms, each of which is used for executions. Upon entry into the room, there is an open area of 8m × 4m, which contains three cells to the immediate right, on the south-east wall. To the left is a room 3m × 3m. This room contains 10 nooses made of beige-coloured rope, which line the north-east wall. There is also a small table in the back left-hand corner of this room, where the detainees are ordered to stamp a statement documenting their execution and last wishes. The nooses in this room are tied to a

metal pipe that hangs, horizontally, from the ceiling. The platform on which the victims stand is made of steel, and it has concrete stairs leading up to it. The platform is 1m high, and its top, a steel plate, is fixed in place with a lock and pin. When the order of execution is given, the pin is removed, which causes the platform to swing down toward the front and the victims to fall downward … After the victims are dropped or pushed, they usually hang for around 15 minutes. At this point, the doctor in the room indicates which detainees have not yet died. These victims are pulled downward by the officers' assistants, which causes the victims' necks to break.[85]

When the executions are over, the bodies are transferred to Tishrin military hospital for documentation and burial. The same process applies to the bodies of those who died under torture. Abu Ras witnessed this process:

On Tuesday, 26 August 2014, we were being transported to the court. They walked us past the body storage room under the watchtower near the kitchen. They took along with us three sick detainees and about 15 bodies. They piled them next to us in the 'meat refrigerator' car. We first stopped at Tishrin military hospital, where I and my colleague transferred the bodies to the hospital prison with our own hands. It was a three-room section within the hospital wall, about 300 metres from the main building. In the centre was an administrative office, with a cell to the right and one to the left. We put bodies in front of them outside the section, right in the open. They started numbering, photographing and bagging them.[86]

Systematic extermination of detainees

Saydnaya inmates did not only die on the gallows. The prison programme is designed to be a slow journey to death. The tale of the 1980s Palmyra prison was repeated in Saydnaya throughout 2011–2020. The detainee begins his bloody imprisonment tale from the first moment he sets foot in the prison with the 'reception party' which might claim his life. Huzaifa al-Jassim's experiences represent so many others': 'Military Police greeted us with indiscriminate beatings all over our bodies. We went down about ten steps. They told us to keep our faces to the floor. Someone in charge came to pick us up. He asked for personal papers or any other belongings. Nobody had anything. All that was handed over in the branch remained there. I thought we were in the Fourth Division. I didn't know where we were. The officer arrested with us tried to raise his head to hand over the court paper to the person in charge, but the latter beat him, breaking his arm. After taking our personal belongings, the prison doctor asked us about our illnesses. Whomever said they were sick were beaten by the doctor or the adjutant who played the doctor's role.'[87]

That was the initial reception. Al-Jassim continues:

They untied the chain that was binding us together. They had every 5–6 detainees stand at the top of the stairs, then the adjutant and his colleagues pushed us downstairs. In the basement we had to take off all our clothes. They gave us instructions forbidding lifting our heads up or removing our hands from our eyes under any circumstances. We were completely naked, standing behind one another with our heads bowed. The military policeman called us by the name. Every person who came forward received 30–35 blows on his back with an iron pipe. The young man who was arrested with me moved his head during the beating, so the adjutant ordered the police to leave him to the end for him to discipline. They pushed me into a 2 m² solitary cell, which had a toilet at its end. I found the officer arrested with us being tortured inside the solitary cell. After a while, a man arrested on the same charges as I joined us. His body became blue, and he was bleeding from his ears, legs and back.[88]

Detainees were crammed, often naked, into those solitaries for two weeks as a first-instance punishment. Saydnaya prisoners were forbidden from having shoes. These were all piled in the reception yard and the detainees could see them on the way to their solitary cells. Muneer al-Faqeer suffered horrible treatment at Saydnaya:

10 of us were crammed naked in the toilet of the solitary cell. We spent our entire first night in it. In the morning they dropped our clothes in from the Judas window. They gave us the prison instructions, which could be summarized in that everything in the prison was done only by order of the ward sergeant. Whispering and talking were forbidden. It was our duty to teach new detainees these instructions and information. When any military policeman passes in the corridor of the solitary cells, we must kneel and close our eyes with our hands and face the wall. When the door or the Judas window are opened, we must get into the toilet. After giving us full instructions, he asked us: 'Whose sons are you?' The answer should be loud and clear: 'We are sons of bitches.' If our voice was low or if he didn't like it, we had to undergo a horrible round of torture.[89]

Living with orders

Life in the red prison of Saydnaya and the security wing in the white building, before its closure in 2015, followed a series of commands. Those uniform orders applied to both solitary cells and dormitories. The day began with the command 'sit', which meant waking up, usually after dawn and before sunrise. Detainees sit in the solitary cells waiting for the rest of the commands. In dormitories they gathered the blankets in the middle of the room in the manner ordered by the prison management, or they gathered them in the inner corner of the dormitory. The blankets had to rolled up and then carefully stacked together. Then came the command: 'Pay attention to your name', which referred to those who are wanted in court or are to be removed from prison or taken to the hospital. This is followed by the command: "Bring the dead bodies you have", which meant preparing the bodies of those who died during the night to be taken out when the door of the cell or dormitory is opened. The head of the dormitory must declare the number of the dead and the number of the dormitory.

Food was distributed collectively, all meals in one go, breakfast, lunch, and dinner. The soldiers pushed the food bowls into the solitary cells through the lower judas window. The door of the room is opened to bring the food in and take the bodies out at the same time. The arrival of the food did not mean we could immediately start eating. We had to wait for the instruction "breakfast", meaning eat breakfast. There was a command for lunch and dinner too. If the sergeant in charge of the wing forgot to give the order, we remained without food; this often happened. The roll call is also conducted through a command: 'Number? Out? In?' The head of the dormitory or the solitary had to accurately answer these questions.

The command closest to our hearts was: 'Move to sleep.' It meant go to sleep immediately. The sergeant checked the dormitories one by one through the judas window. None of the detainees should be seen to be awake or he will be punished. Sleep command was about two hours after the sunset. Exceptional commands came after lunch or in the middle of the night; it was: 'Sit down and hear your name." We later learned that it was to take those for whom execution orders were received.[90]

The number of detainees in each solitary cell ranged between nine to 12 men. Huzaifa al-Jassim described the inner structure of the cell:

The Sergeant instructed me to be the 'pimp' of the solitary, meaning the head of the cell, the '*shawish*'. I made the mistake of standing facing the door when the Sergeant was giving the roll call command. When the food was being distributed, he opened the judas window at the bottom of the door, which is usually closed by an 8-mm metal pin. He put the food and asked me to take it, then ordered me to extend my hands. He hit me, breaking a finger in my right hand and two in my left.[91]

Solitary cells were not only used to receive new guests in Saydnaya. They also hosted those punished from dormitories or those returned from the Military Police headquarters in Qaboun. Al-Jassim observed this:

They brought a new person to the solitary cell. He was returning from the court in Qaboun to prison. His body was bluish and burned with melted plastic.

That's when I considered what I went through was normal. We tried to help him, we gave him some of the available water and fed him some bread. A few days later, he partially regained his consciousness so we asked him if he knew where we were. He said we were in Saydnaya prison, unless we're in the Fourth Division.[92]

The duration of the punishments in the solitary cells could often exceed two weeks, sometimes they were up to a month or even longer. Those in the solitary cells pray that national events or holidays do not happen during their stay there. 'During the holidays, the solitary cells are opened, flooded with cold water, and left like that until an inmate dies from the cold.'[93]

Detainees in the solitary cells suffered more hunger and thirst than those in the dormitories. One detainee, who preferred to remain anonymous, remembered: 'They brought six loaves of bread and half a kilo of cooked bulgur for 11 detainees. Water was often cut off. One of us dared to tell the Sergeant about the water, so he ordered him to stretch his feet out the door through the lower judas window, beat him on his feet until they bled. We got running water for only half an hour a day. Once water was cut for three days. Our odor became disastrous.'[94] Days passed in solitary cells filled with hunger, thirst, constant torment and silence. Muneer al-Faqeer witnessed this: 'Hunger caused me a conditional reflex. When the soldiers threw the bread bag on the floor, I felt joy. This has continued with me to this day. When I watch a man put bread in front of me, I get happy. Hunger was real and catastrophic in Saydnaya. No meat or chicken in the solitaries, but only in the dormitories, yet scarce, of course.'[95]

Belief in religion grew among detainees caught between death and violence; however being seen to pray in prison could cost a detainee his life. Muneer al-Faqeer narrates: 'We trained ourselves to pray with our faces to the wall opposite the judas window of the dormitory. As soon as the window was opened, we adjusted our prayer position into the instructed position of kneeling.' Prisoners spent their day whispering inside the solitary cells if they could. 'We had mostly religious and historical conversations.' The detainees in the solitary cells seized the opportunity 'to shower in the toilet so that the police couldn't hear the sound of water and then punish us. We did everything in complete silence and without drawing attention. We peeped onto the corridor through a hole in the door and sometimes spotted sergeants taking off their military boots and walking towards the solitaries to watch us without us knowing. Amid the silence and stillness, we would hear the sound of a door of a solitary being suddenly opened and torture beginning.'[96]

Dormitory life was not much different from the solitaries, except in terms of space and some light from an electric bulb. Imad Abu Ras stated:

During the roll call, we knelt behind each other in rows of fives on the left side near the toilets. Then the Sergeant called out the violators. Three must be taken out of each dormitory to be punished. Every day three of us came out, because in reality there was nothing to breach in Saydnaya, but that was only an excuse for imposing punishment. If no violators came out, the head of the dormitory and his aide were

Figure 8.4 Imad Abu Ras before and after detention, from his collection.

punished and may perish under torture. The average penalty for the violator is 70 to 80 cable strikes.[97]

Hunger and thirst did not end when you arrived at the dormitory. Nothing made a bigger impression on Muneer al-Faqeer than hunger:

> Hunger reached catastrophic limits. As hunger levels rose, our imaginations hovered around food and the details of cooking. We learned all sorts of cooking in our imagination, even those foods that we never knew how to make. We developed bread-specific equations such as the quarter, the quarter of a quarter, the fifth and the sixth of a loaf. As days rolled, food trade emerged, namely selling your food share by the currency of bread. We spent most of our days with trading and price control. Discussions inside the dormitory were almost like a market where items are sold in the currency of bread. The moment the food arrived we started guessing its kind and immediately initial food trades began among us. However, the entry of food was also used as an opportunity to torture us.

The charges that the head of the dormitory was supposed to accuse his colleagues of so they received punished were: whispering, talking or crossing the toilet line – the line between the toilet and the dormitory space. The charge of approaching the door of the dormitory could mean death.

Once during the punishment, the military policeman hit me with a hard object on the head, so I passed out. When I regained consciousness, he ordered me to go to the toilet. I crawled with my eyes closed, of course, and hit the bathroom wall. I kept crawling and bumped into the wall again and again until I finally found the door. My colleague had preceded me and was crammed into the toilet bleeding heavily. My blood and his covered the bathroom floor. After they left, the rest of the colleagues came to take us out of the toilet and care for our wounds.[98]

With the arrival to the dormitories, the detainee's desire for life grows. Prisoners strive to maintain this desire by resorting to different methods, as Al-Faqeer did:

Such as daily walks for long hours with the aim of keeping the body in an acceptable shape after being subjected to the catastrophic conditions we were living in. We had religious, scientific, and cultural discussions and reviews. I often wrote on the floor tile or in the air. I turned pages in the air. Colleagues thought I went crazy, but it was my way of investing time. In the afternoon, the sun approached the dormitory window. Everyone came close to the door, which was a dangerous stunt. But we had to search for lice on daily basis, before returning to our spots. Then came the command: 'All sleep you bastards!' That was the second most beautiful sound for us in Saydnaya after the sound of the bread bag on the floor. Sleeping was an escape from the reality we were living in.[99]

The sound of the bread bag changed with time in Saydnaya. After 2013, the management stopped providing bread in plastic bags after the suicide of one of the detained officers in the white prison, as Abu Ras remembered: 'The rooms of the security wing in the white building had metal shelves fixed to the walls. We used them to place our blankets or the few things we had. These shelves were completely removed after a captain arrested in this prison executed himself using empty, nylon bread bags. He made them into a rope and executed himself. Shelves were removed and bags for bread were cancelled.'[100] In fact, the security wing of the white building was completely abolished in 2015. The third floor was assigned to the judicial military prisoners, and the remaining sections were used to isolate tuberculosis patients transferred from the red building.

In the red building, the number of detainees in each dormitory ranged between 30 and 35. The number was always changing due to new arrivals, executions, killings under torture or releases. There was no hot water except in the wing bathrooms, which occupied dormitory number 11 of each wing. Khaldoun Mansour testifies:

Throughout my stay in Saydnaya, which lasted over a year, we were taken to the main bathrooms three times only. They took us out completely naked, even without briefs. Everyone had their back bent forward with their hands on their eyes. Two times out of the three we were there I did not have time to wash the soap off my head. Bathing was under count, and its duration did not exceed one minute. The water was unbearably hot. We seized opportunities to shower in cold water in the dormitory.[101]

Even cold water was rare in Saydnaya, according to M.Sh.:

> They re-cut the water for five days. On the first day we grew thirsty; by the second
> it became disastrous. By the third and fourth days we lost the ability to move or
> speak. On the fourth day the warden asked how long the water has been cut, the
> head of the dormitory answered that it had been four days. He ordered him to
> remind him on the fifth day, on which he brought a small bucket of water and
> splashed it on the floor of the room. We drank water from the floor of the room. It
> was the best water I've ever had in my life.[102]

Speech was forbidden in Saydnaya, but the detainees perfected the art of whispering
to communicate with each other. Abu Ras talks about it: 'In 2013 there was a "continue
whispering" command from the head of the dormitory after being reassured that the
sergeant of the wing moved away. The head of the dormitory was killed under torture
for allowing us to whisper. In 2014, the command became "continue to sign", which was
the only language we could communicate through, only moving our hands.' Most
Saydnaya detainees believe that 2014 was the ultimate year of death. At the beginning
of the year, Brigadier General Mahmoud Maatouq took over Saydnaya. After that,
'detainees entered the prison completely naked and flayed from beating and torture.
The new detainees remained in a deplorable state for days, where we had to carry them
to the toilet due to their inability to move'.[103]

However, 2013 also saw a lot of misery, especially on the day that former Prison
Director Talaat Mahfoud was killed by members of the Free Syrian Army. The detainees
suffered exceptional violence from then on:

> They practiced all forms of bloody torture. They entered our dormitory and beat
> us so violently until we all bled. One of us remained without bleeding wounds. One
> of the officers asked his colleague to go out to another dormitory to torture the
> rest, but the latter refused, shouting at his colleague: 'This prisoner hasn't bled yet!'
> We remained a whole week without food afterwards. They just threw us a quarter
> loaf of bread per prisoner. Not to mention the continued daily torture.[104]

Daily punishments, changing managers and their methods were not the only
sources of suffering. In our interview with him, Khaldoun Mansour said that he 'got an
internal fever and miraculously survived. Two of the officers arrested with me in the
same dormitory died of this disease in wing C-left first. Our body temperature rose
dramatically. This heat hit the brain and internal organs. Internal fever can quickly kill.
We did not know the source of the disease, as there was no health care or attention. We
expected it to be a bacterial infection from the food'.[105]

Internal fever, scabies, lice, and torture injuries were followed by tuberculosis in the
winter of 2014. Abu Ras explained:

> The first infection in our dormitory was a young man called Mandoub from
> Palmyra. He lost his appetite and showed symptoms of jaundice. We tried to force
> him to eat and drink fluids but his cough became severe. We didn't dare tell the

prison doctor during his rounds. Our experience with him is limited to torture. Once he trampled me under his feet for requesting some painkillers. However, infections started spreading and we had 4 sick men in the same dormitory. The first patient went to the doctor, but to no avail as we expected. As the situation developed, the head of the dormitory took risks and told the wing sergeant that the situation was difficult and that the sick were sometimes bleeding from their noses. The numbers of the infected began to rise, but the prison administration did nothing. By the end of spring, cars arrived, I think they were from the Red Cross. Those cars parked in the prison yard and started examining all the inmates. They examined the chest and eyes. Afterward the large area of the white prison was turned into a quarantine place to isolate tuberculosis patients. By the time I left Saydnaya, in October of 2015, tuberculosis had claimed the lives of many detainees.[106]

Physical illnesses, constant torture, hunger and being fully alert all the time, damaged the mental health of the detainees, says Abu Ras: 'Some of us lost the ability to tell the exact date. Many "switched off" and died in prison. Some developed a mental state where they completely forgot everyday things such as the names of days, time and short Quran verses that they memorized by heart since childhood.' The reality of the prison was reflected by the Military Police operatives who had become more violent and bloodthirsty. They completely objectified the detainees, as evident in their unjustified violent practices in everyday prison life. Some rare officers showed sympathy. 'Enlistee Haitham Mashaal, from rural Aleppo, was one of the wardens nicknamed *Al-Hanoon* [the kind-hearted]. We gave him this nickname because he never insulted or hit anyone. After a while, we found out they arrested him for giving a Quran to an old man in a dormitory. He was transferred to the District Branch 227, then 215 to finally return to Saydnaya as a prisoner, like us. His former colleagues, police officers, tortured him daily in the wheel, which in Saydnaya was a different prospect than that used in the security and intelligence branches.'[107]

The wheel, the well-known torture device used in all branches of the Syrian military and intelligence prisons, had received an upgrade in Saydnaya. It was the same traditional method of placing the detainee inside the wheel of a car and fixing his legs using a solid metal tube inserted between the wheel and the bend of the detainee's knees. They called that tube *Al-Qares* [the biter]. The sound of the tube falling to the ground struck terror into the hearts of most prison inmates. What was new in Saydnaya was the cable, made from the 'outer casing of the wheel. It was cut about 10 cm wide and about 1.5 metres long. They put us in the wheel, fixed our legs with the tube, sometimes tying the two big toes with a rubber band called the "bird's tie". This tie completely prevents the movement of the feet. When they dropped the Al-Qares on the floor of the wing we were sure that what awaited us was a massacre. Seven or eight soldiers would enter the dormitory and take us one by one to the wheel'. These rounds of torture killed at least one or two detainees in every wing. 'The death of any of us did not inflict sadness or grief. Our death was a joy of salvation for us, and at the same time our colleagues were happy to share our food. Saydnaya killed humanity within us and turned us into a different type of human beings.'[108]

The 'suicide'

They often punished us by cramming us over one another in the toilet of the dormitory. However, on Tuesday 20 October 2015, they chose a different punishment for a 40-year-old man. A very cultured, educated, and polite man. He was a giant, with big bones, head, and features. He was punished by kneeling in the middle of the dormitory and raising his hands up. The warden forgot him for a whole day and the head of the dormitory couldn't break the punishment without permission.

Fatigue and exhaustion consumed the punished man, and his knees were crushed under his body weight. The next day, 21 October, he remained in the punishment state. He begged and pleaded to the head of the dormitory to break it, but to no avail. The head of the dormitory was too afraid to break the punishment as he might be punished. He couldn't ask the sergeant to break the punishment either for fear of punishment. The punished man started crying like a child from the pain, but to no avail. I didn't know what I did then, and why. I stood up, put his hands down and told him to sit in his place. I went into an argument with the head of the dormitory, but I asked him to knock on the door and ask for the warden on duty. After a long argument, the head of the dormitory did what I asked. When the warden came, I expected to receive 15 or 20 cable blows through judas window. The warden could only open the door of the dormitory in the presence of the chief of the wing, and he was not present then, so the military policeman could just hit me in such a fast way.

'Sir, I have a detainee who refuses to obey orders,' the head of the dormitory told the policeman the moment he opened the Judas window. He immediately ordered me to go to the Judas window. I explained to him what had happened. He gave me a threatening promise that he will be back. Until this day, I still don't understand what was going on with me? It looks like I subconsciously decided to commit suicide. When the policeman came back with the wing chief, I asked him to meet the prison Security Officer. They immediately started beating me in every possible way and I started bleeding all over.

The prison doctor came after they told him what was going on. I said to him: 'I know sir that you're a doctor. I want the Security Officer.' I recognized him from his voice. Keeping our eyes shut shielded us from execution, so we relied on hearing. Whoever opened his eyes was killed under torture. After talking to the doctor, they started beating me again. They blindfolded and handcuffed me and took me down to the ground floor. I don't know who met me there. I believe he was a high-ranking prison officer. He asked me: 'What do you want?' I told him my roommate's story. He asked why I was only telling him this now; why did no one ever tell him about such behavior? I didn't know what to answer being handcuffed and kneeling with blood pouring from every point in my body. I was in a humiliating state but continued to speak for no apparent reason for this confrontation that was going to cost me my life.

I told the officer all the incidents that I knew; I said everything. I held the head of the wing responsible for what was going on. They called for the head of the dormitory. The officer asked him for the details and realized I was being honest. At that point, I was kneeling and facing the wall. The sergeant, chief of the wing, took advantage of this time and stood behind me, pressing his feet on my toes. He threatened to kill me and that this was the last day of my life. The officer went up along with the doctor and about 10 operatives. The officer questioned my dormitory's detainees in my presence. After long minutes of fear ridden silence, one of them dared and confirmed the veracity of the things I had told the officer.

The officer ordered the head of the dormitory to be taken down to the solitary cells as punishment and ordered the sergeant chief of the wing to punish me with thirty lashes for remaining silent all the previous days. As soon as the officer left, the chief of the wing came back with the wheel and the tube and I received about 200 lashes after all the beatings I had been subjected to all day and then thrown into a solitary cell. In the two days prior to this incident, water was cut off from our wing and I didn't drink at all. That night I spent in the solitary cell, I couldn't sleep, not from pain, but of thirst. The next day at about 7:30, the door was opened, and I walked out of the solitary cell wobbling like a seal because of my injured feet and my catastrophic condition. That was my last night in Saydnaya prison. I was transferred to the State Security Department to be released in a deal between the Free Syrian Army and the regime army. I went out into a life that I never expected I'd see again.[109]

While awaiting execution, death under torture or release, some of Saydnaya's detainees had the opportunity to receive visitors:

It was once every two or three months and was through the net and no more than a minute or two. During the visit we were hit on our way there and on the way back and upon concluding the visit. It was forbidden to mention any names. The only permitted question was 'How's it going?' 'How are my dad, mom, my brothers and sisters?' You should only tell them that you're okay. The beating that followed the visit was so severe that some died during this torture session. You had to smile at your parents and reassure them just after being beaten. Visiting was difficult. They took the money our parents brought and put in the personal belongings' unit. When I returned to the dormitory, my colleagues showered me with dozens of questions upon which dozens of analyses would be based, dissecting each gesture and phrase my visitors have uttered. The visit was like dreams. Every day we spent time analyzing our dreams. Dreams presented an opportunity for interpretation, analysis, and hope. Most Syrian detainees interpret dreams. It is a skill passed down among prisoners.[110]

9

Civil Prisons

Introduction

This chapter examines the civil prisons, in particular the Citadel Prison, Karakon Sheikh Hassan, Aleppo Central Prison, Damascus Central Prison, Adra Prison, and the Qatana and Douma Women's Prison. The collective experience of detainees in Syrian political and security prisons varies drastically between military and civil. Civil prisons fall under the Ministry of Interior and include a special section for political detainees and prisoners, which is run by the Political Security Division in the Ministry. These prisons are known as 'Justice and Correctional Institutes' as stipulated in Decision no 1222 of 20 June 1929.[1]

The civilian judiciary has its own prisons, usually in old castles in cities with central locations, such as Damascus' Citadel Prison. From these prisons, a Department of Political Security often operates, and when there are clashes between the opposition and the regime, the intelligence services also use these prisons. However, the Ministry of Interior remains responsible for the administration and finances of civilian prisons at all times. Almost every province in Syria has a department and thus a prison. There is one special case, Karakon al-Sheikh Hassan, a prison that belonged to Political Security and was also managed by this department. This was not only a prison, but it also had an investigation department. These were closed down towards the end of the 1980s.

Despite this structure, there is overlap between the powers of the security services and those of the judiciary. There are dozens of cases of detainees who came from the twin military intelligence services and underwent a military trial but were held in a civilian prison. However, the opposite is unheard of: a prisoner in a military prison cannot in any way be under the authority of a civilian judiciary. This is because of the special authority of Military Intelligence and Air Force Intelligence over all state security forces. The far-reaching influence of the military judiciary, which is considered the highest legal authority in the country, also plays an important role here.

Historical background

The Ottoman Empire governed Syria for many centuries, during which the Ottoman authorities developed and established a number of prisons, including several that continued to function as civil prisons after the empire collapsed in 1923.[2] Under the French mandate, the colonial authorities imprisoned a large number of anti-colonial activists in these prisons, a practice that was inherited in the immediate post-colonial period, notoriously characterised by a fragile democracy, fierce elite competition, and a number of military coups and counter-coups. During this 35-year period following the Syrian declaration of independence (1945), one faction among the Syrian political elite could first take power, but then quickly also end up imprisoned.[3] This cycle of instability came to an end in 1970, when Hafez al-Assad seized power; ever since, the civil prisons in Syria lost their relevance to the Intelligence branches, and the military prisons.

In 1970, following Presidential Decree no. 1643, the Prisons Department was tied to the Assistant Minister of Interior, following Presidential Decree no. 1643. With the restructuring of the Internal Security Forces, the functions, branches and sections of the Prisons Department in the governorates were set. Prisons were divided into three categories: the branches, that is central prison, which in Damascus is Adra prison, the central prison of Aleppo, known as Al-Musalamiya, and the central prisons in Homs, Lattakia and Hasakeh. The sections are also prisons, but smaller. They exist in all provinces except those with central prisons. Examples of these are Tartous, Swaida'a and Hama prisons. Those are mistakenly referred to as central prisons. Then comes police stations which are spread in all areas and some large districts. Then correctional facilities for juveniles, which fall under the Ministry of Labour and Social Affairs.[4]

Theoretical principles for the management of civil prisons

On paper, all civil prisons in Syria are used by the civil judiciary. Civil courts of all types are the authority that detains the legally convicted in civil prisons. However, those prisons are not managed by the Ministry of Justice, nor do they fall under it. They are managed directly by the Ministry of Interior. Based on the foundation and administration laws and rules of these prisons, the Internal Security Forces group prisoners based on their gender. The majority of central prisons are designated for men. There were two civil prisons for women, in Douma and Qatana formerly. Those were closed, and their inmates transferred to Damascus central prison for women 'Adra – Women Section'. After separating men and women in prisons, another grouping happens inside those prisons according to the age; adults and juveniles. Then, the prison management separates the 'convicts' from the 'detainees', and makes another distinction based on the type of the crime; murder, theft … etc. Political prisoners have their own wing which falls under the prison administration, but with the direct supervision of the Political Security Division.

Based on the laws and regulations, the Prisons Department in the Ministry of Interior, and through its branches in the governorates, should provide its 'residents' a number of services, most notably nutrition. However, 'despite prison regulations' reference to food provision, with meat added once a week and on feast days, in reality food in Syrian prisons is, in general, bad. That food doesn't contain enough nutritional value to maintain the health of the prisoners. The poor inmates find themselves forced to provide services to their rich fellow inmates in exchange for very small sums of money, which is very degrading. Food brought by prisoners' families during visits is often looted. Even what a prisoner buys from the prison market is subject to the piracy of the guards without any monitoring or control.[5]

As per the laws, the management of those prisons should provide hygiene, health care and adequate space for prisoners. However, 'the majority of prisons in Syria are built following security consideration, with no regard to health-related ones'. The laws stipulate the provision of a small metal bed for every prisoner, in addition to a cotton-filled mattress, a pillow and covers. The rules also stipulate the provision of heating, lights and health care. 'But there is a real problem in enforcing the law when it serves the interest of the prisoner. Syrian prisons are known to be crowded. Most prisoners sleep on the floor. Some don't even get one blanket. Often a veteran rents the bed he/she obtained due to seniority to a new detainee in exchange of money.'[6]

Overcrowding and poor care and management caused the spread of diseases and fights among prisoners. 'Two rooms in Hassakeh central prison caught fire in mysterious circumstances in 1993 killing dozens, including Kamal Haso Farhan and his two sons, which showcases poor services and the piling of people in small rooms.' Prisoners' testimonies confirm that detention rooms designed to fit five people, house over 40 or 50 prisoners. All these rooms are damp and unsanitary, with internal toilets and scarce running water. Their inmates suffer lack from lack of movement and poor sleeping conditions, in addition to skin diseases, rheumatism, pneumonia and hemorrhoids due to bad food. With the lack of proper health care, many of these diseases turn into chronic illnesses that are hard to cure.[7]

This approach to management applies to all other prisoners' rights. Visits are a way to receive bribes and blackmail the prisoners and their families. Possibilities to continue education or work in such institutes are almost non-existent. Political prisoners are forbidden from continuing their university education or sit exams. They are only allowed to sit State middle and high-school exams.

The Citadel Prison

'He went out in the morning
Coughing was so fierce
His feet were strolling towards the last curb
Before he was escorted by smiling guards
Clutching their weapons under their coats
And handed over to the prison's gate.'[8]

In the northwestern corner of the old city of Damascus stands a large medieval limestone stronghold, laced with ornamented curtain walls and fortified gates. Tourists used to stroll around this redoubt, about which the official website of the Syrian Directorate-General for Antiquities and Museums has nothing more to say than that 'it went through many stages of civilization throughout its long history'.[9] However,

Figure 9.1 The Citadel Prison, Google Maps.

the Damascus Citadel Prison was much more than that, most importantly, it was the last of the citadel prisons in Syria. The Ottomans used it as a garrison and, from 1830 occasionally as a prison, but it laid in disrepair and disuse from the 1880s.[10] During World War I, it was briefly used as a prison, and some of the most prominent Arab-nationalist political activists were imprisoned there: Shukri al-Quwwatli (1891– 1967), later president of Syria, was arrested and tortured in the Citadel by the Young Turk authorities in 1916.[11] The French occupation of Syria revived the Citadel and repurposed it as a prison. Throughout the mandate period, the French authorities harshly suppressed anti-colonial demonstrations and imprisoned Syrian activists in the Citadel prison. For example, in April 1922, Syrians organized a strike and mass demonstrations in the old city of Damascus. The French responded with violence, killing demonstrators and imprisoning dozens of them in the Citadel Prison and on Arwad island off the coast of Tartous.[12] The French also machine-gunned demonstrators from their vantage point in the Citadel, on several occasions killing dozens and wounding hundreds more.[13] Some insurrectionists attempted to free their rebel comrades imprisoned in the Citadel, such as Abu Ali al-Kilawi. The issue of detainees remained an important topic in the anti-colonial struggle; in 1936, a Syrian delegation visiting Paris demanded first and foremost that all political prisoners be freed.[14]

After independence, the Citadel was turned into a civil prison. With the arrival of the military to power in Syria through the 1949 coup, some political prisoners were placed in the Citadel Prison. One of them, Jurius al-Hames, wrote: 'I remember that during our detention between 1952 and 1953 we formed workshops to teach the illiterate.'[15] During that period, the fifth tower in the Citadel and Karakoun Al-Sheikh Hassan, in addition to the Mezze military prison, were used to detain political opponents in Damascus. Much of this changed when Hafez al-Assad seized power in 1970 and began modernizing his Gulag. He kept detainees in some of the Citadel's towers despite their dangerous state of near-collapse due to a lack of maintenance and restoration. But the Citadel prison was shut down towards the end of 1985, following the opening of the political prison of Palmyra in 1980, Damascus Central Prison in 1985, and predating Saydnaya prison in 1987.

The old city of Damascus, including the citadel, was listed as a UNESCO World Heritage Site in 1979, which might have been the only case in which a UNESCO World Heritage Site included an active prison. Since 1980, the Citadel Prison administration separated political and judicial prisoners by building a high wall between the two sections. Adnan al-Miqdad narrates:

> When you enter the main gate, there are stairs that go up the tower. We were in the 5th tower, two floors above the ground. It was the first time we saw the citadel from the inside. There were dormitories and breathing spaces for judicial prisoners. However, they took us straight up the tower, to the section of Political Security, away from judicial prisoners. There is a high wall between us and them. We entered the tower which had a small breathing space and a large dormitory that can house about 200 detainees. The dormitory was big and spacious, 20 metres wide and a little over 20 metres long. Solitary cells were in the base of the tower, as well as a room housing four detainees from Iraqi Baath. Entering the tower was through a big iron door. Our dormitory comprised of sequencing stone arches. Each arch could be an accommodation or sleeping space for two. There was a high bench on each side of the dormitory. They formed two group beds for the detainees. The detainees used the benches and the arches as spaces to sit and sleep. There were no beds in the Citadel Prison; we used the benches and the floor.[16]

There was no change to the performance of the Citadel Prison after Hafez al-Assad took power in 1970. The prison remained civil, mostly assigned to judicial prisoners, run by the Ministry of Interior and subject to the rules and regulations of civil prisons. Moving to the Citadel Prison from the security branches indicated the end of the 'detention' phase and the beginning of the 'prisoner' life. However, as Mohammed Adel Faris wrote:

> everything in the prison is a tragedy created by the tyrants. When we look at the Citadel Prison, we find that the issue of using the toilet is solved from one end but tangled from another. There was a toilet in the dormitory we were in, so there was no need to ask permission of the warden to visit the toilet! However, at times we were 56 prisoners in that dormitory, in fact, at some point we were 81, all using one toilet! At any time of the day or the night, even at 2 or 4 in the morning, the prisoner had to book a turn among those waiting. He could be preceded by 10, 15 or even 27 other prisoners! And he had to wait . . ."[17]

The large numbers of prisoners in the dormitories in the Citadel Prison made sleeping, washing up and privacy extremely complicated. Shaving was done in a salon run by specialized judicial detainees for a fee. Health care in the Citadel, al-Miqdad remembered, was through 'doctors you could meet once a week. I had hypertension, and they provided me with medicine. Emergencies in the Citadel Prison were transferred to the al-Muwasa civil hospital'. The differences between the Citadel prison, Palmyra prison and the intelligence branches of various departments were vast. These differences were not only about better food quality which was prepared in the Citadel kitchen or allowing the purchase of personal and food items from outside the prison, but opening visits to all prisoners. Al-Miqdad recalls:

> My family didn't know where I was until three-and-a-half years later. I sent them news to visit me in the Citadel through the families of my visited fellow prisoners. The visit was in a small room with two sets of nets, me on one side and my family on the other. Between the two nets stood an officer monitoring the conversation. The visit lasted about half an hour, sometimes less. I learned later that my family paid money to be able to visit me.[18]

Life in the Citadel Prison was not limited to the basic details of everyday life like eating, shaving, and washing up. Prisoners invented their own methods of entertainment and made up ways to pass the time. Faris writes: 'We held two Quran recital sessions a day, we also had various classes in interpretation, jurisprudence and Hadith.' With a prison library, containing 'the mothers of all books, we used to borrow the books we needed'. Prisoners also benefited from each other's expertise:

> I remember that one of our fellow prisoners who was a specialized doctor gave us a number of medical lectures on interesting topics such as sleeping. Civil prisons are different to the intelligence prisons, in that when the prison administration and police officers inspected the items brought to the prisoner, they looked for drugs and knives. Since these items were not interesting to us, and were not things our families would bring us, everything was allowed in: clothing, food, books, pens, and notebooks. We even had a fellow prisoner from Hizb al-Tahrir who received the Party's publications.[19]

In the early 1980s, television was allowed in the Citadel Prison, but the library remained the focal point of interest for the political detainees. Al-Miqdad:

> Television was entertaining, but the Citadel library was good and beneficial. I prepared for my return to higher university studies in the Citadel. There I studied English and Arabic languages, and we read all the books in the library. We had different specializations, so there were various workshops, seminars and arguments and even political discussions. Most prisoners spent their days reading as most of us were educated and intellectuals. I wrote 4 collections of poems in the Citadel Prison.[20]

The Citadel's political prisoners were from different ideological tenets. Among these, there were members of the Muslim Brotherhood, Iraqi Baath Party, and leftist currents opposing the regime. The prison also hosted in the 1980s 'eight of the Free Officers who tried to coup Hafez Al-Assad in 1973 but got arrested. They were about 200 officers of various military ranks. By 1980 only 8 of them were left. Arrested with us too were some unions members, transferred from the General Intelligence Department to the Citadel Prison'. The political section of the Citadel Prison was under the management of the Political Security Division. 'The wardens in our section were from Political Security. They were six operatives, with every three doing a 12-hour shift.

They opened the doors for 'breathing' at 7:00 and closed them at 19:00. When the 'breathing' time ended, we went back to the tower to sleep; we spent the whole day outside the dormitory.'[21]

The Syrian Ministry of Interior handed the Citadel Prison to the Damascus Archeology Department in 1985. As the prison has been closed for some time, there is no documentation about its management. Al-Miqdad remembered: 'During our time in the prison we had Ahmed Haydar as a Prison Director, succeeded by Brigadier General Suleiman Seedo who was the first director of Damascus Central Prison: Adra.'[22] The lack of documentation of the names of civil prisons' directors indicates they did not play any influential role in the lives of the political prisoners. The detainees of military security prisons on the other hand, remember very well the names of the Directors who were in charge from the first day of their arrest until the moment of their release. However, the Citadel detainees do not seem to remember any details about the management of the civil prison. Detainees often do remember the names of the adjutants supervising Political Security sections in those prisons as they were in daily contact with them.

Karakon Al-Sheikh Hassan

Al-Sheikh Hassan prison differs from the Citadel prison because it is a branch that directly fell under the Political Security Division. So, unlike the Citadel, Al-Sheikh Hassan was not a civil prison with a political section, but a civil political prison in the literal meaning of the word. In addition to being a political prison with two large dormitories and about 14 solitary cells, Karakon Al-Sheikh Hassan was an investigation branch under the Political Security. The Arabic word *karakon* comes from the Turkish original term *karakol*, which meant 'police station' in the Ottoman Empire and still has the same meaning in Turkey. The prison's beginnings date back to the Ottoman era in Syria. Later on, it continued to function as a police station in the French occupation era and the early days of independence:

It was converted from a police station to a prison for political detainees under President Adib al-Shishakli in 1953. After 1963, a second floor was added to the prison making it a two-story structure. The prison was rectangular in shape and surrounded by a very high fence. The prison building was separated from the fence by a narrow corridor of about 1.5 metres wide. This formed a breathing space, which detainees used twice a day.[23]

Sheikh Hassan prison building was located in the historical Midan district in central Damascus, on the edge of a cemetery called Bab al-Sgheer cemetery. It consisted of two sections that differed in architecture, function, and history. Ratib Shabo described it very well:

The first section was in the form of a Damascene house with rooms spread around an open courtyard containing a fountain in the centre. That's from an architectural view. Functionally, this was the administration building. Historically it was most likely the Ottoman section of the prison. The second section was functionally the prison building. It contained two dormitories, a bottom one and a top one. In front of each dormitory stretched two rows of opposite cells, each row contained seven cells.

Historically, the construction of this section dated back to the post-Ottoman era. It was said that part of it dated back to the period of French occupation and the other to the period of national governance. What is certain is that Karakon Al-Sheikh Hassan was an Ottoman building that reflected a French character in some of its parts. Architectural similarities could be drawn between the ground dormitory in the Karakon and the fifth courtyard dormitories in Palmyra prison: 'In both places there were three levels of floor height, for the toilet, the entrance, and the dormitory yard. It appears to be French architecture, as compared to the fifth courtyard in Palmyra prison, which was probably a French architecture, evident in the height of the ceilings, the shape of the windows and their height.'[24]

The basement of the prison building was abolished by the beginning of the 1970s. Only two floors of building remained, and these were above the ground:

> At the end of the cell lined corridor, was the dormitory. Residents of the dormitory were people whose interrogation had ended and thus became under indefinite martial arrest. Residents of the dormitory were political detainees in a relatively stable condition compared to the inmates of the solitary cells, who were still undergoing the process of interrogation and were yet to receive either a release, a transfer to the quagmire of martial detention or something worse.[25]

The exterior of the prison contained a small room located to the left of the entrance to the prison called 'Dormitory no. 1'. Next to it were two rooms assigned for torturers, housing various tools of torture. In the western section of the old building were the bedrooms of the prison guards. Torture was carried out on the inmates of solitary cells, for they were under interrogation: 'Each solitary cell was 2x1 metres, had a reinforced concrete bench, a toilet and a water tap. Light entered it from a small skylight overlooking the outside corridor.'[26]

Stench of the solitary cell

The first thing that strikes you is the smell of the place: a mature musty stench, which still takes me back to the cell the moment I come across it! Then the place shocks you: Do you spend your days next to a toilet hole? You later learn that having a toilet hole in the cell is a luxury. Do you sleep on this dirty insulator and cover yourself with this dirty blanket? Do you sleep without a pillow? How can you spend an hour in this narrow space, let alone days or months!? After the revolution of your senses over the nature and smell of the place subsides, the feeling of isolation begins to take over, rivalled only by the anticipation of interrogation and speculation over the reasons behind your arrest. The most daunting experience of a prisoner in the solitary cell is when they close the skylight. The skylight of the cell is so much more precious to its resident than one might think at first, so much so that a prisoner dreams of having some sort of power or authority to use not for his release, but to force the police to keep the skylight of his cell open. Direct need obscures the important one. By the way, this is a psychological characteristic in humans that police adjutants are better in taking advantage of than officers. The long experience of daily direct contact with prisoners led the adjutants to the conclusion of two fundamental things. The first is that the prisoner's demands do not end, and that once he gets his demand, he starts thinking about the next one, and so on in an endless chain. The second is that an insisting daily demand keeps the prisoner occupied from a bigger one. Therefore, once a prisoner's life is settled in a reasonable condition, the police will take advantage of any minor issue to withdraw the prisoners' gains, taking the claim game back to square one, in an endless circle of claim and delayed response, then confiscation again and then claiming again and so on . . .[27]

The regime of Hafez Al-Assad engraved Al-Sheikh Hassan's prison in the collective memory of Syrian political detention by transforming it, as al-Hames writes, into:

'a repository for victims whom he wanted to terrorize or liquidate. An example of this was the assassination of Syrian officers Salim Hatoum and Badr Juma after their brutal torture. A number of Muslim Brotherhood members were also executed and tortured. Members of the Bar Association in Damascus and Aleppo, members of the association for the defence of human rights in Damascus, as well as hundreds of our fellow citizens, doctors, engineers, workers, students and intellectuals, were also arrested in this prison. Those who managed to come out of this prison alive often had permanent disabilities like no other in the world.'[28]

The conditions of solitary inmates were similar to those of the political security division in terms of interrogation and torture. As for the inmates of the dormitories, their lives were somewhat different, as there was no torture and no interrogation. The moment you entered the dormitory you became 'happy for your salvation from the cellar and from the interrogation process. The happiness of mixing together with fellow inmates of the new batch. The happiness of mixing with the prisoners who were before us in the Karakon. Their happiness with the arrival of "new blood" rejuvenated their lives for some time and slightly shook their idle time. Our happiness to see the goodness of the dormitory: the vegetables, fruits, tea, coffee, maté, and cigarettes after such a long time. The collections of happiness added to our entry to the dormitory a festive atmosphere'. The collections of happiness did not hide the exciting and unique world of the dormitory, 'a display cabinet showcasing various types of human beings. Different ages, various psychological and intellectual backgrounds, and then you enter the display cabinet and become a part of it'.[29]

Prison turns many things of no value into irreplaceable items in its strange world. Shabo describes these:

> Wooden boxes, became a kitchen. Cartons became cabinets hung with ropes and nails on the walls. Buckets, became lamp shades, hung from the ceiling in a way that enables them to be reeled up when sleeping, to shade the light bulbs suspending from the ceiling.' In addition to changing the names of objects in prison, the form of life morphs into a special and unique style: 'One of the old prisoners got up and fixed his light blouse under his pajama pants, as if preparing to perform a task. He took a few rushed steps into the open space of the dormitory as if he were heading to a specific destination. Instead, he turned and walked a few quick steps in the opposite direction with a very serious look on his face. He turned back again and paced again, and kept toing and froing. His movement to a first timer would have seemed like a sort of madness or mental disorder. But with time you realize that it is the most common and familiar movement in prison. It is a kind of exercise to move the stagnant blood in the prisoner's veins; you could call it a stroll or a prison walk ... In the dormitory, a person's bed was his home. When someone sat on your bed it was as if he entered your house and you must show him proper hospitality. A full but miniature life, that would grow or shrink according to prison conditions improving or worsening.[30]

However, daily life was run by strict rules and regulations, 'a kind of great commonality among individuals. A schedule for sleeping, napping, and eating, forced labour duties, shower system, laundry system, wood or olive seed burning system, times to turn on the gas mini-stove, and times where smoking is banned, etc. The lights were obscured by the buckets (the lamp shades) at 23:00, the official time of sleeping'. It is clear that while there was no communication with the outside world; the prisoners, however, found their way to endure the prison:

> 'An early wake-up table, a joyful session when a prisoner with a nice voice and good singing techniques came along, or storytelling sessions in which a prisoner told the story of a novel he read or a movie he watched, or political debate sessions that were often absurd and to a large extent folkloric, or memorizing poetry and proverbs matches and charades.'[31]

These sessions were based on the availability of the gas mini-stoves in the dormitories:

> They disturbed us with their sound and smell and poisoned our blood with their gas emissions, but they were the blood line of our lives. The police were aware of this, so the first method to pressure us and the first penalty was to pull out the

mini-stoves. The attempted suicide of a prisoner in the dormitory by a gas mini-stove was a readily available excuse in the hands of the police. Taking away the mini-stoves meant falling into an abyss of frustration, lethargy, snub, and gloom. No tea, no coffee, no maté, no cooking, nothing.

Mini-stoves had a greater functional role than just making tea and coffee, and the biggest burden was the weekly bath day. However, the mini-stoves and poor ventilation in these dormitories caused suffocation cases that had to be addressed: 'In times of extreme air stagnation and increased pollution to the point where breathing became difficult, the dormitory came up with the invention of ventilation with wet sheets. We wet one of the cotton sheets with water and four people held it from its four corners, and moved it gently up and down to stir and humidify the air.'[32]

Prison life was completed by daily 'breathing' in the courtyard, which was a square-shaped corridor that surrounded the Karakon building:

It was the walkway jammed between the prison building and a four-metre-high fence that surrounded the prison building and was topped by a 2 metre-high barbed wire. Standing in this walkway, you could see nothing from the outside world unless you looked up to see the sky. But from one corner of the square walkway, the north-eastern corner, if you stood there and raised your head slightly and looked to the West, can could see the head of a huge Eucalyptus tree. That was all that was available to us from the romantic world.'[33] Prisoners got ready for 'breathing' time by wearing their best clothes, similar to the way they did when receiving a visit:

As we were veterans, we could receive visits once every two weeks, which was similar to the visiting in the Citadel prison. The visits were heavily monitored. A security operative sat between the family behind the net to the right, and the detainee behind the net to the left. The operative listened to everything being said and prevented any coded or incomprehensible word. The visit was limited to one member of the detainee's family and did not take more than 10 minutes.[34]

Life in Al-Sheikh Hassan's prison was characterized by a lack of connection with the outside world because the authorities blocked newspapers, television, and radio. They did, however, provide prisoners with their food requests through the invoice system: 'There were invoices, and the warden took our requests of vegetables and fruits daily and brought them to us and we paid him for them.' The management of the Karakon was committed to health care, which overall was good; there was a modicum of acceptable treatment.[35] However, this management approach did not apply to everyone. Everyone lived in very harsh conditions as a result of the overcrowding, especially between 1982 and 1985. This prompted the prisoners to strike, demanding that they be transferred to the political wing of Damascus' central prison, Adra.

The strike

'Would you even place cows in such conditions?'

'Who told you you are better than cows?!' The officer answered as if he were ready
for this question ... The authority loaded words of the officer, who was apparently
provoked by the tone of Abu Muhammad's question, were a clear challenge that had
to be answered. We had no way to respond but to strike. Within a short period
of time, the three main blocs of the prison (Politburo, Communist Labour,
Democratic Baath) agreed to carry out a strike. The main request of the strike was
the transfer from Al-Sheikh Hassan prison to Damascus central prison Adra,
without being distracted by secondary demands. At first, this officer summoned
what could be called the 'strike committee' and met with each separately. He made
sure to give gestures of pressure and intimidation, deliberately placing a wheel and
a bamboo stick near the door of the room where he met us. The officer then
introduced a new tactic, which was to suggest that continuing to strike might lead
the branch to intransigence, because the branch did not like to respond under
pressure. He alluded that lists were being prepared in the branch and names would
be proposed for a forthcoming release. The officer was already able to crack the
wall of the strike, and when he touched that, he immediately asked that we inform
him of our decision to continue or stop the strike, and that we take the decision
before him.[36]

A few months after the strike, the decision to transfer political prisoners to Adra prison
came, in the late summer of 1985. Al-Miqdad remembered the end: 'Karakon Al-Sheikh
Hassan was de-commissioned as a political prison with the opening of the political wing
of the Damascus Central Prison, where I was transferred and remained until my release in
1995. In fact, the Karakon cannot be compared with the prison of Adra.[37]

Aleppo Central Prison

The prison is harsh, and harsher are its soldiers
Wood beams standing tall
With hearts that do not beat, and do not feel
Oh, the cuffs around my wrist
Over a quarter of a century ago
Oh God, how long will the wind keep on drifting us
And when will morning shine in our homes
And when do tyrants' grudges dry up
And the night of the haters goes away?
God, we remain patient ...[38]

Figure 9.2 Aleppo Central Prison, Google Maps.

Jurius al-Hames was a prisoner in various Syrian prisons. Before moving to Damascus central prison (Adra), he was taken to Aleppo Central Prison (al-Musalimiya), which 'was built during the unity between Syria and Egypt. That is, under President Gamal Abdel Nasser, when the Security Administration in Syria was in the hands of the infamous officer Abdelhamid al-Sarraj. The prison was designed by German experts'.[39] The prison's main structure resembles the Mercedes sign, similar to Saydnaya military prison. However, Aleppo prison is older, it was built between 1958 and 1960. Like other civil prison, it is considered a standalone branch that follows the Ministry of Interior. It is headed by a brigadier who manages it with 25 officers. All members of the management follow the Internal Security Forces, except for the detachment responsible for the political wing who follow the Political Security Division with members from other security departments, such as Military and General Intelligence.

Geographically, the prison is located north of the city of Aleppo, next to a Palestinian refugee camp, and about three km north of al-Kindi hospital. The prison is close to the town of al-Musalimiya, from which it took its popular (but not official) name. Currently, the structure consists of three buildings:

- The old construction: shaped as a Mercedes sign, consists of four floors. Each floor contains six suites, each comprising ten rooms. Each room normally houses 25 prisoners but, with the start of the revolution, the number of prisoners in each room increased to over 50. The first floor was designated for food and administrative services. The second floor was reserved for detainees. The third floor was for convicts.[40]
- The second building: newly constructed, after 2013. It was reserved for detainees accused of drug abuse and trafficking.
- The third building: the annex, located in the eastern courtyard of the prison. It houses the women's prison and the juvenile prison. It was later used for protesters.

After the outbreak of battles in the vicinity of the prison, all inmates were moved to the old building.[41]

Like other civil prisons, Aleppo has a political wing run by a special detachment consisting of personnel from various security departments. The detachment is often headed by a First Adjutant from the Political Security Division. The wing includes nine dormitories each 8 × 5 metres. Their fronts, Mohammed Berro writes, 'are walls of bars. They allowed us to see the operatives who came to bring and distribute food. They also allowed the members of the security detachment who came to check up on the inmates to see everyone in the room'. This wing received special treatment following the popular movement against former President Hafez al-Assad between 1976 and 1982: 'We, the "political wing" as all prisoners called us, or the "state security wing" as the Prison Director called us, did not have the right to 'breathe' or receive visits. We did not even have the luxury of opening the doors of the rooms to allow prisoners to visit each other.'[42]

Despite this biased treatment, the difference between the prison and the cellars of the security branch remained significant. Berro stated: 'This move [from the latter to the former] was equal to half a release. Space was much bigger, there was light, access to the toilets was available inside the room, even the food was considered relatively clean and plentiful compared to the food of the General Intelligence Branch.' Life in Aleppo prison seems less harsh; however, it was subject to a strict regime: 'It was their daily routine to conduct a morning and evening roll calls, which usually took place when the head of the detachment, who was at the rank of First Adjutant, entered. He had a counterpart who shared controlling and supervising political detainees, in 12-hours shifts each. As soon as we heard: "Prisoners! Roll call!", each one of us stood on his bed. The adjutant passed along and visually counted us from where he stood. They rarely showed aggression.'[43]

Prison life takes shape over time and detainees find their way to communicate with the rest of the inmates of the wing and the prison. Mohammed Berro participated in this communication and became an expert in it over the years: 'This connection was established through a person assigned from our side with a counterpart from theirs, through the air vents in the toilets of our rooms. Through these openings, tools, money that the parents smuggled in, and some of the necessary goods, were exchanged. But most importantly was the transfer of the news which we got fresh every day, through their weekly contact with their families and the availability of radios at their side.' It was clear that all methods of communication, newspapers, radios, and visits, were forbidden to the inmates of the political wing at the time.[44]

Extinguishing the moon

The sudden calm did not last long. At the end of June, news of the massacre in Palmyra prison reached us ... Hours after the news reached us, a violent and swift movement took place. All rooms were thoroughly inspected ... That day we felt that they were preparing for another massacre, maybe close by.

That night, for the first time, a First Lieutenant came and ordered all prisoners to take off their clothes except for their underwear. After midnight they took us down to the 'breathing' yard. There was a large group of torturers, carrying serrated quad cables, which left deep grooves in our backs, chests, faces and forearms for many months. The feet were cracked and made to bleed by the rough concrete ground, which grew at the edges of dense bushes of Syrian Thistle – a type of a thorny plant with sharp spines that cause excruciating pain – upon which we are ordered to roll with bare chests and backs.

After the torturers grew tired of watching us roll or crawl over thorns and sharp stones, the First Lieutenant and his guests started inventing ways to torture us. It was a moonlit night, so they ordered us with a fake firmness to blow the moon with all our might to extinguish it! We spent ten minutes blowing with all our might so as to blow its light off ... They then ordered us to gather by the huge wall, and start pushing it hard so as to push it back by a metre!

After two hours of constant torture, they returned us to our rooms with lacerated skin, dripping a mixture of blood and sweat. We spent the whole night helping each other pluck out the thorns from the backs and chests.[45]

The conditions of prison inmates accused of affiliation with the Muslim Brotherhood worsened. Mohammed Berro narrates:

'They changed how they called us: from "prisoners" or "sons of Adam" [a customary reference to men in the Arab world] to "animals" or "sons of [bitches]"! The daily evening greeting was: "You animals, get ready for your skinning." Food quality drastically deteriorated. Sudden aggressive attacks became more frequent. Each one was a declaration of a massacre or a blood bath committed by the regime forces in Aleppo or any other Syrian city. Torturing us gave them a feeling of safety and security.'[46]

Daily torture in Aleppo prison stopped due to the transfer of Muslim Brotherhood detainees in the fall of 1980 to the Palmyra military prison. However, the prison administration maintained its harsh treatment and tightened living conditions for inmates in the political wing. In 1982, Osama Mohammed al-Askari al-Ashour narrates, 'everything was forbidden in the political wing, so we went on strike to improve the conditions of the prison'. However, the detachment in charge of the political wing resorted to violence to break up the strike:

Participants in the strike were tortured. They used the wheel, batons, and the Magic Carpet which was placed in the wing's detachment. Then we were taken to the solitaries in the prison cellar. It was very cold; the temperatures were below zero. They left us in dark solitaries with nothing but our underwear. Standing on the floor was difficult and leaning against the wall was impossible. We were deprived of sleep. The next day they brought the bread, so we put it under us to separate us from the cold floor hoping to get some sleep. We were about 15 detainees and remained in the solitaires for more than 17 days.[47]

Despite the strike, many things remained off-limits for the inmates of the political wing. Al-Askari told us: 'Books were banned. We had to smuggle them. Pens were impossible to bring in. Banning writing materials was a prison custom. This came after a former Muslim Brotherhood prisoner wrote the names of those who tortured him on his clothes that he sent to his family to wash. This got discovered and the pen became as dangerous as a gun.'[48]

Abu Hamdan's *oud*

Abu Hamdan lined the wood planks from an old fruit box, which he smuggled into the dormitory, on the tiled floor under the mattress. He laid on the bed crossing one leg over the other. Then he sat in the kitchen so that the warden would not see him or hear the noise. He started punching the ends of the aluminum pot with a nail, using the chopping board as a hammer. He finished punching the pot as planned. Abu Hamdan continued his work on the wood from the fruit box. He contemplated the lengths, sensed their durability, and chose the best fit for the neck. He used the nail to draw on the planks. He placed the worn-out planks firmly in the centre of the pot to make it easier for him to carve the circle of sounds. Abu Hamdan crossed the corridor returning from the visit, waving his hands, and cheerfully greeting the prisoners of the dormitories. Abu Hamdan entered the kitchen and pulled the strings, which his mother brought him, out of his pocket, and started working. He stayed until late at night in the toilet.

The next day, at sunset, Abu Hamdan pulled the oud out of the burlap bag he sewed and asked those sitting next to the mesh to monitor the corridor. He tuned the strings. Just before he started playing, he looked at everyone with a big smile and blushed cheeks. Then he began to sing: 'O sweet-voiced person, go ahead, give us the melodies!' The tune was fresh and smooth enticing us to participate, however the surprise of how successful this oud turned out to be and what a good player Abu Hamdan was kept us silent and astonished. The ecstasy took over Abu Hamdan, and his face lit up with joy. He held the oud again, tuned it, and started: 'I long for the bread, for the coffee that my mother prepared.' No one was exchanging looks. They were all absorbing the melody and drowning in it. The faces looked thinner than they were. 'What longing and what rubbish?! Hand the oud over!' The sound of the warden fell upon us like a thunderbolt. The warden took the oud in his hands, looked at it and picked the strings with his fingers then smiled sarcastically. He looked at the faces and saw them pale, watching him with repressed anger; probably he saw nothing. He giggled and weaved the oud against the bars completely smashing it and went on giggling.[49]

The conditions of political prisoners in Aleppo prison continued to be such a tug-of-war for the next nine years. It can be said that their conditions improved slightly and gradually. Bakr Sidqi narrates: 'The situation was excellent, compared to any other prison. There were books, daily "breathing" for about two hours, and for the rest of the day the doors of the dormitories remained open to the corridor of our wing until 19:00.' Even the visits 'were regular on a monthly basis, until the head of the Political Security branch in Aleppo changed, and Hashim Saleh arrived, who stopped the visits altogether, then allowed them again after a while, but only through connections and exclusively through his office. It went on like this for about a year, after which visits returned to being monthly'. The details of daily life such as food and the invoice system to allow prisoners to purchase items from outside the prison showed there was a lot of corruption and bribery among the prison personnel. At times, however, this corruption reflected positively on the lives of prisoners.[50]

The number of inmates in the ward would fluctuate according to the arrest campaigns waged by the Political Security Division. There were 15 or 16 prisoners in each room. There were no beds in Aleppo prison, everyone slept on the floor. There were no gas mini-stoves either. Bakr Sidqi resumes: 'As a result of the constant demand they gave us the mini-stoves, but one of them exploded once so they pulled them back out. They allowed electrical heaters, but then banned them.' Banning and permitting items was tied to events and at times to the mood of the detachment responsible for the ward, according to Sidqi: 'On the day of a fire in our ward, an investigator from the Political Security branch came to look into the matter. He beat us all to know how we got the gas mini-stoves, which indicates the conflict in powers and decisions between the detachment and the branch.' However, the ban on the mini-stoves prompted prisoners to think about solutions and devise their own methods to provide a source of heating for cooking and making tea and coffee. 'We invested the frying oil we bought through the invoice system to make small stoves. Although they emitted a lot of smoke, we kept using them for years before they found out about us and prevented us from buying frying oil.' In 1991, about 90 per cent of the wing's inmates were released following the 'grand pardon': 'Security kept 18 detainees, and I was one of them. We were all transferred to Damascus central prison Adra, pending the sentence of the State Security Court, before later being transferred to the Palmyra military prison.'[51]

The first mutiny

Aleppo Central Prison has been largely absent from the political scene since 1991. After the Saydnaya military prison mutiny, a number of its inmates were transferred to Aleppo, and their designated wing became known as the 'Salafist wing'. After the Syrian Revolution in the spring of 2011, Aleppo prison returned to the forefront by becoming a warehouse where security forces held protesters and revolutionary activists. The number of political prisoners in Aleppo increased as the revolutionary tide reached the city in 2012. During that year, the Syrian Revolution started morphing into a form of armed conflict between Syrian regime forces and armed opposition forces. Military forces of the regime of all forms and affiliations used the prison grounds and buildings as their camp. Medium and heavy military equipment such as cannons and tanks spread all over the prison and on the roofs of its buildings. A Violations Documentation Centre report notes: 'The provocations of prison and army operatives of political detainees began in Aleppo Central Prison. The treatment of prisoners by the operatives and officers gradually worsened. This led to the first mutiny in the prison on 23 July 2012.'[52]

After the Taraweeh prayer that day during the holy month of Ramadan, the insurrection began:

> Fully armed regime forces fired heavy fire and tear gas at prison inmates. The attack lasted about two hours. It resulted in massive destruction of the prison. 35 prisoners were killed and more than 50 wounded. The attacking forces arrested over 500 prisoners and sent them to the prison cellars. They were all severely tortured and their screams filled the prison for 24 hours. They crammed them into very narrow places, stripped them of all their clothes and opened sewage pipes on top of them to increase their suffering. The police took control of the prison and the next day they brought down another batch of prisoners to interrogate, which lasted a whole week during which some prisoners died as a result of high electrocution. They stunned them right over the heart. Over 50 prisoners were killed during that week, especially when regime forces stormed a dormitory and carried out summary executions of many of the detainees.[53]

After the first mutiny, the detainees' sentences were increased by an additional six months without any legal basis. New charges were filed against prisoners arrested on criminal charges. The Prison Administration banned visits, communications and any form of exercise as punishment. The suffering of detainees did not end with increased sentences or a long list of prohibitions, as the prison became a battleground between opposition and regime forces:

> On 15 May 2013, the Free Syrian Army, which was besieging the prison in preparation for breaking in, launched its first attack on the prison. The prison was bombed with mortars. One of the shells hit a cell with prisoners, on top of which regime forces installed a DShK. This killed 3 prisoners, and wounded others. When the prisoners called for medical help, an officer called Mohammed Baroudi opened fire on them. Two prisoners were wounded, the first in the leg and the second in the shoulder. Six prisoners and a large number of prison police officers were killed in the attack. However, on 23 May 2013, the Free Syrian Army waged its biggest attack. Forty-four prisoners were killed because regime forces used prisoners as human shields.[54]

The second mutiny

From the beginning of March 2013:

> food supplies started running out significantly as a result of military operations around the prison, the blocking of roads leading to it and the start of the Free

Syrian Army's attempts to break into it. In May 2013, fuel for the prison furnace ran out. Thousands of prisoners had no food for two days and the "flour crisis" started. Each prisoner was allocated a cup of flour a day, from which had to make his own bread by burning his clothes and personal items to cook his food. Diesel was available to prison officers, the police, and army personnel. Military vehicles, including tanks, operated continuously on diesel within the vicinity of the prison.[55]

The acute shortage of food, and smoke from burning fabrics and furniture impacted the health of the prisoners: Between May and July 2013, disease spread very quickly, especially tuberculosis. On 10 July 2013, flour was completely cut off. Prisoners were left without food for three days and nights. This pushed the prisoners of the first and second wings to insurgency in response to the dire conditions. Regime forces met this with brutality, using live bullets; six people were killed instantly and dozens were injured.[56]

The Free Syrian Army reached an agreement with the Syrian Red Crescent to bring cooked food into the prison. The deal was to release '10 prisoners every time food was brought in. Prison administration stole the bulk of the food and all the medicine that was entering through the Red Crescent. Medicine was sold again to prisoners, but at crazy prices'. The agreement lasted three months, before it broke down as a result of a dispute between the Free Syria Army and regime forces stationed in the prison.

> Food was cut off for nine days, so they fed the prisoners rotting bread ("green bread"), allocating to each prisoner half a loaf per day. After consuming all the "green bread", food was completely cut off for four days.' The rotting bread and lack of healthcare caused 'severe diarrhoea and complete panic among prisoners after more than 50 people died, 23 in one week during the first days of October 2013.

From late April 2012 until 10 October 2014 'the prison saw the deaths of more than 600 prisoners. About 300 of them were buried in the prison's eastern courtyard'.[57] The bodies of some of the other victims were handed over to their families, such as political detainee Ahmed Hamdo al-Mahmood, who died from poor healthcare and hunger, after over a quarter of a century of detention without trial.

At the end of 2014, major battles took place around Aleppo central prison between the rebels and Assad's army; the area around the prison was one of the bloodiest battlefronts in the north of Syria. The prison changed hands a few times: the Assad regime lost and then regained control of the prison, together with the entire city of Aleppo in late 2016. With the end of the military battles, the regime renovated the prison. At the time of writing, Aleppo prison was still functioning as a civilian prison.

Figure 9.3 Ahmed Al-Mahmoud – in Aleppo central prison, from a private collection.

Damascus Central Prison

The Assad regime uses Damascus Central Prison as a model civil prison and correctional institution. It is the largest civil prison in Syria and the most privileged in terms of services and space. The prison administration therefore adopts more gentle methods in dealing with prisoners to maintain the role of the prison in the propaganda machine of the regime. The prison and its inmates appear on Syrian state television and the website of the state news agency SANA; this has become more frequent since 2016. Of course, media appearances are limited to judicial inmates – and not political ones.

Damascus Central Prison, which opened in 1985, is located in Adra, a city 20 km northeast of Damascus. It spreads over an area of 10 hectares and contains several buildings, yards, and unused land. The prison consists of several buildings. The main

Figure 9.4 Inside Aleppo Prison, Syrian Government TV.

Figure 9.5 Damascus Central Prison, Google Maps.

Figure 9.6 Damascus Central Prison, from SANA, the Syrian news agency.

Figure 9.7 Kurdish Prisoners, International Institute of Social History, Bogaers archive.

block of the prison consists of 12 wings. Each wing has 12 rooms, with some exceptions, such as the first and tenth wings, which each contain six rooms. This is also the case in the second wing, known as the 'political wing'. The Political Security Division oversees this wing through a prison-based security detachment.

Prison wings are divided according to the crimes and charges of the inmates. However, the first wing is theoretically designated as an educational school, while the tenth is intended for transit prisoners, known in Arabic as 'al-tasfir'. The area of each of the prison rooms is approximately 55m². About 50 inmates are housed in each room, but in cases of overcrowding, the number can exceed 100. Beds are distributed according to seniority or the importance and financial capacity of the prisoner. Corruption plays a big role in daily prison life from beds and rented sleeping spaces to the prison market. Faiq al-Mir, interviewed by the Syrian Commission for Transitional Justice, said:

> After about 10 days of sleeping on the floor with one blanket, one of the prisoners agreed to rent me his place, which is a space between two beds. That space was 90 cm wide and 180 cm long and cost 500 Syrian Pounds (then USD $10) per week. Renting beds was very common in Adra prison. Their owners rent them to newcomers who are elderly, sick, or well-off. Weekly rental prices at the time, in 2007, were around 700 Syrian Pounds (then USD $14) for the top bed and about 1,200 Syrian Pounds (then USD $24) for the bottom one. The person who rented me his space was summoned and threatened with transfer, he also lost his space.

That was the destiny of anybody who connected with, or helped, political prisoners in prison. The same thing happened to a person who gave his bed to journalist and political opponent Fayez Sara. He was summoned, interrogated and then transferred to another wing.[58]

Each wing has a 'breathing' yard that includes a market which falls under the Prisoners' Welfare Association. The prison also includes a clinic, and patients from each wing have a weekly opportunity to visit. However, the clinic is poorly equipped and offers limited medical services. Critical cases are transported by ambulance to the Police Hospital in the city of Harasta near the prison. Adnan al-Miqdad recalled:

Medical care was available and good ... Compared to the Karakon, which was buried behind high walls, or the crumbling Citadel prison, Adra prison was an open and modern place. We spent most of our days reading and playing sports. Our lives were close to normal, as if we were judicial prisoners. But they didn't let us complete our university studies in prison. We were only allowed to take the high-school exam through a centre inside the prison.[59]

Following the opening of Damascus central prison as an alternative to the Citadel prison, the regime also decided to close Sheikh Hassan prison and transfer its inmates. Ratib Shabo told us:

We went up one staircase, we turned to go up another one, then went through gates of iron bars painted silver. We walked through, inspecting what we see in anticipation, trying to configure this place which will consume an amount we don't know yet out of our lives ... After a while we arrived at our allotted place. A wing on the second floor of Damascus Central Prison. It was actually a half-wing, with dormitories laid out on one side only, unlike other full wings. Windows overlooking outside the prison were sealed with concrete blocks ... The interior windows overlooking the other prison yards were also blocked with perforated iron sheets containing soft holes, through which you can only see if you squint through the hole.[60]

The political wing was isolated from the rest of the prison wings; it had its own, small courtyard. However, it was a big wing. Shabo describes it:

A 150-metre-long corridor on a North-South axis, bordered on the West by a concrete wall, and on the East by six double-numbered dormitories beginning with the second dormitory and ending with dormitory 12. Dormitories were separated by a long space that equals to the length of the breathing yard, with a mesh in the middle. The dormitories were not attached wall-to-wall, but rather spaced. Each dormitory had wall-to-wall windows, located just below the ceiling, overlooking a breathing space. Our courtyard was located at the northern end of the wing. The windows of the corridors of the judicial wings that overlooked it were blocked by perforated iron sheets similar to the ones sealing the windows of our wing's corridor.[61]

For prisoners, moving to a new prison was different from moving to a pre-inhabited prison. The difference between the two was visible on the mental wellness level as well in everyday life. Shabo narrates again:

> You had to start from scratch ... The positive transition from the investigation branch to Sheikh Hassan prison was contradicted by the arduous transition to Adra prison. It was the difference between being a guest over a founded and stable system, and you starting to establish a system with many elements missing. It was a big difference! Spacious dormitories were empty except for a number of single mattresses of bare sponge stacked in a seating block. Nothing comforts the soul like the big space and the expectation of a better prison life. Once the mattresses were raised on iron structures called beds, the area under the bed became a solution to a dilemma often experienced by the prisoner. It turned into a perfect store of items and belongings. The number of prisoners increased, and prisoners had to sleep in bunk beds in the dormitory. New iron beds rose above the existing ones. Spaces between the beds shrunk. The dormitory turned into a crowded human storehouse, full of disputes, grudges and small intrigues, and also with friendships, study, handcrafts and dialogues.[62]

According to Bakr Sidqi, prison spaces and overcrowding weakened the supervision a little: 'Every prison has its own traditions ... Damascus prison was more crowded than Aleppo prison and so the treatment was better. TV was available, exercise was daily, and the library was open. In Aleppo we went through circumstances that caused us to lose many of the privileges that we achieved with the strikes. Life in Adra was more luxurious than in Aleppo.'[63] The management of the Adra prison detachment was good and better than that in Aleppo:

> It was managed by a Captain, not a First Adjutant, a he was a kind and polite man. Several hunger strikes took place to meet certain demands. The Captain dealt with them immediately by discussing with the prisoners and meeting what he could. He controlled his operatives well, unlike Aleppo prison, where the detachment was chaotic. However, the goal of our transfer to Damascus was to transfer us to the State Security court before we were transferred in 1993 to Palmyra prison for refusing to sign a pledge to abstain from political work.[64]

Book fever

Days after our arrival in Adra, the police officers brought us a large folder with titles written mostly in Arabic, some in English and a few in French. That folder was the index of the prison library. It was handled by a prisoner, who volunteered to coordinate the dormitory orders of books. Each prisoner had the right to request only two titles each month, as books were exchanged monthly. Perhaps no place in the world has ever experienced a reading fever like the one experienced in our first period of the Adra phase. Some books were passed around the clock from the hands of a reader whose allotted time had expired, to another reader whose turn had come. Dormitory inmates looked as though they were preparing for an imminent crucial exam. A nap was no longer needed, for calm prevailed ... After a few years of reading, the prison library fell short of meeting our needs. We had to rely on smuggling books through the judicial prison. We could order books through visits, but only those permitted by the 'cultural censorship' of the detachment. In fact, it was a strict monitoring of all aspects, not just political ones.[65]

The library, exercise, and health care were not the only surprises for detainees transferred from the Citadel, Sheikh Hassan, and security branches to Damascus Prison. Shabo remembered: 'Visits ... this was the great blessing of the merciful prison of Adra. Shortly after we moved there, visits were open to all, a visit every two weeks and for two hours. Although the visits took place through two distant meshes and was only for first-degree relatives, and although the voices of visitors and inmate filled the closed visits corridor, so much so that you lost your ability to hear as mixed voices became a deafening buzz that was an extreme opposite to silence, visits brought the flame of life to the prison.' Prison conditions improved with the arrival of Economic Court detainees at the end of the 1980s. Most of those were affluent or influential people, so, 'many things changed for the better, among these was improving the conditions of visits'.[66]

The great release, or the great pardon of 1991, passed through Adra prison as well. Shabo experienced it:

On 14 December 1991, the vast majority of prisoners were released at one go ... The prison system was disturbed after such a large release. Only about 30 prisoners remained in the prison, which housed more than 170 inmates. The doors were closed, and a system similar to that of solitary cells was enforced. Five to six prisoners were placed in each dormitory and inter-dormitory contact was prohibited. The doors opened during the exercise time only, which did not exceed half an hour a day for each dormitory individually. The weekly invoice system was stopped. Joint visits were stopped. The winter of 1991–1992 was the harshest of all the years of imprisonment.[67]

The great release was followed by a wave of negotiations with the rest of the political detainees. Al-Miqdad recalled: 'One of the security committees visiting the prison was headed by the Head of the Political Security Division, Major General Adnan Badr Hassan. The discussion between me and him was heated, so I prepared myself to be thrown in the solitary cell, but the result of these negotiation sessions was that we were transferred to the Supreme State Security court.'[68]

Adra prison had maintained its title of a 'five-star prison' since its opening. After 2005, however, the conditions of its political inmates deteriorated. Ibrahim al-Olabi recalled: 'We were only allowed to go out to the corridor at breathing time, which was only two days a week. We also did not have the opportunity to use the prison's pay phones, there were no beds in our rooms, we slept on the floor.'[69] During that period, 'most prisoners were beaten and tortured by prison guards. Many political prisoners were placed in solitaries which were no more that 2 × 1 metres. All solitary inmates were forbidden to go out to exercise. The small space of the solitaries combined with their dampness caused their inmates to suffer lung diseases such as tuberculosis, asthma, shortness of breath, not to mention infectious skin diseases such as scabies due to lack of hygiene'.[70]

On 25 January 2007, the prisoners mutinied and took control of the prison, using knives, iron bars, chains and gas canisters, overpowering three police officers. The Syrian army and the Fourth Armored Division surrounded the prison. The Attorney General came to the prison personally and threatened the prisoners, via the prison's public announcement system, that he would shoot the mutineers himself if they resisted the army. According to a report by the Syrian Commission for Transitional Justice, 'the prison returned to the control of its administration after a full day of rebellion. There were no casualties during this confrontation, with the exception of fainting and suffocation caused by heavy gas bombs fired at everyone. The administration then imposed punishments on prisoners and harsh measures, some of which are still in force to date. All sharp objects, knives, cups, and metal cutlery were confiscated'.[71] The mutiny was followed by extensive interrogation rounds of prisoners who had been involved.

Adra prison became the scene of another act of resistance on 10 October 2009, when a group of members of the Kurdish-nationalist Democratic Union Party (PYD) announced an open-ended hunger strike to protest about their cruel treatment by the prison administration. The strikers demanded visits to be allowed and contact with the outside world. They also demanded improvements to their living conditions, allowing them to air and open the doors of their rooms during the day. Moreover, they demanded the provision of radio and television sets, similar to the rest of the judicial detainees. But their main demand was to transfer their file to civil courts, and finally, the lifting of the state of emergency and martial law, which had been in force since 1963. They also demanded the annulment of their sentences by the Supreme State Security court.[72]

Following the Syrian Revolution, the conditions of revolutionary detainees in Adra prison varied according to the wing. It became clear that the political wing had reached its full capacity, so the prison administration used different wings to place the new inmates. M.A., a detainee who was arrested during the uprising, narrated: 'They put me in the eighth wing, assigned for those charged with murder. I stayed in Adra for almost a year ... Some old prisoners told me that the prison state has radically changed since the revolution began. With the arrival of the revolution detainees in the prison, its library was revived.'[73]

The prison was somewhat affected by the military action surrounding it. The effects of the battles between the regime army and the Free Syrian Army were reflected in the lives of the prison inmates. Most judicial prisoners did not rely on the prison for their food as they had regular visits; they bought their food outside the prison or it was brought to them. This worked well for the new prisoners, however, M.A. recalled, 'during 2013, the roads leading to the prison were closed as battles around the prison moved closer. Visits were almost completely cut off and the supply of prison markets was significantly reduced. First the tea and sugar went out, then the prices of the goods in the market went up, so most of the prisoners went back to the prison food again. With this shift, food became scarce'.[74] As the battles around the prison ended, things went back to normal. This remains the case today.

Damascus Central Prison for women

Damascus Central Prison, or Adra prison, also contains a prison for women, located just southeast of the men's prison. The women's prison has two sections for female inmates. The first section houses the criminal inmates, also known as the 'judicial prisoners'. The second section houses political prisoners, labeled by the regime as 'terrorists' because they are tried before terrorism courts. Following the end of the State of Emergency on 21 April 2011, President Bashar al-Assad issued Legislative Decree No. 53, which abolished the Supreme State Security court, on the same day. This was followed by Decree No 55 on Combating Terrorism, then, in 2012 by Decree No 22 on the establishment of a court to deal with terrorism cases, which inherited the functions of the State Security court. In essence, only the labels changed, the discourse and practices stayed the same.

All inmates arriving from the security or civil police branches to the Damascus Central Prison for women were placed on the ground floor in a wing known by its functional name, 'the depository'. Ranim Maatouq, a former detainee, narrated:

> The wing had a Head; she was an inmate imprisoned on a big charge and close to one of the prison officers. She was in charge of us. Two weeks later we were transferred to the Terrorism Court. We were taken there in a penal uniform, a long blue robe, and we were all tied in one chain. The judge decided to detain us, so upon my return to Adra prison I was moved to the second floor. I was placed in the homicide wing, where the prison administration allocated two rooms of the wing to the revolution detainees.[75]

The prison, which opened between 2011 and 2012, has five wings. According to J.H., each contans 'a three-metre-wide corridor on either side of which stand six rooms. Each room is equipped with a kitchen, a bathroom, a toilet, beds, a fridge, and a TV. It houses 20–25 inmates. Each wing has a pay phone. The prison also includes an administrative section for officers. It includes twenty rooms, a clinic and a pharmacy.'[76] The prison is run by a Colonel, who reports administratively to the Damascus Central Prison branch, run by a Brigadier. Most of the prison officers are male, except for one female prison warden, who is in charge of the personal belongings department, called Um Ali.[77]

Between summer 2012 and summer 2013, the women's prison was not much different from any security branch, especially the 'depository' section. Brigadier Faisal al-Aqla, who was in charge of the prison, blocked all the benefits that central prisons normally offer. He banned TV, radio, refrigerators, buying vegetables and meat, even banned handicrafts such as making beads and knitting. Phone calls between detainees and their families were strictly prohibited. Parents were also prohibited from bringing books or any kind of food to the detainees. Provocative inspections were carried out with or without him, and in the most heinous manner.[78]

One detainee described what happened in the prison as a 'slow death' in terms of how those who were ill were treated. There were no specialized doctors in the prison to treat the detainees, despite the presence of pregnant women, young children, elderly inmates, and patients with malignant diseases. The prison administration justified the lack of health care by saying that the road to the hospital was dangerous due to clashes and that a telegram had to be sent to a higher authority to get approval to transfer a patient for treatment. The prison witnessed several deaths. A prisoner suffered what seemed to be a 'clot' or a shortness of breath and died immediately afterwards. These difficult conditions prompted a female detainee in May 2013 to attempt suicide by 'cutting her veins in protest for not providing milk for her 10 months old baby, whom she gave birth to during her detention in Homs Central Prison before being transferred to Adra prison. Also, a child died eight days after her birth due to malnutrition and the absence of incubators for newborns'.[79]

After Colonel Adnan Mohammed Suleiman took over the management of the prison, it underwent a series of transformations. According to former detainee R.S., 'prison becomes a five-star stay if you have money. The Colonel was very materialistic and charged money for any service you asked, from phone calls to moving from one wing to another'.[80] However, materialism was not Colonel Suleiman's only vice. Cases of sexual exploitation inside Adra women's prison started to emerge.[81]

The spread of bribery and the exploitation of some women detainees by Colonel Suleiman did not end the violence against women prisoners. Ranim Maatouq explains: 'The detainee Faten Rajab was beaten and another prisoner was held in the solitary cell for two weeks as punishment. The prison director punished me by moving me to a room full of Shabbiha.' Violence and abuse started from the moment of arrival.

'Each girl entered the Lieutenant's room alone, where her belongings were inspected, and she received reprimands and even beatings sometimes. She is then transferred to the detention wing accompanied by insults and jabs of the operatives Abu Taimour and Abu Nagham. Staying in line waiting in fear of what's coming is worse than the beating itself. The moment you enter the wing you feel that you have entered a beehive. I was put-off with the big number of prisoners. As soon as we entered the dormitories, ex-prisoners started helping us with the food and the bathroom arrangements and showering us with questions about what is going on outside and what branch we came from. I remained silent in a state of shock for some time.'[82] As a result of the overcrowding and the lack of beds, 'we had to sleep on the floor. We spread our clothes on the floor and slept on them'.[83]

As the days passe, the prisoner starts to adapt to the prison routine. However, long periods of time with nothing to do sparks prisoners' creativity. As Luna Watfeh recalled:

Sitting idle gives you a bad feeling. So we set up some projects, such as financial support for detainees who do not receive visits. They started preparing meals and selling them to prisoners who had money. Then we established a literacy project for girls who did not know how to read and write. Books and papers were not forbidden in prison then. After the release of the statement that I wrote and smuggled out of the prison on the conditions of the detainees, books and papers were banned\.[84]

Prison papers and letters

I don't remember how the story began. For the first time I am deprived of my children and I am not with them. Coming to visit is dangerous, the road is unsafe. Using the phone for longer than allowed duration is subject to a series of pulling strings. I think about them and write to them and to myself all the time. I put a great effort in prison to get a notebook and a pen. I wrote some letters to my children and secretly smuggled some data and details. I rationed papers and pens, with a sacredness that exceeds that the poor accord to dry bread. I wrote some personal thoughts at dawn of 21 July 2014. Writing became my only friend. I drew on lined paper the details of the last hour of rain: alone I spend it under the weeping sky that shares my grief. Many details come back to mind. Between half past four and half past five. I didn't do the crazy rain dance. I didn't smile as the sky cried. I conjured all of your images. Nour... Maya... Marwa... This time I did not remember the roads of Damascus and my wet steps. I didn't remember its smell and fragrant air. I did not remember a lover and the walks we stole from time. I just remembered my loneliness.[85]

According to most survivor testimonies, the days in Adra women's prison varied between acceptable and difficult, accompanied by a range of mental and physical issues. Women were not locked up alone in prison, but many did have their children or were pregnant the time of their arrest. Luna Watfeh witnessed a woman giving birth in prison: 'One of the prisoners stayed three days in prison after her water broke. After excreting a lot of pressure, she was taken to the hospital but did not return so we did not know what happened to her.'[86] There were many births. However, they were not a primary reason for seeking medical help. J.H., for example, notes: 'Prisoner Hana Khalid, 26, complained of stomach pain. At the roll call time we tried to take her to the clinic, but she fell dead at the door of the wing. They said she died of a heart attack, but she died due to medical negligence. All the time they only gave her painkillers. Since I was a nurse for many years, I don't think she had a heart attack.'[87] The state of medical care generally changed according to the attention the prison administration paid to the inmates and the efficiency of the nursing staff, who were mostly detainees themselves. The clinic in Adra women's prison could only treat physical illness. In cases of mental illness they resorted to specialized doctors at the state-run Neuropsychiatric Hospital Avicenna. Some prisoners were taken to this hospital for various periods, where they received treatment before being sent back to prison.

Visits by inspection committees from the Red Cross or the Ministry of the Interior affected the levels of health care, prison cleanliness and attention shown to inmates. J.H. recalled: 'During my time in Adra, the ICRC committee visited the prison twice. The first visit was in the winter, during which they distributed a sanitary bag and some clothes. The second was in the summer and also included the distribution of some covers, and cleaning tools and products.' The prison administration asked inmates to thoroughly clean the rooms and wings before these visits.[88]

The reign of Colonel Suleiman did not last long, as political prisoners worked hard to file several complaints against him through the inspection committees that visited the prison. He was succeeded by Colonel Raad Reza Salameh in 2016. However, changing the director of the prison did not stop the material relations between some women and officers, nor the usual daily prison system. The doors of the rooms opened at 7:00, then closed at 15:00 for the roll call, and opened again at 18:00. The doors remained open in the summer until 22:00, and in winter until 20:00, after which they remained closed until the next day. However, the Syrian propaganda machine still uses Adra women's prison as a model image for women's prisons.

Qatana and Douma prisons for women

To close this discussion of civil prisons it is important to mention the old, closed women's prisons. Before Damascus Central Prison for Women opened, the authorities relied on Qatana Prison, located 20 km southwest of the capital, and Douma prison, located 9 km east of Damascus. There is not much information about these closed civil prisons. However, it is certain that they shared common qualities in terms of their

Figure 9.8 Map of Douma Women's Prison, Google Maps.

construction and the backgrounds of their inmates. Of course, both prisons were administratively subject to the Ministry of Interior, while a Political Security detachment oversaw the affairs of political detainees.

Qatana

An old traditional Arabic house, built of stones, with rooms, the dormitories, lining its courtyard. The prison had five dormitories, including one room that was more like a solitary cell, which housed the mother of Mahdi Alwani, a prominent member of the Muslim Brotherhood. Heba al-Dabbagh wrote about the prison in her powerful memoir: 'In addition to a dormitory for female political prisoners, other dormitories were assigned in accordance with the charges of the prisoners. Two dormitories were for murder charges, one for marijuana and drugs charges, and the fourth for prostitution charges. The fifth room was more like a solitary cell.' The presence of these dormitories in one geographical space did not mean that inmates were allowed to mingle: 'Mingling between judicial and political inmates was forbidden.'[89]

The political dormitory was a five-metre-long rectangular room located in the left corner of the prison. Its description is identical to that of a traditional room in an Arabic house. It was connected to the courtyard by a stone step followed by a sill. 'Then the floor rises to a higher level. The left corner of the room had the bathroom compartment. There were two windows overlooking the prison courtyard to the right of the door.' It is clear that this room was not always used before 1982, the year it was opened to accommodate the new detainees. Al-Dabbagh was one of them: 'After we went into the dormitory and each one of us learned her sentence, the prison director returned and handed us sponge mattresses, pillows and blankets, one each. They were all old, used, and stinking. Shortly afterwards arguments erupted between the detainees as they battled to get the best mattress, blanket, and spot. Of course, the room was not big enough for all of us.'[90]

Forced labour

After the arguments on spot allocation ended, we were finally able to settle down enough to start cleaning up the place together and set it up as our new home. We noticed that some corners of the room were corroded, and one side of the stone step by the door was broken, threatening any user to slip. We asked the Prison Director, Abu Moutee, if he could allow us some cement so we can repair it, and he agreed. On the second day, he came early and opened the door of the dormitory. The first one out was Hajjeh Um Riyadh. As soon as he saw her and called her name, she fainted. Hajjeh Madiha hurried to her aid and woke her up with some water. As soon as she opened her eyes, she clung to her begging: 'Help me, Hajjeh, they want to take me to hard labour! For God's sake talk to him! Tell him I can't! I have hypertension, I lose my breath easily and won't be able to take it.' The poor thing was crying as if she was possessed. Hajjeh Madiha went out and asked the Director, surprised: 'What happened? Where are you taking her?' The man said with surprise and confusion: 'I swear I did not do anything to her. I only told her to come and take the cement.' As we later learned, because of her poor hearing on the one hand and the fear that was still residing in her, she thought that he wanted to take her to start executing a sentence of hard labour, so she passed out.[91]

Like other civil prisons, Qatana Prison could be considered a 'better' place in terms of accommodation and treatment than the security branches. Visits and even correspondence from the prison to any address in or outside Syria were allowed. Heba al-Dabbagh wrote:

At one point we enjoyed the freedom of postal correspondence. I wrote to my brother's house in Aleppo, my aunt's house, and even Umm Shaima in Saudi Arabia, and I received mail from them all. This did not last more than two or three months after which strict censorship on letters, books and publications returned. Weekly visits continued every Friday and did not stop.

Visits in Qatana Prison were held in a hall dedicated to this purpose. Families were allowed to enter after inspecting what they brought their daughters, be it clothes, food, or gifts. 'Then the visitors were allowed in while we waited. Separating us were two sets of bars, between which was a corridor where policemen walked along monitoring our conversations and interfering in them.[92]

The most famous incident in Qatana Prison was a fire which killed a judicial prisoner. Al-Dabbagh was present when it happened:

Fire broke out more than once. The first fire started in the bathroom of the murder dormitory, killing Fatima, a prisoner accused of killing her husband. The fire spread to the entire dormitory, burning it entirely and almost killing the other prisoners. We called on the warden, Um Debo, to do something, but she didn't respond. When the flames reached the prison yard, the smoke covered the whole place, and the fire nearly engulfed the electrical wires and gas jars in the kitchen next door, the warden finally sounded the alarm. Operatives came trying to find the source of the fire in the darkness of the night but to no avail. Eventually, amidst all the chaos, one of the inmates of the same dormitory extinguished the fire with her blanket. But the fire had devoured a large part of Fatima's body, so she died a week later . .

The causes of these fires were the use of mini-gas stoves to heat bathing and cooking water; they were unsafe equipment.[93]

Douma Prison

Political prisoners were transferred from Qatana to Douma prison in 1985, after which it is believed that Qatana women's prison was closed along with Qatana men's prison that same year. Douma prison was architecturally very close to Qatana prison. Both were traditional Arabic houses built of stone, however Douma prison was slightly larger. The centre of the courtyard was occupied by a water fountain, surrounded by the prison's six dormitories as well as the kitchen, a central bathroom, a clinic and a market. Al-Dabbagh describes the prison:

> The first dormitory from the right was for prostitution charges, and was the largest. It housed more than 100 inmates. Next to it was the dormitory for murder charges. The first dormitory from the left was for marijuana and drugs. It was followed by a room for theft and pickpocketing charges, separated by a room for literacy. This programme was later abolished so the room turned into a common room. The dormitory for political prisoners was at the heart of the structure.[94]

The political prisoners' dormitory was a large room on either side of which was a concrete bench above ground level on which the detainees slept. Duha al-Ashour al-Askari remembered: 'Under the bench there were slots we used to store our personal belongings. A narrow walkway separated the two benches and led to a toilet and a sink that was used for washing as well as an in-house kitchen.' Political prisoners were subject to the general prison system, but any change in their reality was linked to the Political Security detachment. They could not get out of prison even in ab emergency without an approval from the security services, who passed their decision to the detachment. Some of the daily details for political prisoners were also subject to a security decision such as blocking a visit or blocking access to the library. 'The prison had a library outside the inner prison building. It was forbidden to us, and that was a strange paradox. The library was neglected, run by a lazy policewoman. After a big effort I convinced her allow me to put the books in order and coordinate the library. My only condition was that I could read in exchange for my effort. She left me in the library for a few hours, which were the best hours of my day in prison.'[95]

Prison life held many small details, such as cooking, which was done by the prisoners, or knitting and other handicrafts; the common bathroom, which each dormitory was entitled to use one day a week; looking after the children, whose number in prison exceeded 30; taking care of pregnant women and sick inmates, either through the clinic, as al-Askari recalled, 'which was attended by a male nurse until 14:00, or through doctor visits twice a week. Doctors came from the government run Douma hospital next to the prison. Sometimes they brought in specialists if need be'.[96]

Corruption in the police and prison administration was rampant. It was largely visible around food. Al-Askari: 'The food budget for prisons was limited, as they told us. The monthly food allowance per person in the beginning in the 1990s was 20.7 Syrian Pounds (USD $0.5). In 1996, the allocation increased to 63 Syrian Pounds per month (USD $1.5).' These allocations only covered women, with total disregard to their children imprisoned with them. However, those poor figures did not prevent major corruption, which in some cases amounted to 'hundreds of thousands of Syrian Pounds. In addition to stealing food allowances, corruption included illegal visits and acts in violation of prison laws. We knew of the visits of some powerful and wealthy men to their imprisoned mistresses. At times operatives even transported these mistresses outside the prison on the request of these rich people. These corrupt acts only happened around judicial prisoners. The corruption was bluntly visible and outrageous.'[97]

Childbirth in prison

September was my expected due date based on the hospital examination. On Friday, 6 August 1993, I felt strange pains, which I thought were because I was exhausted working in the prison kitchen all day. A fellow prisoner who was a nurse told me that it was labour pains. We informed the operative on duty of the Security Detachment who in turn asked the branch for permission to transfer me to the hospital. He received no response from the branch as Friday was the weekend. Labour intensified so they brought in a trainee doctor from Douma hospital. She had no authority to deliver me in prison and she couldn't do anything. She went back, yet they brought her back to the prison for a second and a third time, and each time she came she told them I had to be taken to a hospital. The prison administration was constantly sending telegrams to the branch to no avail, and they couldn't take me to the hospital at their own risk. On her last visit, the trainee doctor told them that my life and the life of the fetus were now in danger, and that I had to be taken to the hospital. All this while we awaited an answer from the Political Security branch. Prisoners argued fiercely with the political security operative on duty, but then he told them that the branch could refuse transporting me to the hospital to prevent my birth, followed by: 'What would she bring us other than a communist dog.'

At this point I was surprised by what the judicial prisoners did. They started violently knocking on the big, black main prison gate. The noise they made was massive and loud. This confrontation forced the administration to take responsibility and transport me to the hospital. The delay in birth caused me to have a nucleus pulposus hernia, which put me in bed for over a month. But the joy of my fellow prisoners with my little girl took away the pain. All fellow inmates celebrated the birth. Prison officers were sympathetic to the situation and therefore delayed the closing of the dormitory doors until 23:00 instead of 19:00. Each prisoner made me her own birth recovery food according to the traditions of her region.

My child became the joy of the prison. Everyone took care of her. We changed her clothes more than five times a day to see how she looked in this colour or that. Men and women police officers loved her and cared for her. If she got fever, they immediately took her to the hospital, but she would surprise them that there was nothing wrong with her. The doctor told them that she cries and gets sick from staying in the confines of the prison. At this point an internal alarm rang, and I started thinking that she should not stay in prison.[98]

This was not the only birth that took place in Douma prison. Although this child left the prison when she was one-and-a-half, some children remained with their mothers until they reached the age of seven.[99] Imprisonment of women is a penalty that includes their children. There is no information as to when Douma prison was closed, but it was certainly before 2009, when a small section of Damascus Central Prison was assigned to women before a special women's prison was opened there.

Conclusion

Civil prisons do not play an important role in Syrian security life. They certainly exist, but their use for the detention of political dissidents only increased after the uprising in 2011. The heavy reliance on these prisons is due to the huge numbers of detainees as a result of the clashes during the last decade.

The development and change in the conditions of Syrian civilian prisons is evidenced by Karakon al-Sheikh Hassan, which was used as an interrogation centre as well as a political prison – in addition to the Citadel Prison, and the Central Prison of Damascus before the opening of the prison in Adra in 1985. These prisons spread after the mid-1980s and were established in the political and demographic centres of all the governorates of the country. They were used as military sites and bases during the battles of the last decade, just like any government institution under the authority of military units of the security service and the various intelligence services.

Syrian civil prisons are characterized by the fact that they are relatively easy to live in; some inmates even described them as a 'five-star stay'. Indeed, the treatment in these prisons is relatively better, mostly due to the absence, or at least low levels, of torture. Detainees receive acceptable health care there, in contrast to the situation in the military prisons and the detention centres of the security forces. Thus, most interviewees viewed the transfer from a security department prison to a civilian prison as a relief, an alleviation, in fact, almost as a release from prison.

Syrian women's prisons then have their own reality, where corruption prevails and events occur that cross the boundaries of the relationship between guard and prisoner. There are many cases of children born to female political prisoners in Syrian civilian prisons, especially after 2011. Those children generally stayed with their mothers. Children receive their share of their mother's punishment if they remain in prison with them, if there are no legal guardians to care for them outside prison. How these children experienced their stay in prison will be the subject of another discussion.

10

Secret Prisons

Introduction

So far, we have looked at the Assad regime's formal prison system, consisting of three separate, parallel systems: intelligence, military, and civilian prisons. Some of these, like Saydnaya, are officially top secret in terms of their operation and staffing, and any attempt to gain information about them is illegal. Others, such as the Air Force Intelligence prison at the Mezze military airport, are a public secret: everyone knows what goes on there, but no one dares to acknowledge it openly. Nevertheless, all these prisons are formalized by the regime and exist within the official bureaucracies of the security apparatus. A fourth, different category of prisons in Syria is the improvised, ad hoc or secret prison, run by the Republican Guard.

The omnipotent nature of the Assad regime's security and intelligence services, with their unbridled authority surpassing any other state institution, enabled them to control all aspects of life in the country. It became easy for them to turn any government or party institution, hospital, school or military headquarters into a temporary detention centre or even a permanent prison. This kind of abuse or usurpation of public resources was first recorded in the 1980s. At that time, the forces surrounding the city of Hama used schools and hospitals as makeshift, temporary detention centres.[1] These buildings' architectural structures facilitated the imprisonment of large numbers of people, simply by turning the classrooms or wards into cells. Many military headquarters were also converted into temporary detention centres, such as the Hanano barracks in Aleppo during the 1980s, and some of the Fifth Division's headquarters in Daraa during the Syrian Revolution.[2]

This was not a new phenomenon in 2011. In the 1980s there also appeared to be secret prisons that had both security and military features. Al-Tahouneh (The Mill) of the Republican Guard is an example of this. This prison was located in the centre of Damascus behind the state radio and television building. This building was used as a detention centre for members of the Republican Guard, but also served as a prison for rebels and opponents of the regime in the 1980s. The same name was used for the prison in the Republican Guard barracks at the top of Mount Qassioun overlooking Damascus. The new Al-Tahouneh was run by militias operating under the Guard. A detention camp called Deir Shmeil in the Hama countryside was also established after 2011. In addition, the headquarters of the 555th Regiment in the Sumeriya area near Damascus was used as a prison.

Figure 10.1 Republican Guard, from the Syrian Ministry of Defence website.

While there are undoubtedly more of these types of prisons, not much is known about them due to little or no monitoring and documentation. What is clear, however, is that the regime uses secret prisons during periods of unrest. For example, in the 1980s, but also after 2011, it used nearby schools, military headquarters, government buildings, mosques, buildings of trade or agricultural associations, and sports stadiums to temporarily detain prisoners before transferring them to a security force. Unlike official military and civilian prisons, secret prisons are temporary. Due to the lack of supervision in these detention centres, less importance is generally placed on keeping prisoners alive than in military prisons – despite the atrocities that take place there.

The salience of elite troops

A reinforcing factor for this was that the regime has given 'the task of supervising the security strategy to certain military units that has absolute loyalty to the regime'. Reliance on the Republican Guard and the Special Forces is due to the nature of the 'special arrangement used in the appointment of their staff which depends on the Alawite affiliation as a primary factor'. Also, the strength of these military units was due to the nature of the tasks assigned to them: 'The Republican Guard, the Defence Brigades which later became the Fourth Division, and the Tiger Forces that emerged during the Syrian Revolution' are responsible for engineering repression and

Figure 10.2 From left to right: Ali al-Shilli and Suheil al-Hassan, from a pro-regime social media site.

counterinsurgency, ensuring the security of the regime, and carrying out all actions and operations within the society should any signs of threat to this security emerge. These broad powers, in addition to the complex relationship these forces have with the other security services, have given these forces a fluid and limitless nature. Their main objective is to 'support the stabilizing factors of the ruling regime' at all costs and by any means necessary.[3]

The most elitist and best armed of these shock troops is the Republican Guard. Its primary mission is to protect the capital Damascus from any threats, internal or external, and therefore it is the only military force allowed to enter the capital. Not much confirmed information is available on the Republican Guard. Some estimates indicate that it consists of between 10,000 and 20,000 soldiers spread over several brigades. Its officers, some of whom became celebrities in the pro-regime media, receive important shares of oil revenues to ensure their loyalty. The establishment of these forces dates back to the late 1970s, when Hafez al-Assad required mechanized divisions and elite shock troops to repress his opponents from the Muslim Brotherhood and Palestinian militias.[4]

The Republican Guard maintained the trust of presidents Hafez and Bashar al-Assad, both of whom made sure that the leaders of its brigades were selected from specific Alawite families. In addition to the military role assigned to this force, 'the Republican Guard determines the rules and security relations between the intelligence branches on the one hand and between the citizen and the regime on the other'. After the Syrian Revolution, this force became the official front for coordinating military action by various militias: the Iranian Revolutionary Guard, the Lebanese Hezbollah, the Iraqi Shi'ite militias, and the closely associated National Defence Forces (NDF).[5]

In addition to the role of the Republican Guard in military confrontations in the 1980s and after the Syrian Revolution, these forces tackled a range of potential threats to the regime: the 2001 Bedouin-Druze conflict, the 2004 Kurdish uprising, and the 2005 Alawite-Ismaili conflict. These forces consist of a number of regiments and brigades that are functionally separate but administratively subordinate to the Guard command.[6] The Republican Guard is an elite group that runs its own, secret, prison, known as Al-Tahouneh ('The Mill'). In the 1970s, the prison was founded and managed by its precursor, the Defence Brigades. Following the 1984 dispute between Rifaat al-Assad, the commander of the Defence Brigades and his brother President Hafez al-Assad, the administration of this prison was transferred to the Republican Guard.[7]

Al-Tahouneh prison

This prison took its name from the building it occupied, an old mill, located behind the state radio and television building, in the Umayyad Square in central Damascus. Former detainee Mufeed Najm explains: 'Before the 1963 coup d'état of the Military Commission of Baath Party, the building was a private mill of a Damascene industrialist,

Figure 10.3 Map of Tahouneh Prison Old, Google Maps.

Figure 10.4 Map of Tahouneh Prison New, Google Maps.

الدفاع الوطني

Figure 10.5 National Defense Forces, from a pro-regime social media site.

for grinding flour. After the coup, the Baath authority nationalized it as part of nationalizing privately owned facilities and factories. After Hafez al-Assad's coup in 1970, the Defence Brigades seized the mill under the pretext of protecting the radio and television building, then turned it into a terrible prison'. This prison, which housed three underground cells and some above the ground, was run by what was then known as the Defence Brigades Security Branch. The branch and the Defence Brigades were dissolved following the dispute between the Assad brothers, which ended in the banishing of Rifaat to Europe.[8]

This is one of the most secretive prisons in Syria: 'The limited role played by the Defence Brigades Security Branch in the 1980s increased the secrecy of this prison, before it was later converted into a prison of the Republican Guard.' The Defence Brigades had a large role in military field actions in the 1980s. Its Security Branch, however, had a limited role as it had to compete with Military Intelligence. Following the disbandment of the Defence Brigades and the closure of its Security Branch in 1984–1985, the Tahouneh detainees were transferred to various security branches and military prisons pending a final decision about them. That's when the lid was lifted off this prison.[9]

The mill of death

Among the detainees transferred from the Tahouneh to the Mezze military prison was a young Christian man with a doctorate in Economics from France. He worked as a manager of the branch of a French company in Saudi Arabia. The charge under which he was arrested, along with his brother, the film director, was cooperation with the Muslim Brotherhood. Dr. Ghassan Qurayt returned with his younger brother, the film director, to visit their family in Syria. He did not imagine that his brother-in-law, a volunteer sergeant in the Defence Brigades Security would by pushed by greed to blackmail them financially. He asked them for a large sum of money, accusing them of having ties with the Muslim Brotherhood.

They refused to give him the amount he asked for, so he informed the Defence Brigades Security that they had transferred funds from the Muslim Brotherhood organization in Saudi Arabia, to members of the organization in the city of Hama. They were arrested and taken into this horrible prison. There, the chapters of the harrowing tale began, which claimed the director's life, and left its marks etched over Ghassan's body and the soles of his feet, where, more than five years after his arrest, he still could not balance.

In the morning they brought him into our dormitory. He was confused and very skinny. Many circled around him and showered him with the usual questions about where he came from and the charge for which he was arrested. Upon learning his story everyone was puzzled. Over time, when he started feeling reassured and regained some of his balance and health, he began to tell us the facts of that indescribable suffering, both during and after the interrogation. The bad treatment remains consistent for the duration of the arrest. So those who survive torture die of starvation or illness. No one intercedes for you inside this prison, you are left to the mercy of the operatives of the prison, they do whatever they want to you, and no one holds anyone accountable. The management staff of this prison were chosen for having criminal and sadistic minds and were left to be the masters of your destiny. Little food was served twice a day, along with humiliation and beating.

One of those horrifying facts he told us almost crying, was that once while in the toilet he found a small piece of sweets. That piece apparently fell from an operative on the toilet floor. As he was severely hungry and deprived, he quickly picked it up and devoured it. In that terrible, damp prison where you can't distinguish night from day, the detainees were victims of the murderous soldiers of the Defence Brigades Security.[10]

In 2008, the Republican Guard moved the Tahouneh prison to Qassioun mountain, on the road to the Presidential Palace, near Battalion 357. The role of this prison remained internal, that is, to punish violators from among the Guard operatives. With the start of the Syrian Revolution in 2011, groups of local militias were born, such as the National Defence Forces. These were managed largely by the Republican Guard or were under its supervision.[11]

With the rise of the National Defence Forces, the Tahouneh prison went back to playing the role of a security branch, as it was in the days of the Defence Brigades. The National Defence Forces threw in it detainees they kidnapped from their checkpoints in the streets of Damascus, or in cooperation with local or foreign militias. Ammar al-Sheikh Haidar narrates: 'On my way home in Dummar al-Balad area and near the infirmary, two gunmen got out of a Toyota SUV. The quickly jammed me in the trunk. After a ten-minute ride, the trunk was opened. I was blinded by a strong light directed at my eyes before they blindfolded me and tied my hands with a plastic cable tie. I felt that we were at a military checkpoint, where they took my personal information. The next morning, they moved me to a second place.'[12]

It was a large military dormitory divided by metal plates into boxes of equal dimensions, 2 × 2 metres. Haidar continues: 'Each box had a toilet, a water tap, and some blankets. We used one of the blankets to close the hole of the Turkish toilet to sleep on top of it. The inmates of each box numbered between 17 and 24. The number was never fixed as every day we got new people and every day some of us died and they collected their bodies from the cells. Some were taken and never returned back, so we did not know their fate.' Clothes were forbidden in this prison. 'We just had our underpants on. I am an atheist and basically non-religious, but when they lifted the blindfold off my eyes after I entered the box, I felt like it was judgment day. The smell of sweat and filth was disastrous, and you could clearly see lice on bodies and blankets. Scabies spread viciously, and there were always cases of diarrhoea and vomiting. The skin was decomposing, and the festering of the torture injuries was terrible.'[13]

There was no agenda in this prison except torment, either through the known methods or by humiliation or starvation:

Every morning they gave each one of us one small cheese triangle with a quarter of a loaf of bread. The second meal was a very bad kind of tuna. They opened a can of tuna on a nylon bag and gave each prisoner a quarter of a loaf of bread. This scarce and poor food caused diarrhoea that claimed some lives and accompanied the survivors for many years: 'After my release I learned I had a virus in the digestive tract that caused me diarrhoea and constant vomiting. I took highly concentrated antibiotic doses to eradicate the disease'.[14]

As for traditional torture, it was no different from the branches of Military or Air Force Intelligence. Torture was used during the interrogation and as punishment for violations or for the guards' entertainment. People in charge of this prison used the wheel and plastic water pipes to hit the prisoners and they also used electricity to torture. These interrogation or torture sessions were conducted in the presence of some officers, most notably Fadi Saqqar, Commander of the National Defence Forces in Syria, who attended interrogation sessions. But the reality was that some of the Tahouneh detainees were simply kidnapped for ransom. Haidar recounts: 'Some had nothing to do with the revolution but were kidnapped for ransom money, or were taken hostage in place of their relatives fighting in the Free Syrian Army. Some were forced to record televised testimonies confirming the regime's version that the revolution was an armed act of Islamist extremists. After that they negotiated with their families for their release in exchange for large sums of money.'[15]

The 'death mill' continues to mash the bodies of its detainees by either disease, torment, or wound infections with the absence of health care. The screams of detainees being tortured, Haidar remembers, 'fill the air for a long time, then they disappear and we hear the torturer's orders to remove the dead body. The interrogation and torture hall was in the same large dormitory that housed our prison boxes'. Due to the brutality of violence at Tahouneh prison, there are very few survivors, hence rarely any stories come out of that place.

Figure 10.6 Fadi Saqqar, from a pro-regime social media site.

'A dog among us perished'

We had a young man called Mohammed Karzah in his thirties. He was the only one whose name I learned. In the Tahouneh, names were forbidden; we became numbers and we were not allowed to learn anything about each other. We were being watched all the time by cameras inside the cell, so talking was too risky. Mohammed was subjected to violent torture for two weeks, and the injuries were concentrated in the lower part of his body. On the last day they brought him back in very bad shape. A young man who had newly arrived insisted to knock on the door and ask for help. I tried to stop him, but my warning came too late. The warden started a symphony of swearing before opening the door and knowing what the matter was. The warden asked Mohammad why he was injured! He replied, as he was instructed, that he had fallen off the stairs. The warden praised his answer and promised to take him to the doctor. A quarter of an hour later he returned and took him, and two hours or more later he brought him back. The upper part of his body now became similar to the lower part. It wasn't a doctor where he took him, but a death sentence. We tried to clean his inflamed wounds and lower his temperature, but he went into a delirium and started whispering in my ear, with his head on my shoulder. It was then that I learnt his name and that he came from a family known for renovating ancient Damascene houses. He worked in the restoration of these houses using the experience of his family and his studies in the field of Fine Arts. I grew tired and slept, and a little later I felt his body cooling down. I thought he responded to the water bandages, but in fact his temperature dropped because he had died. Keeping a dead body in the cell, the box, was more harmful than death under torture, as we had to knock on the door and call on the warden saying: 'A dog from us perished'. Then they would come and take him out. We never once risked not knocking, for all the time we saw our faces on those dead bodies.[16]

The workers of this prison realize that it is the 'Mill of the Ends'. When you go inside, you are lost; and if you go out, you are re-born. Haidar recalled: 'During the reception party, they bragged, shouting at us as they beat us: welcome to the mill of death.' A rare few entered that place and managed to leave, so its stories remain under wraps to this day.[17] No confirmed information is available on whether the prison is still in use.

Deir Shmeil prison

From the outbreak of the uprising in March 2011, the Assad regime's repression of Syrian society more generally intensified. A crucial aspect of this repression was the use of pro-regime paramilitary groups, popularly called *Shabbiha*, an umbrella term for various militias organically linked to the regime. Their actions were well documented in video clips, leaks, confessions of deserters, and testimonies of victims. The *Shabbiha*'s tasks almost exclusively consisted of repression and surveillance of the civilian population: they stormed neighbourhoods to break up demonstrations, committed property crimes, torture, kidnappings, assassinations and mass killings. The Assad regime stubbornly (but implausibly) washed its hands of the situation: it purported that the militias were allegedly acting on their own, that the government was not directing them, and that there was actually a civil war between equal parties going on in Syria. But for those who dug a little deeper, it was pretty clear pretty quickly that the reality was far from that. It was the Assad regime that spawned, condoned, absorbed, incited, steered, and gradually organized and reorganized the Shabbiha, first in 2011 into the 'Popular Committees', then in 2012 into the 'National Defence Forces' (NDF), which grew out into a large and notorious pro-Assad militia.[18]

From the beginning of the conflict onward, the NDF ran its own secret prison: Deir Shmeil. The NDF operates this prison near the city of Hama in central Syria, in a place called called Deir Shmeil camp. The term 'camp' came from the fact that the location was a training ground for children who are members of the Baath youth groups called the 'Vanguard' (*al-Tali'a*) and the 'Youth' [*al-Shabibeh*] – the two student organizations of the ruling Arab Socialist Baath Party. The prison was founded at the beginning of the Syrian Revolution in 2011 and its founder is believed to be the former head of the Hama Political Security branch, retired Brigadier Walid Abaza.[19] The management of the prison was quickly passed on to former Republican Guard colonel Fadlallah Mikael who ran it until his death in September 2020. Lieutenant Colonel Mouafaq Wannous and Major Fatir Ibrahim shared with Mikael the management of the camp.

The Republican Guard, in coordination with Iran, had formed and trained the NDF. As the war dragged on, the NDF was transformed from a militia to a paramilitary organization into a parallel security institution with its own prisons and authority to investigate and interrogate. The NDF used the infrastructure of the Syrian state and

Figure 10.7 Map of Deir Shmeil Prison, Google Maps.

Figure 10.8 Fadlallah Mikael, from social media, the pages of the supporters of the Syrian regime.

mobilized a large number of young men, many of whom either had a criminal background or were unemployed. None of them joined the NDF out of faith or belief, but in search of an illegitimate source of income. In addition to their looting, these militias also resorted to kidnapping for ransom and acted as sources of information for the army and security services. Their conduct was often based on sectarian spite, intended to prove their loyalty to Assad, but the authorities receiving their reports could not refuse them. Instead, these denunciations are often taken at face value, and based on them, indiscriminate arrests and sometimes murders are committed.[20]

Deir Shmeil camp is located in the northwestern countryside of Hama governorate. According to a detailed report conducted by the Syrian Network of Human Rights (SNHR) specifically on the prison camp, it is located '20 kilometres north of the city of Masyaf. Its area is estimated at about 0.18 km2'.[21] The prison consists of four dormitories and 12 solitary cells.[22] The camp also includes 'buildings with offices for officers,

Shabbiha headquarters, interrogation and torture rooms'.[23] The camp resembles the Tahouneh prison by being more like a security and investigation branch than an actual prison. Therefore, both can be classified as detention and interrogation centres, but with the difference that a stay therein may exceed a year. Both places follow the same entity that used Syrian state facilities and transferred them into 'security agencies that serve the head of the regime as well as personal interests'.[24] The regime's political interests in quelling the revolution and eradicating its activists intersect with the objectives of the private leaders of these security services to hoard money and build wealth through robberies, looting, kidnappings and extortion of local communities. This fatal overlap of interests leads to lots of violence against anyone who is unlucky enough to fall into the hands of the NDF.

Most of the detainees in Deir Shmeil camp come from three governorates: Hama, Homs, and Idlib. The estimated number of detainees in this prison is 2,500, including about 250 children and 400 women.[25] However, these estimates are not accurate, and they fluctuate. The only constant in this facility is fierce violence, as documented by the SNHR:

> On Saturday 25 May 2013, local residents found eight bodies thrown on the side of the road with marks of torture. The bodies were mutilated. People in those areas became accustomed to seeing bodies lying on the side of the road. It is believed that they come from Deir Shmeil, because of the proximity. It is the largest and most notorious place of torture in the region. The bodies belonged to three old men, and two children. One appeared to be 10 years old and the other seemed to be older than that. We couldn't even recognize the rest of the bodies from the severity of the mutilation. After the local residents found the bodies, police officers came and took them to the government hospital in the city of Hama.[26]

Arrest mechanisms and interrogation methods are identical between Deir Shmeil and the Military or Air Force security branches. In some cases, the purposes of arrest vary between the security branches and the NDF, which engage in kidnapping for sectarian or retaliatory purposes or for financial extortion. However, they all stress that the detainee is blindfolded and handcuffed to the back. They also confiscate all electronic devices and steal valuable furniture from the raided houses. Reception at the headquarters of the branches or Deir Shmeil is identical, where the operatives of the headquarters start beating and torturing detainees under the title of 'reception party'. Abu Shaam, a young survivor who was arrested in 2013, testifies:

> The moment we arrived at Deir Shmeil camp, blindfolded and handcuffed from the back, they threw us from the small cargo car we were in. I fell hard to the ground and broke my shoulder. They took us to the second floor. We passed between two rows of operatives who beat us continuously with all the tools available in their hands. They lined us up against the wall, and every few minutes called upon one of us. I entered the personal belongings room where they lifted the blindfold off my eyes. Behind the table sat a Major. They took all my belongings, or, for accuracy, what was left of them after stealing the money I had on me.[27]

Arresting socks

After the Major took my ID card and mobile phone to be kept in the personal belongings department, I was allowed to go to the bathroom to wash blood off my face and hair. After I got out of the bathroom, a NDF operative asked me to take off my clothes and stay only in my underwear. I knew they stole fancy clothes, so I wasn't afraid as my clothes were old. I did, however, try to keep my socks, for they were of good quality, and my feet usually get very cold. I took my clothes off and stacked them over my feet, especially the socks so that they don't draw his attention.

He glimpsed at the tattoos on my body and started asking about their meanings, especially that tattoo with a number. He wondered whether it was my military number in a Free Army battalion or a symbol and a sign of a group. This all was accompanied by insults and beatings, but I kept my feet sturdy on the ground to preserve my clothes, knowing that I will need them in this very cold area. After a futile argument with that guard about my body tattoos and their meanings, he ordered me to walk to the dormitory. When I bent down to pick my clothes off the floor, he noticed my socks and took them by force, refusing my plea for him to leave them with me. It was only at this moment that I felt I was arrested.

He led me to a dormitory on the third floor with the number 201 on its door. More than 40 detainees were jammed in that small room. The moment the door opened, I felt as though I was transported to a strange world. Skinny men with very long beards; the smell of filth numbed my nose. I thought they were Salafist or jihadi detainees, but minutes later I learned that they were people of Al-Salamiyah city and villages, known for their Ismaili majority. They had nothing to do with the Islamists, and some of them had nothing to do with the revolution. They were arrested to be exchanged for ransom money.[28]

Deir Shmeil has its own prison rituals. The newest detainee in the dormitory was subjected to constant torture until a newer detainee comes and so on. Abu Shaam continues: 'The first thing the warden did in the first torture session was plucking my long goatee beard. I remained the new detainee in the dormitory for three days. The warden of our dormitory, Said Jadid, came in every day looking for me like a madman to torture me without reason or order from an officer or investigator. He would close my mouth before striking or would close the dormitory door and start beating me in front of the rest of the detainees.' An additional difference between Deir Shmeil and the regular intelligence branches is that the wardens carry their guns all the time even inside the detention building.[29]

The second difference between the intelligence branches and Deir Shmeil camp was that the interrogation in the latter began exclusively after midnight and continued until the early hours of the morning. Abu Shaam again: 'The warden made his way to the dormitory using a flashlight. He handcuffed me to the back and then blindfolded me and dragged me to the investigation room on the first floor. He opened the door and led me into a warm room. That's how I knew it was the interrogator's room. He put me in a chair opposite the detective, as I expected, for I could see nothing.' After taking the detainee's general information, the civil brief, a pre-official interrogation torture session begins.

> Around three o'clock in the morning the detective ordered the torturer to take me and soak me. The torturer took me out to a terrace near the room. He stripped me down and started pouring cold water on me. The wind that was blowing from the mountains made the situation more difficult. This lasted until the morning. They took me back to the dormitory, where the rest of the detainees helped me recover from the pain and the cold. They gathered around me to give me some warmth before putting my wet clothes back on. These torture sessions were repeated on daily basis for 20 days after my arrest. [30]

The tools and methods of torture used in Deir Shmeil vary. In addition to all the tools mentioned earlier in the operations of the Military and Air Force Intelligence branches, the torturers created their own unique methods, such as mock executions. Abu Shaam recalls: 'In one of the torture sessions, the interrogator ordered me to go up on a table, tied a noose on my neck, and started shaking the table as if he wanted to carry out the sentence. Every time the table shook, I thought it was the end, but he didn't execute me.' The illusion of execution does not mean that the torturer is keen to preserve the life of the detainee. Torture by electricity is carried out by exposing the detainee to the city current (220 volts): 'The detainee is placed in the bathroom with his feet immersed in water. The torturer throws copper cables over the water while standing outside the bathroom. The detainee trembles until the current safety switch turns the current off. The torturer would lift it up again and repeat.' The many deaths resulting from torture in Deir Shmeil were not just a result of electrocution, flogging, or breaking ribs, but also a result of breaking the bones of the detainee using a 'step ladder with two sides that meet at the top forming an inverted V when opened. The detainee is placed between the two sides and the ladder is closed with him inside. The ladder is then laid on the ground and one of the torturers walks over it using his entire body weight. It is a very painful and dangerous process that often causes fractures to the chest and legs'. [31]

The torture of women in Deir Shmeil was no less cruel. A young woman named Samar from Salamiyah was arrested by the *Shabbiha* for organizing a demonstration and was taken to Deir Shmeil. An interview with the NGO Pro-Justice summarizes her ordeal:

> They threw Samar in a barrel of water and began to drown her. Whenever she nearly suffocated, they would raise her head so she can catch what was left of her breath. The moment they raised her head they hit her on the head and body with a cable. This process was repeated dozens of times. They lifted her exhausted, bleeding body from the barrel and then crucified her. The air was cold and her clothes were wet. Her entire body was trembling. It did not stop there. Those savages continued to whip her with all their might from her head to the soles of

her feet. She fainted and woke up in the same room from which she was taken.[32]

Those rooms to which the detainees are returned, the 'dormitories', do not have even the most basic facilities. There are no toilets or blankets to isolate the bodies of the detainees from the cold floor. Their windows are covered only by a metal mesh that does not block the cold air. The wardens cut off the power at 20:00, drowning them in darkness on top of the cold. The food provided to detainees is a continuation of torture. Former detainee and survivor Mohammed al-Tawil recalls: 'It was one meal a day, and consisted of potatoes, or bulgur, and one loaf of bread each. Access to the toilet was only once a day. No second visit was allowed no matter the reason, even if we wet our clothes with urine or feces. Bathing was prohibited.' Torture by beating, starvation, lack of hygiene and cold combined produced a series of diseases. 'They didn't care about the sick and did not give us any medication, nor did they bring a doctor or a nurse. They couldn't care less about our lives. The door of our cell was opened when bringing the food in, and when going out to the toilet.' The reasons detainees died are many, including death under torture, medical negligence, illness, or hunger. 'We would hear the voices of the *Shabbiha* and the interrogators saying: get their bodies out of the camp.'[33]

Deir Shmeil is a notorious secret prison and to find survivors, especially those who are willing to speak about their experiences, is rare. We might never find out the true nature and scale of the secret prisons in Syria. Moreover, an unknown number of Shabbiha and NDF commanders have built prisons in their private homes, often in a basement or an annex. For example, one of the most powerful Shabbiha bosses in the Deir Shmeil area is Ali al-Shilli, who hails from a modest background in a working-class Alawite family in the village of Ain al-Kroum. His militia rampaged through Syria, massacring and arresting demonstrators, committing widespread torture, rape, kidnapping, and looting in rebel communities especially Homs and Hama. His many victims are either dead and buried, forcibly disappeared without a trace, scarred for life physically and psychologically, expelled to Lebanon, Turkey, or Europe, stigmatized due to sexual violence, or terrified of living within a few hours' drive from him. Ali al-Shilli's violent acts have left an indelible, brutal mark on the Syrian conflict. Kidnapping for ransom was one of his special skills, as experienced and narrated by 'Ayman', a public servant who was kidnapped and illegally detained by Ali al-Shilli in the private prison he built in his village:

At 3 o'clock at night, the Shabbiha of Ali al-Shilli broke down our door and stormed our house. They stole all the furniture. They took us to their camp and beat us really hard. Ali al-Shilli personally shot at people's legs ... Then they put me in solitary confinement. But the solitary there is not the same as the regime. I was in a Military Intelligence prison before, but at least they had bathrooms and some food. At Ali al-Shilli's prison, there was no food, nothing. It was worse. I stayed 25 days ... He began torturing me, and broke my leg. My family arranged the ransom of 4 million Syrian Lira. I stayed in Turkey for a year to receive treatment.[34]

In a number of interviews conducted with Ali al-Shilli over social media, he never mentioned his victims, showed remorse, or contended with a guilty conscience. His violence, he claimed, was purely defensive, and if he did kill anyone, they deserved it. For these deeds, he feels he should be rewarded and appreciated, not castigated as a criminal.[35] At the time of writing this book, Ali al-Shilli still lives in Ain al-Kroum and continues to maintain his private prison.

The 555 Paratrooper Regiment prison

The 555 Paratrooper Regiment is located in the Sumariya area, 12 km west of Damascus. The Regiment administratively follows the Fourth Armored Division, led by Major General Maher al-Assad. Theoretically, the Fourth Division follows the command of the First Corps in the Syrian Army. The squad enjoys special training and special support to provide strategic back-up to the regime. The Fourth Division was founded by the brother of Rifaat al-Assad, who commanded the Defence Brigades. Following the feud between the two Assad brothers in the mid-1980s, the Defence Brigades were incorporated into the Fourth Division as a strike force: it has about 15,000 fighters, is mobile, heavily armed, well-equipped and has been responsible for major violence against civilians throughout the Syrian conflict.[36]

Similar to its counterpart the Republican Guard, the Fourth Division has two faces: a military wing and a security wing. In addition to its role at the military level, the Division performs some security tasks and functions. According to the Omran Centre for Strategic Studies:

> it provides the military and air force faculties with an annex of names of candidates to join them. This annex often serves the interest of the Division primarily, then the security branches. This is carried out in coordination with Branch 293 (Officer Affairs) of the Military Intelligence Division. The Security Office of the Fourth

Figure 10.9 Prison of the 555 Paratrooper Regiment, Google Maps.

Division coordinates constantly with all security departments. It is immediately informed of any security incidents in the governorates. It sends its reports, received from its sources and delegates to the main security departments for the necessary actions to be taken which are then reported back to the Office once implemented. The Security Office investigates all complex issues that threaten the cohesion of the security network, and the files of the key people in the regime directly. It plays a big role in the appointments of heads of security branches, especially in Damascus.[37]

Based on the deep-rooted relationship between the Fourth Division and the Military and Air Force Intelligence services, it was not surprising when the former converted some of its buildings to 'deposit prisons' for the Air Force Intelligence after 2011. The Violations Documentation Centre concluded in an in-depth research report: 'The detainees were transferred from the Air Force Intelligence branches after the end of their interrogation to the headquarters of the Fourth Division.' The most prominent and widely used of these HQs is the 555 Regiment, the entrance of which is believed to be located 'behind the Sumariya public transport station'.[38]

This place of detention is characterized as a 'deposit prison', not a security headquarters. Those transferred to the Regiment 'were not subjected to any new interrogation during their stay there. The general feature of the use of this place is the retention of persons whom the regime forces do not intend to bring to justice or release and with whom security interrogations have ended. In addition, it is a place to practice all kinds of torture and abuse of detainees throughout their time there'.[39] These detainees are placed in three underground rooms classified alphabetically (A - B - C), in addition to room no 90 above ground for men and another room adjacent to it for women.[40]

As in the previously mentioned military and secret prisons, the members of this facility receive their inmates with the usual 'reception party' (*hafle* in Arabic). All operatives of the prison wear military uniforms decorated with the emblem of the Fourth Division and their faces are hidden by a military mask. One survivor named Kamal recounts his period at the 555 prison: 'We came down chained in a long row. We started to walk slowly and the closer we approached, the louder the sounds of torture grew. We were beaten with batons and tasered with electrical sticks all over our bodies.' After reaching the prison building, the inspection process began, although all arrivals come directly from the Air Force Intelligence so they don't have anything on them anyway. 'It was just a kind of humiliation. After we were strip searched, they beat us while we were pushed into dormitory C, where we learned that we were in the Fourth Division.'[41]

Dormitory C is the smallest of the three dormitories in the prison basement. Kamal continues:

They jammed us as new detainees into the small dormitory C, in preparation for our transfer to the large dormitories. In dormitory C, which differs from the others in that it doesn't have a toilet, they jammed about 25 detainees. They offered us two meals. The door of the dormitory would open, and the warden brought the food in while we all stood facing the wall with our hands behind our backs and our eyes blindfolded. Torturers beat us with batons and electric sticks. After each meal they should take us out to the toilet. They took us out in rows, crawling on the belly to get to the bathroom. Both detainees would go into one toilet cabin. They should finish in less than 30 seconds together and come back running under the whips. They stomped on other detainees crawling to the toilet.[42]

The situation is not much different in the rest of the dormitories, whether underground or above, except in terms of numbers. The population in large dormitories is 80–100 detainees in an area of about 4 x 5 metres. The number of detainees in the Regiment is about 400–500 prisoners, including a number of women. Former detainee Muhannad al-Ghobash remembers: 'Women were in a designated dormitory above the ground. We would hear their screams every day, especially after our torture parties. The torturers would go up to their dormitory and we would hear their screams getting louder. We didn't know whether it was because of beating or sexual assault.'[43]

The detainees believe that this prison was formerly a military radar unit. Kamal noticed radar rails on the ground in dormitory C: 'The structure is heavily fortified – the walls are very thick and scary. The rooms are more like bunkers. Dormitory B was two rooms that were open to one another, with a very low ceiling, about 2.5 metres. There are no openings for air to come in. If the power went out and the turbine stopped working, breathing became impossible.'[44] Each room had eleven blankets, and each blanket is meant for a group of nine to ten prisoners who group to eat together and share the blanket to sleep. Muhannad al-Ghobash continues:

> The toilet is a hole in the ground that leads to a main sewage pit. That hole is separated from the dormitory with only two walls, without a door or a roof. We would urinate and defecate in front of each other. The line to the toilet is coordinated by one of the prisoners called the 'toilet chief'. Detainees spent their time naturally next to the toilet, talking, eating, or drinking. The first time I arrived at this prison, I spent about 24 hours waiting for some privacy to use the toilet. I waited until the evening without avail. I thought the prisoners at night would sleep and I could go to the toilet. Shortly afterwards I learned that we had to sleep in shifts, therefore so many stayed awake. After that I used the toilet and defecated in front of everyone. Over time, the refusal of new prisoners to use the open toilet made me laugh.[45]

Over time, it becomes clear to the prisoners of the Regiment that the purpose of their stay there is to be subjected to as much torment as possible. Al-Ghobash realized this fairly quickly:

> There were no interrogations, only torture. The wardens came down to us every day after midnight, that is, after they have finished their evening and drinking. They would accuse us of making noise. They ask for 10 people to receive punishment. The head of the dormitory must point out 10 detainees under all circumstances. At first, we thought it was just for a night or two, but after that we knew it was the system of the place. It was decided to divide the inmates into groups of ten to take turns in going out to these sessions. At first, we excluded the elderly, but then the situation became intolerable. These sessions result in the death of some, or cause others fatal

injuries that kill them over time. The party of torment begins with tasers: 'first electric stick, then beating with batons, and flogging with metal cables. Some selfless detainees volunteered to go out in place of the elderly fearing for their lives'. During the preparation of this session and the exit of the punished group, the head of the dormitory is subjected to a quick round of torture that includes some tasers of the electric stick or cable blows. The official punishment session 'lasts about an hour after which the detainees enter the room after having lost their ability to communicate with others because of the severity of the torment'.[46]

However, as Kamal remarked: 'If a quarrel broke out in the dormitory or the sound of the detainees actually rises, about 15 wardens would storm the dormitory and begin to beat us indiscriminately and hysterically'. In addition to punishments at night or those for violations there were some unique punishments, Kamal said:

> During the weekly day for cleaning the dormitory, the wardens ask us to stand pickled in a specific corner of the dormitory and in a rectangular shape. They beat us with batons and electric sticks. After finishing hitting the first row, they ask them to 'form a second layer', that is, to climb on the backs of the second row, so that they can hit them, and so on. After finishing cleaning the first part of the dormitory, everyone has to run to the other side very fast for a distance of no more than 3 metres! Threatened to receive brutal beating if they don't comply, old detainees often trip, and detainees stomp each other.[47]

All that torment was nothing compared to shaving day, which was an irregular process that follows the mood of the wardens. Al-Ghobash was subjected to this violence: 'The fear of this session was so big. Horror would paralyze our joints when the warden surprised us with the shaving order. The news would come down to us like a thunderbolt and the farewell ceremony would begin, as everyone expected their death.' The news came at night, so the fear and horror would last until the morning. While waiting for the doors to open to exit to the shaving, 'the elderly would stay up all night to maintain their place at the far end of the room hoping for a chance to be the last group that go out to shaving. A late exit means greater hope of surviving death, as the fatigue of the torturers alleviated the severity of the torment'. All those preparations came before the door opened with the command 'prepare for shaving'! Then we all get completely naked, and the shaving ceremony begins. We all stand against the wall, blindfolded. We go out to shaving in fours. Going out and back in is by crawling on the belly. The detainees move according to the warden's blows and 'left, right' instructions. A detainee would sit on the shaving chair, and the remaining three are on their bellies subjected to the blows of the torturers. Once done shaving, he joins the rest on the floor while another one site on the chair until they are all done, and they go back just as they exited, so another four had to leave, and so on." These sessions claimed the lives of one or two detainees at the very least. 'Sometimes shaving lasts for two days, which meant more torment and agony of anticipating and waiting.'[48]

The torment was not limited to punishments, shaving sessions, going out to the toilet, torture while bringing in the food or the visit of the health officer. Some actions, if done by the prisoner, meant his inevitable death or the death of some of his colleagues. According to Al-Ghobash:

> If you stood up during shaving or the visit of the health officer, it meant that you have sentenced yourself to death. They consider this an act of disobedience and rebellion that is met immediately with killing. If the warden opened the Judas window and found someone without his blindfold on his eyes, everyone is subjected to a severe and hysterical torture session.[49]

Beating was the direct torment in the lives of prisoners of the 555 Regiment, but the lack of food was an additional indirect torment. Al-Ghobash testifies:

> The food provision was so bad; it was as if we were actually forgotten. Two meals every ten or twenty hours or whenever they remembered. Food was a loaf of bread with olives, yogurt, halvah, jam or boiled eggs. Lunch was soup with rice and sauce, and an often-moldy loaf of bread. Sometimes there were pieces of fruit." The scarcity of fruit prompted the prisoners to "eat oranges with their peels, with dry bread.[50]

Constant malnutrition and continuous torture resulted in health conditions that required special care. Al-Ghobash affirms this:

> Patients prefer not to go out to see the health officer on the day he visited. Often their healthy colleagues went out in their place. For example, seven detainees who claim to be sick would come out to sit next to the door of the dormitory near the toilet. During this health check the rest of us would be crammed into the opposite corner. When the warden made sure the instructions were executed, he would open the door and operatives would come in and start beating the prisoners crammed in the corner. Meanwhile, the doctor and his companion work their cables on patients, while asking them about their health complaints. The screaming of prisoners reached the sky due to the intensity of torture during those visits. The visit lasted about half an hour, and in any case the medicine given was 'cetamol' pills, or yellow ointment for scabies.[51]

The days in the 555 Regiment can be described as consecutive torment sessions, as Al-Ghobash recalled: 'With time, the sound of the opening of the main prison door threw terror in our hearts even before the wardens arrived at the doors of our dormitories. We would begin the game of hiding behind one another and trying to prepare ourselves for the expected violence.' This state of panic was a logical result as any daily procedure became a session of agony, be it the provision of food, health checks, shaving, or the ongoing night-time punishment. Just existing inside the dormitory was punitive:

> Closing the eyes was mandatory all the time with the blindfolds. The shower duration was two hours for 100 prisoners and once a week. We showered inside the toilet space using cold water and some pieces of military soap. We went into the bathroom in threes or fours, with one piece of soap that frantically moved from

one head to the other so we can finish the shower in less than a minute ... Once they brought us rotten food. We had severe diarrhoea to the point of anal bleeding. Some detainees died as a result, and those in critical condition were taken to the military hospital, but they never returned.[52]

At the time of writing, the Fourth Armoured Division is still very much active, and the 555 Regiment prison is still in operation.

Conclusion

This chapter has examined three large, secret prisons in Syria and their differences. Some prisons are both detention and punishment prisons, such as Regiment 555, while others are both prisons and interrogation centres, such as Al-Tahouneh Prison in the Defence Brigades era and in the National Defence Forces era. A second difference is the affiliation of these prisons: Regiment 555 has a clear function and connection, while Camp Deir Shmeil is a secret prison and interrogation centre run by the shadowy Shabbiha militias (and later the National Defence Forces) in Central Syria.

Reading about the reality of Al-Tahouneh prison and the nature of the relationship between the National Forces and the Republican Guard indicates the Assad regime's approach to its central pillars of support. The regime has established the paramilitary group NDF led by its intelligence and elite forces to protect these backbone formations from decay. The creation of a militia led by these services increases their ability to directly fight the civil war and to commit crimes without directly dirtying their own hands. By allowing current and former officers of the Republican Guard or other intelligence services to hold leadership positions in these militias, they remain under their control, but without a direct hierarchy. The regime must have thought that these irregular militias could easily be disbanded after the end of the war, but it is impossible to disband the Republican Guard or the Fourth Division or indeed any of the security and intelligence services, because they are an integral part of the Assad regime's structure.

Secrecy plays a role in all authoritarian regimes and aims to shield the ruling regime from public scrutiny, mask its strengths and weaknesses, and maintain an apparent element of surprise. As a totalitarian intelligence state, the Assad regime is shrouded in paranoia, censorship, and a high degree of mistrust – especially regarding its (secret) prisons. Assad has shrouded his regime with secrecy to maintain an edge over the opposition, potential rivals among the elite, and foreign rivals and enemies. This secrecy is deliberately maintained by the regime to conceal the infrastructure of the prisons and is a central element of Syrian prisons. It has a clear function: it gives the regime the ability to increase its violence against the Syrian population. Extrajudicial killings or deaths because of torture and the practice of openly exchanging prisoners for money have become the order of the day. These kidnappings and ransom operations are one of the sources of income for the perpetrators. Finally, we must emphasize that these three prisons are not the only secret prisons in Syria. However, they are the only ones we have been able to identify from the testimonies of survivors. There are other secret prisons, but we do not have reliable information about them.

Part Two Conclusion

This part has provided an overview of three categories of prisons: military, civilian, and secret. The three military prisons Mezze, Palmyra, and Saydnaya constitute a veritable topography of terror in Syria.[1] The violence that the Assad regime perpetrated at those three sites was not matched at any other point in Syrian history, and only has a few counterparts in the Middle East, most notably in the prisons of Syria's Baathist neighbor Iraq. The brutality, systematism, and impunity that surrounds Syria's archipelago of prisons is exemplified best by these three examples. They straddle the rule of Hafez al-Assad and his son Bashar, and most likely will extend into the future of the country. Each of the three prisons has been characterized by specific conditions and contexts: whereas Mezze was the prison of the political elites, Palmyra was that of the disallowed political opposition that existed outside of the strict confines of Baathist Syria (especially Communists and Islamists), and Saydnaya prison has rightly been called the microcosm of Syrian society because anybody could find themselves there at any time. But these three military security prisons in Syria also have a number of aspects in common, for example their societal impact and broad-based cultural legacy. Any Syrian in the past half-century would shiver at the mere mention of the words Mezze, Palmyra, or Saydnaya, and their directors gained their horrific reputations from the catastrophic levels of violence they exacted on their inmates. And finally, the rich prison literature of Syria has been shaped, fundamentally, by the collective experiences of the detainees in the three prisons.

Several paradoxes have unfolded in the history of these prisons. Saydnaya between 2005 and 2010 produced dozens of jihadists, while that was not the case in 1980s Palmyra, even though it was a hub of the Islamists. The experiences of regime management of Islamist files are similar between 1975–1979 and 2005–2012. In 1975, the regime detained Jihadist-Islamist leaders and a number of their supporters, mostly young men, but then released them after the confrontation with the Islamist movement intensified in 1979. Most of the released detainees, not surprisingly, ended up taking up arms against the regime. In early 2005, the regime arrested a number of jihadists returning from jihad in Afghanistan and Iraq and detained them in Saydnaya. Those same men later went on to mutiny in 2008 and some were killed. All of them were released at the height of the regime's confrontation with the widespread popular uprising of the Syrian Revolution in 2011. Most of those released became leaders of militant Islamist factions, some of which were very radical such as Jabhat al-Nusra, while some even joined ISIS. It was almost as if the regime was using its prisons to detain, torture, and radicalize men, in order to choose, perhaps even create, enemies that would prove useful at a later stage in the field. Indeed, the story of Assad's prisons is a cautionary tale on how the regime politicized its prisons by detaining political groups that would not only improve its domestic security, but also its reputation abroad (such as Palestinian militants in the 1980s, or Jihadists in the 2000s). In a way, its prisons were a social experiment in which the regime tested how Islamists would respond to various policies. From this perspective, the Syrian Gulag has been even more influential at the national, regional and global level than we have previously imagined.

Our Children in the World

Our Children in the World was a programme which aired every Saturday night on state radio. It became a form of communication between prisoners and their families who were not allowed to visit. This would not have come to light were it not for the fact that leftist inmates at Saydnaya Military Prison stuck their necks out and offered to help. They received monthly visits, which were not allowed to last more than 20 minutes and were always under the strict supervision of the guards. Some of them took the risk of passing on to their own loved ones information about prisoners who were not allowed to receive visits. They then had to pass on the information to the relatives of those inmates, who were given pseudonyms, and who could communicate with their families via the radio programme.

The families of leftist prisoners often travelled to different Syrian cities in search of the parents of prisoners who were deprived of visits. Confirmation that they were able to reach the desired address came at the next visit, a month later. Then, every Saturday night, the inmates began intently listening to the radio programme 'Our Children in the World'. This was often like searching for a needle in a haystack. Communication was difficult assuming the prisoner's family had a phone line at all. If they were lucky, after dozens of attempts, they had to wait for an appointment to record their message, which could take a month or longer. After the audio clip was recorded over the phone, it would make its way to editing and processing in the studio, after which it would be included in an episode of 'Our Children in the World'.

The presenter of the programme, Amal Dakkak, always began her talk with a sentimental introduction in which she talked about the longing of the absent and the agony of the waiting, who had been separated for months and weeks. She had no idea that there were people listening who had been gone for more than ten years, without hearing a single message about whether their parents were alive. One of the mothers addressed her son, 'who is studying in Canada': the prisoners' wing in Saydnaya called out the name of her son who had been waiting for that moment. She told him of her love and separated each sentence from the next with a cry, indicating that she had long since exceeded the limits of her patience. She told him about his younger sister's marriage, the birth of her three children, that five years ago she knitted him a wool sweater but had no way to send it, and finally she had sent it, letting him know that his gift would arrive with the next visit to the friend who had delivered his message, and that it may even have arrived before the programme was broadcast.[1]

Conclusion

Afterlives from behind the sun

The trauma centre in Amsterdam's Diemen district is a drab, 1960s building with nondescript flooring and furniture. It looks out onto a residential area where high-rises are rapidly emerging to accommodate the housing demand in the city. It had been raining all day – one of those typical grey days. Akram sat in the waiting room, motionless and a touch nervous, not knowing what to expect and hoping not to be recognized. This was no unfounded fear, as the room was packed with Syrians who whispered to each other in all dialects: Damascene middle-class, Deir ez-Zor countryside, the distinct coastal tongue, and Arabic with Kurdish accent. 'There it is,' Akram thought to himself, 'Bashar al-Assad finally did manage to bring Syrians together – in the waiting room of the trauma center.' When they called him in, a kindly middle-aged Dutch woman with salt-and-pepper hair and gentle, understanding eyes guided him to a small room. This is where he would spend his Friday mornings for the next year, hoping to improve his life and stave off a not unlikely suicide.[1]

Akram's life had changed forever after he was arrested by the Air Force Intelligence in 2011. The regime's repression of the uprising had intensified, a civil war had started, and escalated. In 2013 he gave up and fled Syria to Turkey, where he took a dingy boat with 30 others to a Greek island, walked across Central Europe, and arrived in the Netherlands in the summer of 2015. He had never even been in Western Europe before, but thought he knew a lot about the Netherlands: a developed democratic country with good public facilities, nice people, and most of all, what he lacked in Syria: freedom. The first few months were a honeymoon: he took drugs, attended dance music festivals, slept with girls, and thought he was having the time of his life. Until one day, driving back from a late-night party, the Dutch traffic police was doing routine checks for drinking and driving. He had indeed been drinking and driving, but that is not why he froze, had a panic attack, and crashed his car against a lamp post. It was the sight of a checkpoint with uniformed men that triggered his trauma. Akram began to neglect his health, his apartment became a mess, he suffered inexplicable headaches, and stopped sleeping at night because of the incessant, suffocating nightmares. Instead, he self-isolated, smoked cigarettes, drank *araq*, and browsed the internet endlessly and aimlessly. In the end, the few friends he still had left convinced him to see a therapist and made him an appointment. Again, his life took a new turn.

Meanwhile, in Damascus, Amjad sat in his lavish office and called for coffee to be brought in. The years had been good to him: he had climbed up the ladder in the Syrian intelligence services and was now a Lieutenant Colonel in the Air Force Intelligence. The heavy torture work was now done by the *shabaab*, the younger guys who had enthusiastically joined in 2011. Amjad himself hardly got his hands dirty anymore, except if there were high-profile arrestees or special tasks that required exceptional discretion and clearance. His competitors feared him, his colleagues respected him, and his underlings loved him – to them, he was now the 'boss', the *moallem*. The raise he was given, the kickbacks he enjoyed, and other economic benefits allowed him to renovate his house in the upscale Damascus area of Muhajireen and buy a nice plot of land near the city of Masyaf, right next to a famous general's palace. He joined in on large 'security conferences' with the Iranians and the Russians (and had indeed started to learn Russian) and sat in on secret meetings with the Air Force Intelligence top brass. Now, Jamil al-Hassan not only knew who he was, but would also send him a bouquet of flowers when he got his promotion. Most of the southern Damascus suburbs were under his control, and it was no exaggeration to say that not a leaf could move without his permission. The hundreds of people he had killed, the thousands he had tortured, it was all water under the bridge. By the year 2021, he was senior enough to have American sanctions issued against him personally for crimes against humanity. He didn't care; he wasn't leaving Syria anyway.

Explaining the Syrian Gulag

Why did the Assad regime set up such a huge prison industry? Answering this question is a daunting task because it requires much more research, especially in the regime's inner workings, deliberations, and calculations. An important element in the answer lays in the tension between permissible and impermissible politics and violence. In Assad's Syria, there is a finite set of authorized forms of politics. The Baath Party is obviously the leading party, but the Syrian parliament (the 'People's Assembly') also contains other political parties: the Syrian Social Nationalist Party, the Communist Party of Syria, the Socialist Unionists, the Arabic Democratic Union Party, the National Vow Movement, and the Arab Socialist Union. These are all part of the National Progressive Front of legally licensed parties which support the Arab-nationalist and socialist orientation of the government and accept the leadership of the Baath Party. These parties are often called the 'sham parties' (أحزاب شكلية). The Assad regime tolerates these parties because they submit to the Baath Party and never challenge it in a serious way. It directs its coercive apparatus against any and all parties and people who take political positions outside of this authorized box of politics. This includes Communists, Muslim Brotherhood (the *Ikhwan*), liberals, Salafists, the unaffiliated revolutionary youth of 2011, and violent insurgents. Anybody in this second category is subjected to severe forms of mass violence: intimidation, detention, torture, killings.

Having declared much of the Syrian political spectrum illegitimate, it was a logical step for the Assad regime to target those dissident social and political movements en masse. The regime's extermination of dissent is about extinguishing all activity in the

National Progressive Front Ba'ath Party	Muslim Brotherhood

<table>
<tr><td colspan="3">National Progressive Front
Ba'ath Party</td></tr>
<tr><td>SSNP</td><td>PYD</td><td>ASU</td></tr>
<tr><td>NVM</td><td>SU</td><td>CPS</td></tr>
</table>

Muslim Brotherhood
Communists
Liberals
2011 Revolution
Kurdish opposition

Figure 1 Permissible and impermissible politics in Assad's Syria

realm of impermissible politics: prohibiting it from publishing and organizing, shooting it off the streets, beating it out of the person, exorcizing it even at the individual level – in Assad's prisons, detainees were not allowed to discuss politics even in their prison cells. The regime aimed to remove every inkling of genuine politics from society, because it was and is at war with society. It is here that we understand how the Assad regime used the Gulag to shape and mould its society.

The Syrian prison system does not offer parole, reintegration, or rehabilitation programmes after release from prison, neither in the civil prisons, nor in the intelligence and military prisons. Hence, there is truth to Salwa Ismail's notion that the prison camps 'had as their objective the unmaking of certain political subjectivities, specifically dissident subjectivities that were construed as inherently threatening to the health of the body politic".[2] However, there is more going on than unmaking, as the detainees are not necessarily allowed to abandon those subjectivities, but the regime intends to destroy the political group as a group. The forms, duration, and logic of the mass violence directed against these opposition groups follow the intent to make the groups disappear, not the individual persons per se. Furthermore, particularly telling is the essentialization or racialization of those political identities, for behavioural escape is well-nigh impossible. Even the children of the detainees are targeted: after all, a child of a Communist or Islamist can only end up becoming a Communist or Islamist, therefore must be surveilled and imprisoned for the slightest infraction. After 2011, the prison system thus became an essential aspect of the repression of the uprising, and therefore part of the regime's counterinsurgency strategy. As such, it fulfilled a broader objective than mere imprisonment. This means that Assad's Gulag was in no way marginal to Syrian society; on the contrary, it was central to creating a Baathist political culture.

The Argentinian social scientist Daniel Feierstein argued that the Videla regime's repression in the 1970s was aimed at 'social reengineering', a comprehensive strategy that aimed 'to achieve its objectives in a war that could not be won by military means alone but only through kidnappings, disappearances, torture, and the systematic destruction of the civilian population – in other words, through genocidal social practices'.[3] If it is violence that defines the nature of Syria's prisons, then we can take note of the prominent chronicler of the Nazi camps, Abel Herzberg, who once wrote: 'A concentration camp means torture until death'.[4] This pithy definition of the Syrian Gulag echoes what Amnesty International concluded in a long report on Saydnaya prison, namely that the inhuman treatment including torture, the deprivations, and the weekly mass executions amount to an extermination of detainees.[5] The Rome Statute defines the crime of 'extermination' as 'the intentional infliction of conditions of life, inter alia the deprivation of access to food and medicine, calculated to bring about the destruction of part of a population'.[6] Therefore we can conclude that Assad's prison system does not merely exist to imprison, discipline, and punish, but to exterminate.

Torture

Why does the regime torture people so violently and massively? Scholars and activists have produced a wealth of knowledge on torture as an interrogational, penal, judicial, and terroristic phenomenon.[7] Torture assaults the masculinity of the victimized men and shapes the body politic by 'writing violence' on the bodies of the victims. It is meant to discipline, punish, and terrorize the population and deter it from conducting any form of opposition politics. The Assad regime's half-century career in torture does not exist to extract information, but to impose information, to reaffirm the preexisting narratives that the regime's torture bosses have before they enter the torture chamber. But to what extent is the Syrian Gulag a form of deterrence? Does the regime really believe that detainees repent and relinquish their opposition after being tortured? Do survivors tell stories that deters society from becoming politically active? According to the testimonies in our interviews, survivors most often returned to anti-regime activism, knowing well they would be arrested and tortured. To what extent torture precludes others from becoming politically active was perhaps best refuted in the mass demonstrations of 2011: the protesters knew well what was in store for them if they were arrested.

Other open questions relating to torture remain, starting with sectarian hatred. Our interviews show a paradox that was clearly noticed in an early Amnesty International report of 1987: 'Sometimes torture serves as an expression of sectarian hatred. For example, [name] was severely tortured because he was in the leadership cadre and a Sunni. The reverse also occurs, for sometimes the Alawite prisoner is tortured more. This happened to [name] because he had, in the words of some officers, "betrayed his sect".'[8] This motif appears in our interviews as well, but there is no conclusive picture of how exactly sectarian hatred plays a role in the Gulag. In any case, the regime knows its detainees better than they know themselves and manipulates their religious taboos and cultural sensitivities. In the words of one former detainee, the regime is a 'master sociologist'. For example, when the torturers force their victims to bray like donkeys or bark like dogs, they most likely know that the victim assumes that within the Alawite religious doctrine of reincarnation, Sunnis are to be resurrected as the lowliest of animals, and therefore they are forced to imitate those animals. But neither survivors nor researchers can know for sure; only the perpetrators know.

Another question that remains is the extent to which torture is a means versus a goal. The Mukhabarat officers who torture for a living together make up Assad's machine of death. The year 2011 was not a turning point for them, but only meant more of the same work. Killing or torturing for Assad was a form of relationship management: the more you torture, the more you demonstrate to others that you support him. Like any other bureaucracy, the Mukhabarat bureaucracy simply needs to sustain itself in the broader landscape of Assad's tools of repression. The competition between the four main intelligence agencies leads to a form of mutual radicalization, and a rush to legitimize their own existence and expand their power base. They have a self-serving interest in keeping the prison system afloat, so they torture people to keep their jobs.[9] As a perverse effect, the Gulag then produces enemies (imaginary and real), rather than eliminate them: someone was tortured, therefore he must have done something against the regime. Torturing and extracting confessions are then presented as retroactive evidence of opposition against the regime, and hence *ipso facto* a legitimization of the Gulag.[10]

The Syrian Gulag is also a form of rent-seeking, best exemplified by the practice of extortion. The Mukhabarat has been extorting Syrian society for decades, for example in setting up checkpoints or soliciting bribes for various economic activities. This extractive and parasitic attitude toward Syrian society manifests itself especially in the Gulag. Mukhabarat officers use emotional blackmail when promising detainees benefits or an early release, or their family members information on the whereabouts of their loved ones in jail. Desperate family members pay millions of Syrian Lira in hefty bribes to a seemingly sympathetic officer from the intelligence agencies, believing he will do his best to look for or after their son, brother, father, etc. Some officers might even try, but the vast majority are duplicitous and capitalize on the family members who have pinned their hopes on him. They know they are unwilling and unable to deliver anything meaningful in terms of information or support, but manipulate the families to squeeze payoffs out of them. As the father of one Syrian detainee said: 'Detention is expensive. If you have a detainee [in your family], it means that the same officers who are responsible for your pain enjoy your money.'[11]

Finally, the broader impact of the Gulag on Syrian society is an underexamined topic. This impact was first and foremost felt in the families, as 'detention stoked feelings of anguish among relatives, colleagues, and friends about the fate of the detainees and the kind of suffering they were likely to be enduring ... Family members, up to fourth-degree relatives, were screened out of public employment and faced restrictions on movement and travel. They were also subject to enhanced surveillance and monitoring, being cast as members of a risky population'.[12] Syrian lives are full of such micro-tragedies. S.I. is a middle-aged Damascene who was bullied during most of his youth as 'Abu Mahbus' (أبو محبوس) because his father had been arrested and detained by the Mukhabarat. Growing up without a father made him a target among the neighbourhood boys.[13] Countless others like him never processed the trauma of an absent parent; many of them never became a parent as a result. The broader impact on Syrian culture and society requires a much bigger research agenda than we could have covered in this book.

The silent chimneys of Saydnaya

In May 2017, satellite photos emerged showing a newly built, small annex on the Saydnaya prison complex. Various satellite images show white smoke bellowing from a chimney sticking out from the building; it is not unlikely that the Assad regime built a crematorium to be able to dispose of the many corpses that Saydnaya produces each week. When the regime was confronted with this information, the Syrian Foreign Ministry issued a blanket denial that the 'accusations against the Syrian government of a so-called crematorium in Saydnaya prison, in addition to the broken record about the use of barrel bombs and chemical weapons, are categorically false'.[14]

For over a decade, human rights groups, international media, governments, and various international organizations have exposed, documented, and critiqued the crimes of the Assad regime. None of this coverage and advocacy appears to have made a notable impact on the regime. On the contrary, knowledge dissemination about the violence only seems to educate the regime on how to hide its crimes better. When the UN Human Rights Council published its first comprehensive report in 2011 on the regime's repression, Syrian ambassador to the United Nations, Bashar Jaafari, rejected the methods, findings, and implications of the report, and attacked the integrity of the then United Nations High Commissioner for Human Rights, Navi Pillay. Jaafari also attacked very well-documented reports of mass executions at the prison.[15]

The *New York Times* journalist Anne Barnard personally travelled to Damascus and was allowed a perfunctory, choreographed visit at an intelligence branch. She stood in front of a number of detainees who were instructed to declare there was no maltreatment, and the head of the branch sent her off with a handshake and a smile.[16] Pressure can even backfire. Layla Shwaikhani, an American citizen, was arrested in Syria in 2016. At America's request, the Czech ambassador Eva Filipi interceded, spoke to her in Saydnaya prison, and even pleaded with Ali Mamlouk. A few days later Shwaikhani was executed.[17] Meanwhile, the chimneys of Saydnaya smouldered on. In 2021, satellite imagery emerged that solar panels had been placed on the prison roof.

With the regime having achieved military victory in the civil war, the Syrian Gulag has fully consolidated. The half-century-old stalwart system has proven its value in the repression of the uprising, and the regime has rewarded those that have kept it running. The naïve notion that 'the situation in Syria is quiet now' or that 'there is peace' entirely misconstrues the problem. The fact that there are no military battles only means the regime is in firmer control, which means not less but more violence, because it allows the silent extermination of the Gulag to continue. This impact is not just felt inside Syria. By now, the Syrian Gulag is a global phenomenon: its victims are spread across the world and its perpetrators are being indicted in Europe. Indeed, they are everywhere among us.

To Err is Human

1. A Kurdish teacher from Qamishli is stopped en route to Hasaka in 1987 and is arrested by the State Security. He is taken to Damascus and severely tortured: he is folded into a car tire and beatenon the soles of his feet with sticks and a whip, hung from a ceiling by his wrists, and electrocuted by his genitals. During the torture, they ask him about his cousin who is studying in Romania. Delirious with pain, he swears that he has no cousin in Romania, but he is subjected to even worse torture. After a few days, it turns out that they arrested the wrong person based on an identical first and last name. They apologize to him and release him. All he takes away from the regime is scar tissue on the soles of his feet and months of nightmares.[1]

2. At the height of the civil war in 2014, an Alawite man drives his car through a disputed area and encounters a Free Syrian Army rebel checkpoint. The rebels take him prisoner to verify his identity, but he is familiar with Islamic traditions and pretends to be Sunni for two weeks. Then the regime recaptures the area, arrests him, and sends him to the Military Intelligence branch, where he is tortured. He assures them that he is pro-Assad and begs them to call related army officers to prove his Alawite identity. After two days of torture, they believe him and call someone in Latakia; it turns out that he is indeed one of them. As an apology, he is given a shawarma sandwich. After his release, he declares, "Those two days in the Mukhabarat prison were worse than the entire two weeks with the rebels." Nonetheless, he remains pro-Assad.[2]

3. Nour is driving through his hometown of Homs in 2012, where violence and polarisation are escalating sharply at the time. The Mukhabarat have checkpoints everywhere, where they pick people out of traffic and send them to prison. Nour's cousin is a prankster and earlier that day sent him a satirical message in which he does a superb imitation of Bashar al-Assad's voice. Nour stumbles upon an Air Force Intelligence checkpoint and he is gripped by fear. The intelligence officer takes his phone and begins scrolling through his contacts, photos and messages. He clicks on the mocking sound clip, thinks the voice is really from President Assad himself, and mistakes Nour for a pro-regime loyalist. Who else would have a speech from Assad on their phone? 'Good man, drive on'.[3]

Appendix 1: Biographies

Walid Hamid Abaza (1949–2017), from the village of Ghassaniya in rural Quneitra; of Circassian origin, Sunni. He headed Political Security in Hama from 1978 to the early 1990s, after which he moved to the capital to hold various positions, including deputy head of Political Security and secretary of the party department in Quneitra governorate. He contributed to the establishment and formation of the National Defense Forces, particularly the Deir Shmeil prison in rural Hama after the 2011 revolution.

Riyad Habib Abbas, alias Abu Ali/William (1967–), from the village of Ein Qayta in the Jableh district of rural Latakia; Alawite. He began his career as an officer in the presidential convoy and was then promoted to bodyguard of Hafez al-Assad in his final years. After Assad's death in 2000, he was transferred to the Military Police, where he became commander of the Military Police in Aleppo in 2010. In mid-2013, he was

Figure A1.1 Riyad Habib Abbas, from a pro-regime social media site.

appointed Head of Political Security in Aleppo and in March 2018 Commander of the Military Police.

Ahmed Aboud (1947–), from the village of Qurfays in rural Latakia; Alawite. He has been the head of Division 293 of the Military Intelligence for more than 20 years. He is a cousin of Ali Douba and has close ties to Rifaat al-Assad.

Fouad al-Absi, alias Abu Riyad, from Zamalkeh in Eastern Ghouta in rural Damascus; Sunni. He was a senior officer in the police force. From 1984 to 1987 he headed the General Intelligence Service and then became governor of Damascus.

Michel Aflaq (1910–1989), from a middle-class family in Damascus; Christian. Played the biggest role in the founding of the Baath Party and the development of its Arab-nationalist ideology. Removed from his position as party leader in 1966, he fled to Lebanon and then to Iraq, where he befriended Saddam Hussein and was allowed to write and publish. A court of Hafez al-Assad sentenced him to death in absentia, along with former Syrian President Mohammed Amin al-Hafiz.

Jawdat al-Ahmad, alias Abu Ghassan (1962–), from the town of Qardaha in rural Latakia; Alawite. He began his career as an officer in Air Force Intelligence, where he was part of the intelligence coordination of the chemical weapons programme from 1985 to 1995. As an Air Force Intelligence officer, he was appointed head of the Research Division in 2003, head of the Eastern Region Division in 2009, and head of the Central Region Air Force Intelligence Division in late 2010. Is known for his close ties to Bassel al-Assad.

Louay al-Ali (1965–), from Al-Qalayie in rural Jableh, Latakia region; Alawite. He has progressed from an officer in the Suwayda Division of the Military Police to becoming head of Division 245 in Dara'a in 2011. In 2018, he became head of Military Intelligence Division 217 in Suwayda. Is known for his restlessness and ruthlessness. Related by marriage to Ahmad Aboud and Ali Douba.

Nasser al-Ali, alias Abu Jihad (1960–), from the village of Makta'a Hajar in the Manbij district of rural East Aleppo; a Bedouin, Sunni. In the 1980s, he attended the police academy. After graduation, he was assigned to Political Security. After the revolution, he was head of Political Security of Aleppo with the rank of chief inspector but was transferred to Dara'a as the successor of chief inspector Atef Najib. After the opposition factions entered Aleppo in the summer of 2012, he was transferred back as head of the Aleppo department. In 2013, he was transferred as head of the Tartous department for a few months; he was appointed head of Political Security in Damascus in the same year. On 7 July 2019, he was appointed head of Political Security, succeeding Husam Louqa.

Bashar al-Assad, alias Abu Hafez (1965–), son of President Hafez al-Assad; Alawite of the Kalbiyah clan. When his older brother Bassel died in 1994, he was called upon to prepare to replace his brother as the future president of Syria. He joined the armed forces and was ushered through the ranks until he was named first general, then commander-in-chief of the armed forces and then president of Syria on 11 June 2000,

Figure A1.2 Bashar Al-Assad, SANA.

a day after his father's death. He graduated as a physician in 1988, went to Britain in 1992 to specialise in ophthalmology. He returned to Damascus in 1994 to prepare for the presidency, which he holds to this day.

Hafez al-Assad, alias Abu Bassel (1930–2000), from the town of Al-Qardaha in rural Latakia; Alawite of the Kalbiyah clan. He attended the Military Academy in Homs in 1952 and the Aviation School in Aleppo in 1953. He was then chosen to attend aviation training in Egypt in 1955 and 1956. He held several military posts, especially after 1963, when he participated in the coup with the Baath Party Military Committee. He led the air force and then served as defence minister until he overthrew the government in 1970, established a personal regime, and remained president of Syria until his death.

Maher al-Assad, alias Abu Bassel (1968–), brother of President Bashar al-Assad. He completed his studies in mechanical engineering at Damascus University and entered the Military Academy, where he graduated as lieutenant engineer chief. He joined the Fourth Division and became its commander. Has a reputation for being impulsive and ruthless.

Rifaat al-Assad, alias Abu Rebal (1937–), from the town of Al-Qardaha in rural Latakia; Alawite of the Kalbiyah clan. Brother of President Hafez al-Assad. He was commander of the commandos and paratroopers in the Damascus area and the two major air bases at Mezze and al-Dhumeir (1966–1970) and was commander of the Defence Brigades (1965–1984) who carried out the massacre at Palmyra Prison in 1980

Figure A1.3 Mahed al-Assad, from a pro-regime social media site.

on his orders. He played a prominent role in the siege, storming the city of Hama in 1982. He lived in Europe since late 1984 and returned to Syria in 2021.

Noureddin al-Atassi (1929–1992), from the city of Homs; Sunni. He was president from February 1966 to October 1970, when he resigned all his positions in protest against the army's interference in politics and the actions of Rifaat al-Assad. He then spent 22 years in Mezze prison on the orders of Hafez al-Assad. He was released after he was diagnosed with cancer, but died of the disease shortly thereafter.

Ahmad Adnan Dabbagh, alias Abu Abdo (1932–1980), from the city of Aleppo; Sunni. Was married to the aunt of Asma al-Assad (Bashar al-Assad's wife), Saadat al-Otari. His son is a prominent entrepreneur; his company focuses on the digitization of government services in Syria. Little is known about him, but he was director of General Intelligence between 1970 and 1976 and then minister of the interior until 1980. He played a central role in the repression of the 1970s, when arbitrary arrests and confiscation of property were the order of the day. In a public announcement, he blamed a member of the Muslim Brotherhood for the murder of 32 cadets from the artillery school in Aleppo in 1979. He died in 1980.

Ghazi Dayoub (1958–), from the village of Ain al-Sharqiyah in rural Jableh; Alawite. Took over the investigation of the Military Police in Aleppo and was put in charge of the political prison in Palmyra from 1996 until 1998.

Turki Alam al-Din (1943–), from the town of Al-Quraya in rural Suwayda; Druze. He joined the Internal Security Division 251, headed by Mohammed Nassif, where he was in charge of the Religions Division, then the Parties Division and the Interrogations Division, while he was in charge of the detachment of the City Division.

Ali Douba, alias Abu Mohammed (1933–), from the village of Qurfays in rural Latakia; Alawite of the Matawrah clan. Served in the Air Force and as military attaché to the embassies in the United Kingdom (1964–1966) and Bulgaria (1967–1968). Supported the coup of Hafez al-Assad in 1970 and was deputy director from 1971 to 1974 and then director of Military Intelligence until 2000. Was promoted to general in 1981 and played a key role in the violent suppression of the Muslim Brotherhood uprising in Hama in 1982. Notorious for ruthlessness, physical violence, corruption and sexual assault. Forced into retirement by Bashar al-Assad in 2000 because of he

Figure A1.4 Ali Duba, from a private collection.

and his sons' involvement in a number of financial and criminal scandals, including car theft, kidnapping for ransom, trading in artifacts, and molestation of detainees' wives. Has a sarcastic sense of humor and avoids social circles.

Rasmi al-Eid,[from Dara'a; Christian. He was director of Mezze prison from the early 1970s until 1976 and then became head of the Military Police department that supervised all military prisons, succeeding Ali al-Madani.

Mazhar Faris (1940–), Alawite. He graduated from the Military Academy in 1963 as a lieutenant in air defence. He rose through the military ranks and was appointed commander of a missile battalion in the November 1973 war. He later transferred to Military Intelligence. In 1976 he was appointed head of the Reconnaissance Committee in Lebanon, head of Military Detection Division 248 in Damascus and then head of Palestine Division 235.

Faisal Ghanem (1950–), from the village of Bisnada in rural Latakia; Alawite. Led the Tadmor political prison from its opening in 1980 until 1984.

Rustom Ghazaleh (1953–2015), from the village of Qarfa in the district of Daraa; Sunni. He graduated from the Military Academy in Homs and was appointed to the battalion of armoured vehicles. He served as Security Supervisor in the town of Hamana in the Lebanese mountains, then led the Syrian Military Intelligence detachment in the al-Hamra district of Beirut, before being appointed by President Bashar al-Assad in 2002 to succeed Ghazi Kanaan as head of Syrian Military Intelligence in Lebanon. He left Lebanon in 2005 to be appointed head of Division 227 of the Military Intelligence Service, and then head of Political Security in 2012.

Marwan Hadid (1934–1976), native of Hama; Sunni. He trained in agricultural engineering at the Egyptian University of Ain Shams, where he graduated in 1962. He joined the 1964 anti-Baath uprising in Hama, which led to the regime's troops shelling the Sultan's Mosque. After the 1967 defeat, Hadid and other young fighters went to Jordan in 1968, where they joined Fatah, the main branch of the Palestinian resistance movement. He received commando training in one of the camps. After Assad came to power in 1970, Hadid returned to Hama and founded the Fighting Vanguard here. He was arrested in 1975 and died a year later in Mezze prison.

Mohammed Amin al-Hafiz (1921–2009), from Aleppo; Sunni. Was Syria's first Baath president from 1963 and was deposed in Salah Jadid's coup on 23 February 1966. He remained in prison until 1967, after which he was exiled to Iraq. In 2003, he returned to Syria, where he remained until his death.

Naji Jamil al-Hamid, alias Abu Ayad (1932–2014), from Deir ez-Zor; Sunni. He graduated from the Military Academy in 1954 and trained at the Royal Air Force Technical Academy in England. He was vice commander of the Air Force in 1970 and was in charge of the Air Force from 1971 to 1978, during which time he was head of National Security. As a member of the Supreme Security Committee he was involved in the interrogations at Mezze prison. He retired from the army due to a personal dispute with Rifaat al-Assad.

Omar Hamida (1935–2021), from a clan living in the Bab al-Nayrab neighbourhood in the city of Aleppo; Sunni. In the early 1980s until the late 1990s, he headed the General Intelligence Service in Aleppo. Was known for his brutal torture methods.

Ali Haj Hammoud (1944–), from a family in Homs; Alawite. Between 1976 and 1982 he was a member of Syrian Military Intelligence in Lebanon and was Minister of the Interior between 2001 and 2004.

Jamil al-Hassan, alias Abu Khalid (1952–), from Al-Qarniya in rural Homs; Alawite. He entered the Military Academy in 1972 and specialised in air defense. He rose through the military ranks, becoming an officer at Mezze Military Air Base in 2007 and a Major General in early 2009. From July 2009 to 2019, he served as a director of Air Force Intelligence. Considered one of the Assad regime's most ruthless security chiefs, he was responsible for the violent suppression of the uprising through mass torture, enforced disappearances and the creation and support of militias such as the Shabbiha groups and the Tiger forces.

Adnan Badr Hassan (1937–), from a peasant family in al-Mukharram al-Fuqani in Homs; Alawite of the Khayati clan. Commander of the Ninth Mechanized Infantry Division and head of Political Security from 1987 to 2002.

Nazih Hassoun, alias Abu Anees (1952–), from the village of al-Quraya in Suwayda; Druze. He served in the Air Force Intelligence Service in the 1980s and was promoted to deputy head of its Investigations Division. By 2011 he was in charge of military operations on the Syrian coast and in December 2012 he was appointed deputy head of Political Security under Rustom Ghazaleh. After Ghazaleh's death in 2015, he became head of the service and remained so until 2017.

Nizar al-Helou, alias Abu Hussein (1942–2016), from Safita in rural Tartous; Alawite. He headed Division 227 of Military Intelligence before the Fighting Vanguard's escape from the division in 1983. After this incident, he was dismissed and succeeded by Hisham Ikhtiyar. Is related by marriage to Mohammed Haidar and Hassan Khalouf.

Ibrahim Howaija, alias Abu Modar (1932–), from the town of Ayn Shiqaq in rural Latakia; Alawite of the Haddadi clan. He headed the Air Force Intelligence Service from 1987 until his retirement in 2002.

Hisham Ikhtiyar (1941–2012), born in Damascus; Shiite. He headed Division 227 of Military Intelligence in 1983 and was head of General Intelligence from 2001 to 2005. At the same time, he was a member of the National Leadership of the Baath Party and its Central Committee and security adviser to the President until he was killed in the crisis cell bombing in 2012.

Izzaddin Ismail (1947–), from Bassetwer in rural Latakia; Alawite. He was responsible for security at Mezze Air Force Base before heading Air Force Intelligence in 2002 until his retirement in 2005.

Ghassan Jawdat Ismail, alias Abu Bassel (1960–), from the town of Janeinat Ruslan in the Dirkush area of rural Tartous; Alawite. Deputy Director since 2018 and Director of

Figure A1.5 Hisham Ikhtyar, AFP.

Air Force Intelligence since 2019. His name became known upon his appointment as head of the service's Special Missions Division as superintendent.

Salah Jadid (1926–1993), from the village of Dwayer in rural Latakia; Alawite of the Haddadi clan. In his early youth he joined the Syrian Socialist Nationalist Party and then switched to the Baath. He was a member of the Military Committee of this party. He personally led the coup of 23 February 1966 that deposed President Amin al-Hafez, and from that day became the de facto ruler of Syria until the coup of his comrade Hafez al-Assad in 1970, after which he remained in Mezze prison until his death.

Ghazi al-Jehni (1950–1998), from the village of al-Masoudiya in rural Homs; Alawite. He headed Tadmor prison as Ghanem's successor until 1994, when he became incurably ill, leaving the prison in 1996. Two years later he was killed in a traffic accident in the city of Homs.

Abdul Karim al-Jundi (1932–1969), native of Salamiyah; Ismaili. Graduated from the Military Academy of Homs. Was a member of the Military Committee of the Baath Party, served as Minister of Agrarian Reform, and after Salah Jadid's coup in 1966 was appointed by him to head the National Security Bureau of the party's National

Figure A1.6 Ghassan Joudat Ismail, from a pro-regime social media site

leadership. Was known for his violence and brutality. Expanded the regime's intelligence services significantly in 1967 and recruited an army of young informants. Numerous arbitrary arrests and atrocities took place and stories of torture never before seen in Syria circulated. During a conversation with the head of military intelligence Ali Zaza that ended in an argument, he committed suicide by means of a gunshot.

Ghazi Kanaan, alias Abu Yaroub (1933–2005), came from Bihmarra in rural Latakia; Alawite of the Kalbiyah clan. He was a key figure in Military Intelligence. He headed Military Intelligence in Homs from the early 1970s until 1982, after which he led Military Intelligence in Lebanon for many years. He returned to Syria in 2001 as head of Political Security and was appointed Interior Minister in 2003 until his death in 2005. The Syrian government stated that he had committed suicide in his office. Sources revealed that his death was likely the result of a failed coup to overthrow Assad with the support of the US intelligence agency CIA, with which he maintained close ties.

Hassan Khalil (1945–), Alawite. Deputy Director from 1993 and then Director of Military Intelligence from 2000 to 2005.

Mohammed Nassif Kheirbek, alias Abu Wael (1939–2015), from the village of al-Laqba near Masyaf; Alawite of the Kalbiyah clan. Graduated from the Military Academy and appointed to the General Intelligence Service, where he played a key role in clearing out Hafez al-Assad's opponents after 1970. Since the mid-1970s, he headed the Internal Security Division 251 of the General Intelligence Service. He is considered one of the godfathers of the security and intelligence services in the Assad era, a close confidant of Hafez al-Assad and a mentor to Bashar al-Assad.

Mohammed al-Khouli, alias Abu Firas (1937–), from Beit Yashout in rural Latakia; Alawite of the Haddadi clan. He is considered the spiritual father of Assad's intelligence service. He was deputy chief (1964–1970) and then head of Air Force Intelligence (1970–1987). Between 1971 and 1973 he trained in East Germany with both the Air Force and the Stasi. Under his leadership, Air Force Intelligence grew into an all-powerful apparatus that was largely independent of control and responsible for assassinations of opposition members abroad. He was transferred as vice commander of the Air Force until mid-1994. During this period, he exerted great influence on Hafez al-Assad as his security adviser. Retired in 1999.

Husam Louqa, alias Abu al-Nour (1964–), from the town of Khanaser in rural East Aleppo, of Circassian descent; Sunni. He graduated from the Military Academy in 1984 and was posted to the Ministry of Interior in 1987. He climbed the ranks until he became head of Political Security in Homs in 2004. In 2009, he was transferred to the department's headquarters in Damascus. After the revolution in 2011, Louqa was appointed head of Political Security in Hama and at the end of the same year he was transferred to the head of Political Security in Homs as deputy head of the Military and Security Committee in the city, where he was responsible for the siege of Al-Waer. On 29 November 2018, he was appointed Head of Political Security and on 7 July 2019, Director of General Intelligence.

Mahmoud Maatouq, alias Abu Sam (1970–2018), from the village of Fido in the southern countryside of Latakia; Alawite. He graduated from the Military Academy as a first lieutenant, and served in the Military Police. He played a central role in quelling the Saydnaya prison uprising in 2008. He led it from 2013 until the year he was killed in fighting between the regime and opposition forces near the town of Harasta in the eastern countryside of Damascus.

Ali al-Madani, alias Abu Tamim (1932–), from the city of Hama; Sunni. Headed the Military Police between 1966 and 1976, after which he was director of General Intelligence until 1979. Related by marriage to Naji Jamil.

Mohammed Mahalla, alias Abu Ali (1959–), Alawite. He served in the Republican Guard, rose to superintendent. He was seconded to Political Security in 2009, where he assumed the position of head of the Information Department and was subsequently appointed deputy head at the rank of major general. In 2015, he was transferred to Military Intelligence, of which he became deputy head and then head from April 2015 to 2019, when he was appointed as the president's first security adviser.

Talaat Mahfouz aka Abu Ous (1958–2013), from the village of Breikhiyeh in rural Tartous; Alawite. Climbed up through the ranks of the Military Police, became commander of conscripts or graduates of a bachelor's degree in law, and participated in mandatory military service at the Military Police Academy. Was transferred to Tadmor prison in May 1998 as Dayoub's successor, where he remained until the closure of the political department. Later he was put in charge of the Military Police in Latakia, before being asked to lead the Saydnaya Military Prison during the 2008 mutiny. He remained there until the day he was killed in an ambush by members of the Free Syrian Army. Known as the lion of Saydnaya and Tadmor prisons.

Abdul Salam Fajr Mahmoud (1959–), from the village of Al-Foua in rural Idlib; Shiite. He was a long-time office chief to the director of Air Force Intelligence. In 2010, he headed the Air Force Intelligence Department in the Southern Region and in 2011 he was appointed head of the Air Force Research Division, based at Mezze Military Airport.

Hafez Mohammed Makhlouf (1971–), nephew of Hafez al-Assad's wife, Anissa; Alawite. He joined the General Intelligence Service, climbed until he came to head Division 40, which follows Division 251. He remained here until 2014, when he was relieved of his duties and reportedly moved to Belarus. Played a central role in the violent repression of demonstrations in 2011. Injured in the bombing of the crisis cell meeting on 18 July 2012.

Ali Mamlouk, alias Abu Ayham (1946–), born in Damascus to a family that had migrated from the Alawite province of Alexandretta (since 1939 the Turkish province of Hatay). He studied at the Military Academy and specialised in chemistry. He began his career in the Air Force Intelligence Service at the side of Mohammed al-Khouli. As head of the research division of this service, he was jointly responsible for the security of the chemical weapons programme between 1981 and 1997. In 2005, he became head of the General Intelligence Service. He worked on developing this service, providing it with new surveillance methods and adequate training, including establishing an institute to train officers in modern intelligence methods. He led the National Security Agency from the summer of 2012 until the summer of 2019, where he was presumably appointed as security adviser to President Bashar al-Assad. Known for the contrast between his calm demeanor and his ruthlessness. For decades one of the most powerful men in the country.

Mohammed Mansoura, alias Abu Jasim (1950–), from the village of Hamam al-Qarahleh in rural Latakia; Alawite. Hafez al-Assad appointed him head of Military Intelligence in the Jazirah region based in Qamishli in the late 1970s. He then worked for two years at the command of Palestine Division 235 in Military Intelligence. He was appointed assistant to the head of Political Security, which he headed in 2005 until Ghazi Kanaan succeeded him in 2008. He led the suppression of the 2004 Kurdish uprising, mobilising and arming Arab tribesmen.

Qusay Mayhoub (1961–), from the village of Dargamo in the Jableh district of Latakia; Alawite. He entered military service at a young age, where he joined the 32nd batch of the Air Defense Academy, and then, after failing to become a pilot, went to the Air

Force Intelligence Corps. In early 2011, he worked as an assistant to the head of this service in the Southern Region. When the Syrian revolution began, he was sent to Dara'a as the head of Air Force Intelligence to put down demonstrations. Later he was transferred to this service in Damascus. He became the right-hand man of the department's director, Jamil al-Hassan, and was assigned to the Badia sector and the area around Damascus International Airport.

Kifah Melhem, alias Abu Haidar (1961–), from the village of Janeinat Ruslan in Tartous; Alawite. He served in the Republican Guard under the command of Bassel al-Assad. Was transferred to Military Intelligence in 2006. He was head of Military Intelligence Division 248 until 2012, where he headed Military Intelligence in Aleppo, and then was head of Intelligence in 2014. In 2015, he was appointed deputy head of the division and then head of the Security Committee in the Southern Region, before heading Military Intelligence from 2019 to the present. Is known as the engineer of the Syrian regime's military strategy in Aleppo, overseeing the formation of tribal militias. Responsible for the 2013 Queiq River massacre in which more than 200 men were killed by Air Force Intelligence. He is the brother-in-law of Ghassan Ismael.

Fadlallah Mikael (1965–2020), from the village of al-Rabiah; Alawite. He graduated from the Military Academy, specialised in infantry and served in the Republican Guard, where he was discharged for unknown reasons. After the revolution broke out, he was asked to form militias in the provinces of Idlib and Hama. He directly supervised the prison at Deir Shmeil camp until his death.

Bashir al-Najjar (1945–), from a middle-class family in Damascus; Sunni. He was director general of customs and headed the General Intelligence Service from 1994 until his arrest in 1998 on corruption charges.

Abdul Karim al-Nahlawi (1926–), from Damascus; Sunni. He graduated from the Military Academy in 1950 as a second lieutenant. During the Syrian-Egyptian union from 1958 to 1961, he was deputy director of human resources in the First Army, the Army of the Northern Province (Syria) was. He led the military movement that ended the Syrian-Egyptian union in 1961. After the coup by the Military Committee of the Arab Socialist Baath Party and the seizure of power in Syria in 1963, Al-Nahlawi was expelled from the army along with a number of officers who had participated in the separatist movement. He moved to Saudi Arabia where he worked as an accountant.

Mohammed Omran (1922–1972), from the village of Al-Mukharam al-Fuqaney, Homs; Alawite, of the Khayati clan. Graduated from the Military Academy of Homs. He was a member of the Military Committee of the Baath Party and commander of the small shock troops that protected the Military Committee and later became the Defense Brigades led by Rifaat al-Assad. After he was assassinated in the Lebanese city of Tripoli, fingers were pointed at President Hafez al-Assad.

Barakat al-Osh, alias Abu Balsam (1950–), from the village of Damsarkho in rural Latakia; Alawite. Took over the management of the eastern section of Tadmor prison, the judicial prison, in the early 1980s, and was deputy director of the two sections here at the same time. He was transferred to the leadership of Saydnaya prison from its opening in 1987 and then to the leadership of Mezze military prison until its closure in 2000.

Abdel Fattah Qudsiyah (1953–), from the village of Qurayyat in Masyaf district, of Palestinian origin. His ancestors fled to Syria in the late eighteenth century and converted to Alawism. He graduated from the Military Academy and served in the Republican Guard. He was friends with Bassel al-Assad and Adnan Makhlouf. He was appointed head of Military Intelligence in 2009 and held that position until 2012, when he was appointed deputy director of National Security. He is known for his ruthlessness in dealing with his opponents and his sectarianism.

Mohammed Khalid Rahmoun (1957–), from the town of Khan Sheikhoun in the southern countryside of Idlib; Sunni. He graduated from the Military Academy, specialising in air defence. Head of Air Force Intelligence in Dara'a from 2004 to 2011 and of the Southern Region until 2018 when a decree was issued appointing him as Minister of Interior.

Majid Said (1947–), from a middle-class family in Damascus; Sunni. He headed the General Intelligence Service from 1987 to 1994. Translated books on militarised Israeli society.

Mohammed Adib Salameh, alias Abu Nimr (1953–), from the village of Dahr al-Maghr in the Salamiyeh area of rural Hama; Alawite. He graduated from the Military

Figure A1.7 Adib Salama – on the right, from a pro-regime social media site.

Academy, specialising in air defence, and climbed the ladder until he was head of the Air Force Intelligence Department in the northern region of Aleppo from 2006 to 2016, after which he became deputy director of the department. Had a central role in outsourcing sectarian militias that kidnapped and killed unarmed civilians on a large scale. Known for his ruthlessness and sectarianism.

Fadi Saqqar, aka Abu Malek (1975–), native of Latakia; Alawite. Leads the National Defence Forces (NDF) in Damascus, an irregular militia formed with the support of the Republican Guard and local and regional forces, notably Iran. He was an official with the Consumers Union in Damascus, known for its corruption and arrogance. Sometimes called 'the professor' because of his penchant for lectures.

Abdelhamid al-Sarraj (1925–2013), from the city of Hama; Sunni. He is considered the most important intelligence officer in modern Syrian history and the spiritual father of Military Intelligence and the Syrian security culture. Early in his career, he worked as a gendarme, guarding the Behsita public brothel in the souk of Aleppo. He continued his high school education and attended the military academy in Homs, graduating in 1947. After Husni al-Zaim's coup in 1949, he served as his bodyguard. He was sent to France for specialised training in intelligence. From the early 1950s, he headed the Second Bureau, which later became Military Intelligence. In 1955, Al-Sarraj established a culture of extrajudicial detention. Al-Sarraj climbed up the military ranks until, at the time of the Syrian-Egyptian union from 1958 to 1961, he became the de facto head of what was then called the Northern Province, that is, Syria. In late 1961, he was arrested by separatists led by Abdul Karim al-Nahlawi and imprisoned in Mezze Prison, where the latter imprisoned his opponents. Egyptian intelligence, in cooperation with regional intelligence agencies, smuggled al-Sarraj through Lebanon to Egypt, where he remained until his death.

Mohammed al-Sha'ar, alias Abu Ibrahim (1950–), from the village of al-Hiffeh in rural Latakia; Sunni. Joined the army in 1971, climbed through military ranks and held various positions in Military Intelligence, including in the 1980s that of head of Security in Tripoli in Lebanon and head of the department in Tartous, of the department in Aleppo, of Division 227, and then head of the Military Police. From 2011 to 2018, he was Minister of Interior. He is the only one who survived the 18 July 2012 crisis cell bombing.

Asif Shawkat, alias Abu Zaid (1950–2012), from Madihleh in Tartous; Alawite. Husband of Bushra al-Assad, the daughter of Hafez al-Assad. Graduated from the Military Academy, specialising in infantry. Highlight of his career was the Defense Brigades in 1982, after which he transferred to the Republican Guard, where he was responsible for the security of Bushra al-Assad, whom he married in 1995. In 2005 he was appointed head of Military Intelligence, promoted to major general in 2009 and became deputy chief of the Army Staff Authority and deputy defence minister in 2011. He was killed in the crisis cell bombing on 18 July 2012.

Rafiq Shehadeh, alias Abu Tariq (1956–), from al-Sharashir in rural Latakia; Alawite. He served in the Republican Guard. From 1999 to 2000, he headed the guard battalion of Hafez al-Assad. He was appointed head of Military Security in Tartous and then head of Division 293, which deals with officer matters in Military Intelligence. Was deputy head of the division from 2011 to 2012, and then head until 2015.

Hikmat al-Shihabi, alias Abu Hazim (1931–2013), from the town of Al-Bab in rural North Aleppo; Sunni. Attended the Military Academy of Homs, trained in the United States, and obtained an intelligence management certificate in the Soviet Union in 1970. Held various military positions, most notably that of deputy chief (1968–1971) and then (1971–1974) of the Military Intelligence. He headed the Army Staff Authority until 1998, when he retired and left for America, where he resided until his death in 2013. With Abd al-Halim Khaddam and Ghazi Kanaan, he oversaw the Syrian occupation of Lebanon (1976–2005).

Bahjat Suleiman (1949–2021), from the city of Latakia; Alawite. He graduated from the Military Academy in Homs in 1970. He was given command of the Syrian Army's 41st Tank Brigade, and then headed the Internal Security Division 251 ('Al-Khatib') of the General Intelligence Service. In 2009, he was appointed Syria's ambassador to Jordan and remained so until the Jordanian government expelled him from the country in 2014.

Mustafa Al-Tajer, alias Abu Omar (1932–2003), from a small village near Azaz in the countryside of northern Aleppo; Sunni. Was friends with the head of Military Intelligence Ali Douba, so much so that he was sent to Aleppo in the early 1980s to head its department here. Was notorious for extorting family members of detainees and taking bribes. Returned to Damascus to lead Palestine Division 235, the largest division. He remained here until his retirement and died unexpectedly on his farm.

Figure A1.8 Mustafa Al-Tajer, from a pro-regime social media site.

Tawfiq Younis, from Tartous governorate; Alawite. From 2011 to 2016, he was head of the Internal Security Division 251 of the General Intelligence Service. Before that, he worked at this service in the city of Hama.

Kamal Yusuf, alias Abu al-Ayham (1942–), from the countryside of Baniyas; Christian. He headed the Syrian Military Intelligence Service in Beau Rivage, Lebanon. In the early 1980s, he became the head of Military Investigation Division 248, then the head of Palestine Division 235, and then returned as head of Investigation Division 248 until his resignation.

Yousef Zaghin (1931–2016), from the border town of al-Bukamal in Deir ez-Zor governorate; Sunni. He was twice prime minister and twice minister of agriculture. He was arrested in 1970 and released in 1981 after being diagnosed with cancer. He traveled to Europe for treatment and eventually settled in Sweden, where he died.

Mohammed Zamrini, from Bakao in rural Tartous; Alawite. In 2010 he was an officer in the intelligence service of Sa'sa; in 2011 he was appointed head of Military Intelligence

Figure A1.9 Mohammed Zamrini, from a pro-regime social media site.

in Homs, in 2012 he was transferred to the Training Division, and from here in 2015 to the command of the Raid Division 215.

Ali Mohammed Zaza, alias Abu Mohammed (1932–2018), Kurdish background; Sunni. Was classmate of Mustafa Tlass and Ali Aslan at the Military Academy of Homs. Is related by marriage to Mohammed al-Khouli (Al-Khouli's son is Zaza's son-in-law). Was head of Military Intelligence from 1968 to 1971 and is considered one of the closest friends of Hafez al-Assad. Minister of Interior from 1971 to 1976. Played a role in the assassination of Abdelkarim al-Jundi and Ghazi Kanaan.

Mohammed Deeb Zeitoun, alias Abu Raghid (1951–), from the village of al-Jibba in the Qalamoun area of rural Damascus; Sunni. Headed Political Security from 2009 to 2012, after which he was transferred to General Intelligence and remained here until 2019. Known for his ruthlessness and alcoholism.

Nazih Zreir (1941–), from a Bedouin family in the town of Al-Qaryatain in rural Homs; Sunni. He was head of General Intelligence in Homs in 1972, the year Mohammed Omran was assassinated in Tripoli. From 1979 to 1984 he was director of the General Intelligence Service.

Appendix 2: Torture Methods

Back suspension, the Blanco: a torture technique in which a fixed lever often suspended from the ceiling is used. The detainee is handcuffed to the back, then his hands are tied to the lever, lifting his body from their hands.

Burning with cigarette butts or hookah charcoal: a torture technique. Recorded at various periods in the history of Syrian prisons. Used extensively on women, particularly women who have been raped or sexually assaulted. The torturers systemically extinguish their cigarettes in sensitive areas of women's bodies after assaulting them. Burning with flaming hookah charcoal is used similar to the cigarettes on the bodies of detainees, but the flaming charcoal is more painful and harmful.

Burning with hot water: a technique and tool of torture. Hot, boiling water is poured over the body of the detainee, causing burns of different severity. The use of this method has also been recorded frequently on women who have been sexually assaulted.

Burning-ironing: a technique and tool of torture. It involves burning parts or areas of the detainee's body using heated metal bars or melting nylon or plastic to drip onto the detainee's body, leaving scars of varying intensity and impact.

Cold water: a technique and tool of torture. The torturers splash cold water on the body of the detainee after being severely whipped, and place them in a cold area such as an open yard in winter or in a wet and very damp solitary cell for maximum torment.

Crucification: a technique and tool torture. The body of the detainee is fixed to a wooden cross and they are whipped. The use of this method was recorded in Deir Shmeil prison.

Frontal suspension: a torture technique. The detainee's hands are tied to a metal pipe over 2.5 meters metres above the ground, so that the prisoner maintains minimal contact with the ground via the tips of their toes. The commonly used term for this in Arabic is *shabeh*, used to refer to hanging the the body weight of the prisoner on their hands.

Lakhdar Brahimi: a torture tool that spread after 2011. It is a thick plastic green water pipe commonly used in households. Intelligence operatives gave it that name in mockery of the UN envoy to Syria, Algerian diplomat Lakhdar Brahimi.

Mock execution: a torture technique. Used in different periods in Syrian branches and prisons. It is to convince the prisoner that they have been sentenced to death and that the sentence is about to be carried out, or to place the prisoner's head into a noose and swing the chair or table on which they stand, or to convince the prisoners that they are being transferred to the firing field where they will be executed by a firing squad while they are in fact being transferred to another prison.

Nail extraction: a torture technique. A special metal tool is used to extract the nails, to cause as much pain as possible to the detainee and push them to confess. A different method of nail extraction appeared in the history of Syrian prisons, especially after 2011. The method is to violently hit the nail bed with electrical cables causing the nails to fall off or causing blood congestion under the nails thus causing them to fall off over time.

Sexual violence: a torture technique. Used on both men and women, either by direct sexual assault from the torturer himself, or by using tools such as bottles or sticks. This includes other forms of sexualized torture, such as violence directed against reproductive organs or nipples, or threats of rape. The use of these methods was recorded in different periods in the history of Syrian prisons.

Shackles: the traditional metal shackle used by the police to restrain detainees. After 2011, the use of a different type of shackles known as 'the tie' or 'the gatherer' became common. It is a a plastic tie typically used to gather metal rods or electrical cables closer together. They were extensively used by the Syrian intelligence services because of the extremely large numbers of detainees.

Sleep deprivation: a torture technique. It's been recorded in various periods in the history of Syrian prisons. This method is based on preventing the prisoner by all available means from falling asleep, like by placing them in a very cold or flooded solitary cell, or have the guards rotate to ensure the prisoner is prevented from falling asleep. The detainee during this punishment is often forced to remain standing, to make easier to monitor them.

Solitary confinement: the detainee is placed in a tiny cell, sometimes too small to lay down in or stand up in, for a considerable period of time. The lack of human contact and the sensory deprivation have severe negative psychological consequences on the detainee. According to the United Nations, solitary confinement for over fifteen days is considered torture; the regime uses solitary confinement for months, in some cases for years.

Suspension by the feet: a torture technique in which a prisoner is suspended upside down by tying one, or both of their feet to a pipe in the ceiling, a Blanco or directly to the ceiling, leaving the weight of the body on one or both feet.

The bamboo stick: a tool of torture. A wooden stick made from bamboo, widely used by Political Security Division branches to beat detainees.

The blindfold: a blindfold, mostly made of rubber or a piece of cloth. Its function is to shut the prisoner's eyes and prevent them from seeing. These are widely used in all security branches, in military prisons and in Saydnaya after 2011. Long-term use disorients the detainee and reconfigures his senses, as he has to rely more on his hearing. They do not exist in civilian prisons.

The dynamo: a tool and torture technique using a small-sized generator that resembles an old military phone. The torturer quickly turns the axis of the dynamo after connecting its wires to sensitive areas on the detainee's body. With the rotation of the dynamo's axis, the electric current runs through the body of the detainee, causing great pain.

The electric cattle prod: a torture tool. Originally used by peasants to prod cattle, some of its types are used for self- defence or by anti-riot police. It is battery operated, with two electrodes that emit an electric charge that distracts the target person. In prisons and intelligence branches, the electric stick was modified to release a higher electric charge, thus leading to fainting and, in some cases, burning the skin of the tortured detainee.

The German chair: a tool and torture technique using a normal chair. The detainee lays face down on the floor, as the backrest of the chair is placed on the detainee's back and his hands are shackled to the back, wedging the backrest between the detainee's back and the shackled hands. The torturer slowly returns the chair to its normal position. This raises the backrest of the chair, tilting with it the detainee's back backwards gradually. The metal of the chair presses against the bottom of the detainee's back while the chair's feet gradually reach the ground. This method often causes fractures in the spine, which can cause paralysis of the detainee. At best, the detainee is temporarily paralyzed, not to mention the the severe pain caused by this method of torture.

The ladder: a tool and torture technique. It was used in by Military Intelligence during the 1980s. It is a metal ladder with two sides that meet at the top. The detainee is placed between the two sides and the ladder is closed with him inside. The ladder is then laid on the ground and one of the torturers walks over it with all his body weight squeezing the detainee's body. This technique often causes fractures to the bones of the legs, ribs, or other bones of the detainee's body. The use of this technique was recorded again after 2011 in Deir Shmeil prison.

The magic carpet: a tool and torture technique. The prisoner is tied from his four limbs to a wooden board that folds from the middle. The lower part of the prisoner's prisoner's body is lifted up by moving the lower section of the board. The board is fixed in at a right angle while the prisoner is on their back. The jailer can beat the detainee all over their body, especially on the soles of their feet.

The parachute: a torture technique. The detainee is placed on their back, then the torturers, or forced laborers as ordered by the torturers, lift the detainee by the limbs and waist up and down several times, accompanied by counting from one to three where at three they leave them to fall violently to the ground.

The pyramid: a torture technique. The detainee is forced to lay on their stomach and their colleagues are then forced to lay on top of him/her one over the other, centering all the weight on the first prisoner. This method causes fractures in the ribs of the punished prisoner and may lead to their death. This method was used in Palmyra prison.

The wheel: a rubber car tyre, used as a torture tool. There are two ways to use the wheel. The most common one is to tuck the prisoner's legs and head inside the wheel, and then place the prisoner on their back, allowing the torturer to whip them easily. The second method is to push the prisoner's knees inside the wheel and when they appear from the opposite end, the torturer places a metal rod called the 'the biter' (*al-qares*) under the detainee's knees, and then places the detainee on their face. This method was used in Saydnaya prison after 2011.

The whip: is a cable usually used for electrical wiring in buildings, however used in prisons for torture and whipping. It is known as a 'quadruple cable', that is a cable that comprises four thick metal wires wrapped inside a thick plastic casing.

Tying the penis: a torture technique. This prevents the detainee from urinating. The detainee's penis is tied either by using a type of plastic thread, as was used in Military Intelligence in the 1980s, or using a small metal clamp applied to the penis, as is used in Air Force Intelligence since 2011. The penis is released only after the required confession is extracted from the detainee. This technique causes health problems in the kidneys, ureter or penis that can persist throughout the detainee's life.

Appendix 3: Food

Bidon: a water container with a capacity of roughly 20 litres.

Boiled eggs: the eggs come from the poultry farms of the army's Production Department. Similar to potatoes, they are boiled in giant pots and left for a day or two before being distributed. It is prepared by forced labourers in large quantities. Allocations are distributed and the excess amounts are left for the following day and so on. Hard-boiled eggs are served at breakfast with an egg ration per prisoner at best, and at worst the prisoner gets one-fifth of an egg. The egg reaches the prisoner either broken, mashed or rotten due to long and poor storage. Most prisoners in Palmyra and other military prisons ate eggshells after grinding them to compensate for calcium deficiency in their bodies.

Boiled potatoes: the official dinner food in Syrian prisons. It is the classic, well-known boiled potatoes, except the quality of the potatoes used in Syrian prisons is very poor. Potatoes are boiled in enormous quantities in very large pots and are left soaking in water for a long time which makes them mushy, or sometimes they are not boiled enough so they are raw.

Bowl: a large metal or plastic bowl with a capacity of three litres or more. The meal group uses it to take its share of the dormitory food. In high-security branches or secret prisons, the bowl is replaced with one-litre plastic yogurt container used as a bowl by the meal group.

Bulgur: one of the main lunch items in Syrian prisons, especially the military ones. Bulgur is made by cracking wheat after being peeled. Bulgur is nutritious, however when cooked in Syrian prisons it is boiled without any condiments that enhance the taste. It's also often cooked in dirty pots contaminated with diesel or rotting food. The grains used are also of poor quality and filled with gravel and dirt, which makes eating it a daunting task for prisoners. Bulgur remains one of the best foods served as lunch in Syrian prisons compared to other foods.

Giant pot: a large metal pot used to cook food in large quantities.

Halva: halva is a food item that is considered a synonym of Syrian prisons and is always present in prison literature. In folk tales about prison, friends banter each other by saying: 'If you are imprisoned, I will come visit you with a halva box.' Halva is a food substance rich in sugar. It is made from sesame paste and sugar combined with saponaria, a plant from the Caryophyllaceae family used in this industry. All these ingredients are mixed along with some salt and lemon is special machines. The type of halva distributed in Syrian civil and military prisons comes from the halva factory which follows the Production Department of the Ministry of Defence and is considered

Figure A2.1 Halva, from the author's collection.

the worst of all the types produced by the same factory. 'Military Halva', as it is called, differs from others by containing a large amount of sugar and a small amount of tahini. The higher the sugar content, the harder the halva. This decreases the amount of the oily ingredient in it, thus compromising the softness and nutritional value of the halva in favour of refined sugars. This type is devoid any garnish, such as nuts and dried fruit, that is usually added to the other types of halva produced in the same factory.

Jam: a substitute for halva when the latter is not available. Also manufactured in Production Department factories or those contracted with the military. The quality of jam offered in prisons and security branches is of the worst quality in the Syrian market, which is famous for its rich history in manufacturing jams and compotes of all kinds. The types of jam offered in prisons contain much sugar and little fruit, making it cheap to manufacture. Still, it is considered one of the better food items for prisoners when made available.

Labneh: it is dried yogurt that also comes from the Defence Factories or factories contracted with the army. Labneh is considered a good nutritional item if available. However, it is rarely offered in prisons and military and civil detention centres because those in charge of these institutions usually take it for themselves.

Lentil soup: a food item adopted in all Syrian prisons, military and civil. It is the same as the traditional lentil soup but in prison the amount of lentil is very small in favour of large amounts of water. It also does not contain any meat, vegetables, or any flavorings, and is not much more than a thin broth.

Loaf of bread: the main food item in Syrian prisons, and sometimes the only one. The bread used in Syrian security branches and military and civil prisons is what is known

Figure A2.2 Labneh, from the author's collection.

as 'state bread'. This comes from the government-run automatic furnaces after the nationalization of all private automatic furnaces in the country since 1968. Official bread in Syria was made from barley flour mixed with white wheat flour, some water with a little salt and yeast. All army furnaces produce the same bread, even the smaller ones operating in military prisons. These furnaces are generally manufactured and installed by Defense Factories. The bread in Mezze prison was the only exception. The furnace there kept producing *samoon* bread, which resembles a French baguette, until the prison closed. The reasons for this are unknown. Perhaps because the furnace was established during the French occupation of Syria and so kept the same French bread. However, all bread in Syrian prisons is of poor quality with almost zero nutritional value. When consumed for long periods of time it can cause digestive and health problems.

Meal group: a group of prisoners who agree to eat together. Prisoners resort to these groupings due to the difficulty of distributing food individually, either because of its scarcity or because of the lack of necessary tools. These groups are mostly formed by mutual consent or on instructions from the head of the dormitory.

Mini stoves ['babur']: a small cooking stove that uses kerosene to produce heat. It was used in Al-Sheikh Hassan prison and Aleppo Civil Prison before being replaced by a small gas stove. It works by producing heat from burning kerosene through a head using pressure built manually by a process known as 'injecting' with sufficient air doses. The mini-stoves are considered a dangerous and explosive tool, which caused several accidents in Aleppo and Al-Sheikh Hassan prisons.

Figure A2.3 Bread, from the author's collection.

Olives: despite Syria having vast olive groves, the olives served to prisoners are small green olives soaked in water for several days without any additives remove or cure their bitterness. Olives are offered to detainees as breakfast food – sometimes they are the only breakfast item. Prisoners used olive pits to entertain themselves in military prisons, such as Saydnaya before 2011, making small wooden artifacts out of them with the few tools they had.

Red sauce: the food item that often accompanies rice and bulgur, more in the military prisons than civil, and with difference in quality between the two. Sauce in military prisons is water coloured with tomato paste. A large 40-litre pot contains red water with some peas, carrots, chopped eggplant or chopped zucchini. The amount of vegetables in the sauce pot does not exceed one kilogramme. Like other items cooked in large pots, they are often unclean and badly cooked. You may find eggplants with their green tips and carrots uncut and unclean. Often large amounts of dirt and gravel are left in the bottom of those pots as a result.

Rice: a substitute for bulgur when the latter is not available. The rice used is of very poor quality. It is cooked without care, resulting in it either remaining raw, or mashed and clumpy like clay. Like bulgur, no condiments are added to rice; it is often cooked in large, unclean pots. The prison's allocations of rice are half of those of bulgur.

Slicer: is a small and rectangular sardine can lid. The cover undergoes a lot of processing, bending at one end and sharpening at the opposite end to make it usable as a cutting tool. The slicer is an alternative to the officially banned kitchen knife in Syrian prisons.

Small gas stoves: a substitute for the mini stoves. These are gas stoves that are larger than those used for camping and smaller than those for household use. A gas jar is directly connected to a small stove on top of it. Before 2011, gas was used in civil prisons and Saydnaya prison. This stove, similar to the mini-stove, is considered an asset of great value for prisoners, as it gives them the opportunity and ability to warm up prison food and prepare hot drinks and even cook other food if they are available. Gas stoves are considered safer than the mini-stoves. During the mutiny in Saydnaya prison, Islamist prisoners used gas jars as bombs that prevented army forces from breaking into the prison. These stoves were banned after the prison reopened at the beginning of 2010.

The heater: an innovation adopted by prisoners in some military prisons such as Saydnaya or security branches as a way to heat bath water or make tea. The heater is two sardine box covers which, after cleaning, are packed close to each other while maintaining an isolation distance using some plastic pieces at the four corners. Each piece of metal is connected by a wire; the two wires are connected to an electrical source, often a toilet bulb. The temperature of the water in which the heater is dipped subsequently rises.

The invoice/mini market: the invoice is a term relevant to military prisons, especially Tadmor, Mezze and Saydnaya, before 2011, as well as civil prisons such as Al-Sheikh Hassan and the Citadel. An invoice is a grocery list of food and household items that prisoners request from the Prison Administration every week, two weeks or per month depending on the prison. These materials are purchased from the local market; however, prisoners pay up to five or six times more for them. The mini market is

Figure A2.4 Gas heater, from the author's collection.

specific to civil prisons, especially Damascus central prison. It is a shop inside the prison that sells some supplies and sometimes food items. It is managed by one or more prisoners in agreement with the Prisoners' Welfare Committee and the prison administration. A mini market was allowed in Palmyra prison for a very short time and was limited to selling few food items. Saydnaya prison had a mini market in the exercise yard, after 2005 and before the mutiny. It was run by a Military Police officer but was closed permanently at the beginning of 2008.

Yogurt: a food item served as a substitute for sauce, or with potatoes for dinner, or with olives for breakfast. Yogurt is made in the Defense Factories or in factories contracted to the army. Yogurt is often better than other food items because it is pre-packed which ensures it is slightly cleaner. Prisoners receive at most a tablespoon, sometimes considerably less.

Figure A2.5 Yoghurt, from the author's collection.

Appendix 4: Diseases and Medicine

Diseases

Body lice: a permanent companion of scabies. Similar to scabies, lice had a widespread and permanent presence in both civil and military prisons, especially in the security branches. Body lice are small parasites, the size of a sesame seed or smaller, which live in the folds of clothing, especially the underwear, and move between them and the skin of the detainee several times a day to feed by sucking their blood. The most targeted places of the body are those in close contact with the clothing such as shoulders, armpits, waist, and genitals. Lice spreads fast among detainees. It is enough for one infected detainee to enter the prison without being examined and treated for lice, to quickly spread the infection to their colleagues. Detainees carry periodic inspection sessions of their clothes to kill lice and limit its spread. Prison administrations very rarely carry out sterilization measures using kerosene.

Cholera: it is hard to believe that this disease spread in Palmyra prison during the 1980s, since it is considered a pre-modern disease that is almost extinct. This disease is caused by an infection of the small intestine caused by certain harmful bacteria. Its direct symptoms are severe diarrhea with a rapid loss of body fluids and salts. As the condition worsens, it may cause death.

Diarrhoea: one of the major health problems recorded in intelligence branches and military prisons, especially after 2011. Symptoms begin with abdominal pain followed by loose or watery stool. Other symptoms are nausea, vomiting and a pressing need to defecate. Diarrhoea is known to be caused by viral or bacterial infections. Branch or prison administrations did not provide any medicines in individual cases. If there was a mass outbreak, the prison administration increased food portions and distributed tea with boiled potatoes in larger quantities than usual.

Dysentery: an advanced stage of diarrhoea. Cases of the disease have been recorded at different periods, especially since 2011, where mass outbreaks of the disease or its symptoms have been documented in Saydnaya prison and in the security branches. Dysentery is an inflammation disorder of the intestine, especially in the colon, leading to severe diarrhoea containing blood and mucus in the stool. Diarrhoea is accompanied by a fever and abdominal pain. It is often caused by a local infection from invasive germs or the toxic substances that they secrete. The infection is transmitted orally by consuming contaminated food or water.

Fractures: indiscriminate torture and the use of hard tools to beat detainees, especially at the 'reception parties' often causes multiple fractures. These fractures often occur in the limbs, ribs and fingers. They rarely happen to the back, pelvis, thigh, or neck. Most are treated in primitive ways, such as trying to stabilize the fracture using bandages which detainees use to help their fellows. These primitive treatment measures, and the absence of health care, leave visible scars and sometimes some kind of motor disability.

Herpes/boils: the spread of this disease has been recorded widely in various intelligence branches, especially after 2011. Boils are a cutaneous or subcutaneous injury caused by staphylococcal bacteria. These bacteria enter the body through small cracks or wounds in the skin or through the pores. Other skin diseases, such as scabies or lice, increase the likelihood of infection.

Scabies: The most common disease in Syrian prisons. Infections among Syrian detainees have been recorded from 1970 until 2020. Scabies is an inflammation of the skin accompanied by severe itching caused by parasites called the human itch mite. It is an infectious disease, transmitted by direct contact between people. Mostly considered a disease of times of war, where living standards drop, bathing and hygiene become difficult, and people are crowded into barracks, cellars, or shelters. However, scabies became the flagship disease of Syrian prisons. High numbers were recorded both in terms of infections and scale of spread in Palmyra prison and the Military and Air Force Intelligence branches after 2000. After 2011 the same became applicable to Syrian intelligence branches and military prisons. Many detainees believe that scabies caused the death of many of their colleagues, because it reached the bloodstream, which inflicted a slow death. The only method adopted in the fight against this disease by Syrian prison administrations is benzyl benzoate.

Sepsis: due to extreme violence and the use of hard instruments of torture, the skin of the detainee cracks and is cut. These wounds do not receive any medical care or disinfection. Often, the torturer continues to beat the detainee on their wounds, exacerbating their state. Negligence and lack of hygiene cause skin infections around the wound and sometimes deep in the layers under the wound. These infections cause pus and other fluids to ooze from the wound. The skin around the wound thickens and turns into a crust that thickens over time. If a prisoner is electrocuted, or continues to be flogged over their wounded skin, these inflamed wounds may burst, causing a deeper rupture of muscle tissue and sometimes a large, wide cavity in the back or chest. These inflamed wounds cause swelling of the lymph glands and high fever that can reach a state of delirium. These wounds may kill, especially if their condition deteriorates due to deliberate neglect and lack of medical care and hygiene.

'Switching off': psychological trauma suffered by detainees as a result of a combination of conditions of living in the prison, food and sleep deprivation, constant torture and overcrowding. It is a strong form of dissociation: the detainee enters a psychological state akin to cerebral tremor, where the brain 'shuts down' and stops working. It resembles the figure of the 'Muselmann', those prisoners of Nazi concentration camps who entered a state of apathetic listlessness regarding their own fate, and unresponsiveness to their surroundings owing to their severely violent treatment. Cases observed in Syrian prisons, particularly after 2011, are those in which the detainee is awake yet detached from the reality of their prison life. The prisoner travels in their imagination to a parallel or distant world, such as returning home or going to the market. During this short period of time, which does not exceed an hour, the detainee acts as if they were in that place, outside the prison. Some cases of switching off manifested in violence that the detainee inflicted on those around them or by violently knocking on the door of the dormitory or the solitary cell, demanding to be taken out of there to answer the call of their father or mother or to go to the market with their children or spouse. It is one of the forms of trauma that manifests itself *during* imprisonment; after release, several other post-traumatic stress disorders emerge.

Tuberculosis: the spread of tuberculosis was recorded in Palmyra prison for many years and in Saydnaya prison after 2011. It is an infectious disease caused by *tuberculosis bacillus*. Those bacilli spread slowly and widely in the lungs, causing large cheese-like tubercles or lumps that break down the respiratory tissues and form cavities in the lungs. As the patient's condition progresses it causes a bloody cough of bright red colour. In Palmyra prison the disease was recorded in the blood and bones of detainees leading to their death from medical negligence. The doctors among the prisoners worked to implement a treatment plan in agreement with the prison administration, which provided the medicine for fear that the disease would spread to its operatives. The plan was divided into two stages, the first being isolating the infected, the second was providing the right medicine. Some survivors from Saydnaya spoke of the arrival of medical teams who isolated the sick by moving them from the main building, the red one, to the white building. No one has any confirmed information about the state of patients in Saydnaya today.

Medicines

Benzyl benzoate: the only treatment provided by Syrian prison administrations to treat scabies in detainees. It is a liquid produced by condensation of benzoic acid and benzyl alcohol. The most common use of it is as an insecticide and antiparasitic in veterinary medicine. It is also used to treat scabies and lice in humans.

Kerosene: an oil derivative used by Syrian prison administrations to sterilize cells, blankets, and sometimes detainees from lice. Kerosene is a flammable hydrocarbon liquid and has a distinct smell. It is commonly used in the jet engines of aircrafts and some less pure types are used in baking ovens and also as heating fuel.

Paracetamol: the most common white pill in Syrian prison pharmacies. The health officer, in the security branches and military prisons, hands these to all detainees who come to him asking for treatment, that is if they manage to reach him. Paracetamol is an analgesic and antipyretic, generally used to treat fever, headaches and mild aches.

Military soap: the only soap provided by Syrian military prison administrations and various intelligence branches. Military soap is produced by the Ministry of Defense factories and is considered one of the worst types of soap produced from olive oil leftovers and Laurel.

Salt: detainees in various military prisons with tight security resorted to the use of salt, if available, most notably to provide a sterile environment around wounds, and as a substitute for toothpaste. Apart from its obvious use in food, the military prison with tight security and various security branches strive to deprive their detainees of salt.

Appendix 5: Prison Lexicon

Blanket: a poorly made wool blanket intended for soldiers in the Syrian army, used also for prisoners in military prisons. Blankets are often dirty to varying degrees, old and worn out.

'Breathing' (literally from the Arabic original *tanaffus*): a period in which prisoners leave their dormitories to the prison or wing's yard to 'breathe', i.e. take in fresh air, walk and exercise. In Palmyra prison, 'breathing' was a torture trip to the yard where the dormitory was located. In civil prisons there is a dedicated 'breathing' yard for each wing. In Mezze prison, 'breathing' was daily, as was the case in Saydnaya before 2011.

Croak (Arabic: *fatas*): the word used by guards and wardens to describe a death. It is a highly impolite way of describing a death, normally reserved for the death of an animal.

Eternally punished: is someone identified to be subjected for permanent torture, which meant they had to go out for torture on a daily basis at the time of the torture of the marked. This naming prevailed in Palmyra prison in the 1980s and in Saydnaya after 2011.

Forced labourers/municipal workers: mandatory service soldiers serving their judicial sentence in prison. They are tasked with cleaning, distributing food, co-transporting bodies, or sometimes torturing political detainees. After 2011, the term 'forced labourer' also applied to political detainees who were forced to perform these, except for torture.

Head/Emir of the dormitory (Arabic: *shawish*): a prisoner elected by the inmates of the dormitory or appointed by the prison administration to manage the affairs of the dormitory and its inmates. The head of the dormitory serves as a liaison officer between prisoners and the prison administration.

Judas window: can mean different things according to the prison. In the security branches, it means the metal window that closes with a small lid, carved in door of the dormitory or solitary cell, as in Saydnaya prison. In Palmyra prison, it was also the window in the roof of the dormitory covered in a mesh and used by the police to monitor prisoners inside the dormitory.

Marked: identifying a prisoner in preparation for their torture. Marking a prisoner is made by a decision from the warden or the guard on duty on the top of the dormitory who always monitors the prisoners in Palmyra. However, in Saydnaya after 2011, the term 'marked' denoted a prisoner who was caught in any violation during the wardens' surprise raids on the dormitories.

Military Police inspection: on the day the detainee arrives at the branch or any military prison, they are completely stripped of their clothes and then ordered to take a squat position two or three times, to ensure they are not hiding anything in their private parts. This method is known as the 'Military Police inspection' or 'security movements' (*harekaat amniya*).

Night guard: a prisoner, or a group of prisoners who must stay awake all night in two-hour shifts. The duty of the night guard during their shift is to take care of the affairs of the dormitory and answer the call of the police who monitor everything through the roof windows. The expression is specific to Palmyra prison.

On your side [Arabic: *sayyef*]: an order issued by the wardens in the branches of intelligence and military prisons, especially in Palmyra and Mezze, to force prisoners to go to sleep. The way to sleep is by lying on the side one next to the other. Prisoners sleep on their sides next to each other in alternation of head and feet, to make as much room as possible.

Personal belongings: these are the personal items of the detainee. They are confiscated when they are arrested, and comprise money, documents, and items of personal value such as rings, phone, necklaces and watches.

Prison inhabitation: the process of adapting to the prison and everything in it. That is, when the prisoner settles in their prison as if it were their home. The term in Arabic is derived from the term 'incarcerated', which means a person who feels trapped. The modified term, however, refers to someone who starts to feel indifferent about their surroundings.

Reception party: the first round of torture to which the detainee is subjected upon arrival at the prison or branch, and it is often very violent. The function of this rite of passage is to create a psychological alienation between the detainee and the prison with all its human components. The 'party' prevents the prisoner from communicating with their surroundings. It also plays a big role in the degrading the prisoner in front of the warden from day one. It diminishes any prospect of a human relationship between them.

Roll call: changes according to the prison, but generally it is the counting of prisoners in dormitories and wings. In some prisons, such as civil ones, dormitories are closed after the prisoners' roll call in the evening. In Palmyra, the dormitories were always closed, so the prisoners were taken out to be counted and then returned back. In Saydnaya prison before 2011, the roll call took place during the day, after the distribution of lunch, and was not followed by the closing of the doors. After 2011 the situation in Saydnaya became similar to that of Palmyra's during the 1980s but the roll call took place inside the dormitories instead.

Sacrifiers: an expression to denote the volunteers among prisoners who go out in place of their fellow punished inmates, particularly the elderly and sick. The term came originally from Palmyra, then used for the same purpose in the 555 Regiment's prison in the Fourth Division after 2011.

Solitary: a single cell. In Arabic it is referred to as '*salloul*', which is an expression derived from the French term (*la cellule*). Solitaries are often used to isolate punished prisoners in central military or civil prisons, particularly in the Mezze prison from which the term originated.

The black door: a wing in Saydnaya prison – wing B-right, third floor, in which prisoners who have been punished or newly arrived are isolated from the rest of the prisoners. That was in the years prior to 2010.

The line: going to the toilet. It is the wardens' call to the inmates of the solitaries or dormitories of the General Intelligence or those of the solitaries of civil prisons to visit the toilet. The prisoners form a line in front of the toilet door, hence the expression.

Train: an expression used to describe the sleeping position of prisoners in times of high congestion. Prisoners sleep by overlapping, where they lean their back on the abdomen of a colleague, sitting between their legs, while having someone place their back on their abdomen and so on, thus forming a chain similar to connected train cars; they fall asleep sitting. The term was also used in Saydnaya prison after 2011, to refer to the way prisoners were transferred between wings or from solitaries to dormitories. Each prisoner holds the waist or clothes of the colleague in front of them while kneeling and move together as directed by the warden with their eyes closed. The same method had been previously used in Palmyra prison to go to the prison baths but under the name 'the rectangle train'.

Treading place: the prisoner's mattress or sleeping place. This place has great importance in the life of the prisoner. The prisoner's treading place expresses their personality and the geography of their life in the dormitory. It becomes their residence, a place to which they invite their colleagues in the dormitory during the day to drink tea or talk.

Turbine: a large electric aspirator that helps ventilate dormitories and detention cellars in security branches or prisons whose dormitories are located underground. Torturers often turn off the turbine to punish prisoners. This can cause death as a result of suffocation.

Notes

Introduction

1 Roy Walmsley, *World Prison Population List* (London: Institute for Criminal Policy Research, 2015), p. 2, updated for 2023.

2 This figure is based on a combination of published statistics by various Syrian human rights organizations and informed extrapolation. It includes people who were in detention also for a very short period. The highest number given for this period is by the Syrian Network for Human Rights (1.2 million), but it is not explained exactly how this figure is reached. *Ninth Annual Report on Torture in Syria on the International Day in Support of Victims of Torture* (London: Syrian Network for Human Rights, 2020), p. 9.

3 Salwa Ismail quotes memoirs to place this ratio at approximately one in every thousand Syrian citizens: 14,000 prisoners out of 10 million Syrians in 1984. Salwa Ismail, *The Rule of Violence: Subjectivity, Memory and Government in Syria* (Cambridge: Cambridge University Press, 2018), p. 38.

4 *Gone Without a Trace: Syria's Detained, Abducted, and Forcibly Disappeared* (New York: International Center for Transitional Justice, May 2020), p. 1.

5 Ephraim Kahana & Muhammad Suwaed (eds), *The A to Z of Middle Eastern Intelligence* (Toronto: Scarecrow Press, 2009), p. 295.

6 One early report was crystal clear about imprisonment: *Syria: Torture by the Security Forces* (London: Amnesty International, 1987), p. 1: 'Political prisoners are systematically tortured and ill-treated by Syrian security forces. The victims range from students to lawyers to housewives to soldiers. Anyone who opposes the government is at risk... Torture is facilitated by the extensive powers of arbitrary arrest and detention conferred on the security forces by a state of emergency which has been in force in Syria since 1963... These powers have been grossly abused, resulting in thousands of arbitrary arrests. The security forces have arrested people at will, without warrants, without any explanation of why they are being arrested and without reference to any central authority and held them incommunicado for long periods, in some cases for years.'

7 There is a rich scholarship on the Assad regime, both as case study and in comparative perspective. For a thorough bibliography on modern and contemporary Syria, as well as the conflict, see the one compiled by Judith Tinnes at: www.terrorismanalysts.com/pt/index.php/pot/article/view/431/html.

8 See the whole series at: www.youtube.com/playlist?list=PLeMwite1QcQ3JIAdAEsJ_8ySjbjf0weai.

9 Listen to the whole series at: https://branch-251.captivate.fm/.

10 Jaber Baker, as a former six-year-long detainee of Saydnaya, is not only co-author of this book but, as a survivor, also relied on his own memory at times.

11 Daniela Blei, 'We Can't Save Syrians Anymore, But We Can Save the Truth', *Foreign Policy*, 27 December 2018. Available at: https://foreignpolicy.com/2018/12/27/ugur-umit-ungor-syria-oral-history-project/.

12 All photos are available to view at: https://safmcd.org./

13 For an in-depth discussion of the Caesar files, see: Garance Le Caisne, *Operation Caesar: At the Heart of the Syrian Death Machine* (Cambridge: Polity, 2018).

14 *Archief P.B.Ph.M. Bogaers*, Collection ID ARCH02460. Available at: https://hdl.handle.net/10622/ARCH02460.

15 Sune Haugbolle, 'Imprisonment, Truth Telling and Historical Memory in Syria' in: *Mediterranean Politics*, vol. 13, no. 2 (2008), pp. 261–76.

16 Shareah Taleghani, *Readings in Syrian Prison Literature: The Poetics of Human Rights* (Syracuse, NY: Syracuse University Press, 2021).

17 Mansour Omari, 'On the Trauma of Advocacy', *Amnesty International UK blog*, 23 April 2021. Available at: www.amnesty.org.uk/AdvocacyTrauma.

18 One of the first major reports on torture in Syrian prisons alluded to the Soviet Gulag in its title: *Torture Archipelago: Arbitrary Arrests, Torture, and Enforced Disappearances in Syria's Underground Prisons since March 2011* (New York: Human Rights Watch, 2012). Beyond analogy, considering that the KGB trained the Mukhabarat in the 1970s and 1980s, there are very direct transfers of knowledge and practice between the Soviet Union and Baathist Syria. Gerd Linde, *Die sowjetisch-syrischen Beziehungen im regionalen Umfeld* (Bonn: Bundesinstitut für Ostwissenschaftliche und Internationale Studien, 1982), pp. 3–8.

19 Aleksandr Solzhenitsyn, *The Gulag Archipelago* (London: Random House, 2018). His notion of 'prison industry' applies well to Syria and, much like Solzhenitsyn, as long as the archives are not opened for research, we cannot confirm statistics, precise names, and precise dates. Some stories that former detainees have told us are impossible to verify, and some information we present is by nature partial.

20 Anatoly Marchenko, *My Testimony* (London: Sceptre, 1989), p. 23.

21 Varlam Shalamov, *A New Book: Memoirs, Notebooks, Correspondence, Police Dossiers* (Moscow: Eksmo, 2004), pp. 263–8.

22 Hannah Arendt, 'Social Science Techniques and the Study of Concentration Camps', in: *Jewish Social Studies* vol.12, no.1 (1950), pp. 49–64.

23 Michel Foucault, 'Les intellectuels et le pouvoir', in: *L'arc*, no. 49 (1972), pp. 3–10.

24 Ismail, *The Rule of Violence*, pp. 38–9.

25 Yassin al-Haj Saleh, 'The Greater Jail: The Politics of Prison in Syria', in: *Al-Jumhuriya*, 19 February 2021. Available at: www.aljumhuriya.net/en/content/greater-jail-politics-prison-syria (accessed 18 March 2021).

26 Wolfgang Sofsky, *The Order of Terror: The Concentration Camp* (Princeton, NJ: Princeton University Press, 1997), pp. 9, 17.

27 Ibid., pp. 231–4.

Part One The Intelligence Agencies

1   Bashir Zein al-Abidin, *Al-Jaish wa al-Siyasa fi Suriya (1918–2000).*

2   Patrick Seale, *Asad. The Struggle for the Middle East* (Berkeley, California: University of California Press, 1989).

3   Maen Tallaa, *The Syrian Security Services and the Need for Structural and Functional Change* (Istanbul: Omran Center for Strategic Studies, 2016, pp. 160–1).

4   Seale, *Asad*, p .282.

5 The Syrian Human Rights Committee, *The Massacre of Hama* (1982). *The Law Demands Accountability* (2003).
6 Group interview with several security experts.
7 Maen Tallaa, interview.
8 Ibid.
9 Tallaa, *The Syrian Security Services*, pp. 6–7.
10 Maen Tallaa, interview.
11 Tallaa, *The Syrian Security Services*, p.2.
12 Syrian Expert House and SCPSS, *Syria Transition Roadmap*, p.137.

1 The Military Intelligence

1 Faraj Bayraqdar, interview.
2 International Institute of Social History, Bogaers archive, file # 436, M.A.K., 94-1186-II-11, life story, 4 July July 18, August 10, 1994.
3 Abu Ibrahim, interview.
4 Ibid.
5 Ibid.
6 Ibid.
7 A jail located in the Khaled bin al-Walid barracks, and a transfer station of military judiciary prisoners to be transferred to Tadmor military prison. The Baloni at the time had five rooms and about ten solitary cells.
8 Bara'a al-Sarraj, *Min Tadmor ila Harvard* (Chicago: CreateSpace, 2016), pp. 8–10.
9 Mohammed Nader Diab, interview.
10 Abu Ibrahim, interview.
11 Mohammed Nader Diab, interview.
12 Omar Ahmed Hozayfeh, *Behind the Walls of Tadmor* (unpublished manuscript).
13 Baraa al-Sarraj, interview.
14 Interviewer met Hilal in *Al-Quds al-Arabi*, 13 juli 2001.
15 Ibid.
16 International Institute of Social History, Bogaers archive, file # 285, A.B., 95-1268-I-21, Fremdenpolizei Zürich interview with M.T., July 9, 1993.
17 Adnan Misbah al-Miqdad, interview.
18 Ibid.
19 Ibid.
20 Sulaiman Abu al-Khair, *The Road to Tadmor. The Desert Cave.*
21 Adnan Misbah al-Miqdad, interview.
22 Abu al-Khair, *The Road to Tadmor.*
23 This testimony is based on a long television interview on al-Hiwar TV and a personal interview with Mahmoud Ashour, a former detainee in Tadmor prison for over twenty years.
24 Haisam Shamlouni, interview.
25 Ibid.
26 Ibid.
27 Pierre Adam Yohanna, interview.
28 Hozayfeh, *Behind the Walls of Tadmor.*
29 Suleiman Abu Al-Khair, interview.

30 Muhammad Issam al-Dimashqi, interview.
31 Lina Wafai, interview. For a long interview with her as part of the documentary series 'Oh Freedom' (*Ya Hurriya*), see: www.youtube.com/watch?v=F_3cr_aPSTY&ab_chann el=SyriaTV%D8%AA%D9%84%D9%81%D8%B2%D9%8A%D9%88%D9%86%D8% B3%D9%88%D8%B1%D9%8A%D8%A7
32 International Institute of Social History, Bogaers archive, file # 372, O.A.D., 97-1476-I-4, life story, 2 April 1997.
33 Ali Abu al-Dihn, interview.
34 Ibid.
35 International Institute of Social History, Bogaers archive, file # 284, A.A.S., 92-878-I-45, life story, 10 June 1992.
36 International Institute of Social History, Bogaers archive, file # 335, S.A., 95-1378-I-22, life story, 9 January 1996.
37 Jaber Baker was arrested and detained in Palestine Branch from 22 March 2002 until the end of May 2002 before being transferred to the Military Investigation Branch. Baker returned to the Palestine Branch in 2004 after his release journey.
38 Abu Eyad, interview.
39 This movement takes place after stripping the detainee, when he is asked to go down in a squatting position and stand up for several times, to find out if he has hidden something in his rear.
40 Ibrahim al-Olabi, interview.
41 Abu Khaled, interview.
42 It was possible that there was a camera inside recording audio and video, controlled by the prison administration or the interrogator.
43 *Torture Archipelago: Arbitrary Arrests, Torture, and Enforced Disappearances in Syria's Underground Prisons since March 2011* (New York: Human Rights Watch, 3 July 2012), p. 2.
44 An armed Islamist faction opposed to the Assad regime, based in the Eastern Ghouta region in Damascus countryside.
45 Aida al-Haj Yusuf, interview.
46 Ibid.
47 Ali Hamidi, interview. Ali is a young man who changed his gender from female to male after being released from prison.
48 Abu Abdurrahman, interview.
49 Human Rights Watch, *Torture Archipelago*. The interviews on which this report was based were conducted in the fall of 2011.
50 Mutayyam al-Taweel, interview.
51 International Institute of Social History, Bogaers archive, file # 623, X.A., 98-299-II-10/11, life story, 22 February 1999.
52 International Institute of Social History, Bogaers archive, file #123, T.D., 92-957-I-6, 28 September 1992.
53 Ranim Maatouq, interview.
54 Hozayfeh, *Behind the Walls of Tadmor*.
55 Tallaa, *The Syrian Security Services*.
56 Tallaa, *The Syrian Security Services*.
57 The Syrian Network for Human Rights, *The Syrian Holocaust, Branch 215* (2014).
58 Rafif, interview.
59 Ala'a, interview.
60 Human Rights Watch, *Torture Archipelago*.

61 Bassel Mohammed Sounaib, *Spy for nobody*. The author worked in the Military
   Intelligence division for over twenty years before he was arrested by Military
   Intelligence Branch in Homs in May 2012.
62 Ibrahim al-Hariri, interview.
63 Human Rights Watch, *Torture Archipelago*.

2 The Air Force Intelligence

1 Ma'an Tallaa, *The Syrian Security Services and the Need for Structural and Functional
   Change* (Istanbul: Omran Center for Strategic Studies, 2016), p. 14.
2 Patrick Seale, *Asad: The Struggle for the Middle East* (Berkeley, Californië: University of
   California Press, 1989), p. 268.
3 Zein al-Abidin, *Al-Jaish wa al-Siyasa fi Suriya* (London: Al-Jabiya, 2008), pp. 491–2.
4 Garance Le Caisne, *Operation Caesar: At the Heart of the Syrian Death Machine* (New
   York: John Wiley & Sons, 2018).
5 Faraj Bayraqdar, interview.
6 Mohammed Adel Faris, *Because They Said No: A Prison Memoir*.
7 A. Kh., interview.
8 Omar al-Sayyed Youssef, interview.
9 A. Kh., interview.
10 International Institute of Social History, Bogaers archive, file #123, T.D., 92-957-I-16,
    life story interview, 4 November 1992.
11 A. Kh., interview.
12 Omar al-Sayyed Youssef, interview.
13 M. H., interview.
14 Homam al-Youssef, interview.
15 M. H., interview.
16 Omar al-Sayyed Youssef, interview.
17 Homam al-Youssef, interview.
18 A. Kh., interview.
19 Omar al-Sayyed Youssef, interview.
20 A. Kh., interview.
21 Homam al-Youssef, interview.
22 A. Kh., interview.
23 Anonymous, interview.
24 H. S., interview.
25 Ibid.
26 Ibid.
27 Ibid.
28 Ibid.
29 Akram al-Saud, interview.
30 Ibid.
31 Thamer al-Jahmani, interview.
32 Ibid.
33 Muhannad al-Ghobash, interview.
34 Ibid.
35 Ibid.

36 Mohammed Khalil Bostaji, interview.
37 Ibid.
38 S. A., interview.
39 M. H., interview.
40 Ibid.
41 Mohammad Abu Hajar, interview.
42 Abu Zeid, interview.
43 Akram al-Saud, interview.
44 Sarah Abdullah, interview.
45 Ibid.
46 International Institute of Social History, Bogaers archive, file # 463, R.A.S., 92-915-I-48, life story, 30 June 1992, pp. 17–20.
47 International Institute of Social History, Bogaers archive, file # 463, R.A.S., 92-915-I-21, plea notes B.G. Schonebeek, 26 May 1992, p. 1.
48 International Institute of Social History, Bogaers archive, file # 463, R.A.S., 92-915-I-12.
49 Ahmed Hamada, interview. See also the report of the Violations Documentation Center Syria [VDC], 'Escaping Hell'. Available at: www.vdc-sy.info/index.php/en/reports/1379156802#.YK3lv6gzZPY.
50 VDC, *Escaping Hell.*
51 Ahmed Hamada, interview.
52 Ibid.
53 M. Sh., interview.
54 M. Sh., Ahmed Hamada, interviews.
55 Ahmed Hamada, interview.
56 Ibid.
57 Ibid.
58 Ibid.
59 Imad Abu Ras, interview.
60 *Ibid.*
61 Muhannad al-Ghobash, interview.
62 Abu Zeid, interview.
63 *Ibid.*
64 Mohammed Khalil Bostaji, interview.
65 Y. B., interview.

3 The State Security or General Intelligence

1 Former director of Branch 251 prison (anonymous), interview. Tallaa, *The Syrian Security Services*, p. 10.
2 The Syrian Human Rights Committee, *Law on the Establishment of the State Security Administration and Law on Internal Regulations of the State Security Administration* (2004). Available at: www.shrc.org/?p=7451.
3 Tallaa, *The Syrian Security Services.*
4 See the podcast *Branch 251*. Available at: https://branch-251.captivate.fm/
5 Anwar Raslan and Eyad al-Gharib's court cases in the German city of Koblenz brought this branch into the limelight. Raslan and al-Gharib had worked in Branch 251 before they defected in 2012 and fled to Germany.
6 Tallaa, *The Syrian Security Services*, pp.10, 11, 12.

7 Ahmed Matouq, interview.
8 Said Hawwa, *This is my Testimony: This is my experience.*
9 Seale, *Asad*, pp. 524–5.
10 Mohammed Adel Faris, *Because They Said No. Prison Diary.*
11 Ibid.
12 Ibid.
13 Ibid.
14 Salim Abdelkader Zanjir was arrested in 1979 and escaped in May 1980. See his book *End of Line, End of Investigation.*
15 Faris, *Because They Said No.*
16 Mohammed Berro, interview.
17 Ibid.
18 Ibid.
19 Mohammed Berro, *Syrians in Captivity.*
20 International Institute of Social History, Bogaers archive, file # 386, A.M., 92-927-I-23, life story, 18 August 1992.
21 T. T., interview.
22 Yaqoub Bahi, interview.
23 Faris, *Because They Said No.*
24 Ibid.
25 Ibid.
26 Ibid..
27 Ibid.
28 Mufeed Najm, interview. See also his book: *Wings in a Cell.*
29 Ibid.
30 Ibid.
31 Salim Abdelkader Zanjir escaped in May 1980. See his book *What you Don't See.*
32 Heba al-Dabbagh, *Just Five Minutes . . . Nine Years in the Prisons of Syria* (Toronto: Bayan Khatib, 2007).
33 Ibid.
34 Ibid.
35 Former director of the prison of Branch 251, interview.
36 Ibid.
37 Üngör's observations in the case of Anwar Raslan and Eyad al-Gharib, Oberlandesgericht Koblenz, 31 July 2020.
38 A term for military prisons, especially Palmyra, Mezze, and Saydnaya before 2011, as well as civilian prisons such as Sheikh Hassan and Al-Qalaa. The 'bill' is a list of food, supplies and household items that prisoners require from the prison administration every week, two weeks or month, depending on the prison, its administration and its system. These materials come from the local market, but prisoners pay a price that may be five or six times as much.
39 Mohammed Naim Aintabli, interview.
40 Mufeed Najm, interview. See also his book: *Wings in a Cell.*
41 Mahmoud Hilal, interview.
42 Ibid.
43 Yahya Hakoum, interview.
44 Ibid.
45 M. H., interview.
46 Ibid.

47 Colonel Anwar Raslan's statements at the Koblenz court confirm the information. Within a month, the branch had arrested more than 17,000 people.
48 Sumaya al-Olabi en Luna Watfeh, interviews.
49 International Institute of Social History, Bogaers archive, file # 585, L.X., 98-1534-I-50, life story, 24 September 1998.
50 Sumaya al-Olabi, interviews.
51 Mahmoud Hilal, interview.
52 Yahya Hakoum, interview. Based on his testimony, they were in the detention centre under the administration, so they were being taken a long way to be investigated in Branch 285.
53 Ibid.
54 Violations Documentation Centre in Syria, Branch 285.
55 Syrian Network for Human Rights, *Sexual Abuse: 'A Scar of a Lifetime', Rape in Syrian Security Branches: Seven Raped Women in Hama Security Branch* (2015).
56 Human Rights Watch, *Torture Archipelago*.

4 The Political Security Division

1 Sasha al-Alou, *Ministry of Interior in Syria: Reality and reform necessities* (Istanbul: Omran Center, 2019).
2 Brigadier Nabil al-Dandal, televised interview on Orient News. Available at: www.youtube.com/watch?v=rFbItXVNhcc.
3 Tallaa, *The Syrian Security Services*, pp. 16–17.
4 Seale, *Asad*, p. 177.
5 Mahmoud Ashour, personal and televised interview (al-Hiwar TV).
6 Ibid.
7 Osama al-Askari, interview.
8 Ibid.
9 Ibid.
10 Bakr Sidki, interview.
11 Jalal Noufal, interview.
12 Ibid.
13 Rateb Shabo, *What is behind these walls*.
14 Ibid.
15 Mahmoud Issa, interview and his memoirs *The Rain of Absence*.
16 Duha al-Askari Ashour, interview.
17 Ibid.
18 Munir al-Hariri, televised interview: "The Memory of the Syrian Intelligence", *Orient TV*. Available at: www.youtube.com/watch?v=X1ZU6Rmua-4.
19 Duha al-Askari Ashour, interview.
20 Ahmed Maatouq, interview.
21 Ibid.
22 International Institute of Social History, Bogaers archive, file # 411, M.S.I., 91-707-I-42, life story, 5 July, 9 July, 2 September 1991.
23 Mohyideen Kanaan, interview.
24 Ibrahim al-Olabi, interview.
25 Ayat Ahmed, interview.

26 Ibid.
27 Ibrahim al-Olabi, interview.
28 Munir al-Hariri, interview.
29 Osama al-Askari Ashour, interview.
30 A. B., interview.
31 Human Rights Watch, *Torture Archipelago*, p. 2.
32 Ghaith Faris, interview.
33 Abu Hajar – Mazzaj, 'Zahaqna' (24 March 2018). Available at: www.youtube.com/watch?v=1cGEx9q_ZCU.

5 The Military Police

1   Said Hawwa, *Hadha Shahadati, Hadha Tajrubti* (Cairo: Wehbe, 1989).
2   Ahmed Hamada, interview.
3   Ibid.
4   The Syrian Network for Human Rights, *Analytical Study about the Leaked Pictures of Torture Victims in Syrian Military Hospitals: 'The Photographed Holocaust'* (2015).
5   This model is built on the composite testimonies collected for this research, in addition to various human rights reports.
6   Le Caisne, *Operation Caesar*.
7   Ibid.
8   Syrian Association for Missing and Conscience Detainees, 'The Devil You Don't Know. The Dossier of the Torture of Detainees in Syria, Detailed Report between 2013 and 2016' (2016).
9   Ibid.
10 Le Caisne, *Operation Caesar*.
11 Syrian Association for Missing, 'The Devil You Don't Know'.
12 M. Sh., interview.

Poem in Morse Code

1   Interview with the Syrian poet and former detainee Faraj Bayraqdar (1951).

6 Mezze Military Prison

1   Suad Jarrous, *Zoqaqiat Dimashqiya* (Beirut: Riad al-Rayyes, 2011).
2   Ibid.
3   'Sijin Mezze', *An-Nahar*, 11 januari 2000.
4   Jarrous, *Zoqaqiat Dimashqiya*.
5   Ibid.
6   Patrick Seale, *Asad. The Struggle for the Middle East* (Berkeley, California: University of California Press, 1989).
7   Saïd Aburish, *Arafat: From Defender to Dictator* (London: Bloomsbury, 1999), 63.
8   Ezekiel Hameiri, שבויי סוריה סיפורם של ישראלים בצינוק סורי (Tel Aviv: Bustan, 1974); Igal Sarna, *The Man Who Fell Into a Puddle: Israeli Lives* (New York: Vintage, 2004), 140–5.

9 Gideon Raff, *Prisoners of War* (*Khatufim*; םיפוטח), 2010 [TV series]. Official website: www.mako.co.il/tv-hatufim
10 Mihri Belli, *Mihri Belli'nin Anıları: İnsanlar Tanıdım* (Istanbul: Doğan, 1999), vol.2, 228–32.
11 Said Hawwa, interview.
12 Ibid.
13 Abu Ibrahim, interview.
14 Jerios Hames, *Taqneen al-'Itiqal fi Suriya.*
15 Said Hawwa, interview.
16 Mahmoud Tarjuman, *Qissat al-Insan al-Ma'taqal 1976–1985* (Damascus: Damascus Literary Association, 2004).
17 Ibid.
18 Ibid.
19 Mufeed Najm, *Wings in a Cell.*
20 Mufeed Najm, interview; *Wings in a Cell.*
21 Ibid.
22 Ibid.
23 Tarjuman, *Qissat al-Insan al-Ma'taqal*
24 Ibid.
25 Ibid.
26 Interview with Palestinian former detainee Abu Ismail, in: Mohammad Malas, *The Dream: A Diary of a Film* (Oxford: Oxford University Press, 2016), 93.
27 Mufeed Najm, interview.
28 Ibid.
29 Ibid.
30 International Institute of Social History, Bogaers archive, file # 444, M.S.H., 93-1007-I43, life story, 10 and 13 March 1993, pp. 12–15.
31 Mufeed Najm, interview.
32 Mo'bed al-Hassoun, interview.
33 International Institute of Social History, Bogaers archive, file # 411, M.S.I., 91-707-I-42, life story, July 5, July 9, 9 September 2, 1991, pp. 22–24.
34 Mufeed Najm, interview.
35 Ibid.
36 Ibid.
37 Ibid.
38 Mo'bed al-Hassoun, interview.
39 Mufeed Najm, interview.
40 Fouad Aoun, interview; *From Saddam's Hospitality to Mezze Prison.*
41 A.Kh., interview.
42 Ibid.
43 Ibid.
44 Ibid.
45 Ibid.

7 Palmyra (Tadmor) Military Prison

1 Faraj Bayraqdar, *Khiyanaat al-lugha wa al-samt* (Beirut: al-Jadid, 2011).
2 Abdullah al-Naji, interview, and *Hamamat al-Dam fi Sijin Tadmor.*

3 Mohammed al-Tadmori, interview.

4 Ibid.

5 Yassin al-Haj Saleh, *Bal-khalas ya shabab! 16 aaman fi al-sujoon al-Suriya* (Beirut: Dar al-Saqi, 2012).

6 Yassin al-Haj Saleh, interview.

7 "Inside Tadmur: The worst prison in the world?", *BBC News*, 20 June 2015, at: www.bbc.com/news/magazine-33197612

8 Abdullah al-Naji, interview, and *Hamamat al-Dam fi Sijin Tadmor*.

9 Ibid.

10 *Behind the Walls of Tadmor* (unpublished manuscript written by a number of survivors of Palmyra prison from its opening until its closure).

11 *Behind the Walls of Tadmor*.

12 Abdullah al-Naji, interview.

13 Khaled al-Aqleh, interview.

14 These confessions were published in the *Jordanian Documents Book 1981*, printed by the Jordanian Ministry of Media, 25 February 1981.

15 Abdullah al-Naji, interview, and *Hamamat al-Dam fi Sijin Tadmor*.

16 Abbas Abbas, *Tawaqqan ila al-Haya* (Beirut: Dar al-Khayal, 2015). Abbas spent fifteen years in Palmyra and Saydnaya.

17 Sulaiman Abu al-Khair, *Al-Tariq ila Tadmor. Kahaf fi al-Sahra 1981–1986* (Caïro: Dar al-A'laam, 2011).

18 Ibid.

19 Mustafa Khalifa, interview, and *The Shell*.

20 Ibid.

21 Ibid.

22 Ibid.

23 Ali Abu al-Dihn, interview, and *A'id min al-Jaheem: Zikriyaat min Tadmor wa Ikhwaatuh* (Beirut: Dar al-Jadid lil-Nashr, 2012).

24 Mohammed Berro, interview, and *Naj min al-Maqsala. Thamaniya Awa'im fi Sijin Tadmor* (Beirut: Jusoor, 2020).

25 *Behind the Walls of Tadmor*.

26 Mohammed Berro, interview.

27 Ibid.

28 Abbas Abbas, interview.

29 Copy to Come

30 Sacrificers volunteered for tasks such as bringing in the food or anything else from outside the dormitory. They were a group of young men of strong build, who sometimes volunteered to receive punishment in place of the elderly or the sick if they were identified for punishment at night.

31 Abdullah al-Naji, interview.

32 International Institute of Social History, Bogaers archive, file # 454, M.A., 92-984-I-30, life story, January 7 and 20, 1993, pp. 19–24.

33 *Behind the Walls of Tadmor*.

34 Ibid.

35 Al-Saraj, *Min Tadmor ila Harvard*.

36 Mahmoud al-Ashour, interview.

37 Mustafa Khalifa, interview, and *The Shell*.

38 *Behind the Walls of Tadmor*.

39 Ibid.

40 Moubed Al-Hassoun, interview, and *Before Dark*.
41 *Behind the Walls of Tadmor*.
42 Mohammed Hammad, *Tadmor*.
43 Al-Saraj, *Min Tadmor ila Harvard*.
44 *Behind the Walls of Tadmor*.
45 Ibid.
46 Ibid.
47 Abbas, *Tawaqqan ila al-Haya*.
48 Al-Naji, *Hamamat al-Dam fi Sijin Tadmor*.
49 Faraj Bayraqdar, *Khiyanaat al-lugha wa al-samt*.
50 Abu al-Khair, *Al-Tariq ila Tadmor*.
51 Al-Naji, *Hamamat al-Dam fi Sijin Tadmor*.
52 Mohammed Hammad, interview.
53 *Behind the Walls of Tadmor*.
54 Khalifa, *The Shell*.
55 *Behind the Walls of Tadmor*.
56 Ibid.
57 Al-Naji, *Hamamat al-Dam fi Sijin Tadmor*.
58 *Behind the Walls of Tadmor*.
59 Ibid.
60 Moubed al-Hassoun, interview.
61 Al-Naji, *Hamamat al-Dam fi Sijin Tadmor*.
62 Abu al-Khair, *Al-Tariq ila Tadmor*.
63 Ali Abu al-Dihn, interview.
64 Abbas, *Tawaqqan ila al-Haya*.
65 Mohammed Berro, interview.
66 Mustafa Khalifa, *The Shell*.
67 Ibid.
68 *Behind the Walls of Tadmor*.
69 Ibid.
70 Mustafa Khalifa, *The Shell*.
71 Abu al-Khair, *Al-Tariq ila Tadmor*.
72 Abbas, *Tawaqqan ila al-Haya*.
73 Mohammed Berro, interview.
74 Ibid.
75 Al-Saraj, *Min Tadmor ila Harvard*.
76 Mustafa Khalifa, *The Shell*.
77 Al-Saraj, *Min Tadmor ila Harvard*.
78 Ibid.
79 Ali Abu al-Dihn, *A'id min al-Jahim*.
80 Al-Saraj, *Min Tadmor ila Harvard*.
81 Mohammed Hammad, interview.
82 Mahmoud Issa, interview; *Matar al-Ghiyab* (Beirut: Dar al-Khayal, 2016).
83 Abbas, *Tawaqqan ila al-Haya*.
84 Heba Dabbagh, *Just Five Minutes*.
85 Mahmoud Qadi al-Qala'a, *The Trouble*.
86 Interview with Raed al-Nakshibandi, 30 November 2016. Available at:: www.prison-insider.com/en/articles/raed-al-nakshbandi-syrie

8 Saydnaya Military Prison

1 Al-Saraj, *Min Tadmor ila Harvard.*
2 For a visual rendition of Saydnaya using digital methods and oral histories, see the Saydnaya project of Forensic Architecture. Available at: https://saydnaya.amnesty.org/
3 H.M., interview.
4 *Human Slaughterhouse: Mass Hangings and Extermination at Saydnaya Prison, Syria* (London: Amnesty International, 2017). Available at: www.amnesty.nl/content/uploads/2017/02/Human-Slaughterhouse_EMBARGOED.pdf?x82206.
5 Imad Abu Ras, interview.
6 See: https://admsp.org/
7 *Prison of Sednayah during the Syrian Revolution (Testimonies)* (Gaziantep: Association of Detainees and Missing in Sednaya Prison, 2019), p.10; Diab Serriya, 'Qissat Sadiqi al-Shabbih fi Sijin Saydnaya' (6 July 2018). Available at: https://admsp.org/news/%D9%82%D8%B5%D8%A9-%D8%B5%D8%AF%D9%8A%D9%82%D9%8A-%D8%A7%D9%84%D8%B4%D8%A8%D9%8A%D8%AD-%D9%81%D9%8A-%D8%B3%D8%AC%D9%86-%D8%B5%D9%8A%D8%AF%D9%86%D8%A7%D9%8A%D8%A7
8 *Prison of Sednayah During the Syrian Revolution,* p. 17.
9 Ibid.
10 Ibid.
11 H.M., interview.
12 *Out of Sight, Out of Mind: Deaths in Detention in the Syrian Arab Republic* (Geneva: OHCHR, 2016), pp. 1, 17.
13 Abbas, Tawaqqan.
14 Mohammed Saleh al-Saleh, interview.
15 Mohammed Berro, interview.
16 Pierre Yohanna, interview.
17 Mohammed Saleh al-Saleh, interview.
18 Omar al-Sayed Youssef, interview.
19 Hammam al-Youssef, interview.
20 H.M., interview.
21 Ibid.
22 Malik Dagestani, 'Sijin Saydnaya: Intifaada al-Labn,' available at https://www.syria.tv/سجن-صيدنايا-انتفاضة-اللبن.; Mohammed Saleh al-Saleh, interview.
23 Bassam Youssef, interview.
24 Ibid.
25 Mohammed Saleh al-Saleh, interview.
26 Al-Saraj, interview; *Min Tadmor ila Harvard.*
27 Ibid.
28 Malik Dagestani, 'Laylat Sabt al-Nur: Ibna'una fi Saydnaya', Al-Raafed, 9 May 2018. Available at: www.alraafed.com/2018/05/09/1-47/; Jaber Baker's personal experience in Saydnaya prison between 2002 and 2004.
29 Al-Saraj, interview; *Min Tadmor ila Harvard.*
30 Malik Dagestani, 'Qabl riba' qurun, masrah Saydnaya al-sirri', *Al-Jumhuriya,* 10 July 2017. Available at: www.aljumhuriya.net/ar/content/%D9%82%D8%A8%D9%84-%D8%B1%D8%A8%D8%B9-%D9%82%D8%B1%D9%86%D8%8C-%D9%85%D8%B3%D8%B1%D8%AD-%D8%B5%D9%8A%D8%AF%D9%86%D8%A7%D9%8A%D8%A7-%D8%A7%D9%84%D8%B3%D8%B1%D9%91%D9%8A

31 Bassam Youssef, interview.
32 Yaqoub Bahi and his wife, interview.
33 H.M., interview.
34 Pierre Yohanna, interview.
35 Bassam Youssef, interview.
36 Ibid.
37 Ibid.
38 Al-Saraj, interview; *Min Tadmor ila Harvard.*
39 Pierre Yohanna, interview.
40 Omar al-Sayed Youssef, interview.
41 Pierre Yohanna, interview.
42 A.Kh., interview.
43 Ibid.
44 Kheder Ramadan, interview.
45 *Ibid.*
46 *A.Kh., interview.*
47 *Kheder Ramadan, interview.*
48 *Ibid.*
49 *A.Kh., interview.*
50 *Ibid.*
51 *Kheder Ramadan, interview.*
52 *A.Kh., interview.*
53 *Ibid.*
54 Kheder Ramadan, interview.
55 Ibid.
56 Ibid.
57 A.Kh., interview.
58 Kheder Ramadan, interview.
59 A.Kh., interview.
60 Kheder Ramadan, interview.
61 A.Kh., interview.
62 Kheder Ramadan, interview.
63 H.M., interview.
64 Kheder Ramadan, interview.
65 H.M., interview.
66 Kheder Ramadan, interview.
67 A.Kh., interview.
68 A.Kh., interview.
69 A.Kh., interview.
70 Kheder Ramadan, interview.
71 Ibid.
72 A.Kh., interview.
73 'Wathaaiqi Ahdaath Sijin Saydnaya al-Suri' (Tahqeeq al-Jazeera, 3 April 2015), at: https://www.youtube.com/watch?v=tMjczCj9FVY
74 'Ana wa yak, ya Abu Shama / Maher ba'du bal-bijama'
75 H.M., interview.
76 Kh.M., interview.
77 Ibrahim al-Olabi, interview.
78 Amnesty International, *Human Slaughterhouse.*

79 Ibid., p.17.
80 Imad Abu Ras, interview.
81 Muneer al-Faqeer, interview.
82 Muneer al-Faqeer, interview.
83 Amnesty International, *Human Slaughterhouse*.
84 Ibid., p. 22.
85 Ibid., 24–25.
86 Abu Ras, interview.
87 Huzaifa al-Jassim, interview.
88 Ibid.
89 Muneer al-Faqeer, interview.
90 Abu Ras, interview.
91 Huzaifa al-Jassim, interview.
92 Ibid.
93 Muneer al-Faqeer, interview.
94 Sh.M., interview.
95 Muneer al-Faqeer, interview.
96 Ibid.
97 Abu Ras, interview.
98 Muneer al-Faqeer, interview.
99 Ibid.
100 Abu Ras, interview.
101 Khaldoun Mansour, interview.
102 Sh.M., interview.
103 Abu Ras, interview.
104 Khaldoun Mansour, interview.
105 Ibid.
106 Abu Ras, interview.
107 Ibid.
108 Ibid.
109 Ibid.
110 Sh. M.; Khaldoun Mansour; Muneer al-Faqeer, interviews.

9 Civil Prisons

1 Syrian Commission for Transitional Justice (SCTJ), *Al-Sujoon al-Suriya wa Awda'a al-Sujana' Fiha* (Istanbul: Syrian Commission for Transitional Justice, 2014), p. 9. Available at: https://shrc.org/wp-content/uploads/2015/04/SCTJ_Prison_Report_Final_Ar.pdf
2 Emine Gürsoy Naskali and Hilal Oytun Altun (ed.), *Hapishane Kitabı* (Istanbul: Salt Araştırma, 2005).
3 Kevin Martin, *Syria's Democratic Years: Citizens, Experts, and Media in the 1950s* (Bloomington, IN: Indiana University Press, 2015), p. 70.
4 SCTJ, *Al-Sujoon al-Suriya*, p. 10.
5 Ibid.
6 Ibid.
7 Ibid.

8 Adnan al-Miqdad, *Mazaq Sajjeen*; interview.

9 See http://dgam.gov.sy/world-heritage-list-sites-in-syria/damascus/?lang=en.

10 Thomas Philipp and Christoph Schumann (ed.), *From the Syrian Land to the States of Syria and Lebanon* (Beirut: Ergon, 2004), 13.

11 Philip Khoury, *Syria and the French Mandate: The Politics of Arab Nationalism 1920–1945* (Princeton, NJ: Princeton University Press, 1987), 236.

12 Ibid., 125.

13 Ibid., 187.

14 Ibid., 306, 461.

15 Jurius al-Hames, *Mamlaka al-Istibdad al-Muqnin fi Suriya. Al-Sujoon wa al-Ma'taqalaat al-Rahiba* (Ahlen: Dar Baft, 2004).

16 Adnan al-Miqdad, *Mazaq Sajjeen*; interview.

17 Mohammed Adel Faris, *Li'annahum Qalou La. Because They Said No* (2007).

18 Adnan al-Miqdad, *Mazaq Sajjeen*; interview.

19 Faris, *Li'annahum Qalou La.*

20 Adnan al-Miqdad, *Mazaq Sajjeen*; interview.

21 Ibid.

22 Adnan al-Miqdad, *Mazaq Sajjeen*; interview. The testimony provided by al-Miqdad needs verification.

23 Jurius al-Hames, *Mamlaka al-Istibdad.*

24 Ratib Shabo, *Madha Wara Hadhih al-Jidraan* (Beirut: Dar al-Adaab, 2015).

25 Ibid.

26 Adnan al-Miqdad, *Mazaq Sajjeen*; interview.

27 Ratib Shabo, *Madha Wara Hadhih al-Jidraan* (Beirut: Dar al-Adaab, 2015).

28 Jurius al-Hames, *Mamlaka al-Istibdad.*

29 Shabo, *Madha Wara.*

30 Ibid.

31 Ibid.

32 Ibid.

33 Ibid.

34 Adnan al-Miqdad, *Mazaq Sajjeen*; interview.

35 Jalal Noufal, interview.

36 Shabo, *Madha Wara.*

37 Adnan al-Miqdad, *Mazaq Sajjeen*; interview.

38 Ahmed al-Mahmoud, born in 1965, arrested in 1988 and was not charged until his death in Aleppo prison on 1 January 2014. He made this call during the 2013 siege of the prison.

39 Jurius al-Hames, *Mamlaka al-Istibdad.*

40 SCTJ, *Al-Sujoon al-Suriya*, p. 24.

41 *A Special Report on Aleppo Central Prison. The Execution and Fatal Starvation of Dozens of Prisoners* (Violations Documentation Centre, 2014), p. 2. Available at: www.vdc-sy.info/pdf/reports/1398197682-English.pdf

42 Mohammed Berro, *Naj min al-Maqsala. Thamaniya Awa'im fi Sijin Tadmor* (Beirut: Jusoor, 2020); interview.

43 Ibid.

44 Ibid.

45 Ibid.

46 Ibid.

47 Osama Mohammed al-Askari al-Ashour, interview.

48 Ibid.
49 Mohammed Osama Shaker, 'Oud Abu Hamdan', *Hentah*, 26 juni 2015, Available at: https://hentah.com/2015/06/26/3191/. The events of the story took place in 1983.
50 Bakr Fahmi Sidqi, interview.
51 Ibid.
52 *A Special Report on Aleppo Central Prison.* p.6. Available at: www.vdc-sy.info/pdf/reports/1398197682-English.pdf.
53 Ibid.
54 Ibid., p. 7.
55 Ibid., p. 9.
56 Ibid., p. 15.
57 Ibid., p. 11.
58 SCTJ, *Al-Sujoon al-Suriya*, p. 31.
59 Al-Miqdad, *Mazaq Sajjeen*.
60 Shabo, *Madha Wara*.
61 Ibid.
62 Ibid.
63 Osama al-Ashour al-Askari, interview.
64 Bakr Fahmi Sidqi, interview.
65 Shabo, *Madha Wara*.
66 Ibid.
67 Ibid.
68 Al-Miqdad, *Mazaq Sajjeen*.
69 Ibrahim al-Olabi, interview.
70 SCTJ, *Al-Sujoon al-Suriya*, p.32.
71 Ibid.
72 Ibid., p.40.
73 M.A., interview.
74 Ibid.
75 Ranim Maatouq, interview.
76 J.H., interview.
77 R.S., interview.
78 Violations Documentation Center, 'Adraa Women's Prison is Turning into just another Security Branch', september 2013. Available at: www.vdc-sy.info/pdf/reports/1379945097-English.pdf.
79 Ibid.
80 Um Mohammed, interview.
81 R.S., interview.
82 Luna Watfeh, interview.
83 Ranim Maatouq, interview.
84 Luna Watfeh, interview.
85 Ibid., letter from her private archive.
86 Ibid.
87 J.H., interview.
88 Ibid.
89 Dabbagh, *Just Five Minutes*.
90 Ibid.
91 Ibid.

92 Ibid. After many attempts to send news on her location to her family to come visit her, she learned that they all died in the Hama massacre in February 1982. The only visit she received was from her aunt, who was the only surviving member of her family living in Syria.

93 Ibid.

94 Ibid.

95 Duha al-Ashour al-Askari, interview.

96 Ibid.

97 Ibid.

98 Ibid.

99 The veteran Syrian opposition figure Michel Kilo (1940–2021) once said in an interview that he had seen a four-year-old boy who had been born and raised in prison, and had no idea of what a bird was, or what a tree was. Interview with Michel Kilo by Zeina Yazigi, 5 November 2012. Available at: www.youtube.com/watch?v=nE0E16nGpyY [accessed 2 June 2021]. For a theatre play based on the story see: 'The Prison Boy', 10 April 2016. Available at: www.youtube.com/watch?v=KuycpmPULFw [accessed 2 June 2021].

10 Secret Prisons

1   See the YouTube channel of Kamal al-Labwani, who was serving his mandatory military service as a doctor in one of the divisions stationed in Hama. He was asked to examine some of the detainees in a school. Available at: www.youtube.com/channel/UCLkdAJay59EpsEFLcVJji0Q.

2   Mohammed Berro, Mahmoud Ashour, Ola Humidi, interviews.

3   Omran Centre for Strategic Studies, The Syrian Security Services and the Need for Structural and Functional Change (Istanbul: Omran, 2016).

4   Ibid.

5   Ibid.

6   Ibid.

7   Mufeed Najem, interview en Ajnaha fi Zinzaneh (Beirut: Al-Muasasa al-Arabiya lil-Dirasaat wa al-Nashr, 2015).

8   Ibid.

9   Ibid.

10 Ibid.

11 Omran Centre, The Syrian Security Services.

12 Ammar al-Sheikh Haidar, interview.

13 Ibid.

14 Ibid.

15 Ibid.

16 Ibid.

17 Ibid.

18 Uğur Ümit Üngör, "Shabbiha: Paramilitary Groups, Mass Violence and Social Polarization in Homs" in: Violence: An International Journal, Vol. 1, No. 1 (2020), pp. 59–79.

19 Radio al-Kul, 'Ma'skar "Deir Shmeil": Ma'qal Sirri lil-Shabbiha Mustaqil 'an Afra' al-Nizam', 27 January 2016. Available at: www.youtube.com/watch?v=F8l_X3tXgBA.

20 Omran Centre for Strategic Studies, *The Syrian Security Services*.

21 Syrian Network for Human Rights, 'Secret Detention Centres in Syria, Deir Shmeil Camp' (17 December 2014), p. 2. Available at: https://sn4hr.org/wp-content/pdf/english/Secret_Detention_Centers_in_Syria_en.pdf.

22 Abu Shaam, interview.

23 Radio al-Kul, 'Ma'skar "Deir Shmeil"'.

24 Omran Centre, *The Syrian Security Services*.

25 Syrian Network, 'Secret Detention Centres', p. 2.

26 Ibid., p. 3.

27 Abu Shaam, interview.

28 Ibid.

29 Ibid.

30 Ibid.

31 Ibid.

32 'Ma'taqalah ala haafat al-mut: fi jaheem "Deir Shmeil"'. *Pro-Justice*, 16 november 2018, op. Available at: https://pro-justice.org/ar/victims/%D8%A7%D9%84%D8%B9%D8%B1%D8%A8%D9%8A%D8%A9-%D9%85%D8%B9%D8%AA%D9%82%D9%84%D8%A9-%D8%B9%D9%84%D9%89-%D8%AD%D8%A7%D9%81%D8%A9-%D8%A7%D9%84%D9%85%D9%88%D8%AA-%D9%81%D9%8A-%D8%AC%D8%AD%D9%8A%D9%85.html.

33 Wael Mohammed Al-Tawil, interview.

34 Ayman, interview.

35 Ali al-Shilli, interview.

36 Maen Tallaa, *The Syrian Security Services and the Need for Structural and Functional Change* (Istanbul: Omran Centre for Strategic Studies, 2016), pp. 21–22.

37 Ibid.

38 'Shahadaat Hawl Jaheem Ma'taqalaat al-Firqa al-Rabi'a' (Violations Documentation Centre, 2013), p. 1, op. Available at: www.vdc-sy.info/pdf/reports/testimonies-Arabic.pdf.

39 Ibid.

40 Muhannad al-Ghobash, interview.

41 'Shahadaat Hawl Jaheem'.

42 Ibid.

43 Muhannad al-Ghobash, interview.

44 'Shahadaat Hawl Jaheem'.

45 Muhannad al-Ghobash, interview.

46 Muhannad al-Ghobash, interview.

47 'Shahadaat Hawl Jaheem'.

48 Muhannad al-Ghobash, interview.

49 Ibid.

50 'Shahadaat Hawl Jaheem'.

51 Muhannad al-Ghobash, interview.

52 Ibid.

Part Two Conclusion

1   Analogous to the set of Nazi sites of violence: see www.topographie.de/.

Our Children in the World

1   Source: interviews with several former detainees, in particular Mohammed Berro, and personal experience of Jaber Baker.

Conclusion

1   Recent psychiatric research has convincingly demonstrated how deep the societal and personal traumas are for Syrians. See e.g.: Steven Segal et al., "The Syrian Regime's Apparatus for Systemic Torture: A Qualitative Narrative Study of Testimonies from Survivors", in: *BMC Psychiatry*, vol.22, art.787 (2022).

2   Salwa Ismail, *The Rule of Violence. Subjectivity, Memory and Government in Syria.* (Cambridge: Cambridge University Press 2018), p. 39

3   Daniel Feierstein, *Genocide as Social Practice: Reorganizing Society under the Nazis and Argentina's Military Juntas* (New Brunswick, NJ: Rutgers University Press, 2014), p. 135.

4   Abel J. Herzberg, *Tweestromenland: Dagboek uit Bergen-Belsen* (Amsterdam: Querido, 1950): 'Een concentratiekamp betekent marteling tot aan de dood.'

5   *Human Slaughterhouse: Mass Hangings and Extermination at Saydnaya Prison, Syria* (London: Amnesty International, 2017), p.31.

6   *Rome Statute of the International Criminal Court* (Rome: United Nations, 17 July 1998), p. 4.

7   Elaine Scarry, *The Body in Pain: The Making and Unmaking of the World* (Oxford: Oxford University Press, 1987); Marnia Lazreg, *Torture and the Twilight of Empire: From Algiers to Baghdad* (Princeton, NJ: Princeton University Press, 2016).

8   *Syria: Torture by the Security Forces* (London: Amnesty International, 1987), p.4.

9   In some civil wars and counterinsurgencies, such as in Colombia, Northern Ireland, Chechnya, or Turkish Kurdistan, army personnel received higher pay during the conflict, which led some officers to pretend that there were skirmishes to keep the war going.

10 For a similar dynamic in the Indonesian genocide, see: John Roosa, *Buried Histories: The Anticommunist Massacres of 1965–1966 in Indonesia* (Madison, WI: The University of Wisconsin Press, 2020), 85–115.

11 Sultan Jalabi, 'Syria's lucrative detainment market: How Damascus exploits detainees' families for money', *Syria Untold*, 13 April 2021. Available at: https://syriauntold. com/2021/04/13/syrias-lucrative-detainment-market-how-damascus-exploits-detainees-families-for-money/.

12 Ismail, *The Rule of Violence*, p. 54.

13 Interview with S.I., Amsterdam, 4 June 2018.

14 Philip Issa and Bassem Mroue, 'Syria denies US allegations of mass killings, crematorium', *Associated Press*, 16 May 2017. Available at: https://apnews.com/article/damascus-syria-ap-top-news-middle-east-bashar-assad-a037b8ebf0a04f11877ce943b9 97ade8.

15 "Syria Denies Burning Bodies of Political Prisoners", *New York Times*, 16 May 2017, at: https://www.nytimes.com/2017/05/16/world/middleeast/syria-negotiations-prison-crematory.html [accessed 21 January 2021]

16 "The Syrian Conflict According to Assad's Prisoners", *WNYC*, 8 May 2013, at: https://www.wnycstudios.org/podcasts/takeaway/segments/291992-syrian-conflict-according-assads-prisoners ; Anne Barnard, "Inside Syria's Secret Torture Prisons: How Bashar al-Assad Crushed Dissent", *The New York Times*, 11 May 2019, at: https://www.nytimes.com/2019/05/11/world/middleeast/syria-torture-prisons.html
17 "An Inside Look at Political Imprisonment", Council on Foreign Relations, 13 May 2019, at: https://www.cfr.org/event/inside-look-political-imprisonment

To Err is Human

1 *International Institute for Social History*, Bogaers archive, #515, 92-936-II-12, p.11, life story A.M, Z.S.
2 O.H., interview, 12 April 2017, 2 February 2019; Z.N., interview 29 March 2019.
3 Nour, interview, 16 Juni 2018.

Select Bibliography

Al-Haj Saleh, Yassin (2015), *Récits d'une Syrie oubliée. Sortir la mémoire des prisons*. Paris: Les Prairies Ordinaires.

Al-Haj Saleh, Yassin (2021), 'The Greater Jail. The Politics of Prison in Syria', in: *Al-Jumhuriya*. Available at: www.aljumhuriya.net/en/content/greater-jail-politics-prison-syria

Amnesty International (1987), *Syria. Torture by the Security Forces*. London: Amnesty International.

Amnesty International (2017), *Human Slaughterhouse. Mass Hangings and Extermination at Saydnaya Prison, Syria*. London: Amnesty International.

Archief P.B.Ph.M. Bogaers, Collection ID ARCH02460. Available at: https://hdl.handle.net/10622/ARCH02460.

Branch 251 podcast. Available at: https://branch-251.captivate.fm/

Arendt, Hannah (1950), 'Social Science Techniques and the Study of Concentration Camps', in: *Jewish Social Studies* vol. 12, no 1, pp. 49–64.

Barnard, Anne (2019), 'Inside Syria's Secret Torture Prisons. How Bashar al-Assad Crushed Dissent', *The New York Times*. Available at: www.nytimes.com/2019/05/11/world/middleeast/syria-torture-prisons.html

Blei, Daniela (2018), 'We Can't Save Syrians Anymore, But We Can Save the Truth', *Foreign Policy*. Available at: https://foreignpolicy.com/2018/12/27/ugur-umit-ungor-syria-oral-history-project/

Dabbagh, Heba (2007), *Just Five Minutes: Nine Years in the Prison of Syria*. Toronto: Bayan Khatib.

Feierstein, Daniel (2014), *Genocide as Social Practice. Reorganizing Society under the Nazis and Argentina's Military Juntas*. New Brunswick, NJ: Rutgers University Press.

Foucault, Michel (1972), 'Les intellectuels et le pouvoir', in: *L'arc*, nr. 49, p. 3–10.

Ghazzal, Zouhair (2015), *The Crime of Writing: Narratives and Shared Meanings in Criminal Cases in Baathist Syria*. Beirut: Presses de l'IFPO.

Haugbolle, Sune (2008), 'Imprisonment, Truth Telling and Historical Memory in Syria', in: *Mediterranean Politics*, vol. 13, no 2, pp. 261–276.

Herzberg, Abel (1950), *Tweestromenland. Dagboek uit Bergen-Belsen*. Amsterdam: Querido.

Human Rights Watch (2012), *Torture Archipelago. Arbitrary Arrests, Torture, and Enforced Disappearances in Syria's Underground Prisons since March 2011*. New York: HRW.

International Centre for Transitional Justice (2020), *Gone Without a Trace. Syria's Detained, Abducted, and Forcibly Disappeared*. New York: ICTJ.

Ismail, Salwa (2018), *The Rule of Violence. Subjectivity, Memory and Government in Syria*. Cambridge: Cambridge University Press.

Issa, Philip and Bassem Mroue (2017), 'Syria denies US allegations of mass killings, crematorium', *Associated Press*. Available at: https://apnews.com/article/damascus-syria-ap-top-news-middle-east-bashar-assad-a037b8ebf0a04f11877ce943b997ade8

Jalabi, Sultan (2021), 'Syria's lucrative detainment market. How Damascus exploits detainees' families for money', *Syria Untold*. Available at: https://syriauntold.

com/2021/04/13/syrias-lucrative-detainment-market-how-damascus-exploits-detainees-families-for-money/

Kahana, Ephraim and Muhammad Suwaed, red. (2009), *The A to Z of Middle Eastern Intelligence*. Toronto: Scarecrow Press.

Khalifa, Mustafa (2016), *The Shell: Memoirs of a Hidden Observer*. Northampton, MA: Interlink Books.

Lazreg, Marnia (2016), *Torture and the Twilight of Empire. From Algiers to Baghdad*. Princeton, NJ: Princeton University Press.

Le Caisne, Garance (2018), *Operation Caesar. At the Heart of the Syrian Death Machine*. Cambridge: Polity.

Linde, Gerd (1982), *Die sowjetisch-syrischen Beziehungen im regionalen Umfeld*. Bonn: Bundesinstitut für Ostwissenschaftliche und Internationale Studien.

Marchenko, Anatoly (1989), *My Testimony*. London: Sceptre.

Omari, Mansour (2021), 'On the Trauma of Advocacy', *Amnesty International UK blog*, 23 april 2021. Available at: www.amnesty.org.uk/AdvocacyTrauma

Pither, Kerry (2008), *Dark Days: The Story of Four Canadians Tortured in the Name of Fighting Terror*. New York: Viking.

Roosa, John (2020), *Buried Histories. The Anticommunist Massacres of 1965–1966 in Indonesia*. Madison, WI: The University of Wisconsin Press.

Scarry, Elaine (1987), *The Body in Pain. The Making and Unmaking of the World*. Oxford: Oxford University Press.

Shalamov, Varlam (2004), *A New Book. Memoirs, Notebooks, Correspondence, Police Dossiers*. Moskou: Eksmo.

Sofsky, Wolfgang (1997), *The Order of Terror. The Concentration Camp*. Princeton, NJ: Princeton University Press.

Solzhenitsyn, Aleksandr (2018 [1973]), *The Gulag Archipelago*. London: Random House.

Syrian Network for Human Rights (2020), *Ninth Annual Report on Torture in Syria on the International Day in Support of Victims of Torture*. London: Syrian Network for Human Rights.

Taleghani, Shareah (2021), *Readings in Syrian Prison Literature. The Poetics of Human Rights*. Syracuse, New York: Syracuse University Press.

United Nations (1998), *Rome Statute of the International Criminal Court*. Rome: United Nations.

Walmsley, Roy (2015), *World Prison Population List*. London: Institute for Criminal Policy Research.

"Ya Hurriya", Suriya TV. Available at: www.youtube.com/playlist?list=PLeMwite1QcQ3JIA dAEsJ_8ySjbjf0weai.

List of interviews

Name	Method	Year	Code
Bereqdar, Faraj	Online and in person	2019	19001
Abu Ibrahim	Online	2019	19002
Diab, Mohammed Nader	Online and in person	2019	19003
Al-Miqdad, Adnan	Online	2019	19004
Shamloni, Haisam	Online	2019	19005
Abu Iyad	In person	2019	19006
Hilal, Mahmoud	Online	2019	19007
Hamidi, Ali	In person	2014–2019	14001
Abu Abderrahman	Online	2019	19008
Ranim Ma'atouq	Online	2019	19009
Rafif	Online	2019	20001
Ala'a	Online	2015	15001
Ashour, Mahmoud	Online and in person	2020	20002
Al-Ashour Al-Askari, Osama	Online	2019	19010
Sidki, Bakr	In person	2016, 2020	20003
Noufal, Jalal	Online and in person	2019–2020	19011
Issa, Mahmoud	Online	2019	19012
Matouk, Ahmed	Online	2019	19013
Kana'an, Mohideen	Online	2019	19014
Al-Olabi, Ibrahim	Online	2019	19015
Ahmed, Ayat	Online and in person	2019	19016
A. B.	Online	2019	19017
Faris, Ghaith	Online	2019	19018
M. Sh.	Online	2019	19019
Bero, Mohammed	Online and in person	2019	19020
T. T.	Online	2019	19021
Bahi, Yaqoub	In person	2019	19022
Najem, Mufeed	Online	2020	20004
Aintabli, Mohamed Naim	Online	2019	19023
Hakoum, Yahya	In person	2019	19024
M. H.	Online	2019	19025
Al-Olabi, Sumaya (Luna Watfeh)	Online	2020	20005
A. Kh.	Online	2019	19026
Al-Sayyed Youssef, Omar	Online and in person	2019–2020	19027
M. H.	Online	2019	19028
Al-Youssef, Hammam	Online	2019	19029
Anonieme officier	Online	2019	19030
H. S.	Online	2019	19031
Al-Saud, Akram	In person	2016, 2019	19032
Al-Jahmani, Thamer	Online	2019	19033
Al-Ghobash, Muhannad	Online	2020	20006
Bostaji, Mohamed Khalil	Online	2019	19034
S. A.	Online	2019	19035
M. H.	In person	2014	14002
Abu Zeid	In person	2014	14003
Abdullah, Sarah	Online	2019	19036
Hamada, Ahmed	Online and in person	2019–2020	19037
M. Sh.	Online	2019	19038
Abu Ras, Imad	Online	2019	19039

Name	Method	Year	Code
Y. B.	Online	2019	19040
Al-Sheikh Haider, Ammar	Online	2019	19041
Abu Shaam	Online	2019	19042
Al-Hassoun, Mo'bed	Online	2020	20006
Al-Tadmori, Mohammed	Online	2019	19043
Al-Aqleh, Khaled	Online	2019	19044
Abu Al-Dihn, Ali	Online	2019	19045
Al-Saleh, Mohamed Saleh	Online	2019	19046
Yohanna, Pierre	Online	2019	19047
Yousef, Bassam	Online	2019	19048
A. Kh.	Online	2019	19049
Ramadan, Kheder	Online and in person	2020	20007
Al-Faqeer, Munir	Online and in person	2020	20008
Al-Jassim, Huzaifa	Online	2019	19050
Mansour, Khaldoon	Online	2019	19051
M. H.	Online	2019	19052
J. H.	Online	2019	19053
R. S.	Online	2019	19054
Umm Mohammed	Online	2019	19055
Al-Askari Ashour, Duha	Online	2019	19056
S.I.	In person	2018	22001
Al-Taweel, Mutayyam	In person	2017	22002
Al-Ahmad, Bassam	In person	2015	22003
Al-Haj Saleh, Yassin	In person	2015	22004
Massouh, Samer	In person	2015	22005
Kurdi, Mohammed Eyad	In person	2015	22006
Jizawi, Noura al-Ameer	In person	2016	22007
Abu Hajar, Mohammed	In person	2016	22008
Akkad, Ayman	In person	2016	22009
N.A.	In person	2016	22010
Hassan H.	In person	2016	22011
A.S.	In person	2016–2022	22012
Al-Souliman, Rita	In person	2016	22013
O.H.	In person	2017	22014
K. Sh.	In person	2018	22015
Mohammed Abdallah (Artino)	In person	2018	22016
H.K.	In person	2019	22017

Acknowledgements

This book would not have been possible without the cooperation of the many survivors of the prisons of the Assad regime. They answered our questions with patience and responded to our discussions with genuine interest. Some of them have been quoted anonymously, but our gratitude goes out to all, and we dedicate this book to them.

A very special thanks goes out to Lara al-Malakeh for her exceptionally careful and empathetic translations of the Arabic parts of the manuscript. Without her expert eye and commitment, this book would not have reached the emotional and intellectual depth that it has.

We thank Mr. Pieter Bogaers for granting access to his archive, and Dumuzi and Fadia Afashe for their beautiful drawings and painting. Finally, we are grateful to Sophie Rudland, Yasmin Garcha, and Nayiri Kendir of I.B. Tauris, and Paula Devine for their support in the preparation, development, editing, and completion of this book project. This book was made possible with financial support from the Dutch Fund for Special Journalistic Projects (*Fonds Bijzondere Journalistieke Projecten*) and the Democracy and Media Foundation (*Stichting Democratie en Media*).

We could not have completed this work without the unwavering support of our friends and family, and especially the loving patience of Jaber's partner Linda Bilal, and Uğur's partner Ayşenur Korkmaz and son Sami Üngör.

Index